BRANDEIS

BRANDEIS

The Personal History
of an American Ideal

by ALFRED LIEF

1936

STACKPOLE SONS

New York
Harrisburg, Pa.

History

47896.

APR 2 6 1945

E
669
B81L5

FIRST PRINTING, SEPTEMBER, 1936
SECOND PRINTING, OCTOBER, 1936
THIRD PRINTING, OCTOBER, 1936
FOURTH PRINTING, MARCH, 1937

A NOTE OF ACKNOWLEDGMENT

TO those who knew Justice Brandeis in the earlier years and generously contributed their knowledge to this work, the author offers his thanks. His biography is dedicated to them: The late Justice Oliver Wendell Holmes, Judge George W. Anderson, Newton D. Baker, the Reverend Dr. A. A. Berle, Sr., Meyer Bloomfield, Robert W. Bruere, William E. Chilton, Sr., Julius Henry Cohen, Maxwell Copelof, Judd Dewey, Joseph B. Eastman, Elizabeth Glendower Evans, Edward A. Filene, Lincoln Filene, Senator Duncan U. Fletcher, Louis R. Glavis, Josephine Goldmark, Judge James M. Graham, the late Alice H. Grady, Jacob de Haas, Norman Hapgood, Colonel Edward M. House, Frederic C. Howe, Paul U. Kellogg, Judge Julian W. Mack, E. Louise Malloch, Henry Morgenthau, Sr., Henry Moskowitz, Senator George W. Norris, Robert Lincoln O'Brien, Mary Kenney O'Sullivan, Marlen E. Pew, Gifford Pinchot, George Rublee, and Robert Szold. My gratitude should not suggest that they have endorsed my treatment of the material they have made available.

A. L.

CONTENTS

BEFORE THE CURTAIN

WHEN Louis D. Brandeis was nominated to the Supreme Court of the United States in 1916 a financial oligarchy did its best to brand him as unfit. A band of Boston élite raked his record for proof of unprofessional conduct. For four months their concentrated power bore down and prevented confirmation.

Brandeis showed neither hurt nor resentment during the fight. Once the pet of Boston's Brahmins, he had been steadily attacked for the past nine years by Wall Street and State Street—and now he was glad to have it out. He supposed that a racial background of eighteen centuries of Jewish persecution had inured him to such hardship. While witnesses took their stand at the Senate hearings he sat quietly in his Boston office, read law all day long, and accepted no new clients. He abstained from lunching at the Union Club and drove home at midday in his carriage, over Beacon Hill and down to his house in Back Bay.

"My record will stand on its merits," he said.

On one of those days a friend took him for a stroll across the Common. They stopped in front of the *Transcript's* bulletin board and read the latest chalked notice: William Howard Taft, Elihu Root and five other presidents of the American Bar Association had signed a memorial to the Senate declaring him unfit. Brandeis reddened but said nothing and sauntered away from his pillory.

He was sure the opposition was not based on racial grounds. Nor did he believe his old enemies were seeking revenge for his unrelenting campaign against their anti-social system. They feared him for the power he would wield as a justice. The Supreme Court must not harbor a radical!

Twenty years passed, years which brought thousands of controversies. As the court disposed of them, so it molded the social and economic life of the nation. To these cases Mr. Justice Brandeis applied the open mind of an honest judge, the intellectual painstaking of a faithful judge, and the creative competence of a great judge. His courage in being willing to stand often with a small minority, or even alone, cannot be overstated. A general public may not be aware of it, but the vouchsafing comes from one of Brandeis' associates on the bench: "It really requires courage on the part of a judge to stand up against the majority, especially when the law which is being declared unconstitutional is more or less unpopular."

In the following pages the reader may discern a scrupulous effort to present Brandeis with detachment— Brandeis in terms of action. How to appraise his contribution to the growth of the living Constitution is at best a heroic task for those who have stood on the sidelines. Time, waiting in the distance, will know better. But the justices who worked with him obtained the insight of familiarity, and the public declarations of Oliver Wendell Holmes, Charles Evans Hughes, Harlan Fiske Stone and Benjamin Nathan Cardozo attested to his greatness. One of his associates considered as worthy of special emphasis "the wide range of his thinking, the new habit which he has established in the court of making careful examination of all the factual background out of which constitutional doctrine springs, his enormous industry, his unfailing loyalty to the best traditions and highest ideals of the court."

The same colleague said: "Another contribution not so well known from the outside, but well understood by members of the court, is the emphasis he always puts on strict adherence to the proper function of the court—that it should never decide constitutional questions unnecessarily; that it should keep strictly within its jurisdiction; that it should safeguard in every way the power of the court to declare laws unconstitutional from being improperly resorted to or exploited by litigants."

This sheds light on the separate opinion Brandeis wrote in the Tennessee Valley Authority case, declaring that the court should have refrained from passing on it. One of the justices privately expressed a belief that if Brandeis had been on the court under Chief Justice Taney the Dred Scott case probably never would have occurred, or if it had there would have been a vigorous protest. According to Brandeis, the determination of constitutionality is a function legitimate only in the last resort and in a real and vital controversy. He agreed with Mr. Justice Matthews who felt bound in 1885 "never to formulate a rule of constitutional law broader than is required by the precise facts to which it is applied." And be held with Mr. Justice Brewer who wrote in 1892 that it was never intended that a party beaten in the legislature could, by a friendly suit, "transfer to the courts an inquiry as to the constitutionality of the legislative act."

Under the New Deal political rivals sought out the sanctum as a sanctuary. This was hardly to the court's liking. It would suffer in prestige if made an election issue. Its remove from partisan interests must be preserved; its independence untouched. How unwilling it was to be rushed into taking appeals from injunctions against federal agencies appeared when Chief Justice Hughes and Associate Justices Brandeis and Van Devanter objected before a Senate committee in 1935 to a bill which would have destroyed the court's discretion.

The Roosevelt administration brought out the significance of the Supreme Court in the American system of government. These stormy years of experimentation revealed the

fateful power of nine silk-robed men. Would they be their
country's saviors? Or would their juristic logic ignore economic perils and invite a constitutional amendment to restrain them? In this era the importance of Brandeis shone
more vividly than ever. The crusading reforms which his
friends were loath to have him leave in 1916 were trifling
beside his position in the highest court.

The extent of his influence cannot be measured now. We
must wait. But it is a vibrant force—in the discussion of the
conference room, in the controlling opinions which he was
assigned to write, and in the dissenting opinions which hold
a light for the future.

No one has more sternly criticized the court than has
Brandeis. Repeatedly he protested against the members' intrusion of their views on the wisdom of a law. He did not
hesitate on the proper occasions to speak out against their
assuming the character of a super-legislature. He carried on
after Holmes, who had rebelled to the last against stretching
the due process clause to the limit of the sky. And he joined
in Stone's dissent in the case of the Agricultural Adjustment
Act, where Stone said that "the only check upon our own
exercise of power is our own sense of self-restraint. For the
removal of unwise laws from the statute book appeal lies not
to the courts but to the ballot and to the processes of democratic government." Brandeis not only regarded the court as
ill-equipped to perform legislative work; this was not its
business.

He rejected ready compliance with the doctrine of *stare
decisis*—the policy of not disturbing a rule enunciated in previous decisions. The reasonableness of a statute must depend
primarily upon facts. A rule failed of justice in later controversies where conditions were changed or were more
adequately presented. Brandeis said, "The court bows to
the lessons of experience and the force of better reasoning,
recognizing that the process of trial and error, so fruitful
in the physical sciences, is appropriate also in the judicial

functions." These were words uttered in dissent, urging the court frankly to overrule itself.

To say that Brandeis has given us an enduring example is to venture on an appraisal, to trespass on posterity's lot. First we must have the story. And then we may make our estimates and appreciate the fullness of this personal memorandum by his contemporary, the scientist Albert Einstein:

"I treasure the memory of my only visit to him: a person of swift and clear insight, of keen conviction, wanting nothing but to serve society, and serving in the loneliness of great work."

Chapter 1

THE BEGINNINGS OF A LAWYER

IN THE SUMMER of 1877, home in Louisville for a vacation from Harvard Law School, twenty-year-old Louis Brandeis was called out in the militia and given a gun to guard railroad property during a strike. He carried the weapon, but he was sure he did not know how to harm anyone with it. He was handier with a book—and his eyesight was bad.

When the violent wave of railroad strikes ended in that year he returned the gun gladly, for Louisville had most peaceful and delightful associations for him. It was his birthplace. Here he had enjoyed a full measure of boyhood. Father's grain business prospered, and the happy household of four children was rich in cultural associations. Fast horses filled the stable; there were days of hard riding, of languorous loafing on the banks of the Ohio River, waiting for the steamboat *Fanny Brandeis* to glide up to the wharf. There were adventurous evenings with English literature in a room above the drugstore on Walnut Street, where a young bookkeeper had formed a library club.

Mother laid down a taboo: no mention of money or other grubby matters at meals. The family group talked instead of personalities and books, of music and the arts. His older sister Fanny was the musical impresario and the instigator of his career as a violinist. Father entertained with stories garnered on frequent trips through the countryside. Uncle Lewis Dembitz, a learned lawyer in town, was a constant caller and represented the intellectual interests of the family. They had no pew for religion; forebears on both sides of the house had long since broken through the walls of orthodoxy, out of the mental ghetto as well and into the arena of Polish and Bohemian revolt. Such were the spiritual roots of the home. The Brandeises aimed to cultivate the art of living, and the cultural values that made living worth while. And their big house on Broadway became a rendezvous for musicians and other gifted friends.

Despite this, Louis was a boys' boy, running barefoot in hot weather, ringing doorbells at night, teasing girls and little Lord Fauntleroys, coaxing doughnuts from Lizzie the cook, and riding—always riding—for he loved horses. With his brother Alfred, three years older, he enjoyed a rare companionship; in quieter moments together they taught one of the colored servants to read.

Now in '77, with the composure of a well rounded and well balanced youth he was about to make a place for himself in a man's world. His brother was already in the saddle jogging alongside Papa Brandeis on the road to recovering a business shattered in the crisis of Reconstruction.

Father started as a grain commission merchant in '51. As one of hundreds of thousands of German-speaking immigrants who settled in the Ohio Valley, Adolf Brandeis had come to this country three years before to reconnoiter for a small family group of middle-class Jews in Prague, Bohemia, who sought release from political and military despotism and its resultant economic oppression. They thought of taking up farming and moving their pianos, linens and silverware to the American backwoods. Besides this responsibility Adolf, then twenty-six, had a personal interest on which to stake his judgment; one of the expectant hearts in Prague was his fiancée, Frederika Dembitz. He wrote these city-bred folk not to dream of undertaking a farmer's life; but America abounded in opportunities, freedom was everywhere. He took out his first papers in Hamilton County,

FREDERIKA BRANDEIS   ADOLF BRANDEIS

Portraits of Brandeis' parents, made about 1865

Ohio, in October, 1848, and to his Fritzchen he wrote:

> I already love our new country so much that I re-
> joice when I can sing its praises....I have gotten
> hold of a book which contains the messages of all the
> presidents. This week I have been reading of the prog-
> ress made in Washington's day, and I felt as proud
> and happy about it as though it had been all my own
> doing, as though the statistics showed my own yearly
> balance sheet. Afterwards I laughed at myself, but
> there is something in it. It is the triumph of the rights
> of man which emerges....I feel my patriotism grow-
> ing every day, because every day I learn to know the
> splendid institutions of this country better.

The following spring brought the lovers together again.
The group of immigrants gravitated into various occupations, some in Cincinnati, others in Madison, Indiana, where
the Brandeis couple spent their first two years. Then they
moved across the river to Louisville with their infant Fanny.
And they had two more children: Amy and Alfred. As the
West expanded and nature's bounty welled up regardless
of the slavery struggle that occupied men's passions, business
thrived. Louis David, arriving November 13, 1856, was born
on the high tide of the family's affluence. Failure of the
wheat crop in New York State occasioned the first shipment
of Kentucky white wheat to the East, and the contact thus
made by the firm of Brandeis & Crawford with Buffalo
millers led to an extensive trade. While the outbreak of the
Civil War cut off their large business with the South, they
became contractors for the federal government.

Kentucky was a slave state, but in the Brandeis home it
was natural to be abolitionist. Refugees from oppression,
like Carl Schurz and Franz Sigel, the elders did not have to
think twice in siding against slavery. Like millions of other
aliens they drank deep of the principles of Americanism,
whereas most natives sipped a toast only on the Fourth of
July. In those stirring times a gaunt Kentucky-born orator

stood out as the embodiment of American ideals, and in 1860
Uncle Lewis journeyed to Chicago as a delegate to the Republican convention and helped nominate this man Lincoln.

Although the state did not secede, Louisville's heart was
with the South, and the Brandeises were not doing the
popular thing in favoring the North. When Union soldiers
encamped a short distance from the city there were frequent
buggy excursions from the household and two excited boys
ventured along to the campground to help distribute food
and coffee prepared by their mother. Five-year-old Louis
bustled about the baskets. The concentration of soldiery in
the neighborhood became so heavy that railway tracks had
to be laid down in front of their house for army use. At one
time the Confederate troops led by General Braxton Bragg
were reported to be ten miles away. In fear of a raid—and
of what might happen to Northern sympathizers—Adolf
Brandeis hurried his family to the other side of the river.
After two nervous weeks they ferried back and resumed
their comfortable life.

Louis' education began at the age of six, when he was
taken to a small private school conducted by an English-
woman. Two years later he entered the German and English
Academy, profiting by a new system of pedagogy brought
over from Germany. Here a mark of 6 denoted perfection;
he received 5 in penmanship and 6 in everything else. On the
margin of his report card the principal wrote, "Louis de-
serves commendation for conduct and industry." But on
July 4, 1864, his conduct was not strictly exemplary. Instead
of keeping trim and neat for a holiday visit Mother was
planning to make with them, he and Al played with some
dampened flaring powder. They burned their faces black
and soiled their clothes. When he was ten, the Websterian
Debating Society made him a member. The main concern
of this youngest member was not the political issues of the
day, but the accuracy of the treasurer's accounts. Wiry
Louis was ready to battle over a discrepancy of forty cents.

At the Male High School 5 signified excellence and 6 "without fault." He earned 6 in almost every subject; occasionally he was weak in languages, getting 5.9 in Latin, 5.8 in Greek, 5.95 in French, 5.7 in German. They gave him a gold medal for "pre-eminence in all his studies." Fourteen years old, he was the youngest ever to receive a diploma. The excitement was too much for him; when his turn came to make a speech at the exercises he lost his voice. Once out in the schoolyard he pitched into a fight with a bigger boy—all over a girl named Emma.

In 1872 business reverses began to appear in father's ledger like seismographic warnings. Uncle Lewis advised a trip to Europe. Sensing a panic round the corner he suggested that Adolf end the partnership with Mr. Crawford, sell the house, and pack the family off till the depression should touch bottom. They sailed without waiting for a buyer. But first Adolf obtained naturalization papers and foreswore allegiance to Emperor Franz Joseph. Prague was revisited and a good deal of time was spent in Vienna, much to the delight of father, who still loved the gallantry and courtliness of European social life. They wintered in Italy.

To the boys the trip was geography come to life. Patches on the map and foreign place-names acquired the vividness which only experience imparts. Hiking one day in the Bernese Mountains in Switzerland they reached the source of the River Inn. At once Al, who was more robust, proposed that they keep going and track down the River Adda, somewhere nearby; but Louis, resting, exclaimed, "I don't see why I should have to find the source of every damned river in Europe!"

While the rest of the family remained in Vienna with relatives, Fanny being ill, Louis traveled alone to Dresden in '73 to resume his schooling. There he found the Annen-Realschule, a three-story stone structure resembling a hospital more than anything else. He looked it over, front and back, before making up his mind. Inside, the rector, Herr

Job, firmly informed him that he must produce a birth certificate and a vaccination certificate. Louis caught his eye and argued: "The fact that I am here is proof of my birth, and you may look at my arm for evidence that I was vaccinated." Rector Job, an easy victim of the self-confident manner of the slender boy, was a genial soul with a weakness for American ways, and not typical of the sternly ordered administration.

Dresden proved a continuation of the Louisville tradition. A mark of 2 meant *gut* and 1 meant *sehr gut*. The young *Amerikaner* got 2a in Latin, 2b in French, 2 in German, and 1 in each of a dozen sciences. At the end of two years the faculty offered him a prize for diligence and good conduct, and he selected a book called *Charakterbilde aus der Kunstgeschichte.* He did not take singing, religion or penmanship.

Father, urging him to study medicine and remain in Europe, drew a contrast between the ease and culture of life on the Continent and the rough-and-tumble character of America. But Louis' contact with German discipline made him hanker for the freer air back home, the spaciousness, the free-swinging years he remembered. He had been happier there. Nostalgia as much as freedom settled the question, although analysts with a weakness for the dramatic may put a sure finger on such surging influences as the parental migration following the frustrated revolutions of '48 and the march of Union soldiers past the front door in '61. Louis simply wanted to get back. And as for medicine, he had not the slightest taste for it. For as long as he could remember he wanted to be a lawyer. His uncle belonged to the profession and so did the young men who used to court his sisters.

With two hundred dollars borrowed from Al (who had already returned and gone into business) he entered Harvard Law School in '75. The Boston and Cambridge he slipped into were in the afterglow of Emerson. That lamp of learning was not yet out and the elite gathered round its winter

rays. Longfellow and Lowell and witty Dr. Holmes were
on the Harvard faculty. A law student swinging his green
bag of books along the campus might be admitted to the
stimulating company of Brahmins and Athenians, especially
if he happened to be as personable and well-spoken as Louis
Brandeis. One evening at a professor's house he sat in a mute
circle listening to the aged Emerson read a lecture on education. The boy felt spiritually at home with these old American families.

Although the Law School imposed no entrance requirements, most of the two hundred students were graduates of
New England colleges. Louis lacked both a degree and
identity of background. There was a detectable Southern
softness in his voice. The question of his being a Jew never
came up. What distinguished him in the eyes of teachers
and classmates were intellectual qualities.

When he rose in the recitation hall to take part in eviscer-
ating a case the class expected a treat. This black-haired,
blue-eyed fellow, with high color suffusing his olive skin,
had the polish and poise of a gifted actor and the speech
of a man with broad mental grasp. Dean Christopher Columbus Langdell had introduced the case system whereby a
principle of law was learned by studying its embryology;
each stage of development being illustrated by a case, each
case dissected by the student, who was thus enabled to compare it with the next phase of growth and to arrive at conclusions through his own hard thinking instead of by
teacher's fiat. Louis' ease came from thorough preparation.
In the Pow-Wow Club's mock court he had another opportunity to put learning into action. The years at Harvard
were thrilling. Life was italicized. Cambridge was his world
and he was its worldling.

He studied intensively and read till his eyes hurt. His
eye trouble became so severe that the doctor at school advised him to quit law. But he was no more willing to give
up law than to give up his eyes. He took a trip to New

York to be examined by a specialist. There old Doctor Knopf told him, "Suppose your eyes do hurt, what of it? Don't use them too much, that's all." He returned to Cambridge and induced Samuel Dennis Warren and other classmen to read to him. Absorbing legal education by ear and storing it in his head, in turn he tutored others and got worthwhile fees from rich men's sons. Eight hundred dollars of these earnings was put into government 4% certificates, an issue of 1874 floated to enable the resumption of specie payments after the panic.

A rule he set for himself was to limit his wants to the barest minimum in order to be free of pressure for money. By keeping your debits low your credits went correspondingly higher, he reasoned. The result would be a measure of financial independence, relieving him of having to do objectionable things for money needed to sustain a more expensive scale of living. This apparent strain of austerity owed less to the Puritan atmosphere than to close reasoning. Sacrifice and self-denial were not involved; it was choice. He stopped smoking cigarettes, but not to save money; they gave him little pleasure and made him nervous. He also stopped playing violin, knowing that he was not much of a musician and could use the time to better advantage. At the end of the Harvard period, after repaying his brother, he had a capital of $1,500.

In spite of being at the head of his class and breaking the school's record with an average mark of 87, he had a hard time being graduated. There were rules. In spite of leading the vote of the class of '77 as the one to deliver the oration, there were rules. Professor Langdell stroked his troubled beard and sought to straighten out the tangle by sending young Brandeis to President Eliot. This was the first meeting of the bright boy and the mighty president. Dr. Charles W. Eliot expressed himself with irrefutable logic: "The rule is that the orator is to be a recipient of a degree. The rule is that you cannot have a degree before you are twenty-one. You will not be twenty-one until November. Commencement is in June. I don't see, Mr. Brandeis, how you can be the orator."

Mr. Brandeis was not worried. After all, the encounter with the great and liberal president of Harvard University was an exhilarating event, and the world could wait a little longer for its Brandeises. But on the morning of commencement day, in view of his high standing, the trustees decided to award him a degree by a suspension of the rules, and it was *cum laude*. The class orator had already been selected. This did not matter. The eleventh-hour recognition brought as much satisfaction as he needed on that day.

A third year was added to the course and he planned to stay for it. Before the summer trip to Louisville, Dr. Eliot informed him of his appointment as a proctor in the college. This included the privilege of living off the campus and enabled him to room with Sam Warren in a small building behind the Warren family residence in Mount Vernon Street on Beacon Hill. Sam had finished second in the class. They were drawn together by an intellectual kinship; on this and on their congenial temperaments grew a fast friendship, and they put in so many appearances together that they were dubbed twins. But not identical twins; Sam was much the more reserved. The Warrens had numerous social and cultural connections and introduced the popular Brandeis boy. Through them he met O. W. Holmes, Jr., a member of the law firm of Shattuck, Holmes & Munroe. The circle in which he moved was rockbound, but invigorating.

The city of St. Louis, was very much unlike Boston. It was raw and raucous. It had the clangor of a railroad junction, the saltiness of the frontier town. But when the all-important question arose—where should this young attorney root his practice?—the West had a definite appeal. An opening was made for him in St. Louis in the office of James Taussig at 505 Chestnut Street. Besides, his sister, Fanny, was living there, married to another lawyer, Charles Nagel.

Most of the practitioners in St. Louis had merely read law
and lacked the grasp of principles and precision of mind be
longing to a prize pupil of Professors Langdell, Ames and
Thayer. Here was a chance for leadership.

In St. Louis he wrote his first brief. The suit was in behalf of one Martin Michael who supplied wood for a lime
kiln and sought to collect from the owner, insane, whose
guardian was running the business. The work with Mr.
Taussig was varied and gave him contact with railroad problems; it was interesting, of course, but the eight months he
spent in that outpost left his cravings unsatisfied. A bad
case of malaria made the situation worse. Like an engraved
invitation back to civilization came a call from Warren, then
working for Holmes' firm, beckoning Louis to return and
have their names painted on a door. The combination of
Sam and Boston was too strong to resist.

Warren & Brandeis, counsellors at law, 60 and 62 Devonshire Street, in 1879 opened the first modern office in Boston.
They had a telephone and a stenographer. The office was
organized on a businesslike basis and partitioned into many
rooms, each bearing a number. One of their earliest clients,
a man of spirit, looked at the numbered doors and said, "I'll
have a room with a bath." Some of Sam's clients came in
through his father's paper mill. One of Louis' was Ex-Governor Bradley of Rhode Island, whose son he had tutored.
Another connection was Jacob H. Hecht, who had put up
surety for Louis' tuition and was president of the United
Hebrew Benevolent Association. Brandeis argued his first
case before the Massachusetts Supreme Judicial Court for
Hecht, suing a member for twenty-five dollars back dues,
and won it.

When their first year was over the partners found they
had earned a net profit of $1,200 each. They congratulated
each other. It was a fine day for a horseback ride.

Dane Hall, which housed the Harvard Law School when Brandeis entered in 1875

Annen-Realschule, Dresden, which Brandeis attended from 1873 to 1875

Chapter II

CONSERVATISM AND FIRST DOUBTS

COUNSELLOR BRANDEIS never charged more than he thought his services were worth. His clients apparently felt that he did not use his yardstick too liberally, for some of them let him levy on them for gifts to the Law School. It would not have been in character to forsake all other interests to concentrate on building up a practice. He continued to pursue the art of living well. Eager for the stimulus of good conversation he frequently pulled the doorbell of Professor Nathaniel S. Shaler, a Kentuckian, geologist and humanist, at whose hearth he basked in the company of brilliant minds. He had something to contribute, too.

The year 1879 brought him closer to that consummate man of philosophic cast, Mr. Holmes, who was fifteen years his senior. Holmes would dispatch this sort of note to him:

> Can you spare me the time and the self-sacrifice to give me this evening or a part of it and let me read over such notes as I have made for an article on Torts? It still consists of disjecta membra but I want some assistance in making up my mind whether my ideas are ripe for publication.

In another letter Mr. Holmes asked him to "look in on me this A. M. without prejudice to further consultations more at length of an evening."

The Law School needed a new building. After a large donation to the Harvard Corporation had been announced, a conspiracy was set afoot to convince the trustees that the money should be spent in the right direction. Professor James Bradley Thayer told Brandeis about a squib in the *Boston Advertiser* and urged him to second the motion. Brandeis sent a few lines to the *Post* and Warren to the *Transcript*, and thus the semblance of lively public interest was manifested.

Another appeal came from Professor Thayer enlisting him in the collection of material for a course on constitutional law. When Thayer planned to take a leave he proposed Brandeis for his class in evidence; the Corporation was busy and delayed action. The professor kept him posted on each step of progress, and finally Dr. Eliot invited the aspirant to call. The president was confident of approval. But after arrangements had been made Thayer's sabbatical was postponed.

Meanwhile Brandeis had been working with him to create a professorship for Holmes, whose book, *The Common Law*, was just off the press. One day Brandeis read that a former protégé of his, named Weld, had fallen heir to three million dollars; he straightway sent for Weld and persuaded him to part with $90,000. A chair was endowed for Oliver Wendell Holmes.

The new professor enjoyed teaching torts, but within a year he changed gowns to sit on the bench of the Supreme Judicial Court. The school was jubilant nevertheless; it had the new chair, the new building, and a new library fund. Professor James Barr Ames acknowledged its obligation to alumnus Brandeis. Finally Dr. Eliot made the offer of an instructorship in evidence for '83, two exercises a week.

The notification was forwarded to Louisville for what it was worth. Mother hastened over to Uncle Lewis to share her pride and point out that the letter was addressed "Louis Dembitz Brandeis." This was the first time Uncle felt glad that Louis had changed his middle name from David to Dembitz; Grandfather Dembitz, were he alive, would be overjoyed in knowing that one bearing his name had achieved an academic office, for none had a greater veneration for anything connected with a university.

Brandeis' notes for the course were good enough for Judge Holmes to borrow. His fame spurred an associate justice of the Supreme Court of the United States, Horace Gray (lately elevated from the Massachusetts bench), to solicit his help on a citation bearing upon a case in hand.

Professor Shaler admonished him to quit his practice: "You're too sensitive. A lawyer should be made of sterner stuff. You won't be able to stand the gaff of opposition."

True, there was tranquillity in his makeup; perhaps he seemed too gentle to some contentious clients. But wide study had given him self-confidence and overcome the handicaps of a sensitive face and the soft lines of his mouth. His expanding knowledge of industry and business attracted clients as the demands of corporations, increasingly ramified with the industrial evolution following the Civil War, taxed the ingenuity of lawyers. He seemed deft in getting at the core of a problem, sometimes with lightning intuition; yet he worked with the research spirit of a scientist and insisted on having all the facts—from the adversary's angle as well. Only by studying each problem as a whole and reaching conclusions impartially could he feel competent to advise. He would refuse to encourage a committee of entrepreneurs if their proposed course might harm the general situation, because in the long run it would visit injury upon themselves. Besides the legal points in a case he had to have an understanding of the underlying technical processes. Thus he acquired a reputation as a good business adviser, and more business men thought they needed him. It was no part of shyness to refuse a retainer unless full command went with it; nor was it meekness to decline to take on another case from an unpaid account. He could be firm, and that stiff tuft of dark hair sticking out of his close-cropped head was by no means incongruous with his personality.

His zest for practical affairs and admiration for the remarkable abilities of his partner's father led him into a study of S. D. Warren & Company, one of the leading paper mills. That company was a source of business education, one of the first in the country to install a cost-accounting system. With characteristic patience Brandeis mastered the science of accountancy. In the operation of the plant he saw how the ratio of production to plant capacity affected costs; if output fell below a certain percentage the management automatically would know they were operating at a loss. He found a use for everything he learned.

When Harvard offered him an assistant professorship with the promise of an early full professorship he replied:

"I'm not ready for it. I want other experiences first."

"Perhaps we won't be ready when you are," Dean Langdell said.

"That's a chance I'll have to take."

His parents, stopping with him at Plymouth that summer, were disappointed. But their Louis had always made plans for himself.

Railroading was another avenue of revenue in those years. Plenty of litigation resulted from the propensity of financial moguls for riding the iron horse. In representing bondholders of a Maine line he learned something of railroad finance. As Eastern counsel for the Wisconsin Central Railroad Company he argued his first case before the Supreme Court of the United States (November 6, 1889). He was properly reverential. The suit involved taxation of the road's land-grant. He won it, as well as others in a series for the same company. (Chief Justice Melville W. Fuller later remarked to a friend that Brandeis was the ablest attorney he knew of in the East and recommended him.) In the panic of '93 he acted as counsel for the receivers of that road and in subsequent years his work for a reorganization committee took him to Wisconsin for long stretches of time.

Out of a multiplicity of cases arising from the industrial

concentration and the business struggles of that era his income grew rapidly. Like solid Bostonians who enjoyed the comforts of life while their money worked, he put his earnings into safe investments—chiefly mortgages. He took notes of the Warren paper company, placing his money there merely as a convenience; they did not need it. The law firm of Warren & Brandeis swiftly sailed into eminence, and each year Harvard's best men vied to get in. Professor Shaler's admonition was even more amusing in retrospect.

Brandeis' personal expenses were low, in accordance with his first principles of independence. He could afford to reject clients if they happened not to yield to his dictates.

He pursued an active outdoor life wheeling, skating, and canoeing when the Charles River thawed out. Late afternoons it was horseriding. He joined the Union Boat Club and the polo club at Dedham (where Warren had his country home) and was secretary of the Boston Art Club. The young man attended Shakespearean revivals, whenever they turned up, and of course the Athens of America supported concerts—which he could enjoy without a tinge of jealousy for the first violinist. Despite the fullness of these days he had time to write an article for the *American Law Review* on "Liability of Trust-Estates on Contracts Made for Their Benefit." In Boston and its environs inherited wealth and trust-estates were classed among the old traditions.

All these charming associations engendered acquiescence in the established order of things. That which was, was rather right; except that the condition of "the poor" needed amelioration. Soon after his return from St. Louis he paid visits for the Associated Charities for a short spell. If Mr. Holmes had the tolerant air of a skeptic, Brandeis had the curiosity of one who wanted to know the good and the bad; not to wallow in the bad, but to know it existed. In this period he looked askance at the jury system: it was inept, faintly vulgar, untrustworthy—how could untrained men make expert decisions? His faith in the judge was complete.

He made his first break with the past in politics. During the Cleveland-Blaine presidential campaign of '84 he called himself a Mugwump. Pinning an epithet to oneself was a mild form of rebellion, but in his protest against Blaine of Maine he put aside his allegiance to the Republican Party. (He kept, though, a memento of the Harvard days—a flier of the regular Republican candidates headed by Rutherford B. Hayes, a Law School alumnus; this was his ticket.) After the nomination of Blaine he identified himself with the local Independents and Independent Republicans who hired the large dining room of Young's Hotel to stage a demonstration. He had already become active in the Civil Service Reform Association of his congressional district, on the executive committee; civil service reform was a solid plank with Cleveland. From this time on Brandeis was a Democrat in national politics.

Talk was what he relished as much as anything after hours. Not that he was communicative about himself; he liked to draw others out, dip into their interests, store up new information, even if he got it from a boy on the street. He revelled in discussion—at William Dean Howells', where he met George W. Cable and Joseph Pennell; at Barrett Wendell's, or on the river, canoeing. On Sunday boating trips he engaged in long talks with Glendower Evans while Mrs. Evans listened. He had been introduced to the couple on Wendell's doorstep, and pert Elizabeth Evans, seeing what she pleased to think a bright young face, asked the Harvard instructor, "Oh, is that one of your little charges?"–but her husband, who had come through the Law School hearing of the prodigious Mr. Brandeis, recognized the name.

Brandeis would drop in on the Evanses almost every week for dinner and talk. Sometimes only for discussion. He would appear in a dress-suit, not say whither he was bound, and talk till it was time to go. One evening the subject was religion. Glendower was under the spell of Phillips Brooks, a broad Trinitarian, and Louis argued against him. Eliza-

beth, siding with neither her husband nor her guest, said
nothing, but she was thinking this time, in her brisk way,
that Louis was getting the worst of it.   He insisted that
man's mind could not know what was beyond life and he
had no use for religion.   When Glendower pressed the possibility of after-life he picked up his hat and left with a
tart "Good evening!"

It did not end there.   Another time, when they were paddling, Glendower mentioned that he was reading Schopen-
hauer.   Louis showed no enthusiasm.   He spurned meta-
physics.   He preferred practicality.   When Felix Adler
later proposed that he become the Boston leader for the
Society for Ethical Culture, he declined; the world did not
need ethical preachers so much as ethical doers.   He believed
in the contagion of example; health was as catching as sickness.

His first public works were undertaken as the initiator of
a movement to make the Law School the foremost force in
America in the training of lawyers by building up its facilities, publicizing the Harvard system, and attracting students
from all parts of the country.   As an instrument to this end
he conceived the Harvard Law School Association.   Busy
as secretary and general schemer in a project greater than
anything else that loomed at the time, he did not give serious
thought to the offer of local Democrats to nominate him for
the legislature; they had a ward for him where the Republicans had picked a Negro.

He took a month's holiday abroad, traveling as "an eminent
member of the Massachusetts bar," according to a State Department letter of introduction, and meeting Sir Frederick
Pollock, the distinguished professor of jurisprudence at Oxford University.   It was when he came back that Mrs. Evans
showed him the way to public service directly in his field.
This was after Glendower died.   Brandeis had quietly appointed himself a brother and was loyally taking care of her,
never permitting her many civic activities to overtax her

strength. One morning in '87 Mrs. Evans was riding to Benton, to the state reform school, where she was on the board of trustees. With her on the train was another trustee, Lizzie Putnam, an old New Englander who exercised herself over the spreading power of the Irish Catholics. Horrified, Miss Putnam showed her an item in the newspaper reporting that the $10,000 appropriation which the House of the Good Shepherd was seeking from the legislature had been approved in committee. Mrs. Evans saw no harm in that; her good friend Mr. Brandeis was counsel representing the Catholic institution; he had escorted the committee to the home and had the gates thrown open to the visiting Protestants. But it was outrageous, Miss Putnam declared, for the Commonwealth to disburse public money to this sectarian body. The $10,000 would be a foothold. Next year the Irish would ask for more.

The two women wrote letters-to-the-editor in a campaign to show that such appropriations were against public policy and to force a rehearing. Bessie Evans called on Brandeis to reason with him. Triumphantly she repeated a provision in the Massachusetts constitution under which such a grant ought to be forbidden. He merely listened. There was no indication that he was impressed, save what she thought a supercilious smile. But when the committee responded to pressure for a new hearing he was not present. The Good Shepherd's regular Catholic attorney appeared instead (unsuccessfully). Brandeis had notified the client of his new conviction.

"There's such a luminous look about you, you seem to have come from a wrestle with the devil!" his friend exclaimed.

He told Bessie and Lizzie of the principles which this experience had revealed to him: the state should never allot money without controlling its use and a lawyer should not advocate a cause which was against the public interest. Hence appropriations for Protestant institutions which Lizzie Putnam herself had backed should also be discontinued.

Irish immigration had something to do with another public question. In the movement for equal rights for women many zealous and otherwise social-minded ladies took the opposing side. Yes, if suffrage were bestowed upon them they would always vote properly, but they had no such confidence in their servants. For every dependable mistress of a Boston household there would be the votes of three or four Papists. When Brandeis appeared before a legislative committee in '88, retained by the Massachusetts Association Opposed to the Further Extension of Suffrage to Women, he faced Lucy Stone and her cohorts with a different line of reasoning: The present state of affairs was being administered wholesomely; could not men be trusted to care for their wives and mothers and sisters? It was risky to admit a new element of voters who might usher in a change for the worse. Moreover, women had proved themselves negligent in exercising rights they already possessed. The bill before the legislature aimed to give women qualified to vote for members of the school committees the right to vote on licenses for the sale of intoxicating liquors in their communities. The bill was defeated.

The labor movement caught Brandeis' attention in a roundabout way through John F. O'Sullivan, a reporter on the *Boston Globe*. O'Sullivan's articles on free silver were so well written that Brandeis sought him out to correct the error of his advocacy. Brandeis met O'Sullivan's wife, Mary Kenney, the first woman union organizer, who had come on from Chicago with Samuel Gompers' blessing. Many an evening he spent in their house on Carver Street, Jack doing most of the talking—on labor. Together, the O'Sullivans educated him in unionism.

A shoe strike at Haverhill advanced him beyond the academic stage and helped awaken the social conscience of other susceptible Bostonians. A minister's wife opened the door to Mary Kenney and invited the parish to hear her speak on the condition of the workingman. A number of Brandeis' clients were shoe manufacturers, and he appraised the problem from his own viewpoint. To a group of strikers he said, "I believe with you, labor unions are necessary and employers should recognize them. But unions are also needed for the employers' own good." And there the judgment rested.

Disturbing thoughts concerning the freebooting public franchise corporations began to take hold. Why should the people's rights in the streets be given away? He had read about cities in Canada which arranged equitable contracts with traction companies. He thought about this while boating on the river one day with Mrs. Evans. He wondered whether he should take time from his private practice to fight a cause which the public had not yet recognized. He felt he should speak up, for in years to come his conscience would bother him when the people realized their plight and he knew he might have defended them. But Brandeis was still in midstream, thinking.

Politics might yet be the fulcrum, and the enthusiasts who organized the Young Democracy in the legislature to promote reforms deserved support. Again they asked him to run. Failing that, they prevailed on him to study one measure in particular and identify himself with it; his influence, they said, would help tremendously even if exerted incidentally. Another offer came from the Public School Union, which discreetly promised its backing if he ran for the school board on the Democratic ticket.

Before going to the State House in the rôle of reformer he appeared at a hearing of the joint legislative committee on liquor laws in '91 and denounced "so-called temperance advocates" for making politicians and criminals out of liquor dealers. The gentlemen of the Citizens' Law and Order League were closing their eyes to the fact that "liquor is desired by a large majority of the voters of the Commonwealth, and consequently the people will sell it."

Registered as counsel for the Protective Liquor Dealers' Association, he argued for an amendment to a law which prohibited the sale of liquor except as part of a meal. Restrictions enacted by the prodding of temperance workers resulted, he said, in a larger average drink, more excessive drinking, more arrests for drunkenness, the injection of the liquor trade into politics. The law was a dead-letter—"men will not drink because you say they shall not." The only way to remedy the evils of liquor and prevent the abuses of the traffic was to regulate it sensibly. In his quiet style of presentation Brandeis advised, "Make the liquor business respectable." He held pince-nez in hand and used them for emphasis rather than raise his voice.

"You enact laws which the habits of the community will not permit liquor dealers to obey, and as a consequence you invite into the business the professional lawbreakers or those who are ready to become such," he said. A law prohibiting people from taking a drink unless they consented to eat at the same time clashed with the habits of the great mass of the people. The harassed dealers could not comply; for survival they had to resort to someone in authority to protect their interests. "You can remove liquor dealers from politics by a very simple device—make the liquor laws reasonable."

His opponent asked, "Isn't the existence of a statute proof of the will of the majority?"

"No," Brandeis replied. "It is evidence which creates presumption, but the presumption may be rebutted by the facts. When we find . . . that throughout nearly sixteen years that law has been daily transgressed by men of prominence everywhere and ignored by common consent, I say that then this presumption as to the will of the community has been most effectually rebutted and that you cannot reestablish that presumption, cannot rehabilitate it, by merely showing that this or that legislature has refused to remove from the statute book these idle and inoperative words."

There were men in the liquor trade of good financial and social position who desired to elevate it, he said; but they were surrounded with uncertainties and put under fear of persecution. Governor Russell's inaugural message had urged clarification of the powers of the licensing board. If the legislators of the Great and General Court of Massachusetts passed the amendment their hearts would be "cleansed of that insult to republican institutions—the fear of entrusting to chosen officials so trifling a matter as whether in a particular store there shall be tables or a bar."

He argued that no law could be effective which did not consider the conditions of the community for which it was designed. Every law must be a bad law that remained unenforced. These were fundamental truths in legislation.

How Brandeis came to posit them as a spokesman for liquor dealers was a story in itself. In his Kentucky days he knew William D. Ellis, of Bourbon whiskey fame. Taking Ellis offguard one day, he handed him a list of legislators and asked him to check off the names of the corruptibles; Brandeis needed that information for his fellow-reformers in the Citizens' Association. Then he applied his persuasive art to the whiskey king, pointing out the advantage of conducting the liquor business respectably. Ellis had a fourteen-year-old son: the weak spot. Brandeis appealed to him in the name of that boy until tears rolled down the father's cheeks. But Brandeis had to convince the rest of the wholesalers' executive committee that it was to their best interests to give up bribery. Ellis made him repeat the act for them and those gentlemen went away in a somewhat subdued shuffle. After taking counsel among themselves they returned, still chastened, but shrewd. They would stop the practice on condition that Brandeis represented them on a pending bill. First he hesitated. Then he made a stipulation: they must not spend a dollar on legislative matters without consulting him. With this understanding he took the newspapers into his confidence. They were friendly to him at the time. By

assuring them of the honest purpose to end corruption he
induced them to give ample space to the arguments he made
at the hearing.

Naturally the lobbyists were angry and plagued their
former masters, and these uneasy liquor dealers would go to
Brandeis' office almost daily, just to hold his hand.

The bill passed. So did another, authorizing the licensing board to determine the validity of objections of real
estate owners within twenty-five feet of a prospective licen-
see. He argued that if they were allowed to decide for
themselves whether a licensed establishment would injure
their property or the moral welfare of the neighborhood they
would have the power to blackmail.

"Is there a man in Massachusetts so little of a trader that,
when he has goods to sell which he knows the other man
must buy, he will go to the man and offer them to him?"
he asked. "Well, the liquor dealer comes, and what is demanded of him? Not compensation for the damage that
would be done—but a share of the estimated profits of conducting the liquor business."

The relationship of law to commerce, a daily fascination
in his practice, evolved into an abstract idea which he would
sometime mull over during buggy rides to his week-end
resort at Dedham. He arranged with the Massachusetts Institute of Technology to deliver a course on business law.
It would have additional value as an educational experiment;
he wanted to test his belief that law should be taught to
laymen as part of a liberal education, training and enriching
the mind, illumining history and the questions of the day.
The government was said to be one of laws, not of men; yet
not one person in a thousand was taught to understand law.
Above all, with unrest rising in the country, the conservatism which the study of the law engendered would be invaluable to the community.

This unrest reached political proportions. The People's
Party, or Populists, organized a mass assault upon plutocracy

by combining resentful farmers known as the Grangers, who fought excessive railroad rates; Greenbacks, who demanded currency reform and condemned land-grants to railroads; and the Union Labor Party, which had gone into the field shouting corruption in high places and asking voters to leave the old parties in a fight against the control of legislation and judicial decisions by the railroads and giant corporations.

The Republican and Democratic parties were barely distinguishable and ran about even in the popular vote in presidential elections. For twenty-four years since Buchanan the Republicans had held the White House until the Cleveland-Blaine contest and they might have continued in possession of power and patronage for twenty-four more; the vote was close, and Cleveland slipped through because he happened to own a better reputation than Blaine in his home state of New York. The Greenback Party had practically nothing to do with the change. In '88 Harrison defeated Cleveland and in '92 Cleveland defeated Harrison. But in this last election the Democrats had the Populists to thank. The Populists, in their cry against great accumulations of wealth and their demand for free coinage of silver as cheap money with which to pay debts, sapped Harrison's strength in the West and polled more than one million votes.

Here was a portent of discontent. Labor and small business struck out for protection. The conscience of intellectuals called for a change. *Progress and Poverty* by Henry George exposed the state of the nation. An article in the *Atlantic Monthly* tore the veil off the criminal structure of America's marvel, the Standard Oil Company: it was called *The Story of a Great Monopoly*, by Henry Demarest Lloyd, and it vindicated the courage of Editor William Dean Howells by requiring seven printings of the issue. *Looking Backward* by Edward Bellamy, fictional and palatable, swept into popularity and was bellows to the breath of social and economic criticism. While the public groped for remedies, the government at Washington created the Interstate Com-

merce Commission to regulate the railroads and passed the
Sherman Law to curb the trusts. Labor, meanwhile, had
won the blessing of President Cleveland, who favored the
recognition of unions and the arbitration of disputes. The
feeble Social Democratic and Socialist Labor parties had
sprouted, and the Knights of Labor—an attempt at one big
union of all classes of workers—was crumbling when the
American Federation of Labor organized on craft-union lines
to wring concessions from industry.

Brandeis was acquainted with Lloyd. The writer had
come on from Chicago to be near his sons, at Harvard, and
made his winter home on Mount Vernon Street. Between
law and journalism Lloyd took a hand in public questions,
espoused trade unionism, municipal ownership and cooperatives; he had interceded on behalf of the Haymarket anarchists and helped organize the People's Party. He called himself "the people's attorney," but mostly he practiced writing.
At this point he was laboring over a microscopic study of
an anti-social body: wealth. Howells encouraged him.
Brandeis liked listening to Lloyd's ideas and to the musical
voice which rose from under a broad, ragged sweep of mustache.

Having delayed working out the syllabus for his proposed
course on business law at the Institute of Technology, Brandeis thought another postponement would be equivalent to
an act of bankruptcy. He promised to be ready for the
term 1892-93 and scrupulously prepared notes, based largely
on an outline of philosophic fundamentals. Then, abruptly,
he abandoned them. A headline in the morning paper shook
him into a realization of the inadequacy of antiquated laws
governing the new industrial relations. In the light of the
rifle flare at the Carnegie steel works at Homestead, Pennsylvania, he considered his syllabus useless.

The shooting of steel workers at Homestead dramatized
for Brandeis the injustice of the legal supremacy of organized
capital over labor. His friend Mary Kenney had gone down

to Homestead before the company's agreement with the union expired; she saw walls being built around the mill grounds, with apertures for guns. The workers knew what was coming but did not break the contract. The company refused to continue recognition of the union and proposed, like other industrial baronies, to check labor's struggle to equalize bargaining power. Carnegie's next step was to slash wages, and his manager, Henry Clay Frick, hired Pinkerton guards to protect strike-breakers. The union men stood their ground as capital's private army came up the Ohio River on barges and fired their Winchesters, attempting to land.

The abhorrent use of violence in settling disputes plainly disclosed the disparity between the spirit of law and its application. More than that, the law was not adapted to the complex problems of the modern factory system. Brandeis' emotion found an intellectual outlet. Homestead made him a student of economics. He rewrote his notes and taught those young men at Tech a realistic approach, and his lectures proved so popular that he was asked to repeat them the following year.

While Judge Holmes on the bench was showing tolerance toward labor's aspirations, Brandeis' aim was to handle a controversy in such a way as to avoid its becoming a legal issue. He had a strike on his hands as the attorney for a very successful young shoe manufacturer, William H. McElwain. Twenty-five hundred workers walked out at McElwain's plant in Manchester, New Hampshire, in protest against being put on a piece-work basis. McElwain was no money-grubbing capitalist. He believed in paying high wages and providing proper conditions, and thought the new arrangement would work out equitably. Brandeis pried him for figures.

"Are you giving me the average pay for fifty-two weeks or what they earn when they are working?"

The head of the International Boot and Shoe Workers'

Union was called into conference—John Tobin, a big, well-spoken Irishman. Brandeis listened and noticed that the union leader's statement of facts tallied with the employer's. Tobin made a straightforward plea for fair dealing, and when he finished Brandeis said, "You're perfectly right."

Counsel did not know who was the more surprised, McElwain or Tobin. He proposed that a record be kept of each worker's employment; the paramount question concerning the men was not their wages when they were working but what they received in the course of the year to support themselves and families. McElwain had not calculated the workless weeks. Tobin had asked only for adequate compensation for work performed. After all, the shoe industry was seasonal. Neither had seen it Brandeis' way. They understood each other better now and made him their arbiter.

Particular cases were only the spawn of larger social issues whose contours now began to assume a sharper edge. They became an intellectual challenge, and Brandeis planned to spend less time on the private affairs of his clients.

Part of the day's work was to be answerable for one's professional activity. He was summoned in '93 by the legislature's railroad committee to testify at an investigation of the New Haven Railroad, which was charged with wrecking the New York & New England in a plot to monopolize transportation between Boston and New York. Brandeis was alleged to have inside knowledge. He had brought stockholders' suits against the New York & New England, and now its attorney, the esteemed Moorfield Storey, sought to prove collusion between the secret backers of the suits and the New Haven.

A bill of complaint drawn by Brandeis prayed for a receivership: the road was insolvent, its operating expenses exceeded its earnings. And yet the directors had voted an extra dividend on preferred stock, and Brandeis applied to the Supreme Judicial Court for an injunction against pay-

ment of the dividend. It was granted by Judge Holmes.
The next suits were to restrain a proposed bond issue of
$25,000,000; a mortgage was prepared, but court action in
Connecticut held back the issue.

Storey put Brandeis on the grill. Storey (an overseer at
Harvard, who had known him since '77) asked Brandeis
(on the visiting committee to the Law School, appointed by
the overseers) if he had a list of the suits with him.

"No, but I have them in my head very well and I can
state them chronologically."

He had brought them in the name of N. F. Goldsmith &
Company, liquor dealers, who held stock in the New England. Storey asked him another: Who paid the expenses
of these suits?

"That, I think, Mr. Storey, is not a proper question. . . .
I have no objection whatever, I, personally, to telling the
committee everything I know—I think it is probably less
than is supposed. . . ." He was not going to divulge the
confidence of his clients, but would not mind if Mr. Storey
asked them directly. Besides, he failed to see what bearing
this had on the present inquiry, which was the alleged discrimination by the New Haven against the New England
in regard to freight.

What Brandeis knew was this: In 1888 he met a New
York lawyer named William J. Kelly and thereafter represented him in Boston. In '92 Kelly came to him with a
case concerning a new client, Austin Corbin, head of the
Long Island Railroad and a director of the New England.
Corbin became president of the New England and found
the New Haven its chief obstacle to an entrance into New
York City; so he helped build a line parallel to the rival's.
Before leaving for Florida on a vacation Corbin made arrangements for proxies to be collected and the same management re-elected; but he was double-crossed, he said. Self-
benefiting directors held sway, the financial condition of the
New England suffered, fraudulent acts were committed;

Corbin refused to remain on the board if these directors
stayed on. He resigned, but he wanted a receiver appointed
to protect friends whom he had induced to invest in the
road. He needed dummies, residents in Massachusetts, Con--
necticut and Rhode Island, to lend their names to court actions. Lawyer Kelly came up from New York and with
Brandeis went over a list of people who had been stockholders prior to the frauds. This was how Goldsmith came
to be a litigant.

Before Brandeis was called to the hearing at the State
House he attended a stockholders' meeting and demanded
that action be taken on charges of falsification of accounts.
He moved for adjournment pending a probe. Goldsmith
seconded the motion. It was opposed by Charles A. Prince,
representing the accused directors; the charges might be
credible if they came from any other source, said Prince,
but Brandeis and Goldsmith were working for would-be
wreckers of the road, schemers of iniquity. The motion
was carried.

As the legislative hearing continued, Brandeis told Storey
that Goldsmith now authorized him to give the name of the
backer provided the New England agreed not to use the
information in the cases.

Storey smiled politely but triumphantly.—"Nothing can
disclose the character of this litigation better than the statement of counsel that he is afraid that the evidence which
he is asked to give will prejudice him in certain suits which
he has brought."

Brandeis broke in—"I haven't said that I'm afraid."

"Wait a moment! One of us at a time, if you please."

The flurry was over, and Brandeis turned to the committee: "We have protected the community from one of the
nastiest, one of the most disreputable, acts—the floating of
stock, of preferred stock, upon a community by a false
representation of dividends. . . . When we got them into
court they did not dare to oppose the injunction. . . . I put

the question to Mr. Storey first and he said he positively
wanted it for use here, and not in the cases. If that is his
word that he gives you, why isn't he willing to give you
his bond? If it is as good as his bond, let us have the bond.
I want the bond, not because I doubt the word—because I
do not—but I want it because there are, as Mr. Storey said,
a number of counsel."

Storey resented this as an insulting attack and asserted
that the New Haven was trying to cripple the credit of the
New England as a step toward monopolization. Brandeis,
too, was resentful— at the "somewhat sneering way" in which
"my Brother Storey" referred to the litigants as public bene-
factors. Brandeis went on to relate voluntarily that he had
collected fees not from Goldsmith but from Kelly of New
York, acting for Corbin and others. He offered to tell
Storey the amounts of his bills, but there was a courteous
silence in the best professional tradition.

"I am afraid they are too small," Brandeis confessed. "I
am ashamed of them. It is not a large account."

To one of the legislators who asked if the New Haven
was behind the Corbin suits he answered, "I have had nothing to do with the New York & New Haven Railroad Company from the first day to the last."

Viewed objectively, Corbin was an ambitious capitalist
interested in railroads only as pawns to power. It developed
that when he realized the hopelessness of resuscitating the
New England, and being world-weary to boot, he stopped
spending money on the road. J. Pierpont Morgan, William
Rockefeller and other directors of the New Haven asked
him to let them continue the receivership suit and eventually
their line gobbled up its sick and noisy competitor. Storey
dourly observed, "The findings of the Massachusetts legislature were such as might have been expected in view of the
relations between the legislature and the New Haven."

There seemed to be overtones in that remark.

Chapter III

PUBLIC WORKS

SOON AFTER losing one partner Brandeis acquired another. Sam Warren withdrew upon his father's death in '89 to take up the conduct of the paper business. Thus ended ten smooth years of teamwork, but the friendship remained intact and even the name Warren & Brandeis was retained as a monument to Sam's hopes of resuming law some day. Both belonged to the exclusive Dedham Polo Club, numbering twenty members, and otherwise continued in social contact. When the Young Democracy asked Brandeis to take the field with them—"Read this over in your closet," their appeal said, "and do not throw it aside in your office"—it was Sam whom Louis consulted. And it was to Louis that Sam turned for help in handling the Warren estate.

But in '91 Louis found a partner for life. He had been in Washington the year before on Wisconsin Central matters, and he traveled on to see his parents. A girl named Alice Goldmark happened to be in Louisville, returning from a Western trip and stopping to call on relatives on her way home to New York. Adolf Brandeis saw her first and was immediately smitten. He went to his son.

"Louis," he said, "I have just been talking to the girl you are going to marry."

Louis looked at him with a skeptical smile. Still — his courtly father had a reputation for a sharp eye and good taste.

45

Presently Alice appeared. Hadn't they met many years before in New York? His memory was too sure for doubting. She was only a child then and he was ten years older. Now he was thirty-four and she was an interesting young lady. He noted the patrician cast of her features and the delicate coloring. Her face created a soft, thoughtful mood about her; but she was mentally alert, and she had a buoyant spirit and a gift for comradeship. The earnest lawyer talked his very best. In less than two weeks he was on his knees, summing up before a most friendly jury.

Back in Boston he burst with the news:

"Mrs. Evans, I'm engaged! I'm engaged!"

Down in New York the Goldmark sisters were gay with him. They sat down to a bit of genealogy. The girls' father had been a political exile from Vienna, a Forty-eighter, accused of complicity in the murder of the Austrian Minister of War, Latour. Educated to be a physician, he preferred chemistry and invention; during the Civil War he was one of a few manufacturers of percussion caps and cartridges for the federal government. In '68 he returned to Vienna to risk retrial and clear his name. His wife was Regina Wehle. Louis' grandfather, Dr. Dembitz, had married a Wehle, a daughter of Aaron Beer Wehle (1750-1825) whose first marriage was unfruitful and who remarried at the age of forty-one and begot ten children. Regina was one of his granddaughters. So Louis and Alice had a great-grandfather in common.

On a spring morn in '91 he told Mrs. Evans, "I'm going to New York"—just that. There in the Goldmark home he was married to his second cousin by Felix Adler, husband of Alice's sister Helen. They went on a wedding journey to the seclusion of a country place near Dedham—once the estate of landed gentry—and stayed away a whole happy month. He had bought a house in a sedate row at the foot of Beacon Hill; the narrow, brick house at 114 Mount Vernon Street. He sent the keys to Mrs. Evans and

AGED 15

AGED 21

AGED 30

AGED 38

Various stages of the Brandeis youth

bade her unpack the trunks and put the home in readiness. The coal order, the milk delivery and the electric wire to go under the dining-room table he attended to himself, and saw to the testing of wallpaper samples to make sure they were free from arsenic. Bessie had something more to do now; for Alice was lonesome and homesick for her large family. She was not accustomed to Boston's austerity; but there were rounds of interesting company, and soon the gracious wife of the gifted Mr. Brandeis was happy again. He bought a phaeton and a fine horse, King Cole, and off they would drive to Dedham for weekends. Alice wore a red Shaker cloak and sang aloud to the passing countryside.

During their engagement Louis had taught her his design for living; described the Stoic simplicity of his needs, and laid stress on the preservation of independence. He was a Thoreau who did not retire to the woods. Out of his practice he drew $20,000 that year. When they married they fixed their scale of household expense and he opened a separate bank account for her. She agreed that he would be happiest in public causes, working for leisure and using leisure for work. He was worth $50,000. At the rate that they saved money he would soon have a fortune, but his richest possession was a surplus of time.

One of the fruits of expenditure from that account, one which a proud wife might quietly enjoy, was the award of an honorary M.A. degree in '91 for services on behalf of alma mater. His activities were compounded of loyalty to the university, fondness for his profession, and a strong attachment to education *per se*. The avowed object of the Harvard Law School Association was "to advance the cause of legal education and increase the usefulness" of the school, but the underlying aim was to attract more students and make Harvard the capital of legal learning in America, perhaps a National University of Law. The association started in '86, Brandeis enlisting one hundred and fifty alumni in the project. He took on a burden of heavy correspondence.

While a committee was appointed, including Robert Todd Lincoln, to launch the association on the two hundred and fiftieth anniversary of the founding of Harvard College, he looked beyond the duties of a keeper of the minutes and persuaded Holmes to make an oration calculated to bring the school dignified advertising. The publicity would draw the attention of other states and rekindle the fire in former students.

Holmes' theme, "The Use of Law Schools," fitted in perfectly with the plans, for classroom training of lawyers was still struggling for recognition in a profession composed mostly of self-wrought men. Harvard had begun to teach law in 1817 and profited by the glory of Justice Joseph Story who taught while he was a member of the Supreme Court of the United States. She also profited by the fame of Langdell's case system; but the suspicion that the school produced scholars but not lawyers had to be dispelled. Holmes advertised the school in his matchless prose and darted epigrams at "that most hateful of American words and ideals, 'smartness,' as against dignity of moral feeling and profundity of knowledge." Harvard's aim was "not to make men smart, but to make them wise in their calling." She did not undertake to teach law or make lawyers but "to teach law in the grand manner, and to make great lawyers."

"Culture, in the sense of fruitless knowledge, I for one abhor," said this tall, graceful man standing before them. "The mark of a master is, that facts which before lay scattered in an inorganic mass, when he shoots through them the magnetic current of his thought, leap into an organic order, and live and bear fruit. But you cannot make a master by teaching. He makes himself by aid of his natural gifts."

The student body grew rapidly and the faculty put the credit in the right place. The reason why a dwindling number had been attracted to the school before this was the stiffening of entrance requirements and the lengthening of the course. In Brandeis' time candidates for a degree were not required to take an examination and they needed to attend only three of the four terms; afterwards applicants who were not college graduates had to be examined in Latin and in Blackstone's *Commentaries*, and the course was three full years. Soon after the association was formed the enrolment exceeded two hundred for the first time. *Harvard Law Review* began publication in '87, primarily to set forth the work being done under the Harvard system. In a few years income from tuition fees was overflowing, the students numbered nearly four hundred, and a weeding-out process was necessary to prevent the crowding of Austin Hall.

The association also grew—to eight hundred members in two years. Rutherford B. Hayes, Chief Justice Fuller and Joseph H. Choate were among the officers. Holmes consented to be a vice-president. Brandeis conceived the idea of getting a distinguished graduate in each state to serve as a regional vice-president with a younger man as corresponding secretary for the state; to give momentum to the participation of alumni he suggested sending them the *Review* (he was one of its trustees) on a year's free subscription. At the second annual meeting Austen G. Fox was introduced as "one who gallantly bears Harvard's banner in New York." Abbott Lawrence Lowell was on an essay-prize committee. A gift of one thousand dollars was made by the association for increased instruction in constitutional law.

Brandeis urged upon Langdell the idea of giving a course in the peculiarities of Massachusetts law; for one thing, it would help overcome the impression that Harvard's instruction was not practical. The criticism was frequently passed that it dealt too largely with English law, imbuing students with a handicapping disrespect for the decisions of American courts. Brandeis had found in his experience as one of the examiners for admission to the Suffolk County Bar and as an employer of assistants in his own office that ignorance of Massachusetts law was widespread. Obviously the new course would be a departure from the school's policy, but in the growth of schools as in the growth of other institutions the logical order must sometimes be departed from.

Some of the faculty disapproved of such an innovation, but once the innovator gained his point he forwarded a check for one thousand dollars as the first of five instalments pledged anonymously (by his friend and client, Edwin H. Abbot, president of the Wisconsin Central). Then he plowed ground for a supplemental course on New York law. Thus he hoped to demonstrate that the School was not limiting its sphere of influence, but was taking steps towards the development of a National University of Law. Moreover, the incentive for entering Columbia in preference to Harvard would be removed, and the school would get a firm hold on the New York bar. Among the successful lawyers in New York he was sure the school had enough warm friends to raise money. After gathering information from other schools regarding the instruction they offered in patent law, he tried to induce Langdell to consider such a course, pointing out that the large increase in the income of the school presented a choice between adding instructors and adding instruction. Again, he suggested that dissertations be required of candidates for a *cum laude* degree; the quality of the students would be improved.

In addition to sending fifty dollars to the *Review* to be used in stimulating circulation, he contributed three articles and advice. The advice was that there should be a permanent editor-in-chief (a professor) and a permanent business manager; and publication at regular intervals throughout the year. The *Review* should emerge from its period of infancy. If it was to appear no oftener than bi-monthly it should avoid the time already selected by the *American Law Review*, its only rival in the country. The articles were written jointly with Sam Warren and at Sam's suggestion. First came *The Watuppa Pond Cases* and *The Law of Ponds*, inspired by court decisions on the diversion of water by factories for power purposes. (Brandeis engaged John H. Wigmore to look up the facts.) These writings helped revive the controversial question and led to a more intelligent understanding. The third contribution was *The Right to Privacy*, occasioned by violations inflicted upon Warren, whose sensitive nature resented even mention of his family in newspaper society columns.

Sam was married to Mabel Bayard, daughter of the ambassador to Great Britain, and editors thought his affairs belonged in the public eye, and in the camera's eye. He was outraged when photographers invaded his babies' privacy and snapped perambulator pictures. Instead of turning to the courts for redress he turned to Louis. They talked it over and agreed that protection against prurient curiosity was part of the right to be let alone; thoughts, emotions, and sensations demanded legal recognition. The press was overstepping the bounds of decency; gossip was now a trade pursued with industry and effrontery. Brandeis wrote:

> Column upon column is filled with idle gossip, which can only be procured by intrusion upon the domestic circle. The intensity and complexity of life, attendant upon advancing civilization, have rendered necessary some retreat from the world, and man, under the refining influence of culture, has become more sensitive to publicity, so that solitude and privacy have become more essential to the individual; but modern enterprise and invention have, through invasions upon his privacy, subjected him to mental pain and distress far greater than could be inflicted by mere bodily injury.

Successive editors of the *Review* requested further articles, but Brandeis was too busy. Composition was not a light task for this fluent speaker. He wrote, rewrote, transposed, interlineated, scratched out, redrafted, and transposed again.

The council of the Harvard Law School Association held their meetings in his office at 50 Devonshire Street, A. Law-

rence Lowell occasionally attending. Later they met in his
larger quarters at 220 Devonshire. They were preparing a
celebration of Langdell's twenty-fifth anniversary as professor and dean, and Sir Frederick Pollock was to be spe-
cially invited from Oxford—as a master stroke of publicity—
to deliver the oration. The Oxonian asked to see specimens
of discourses at previous meetings, and Brandeis assured him
that none but Holmes' was worthy of the occasion. Would
Sir Frederick be his guest at the Dedham Polo Club? Not
all of the members played polo; some golfed, others rode,
canoed, or did nothing, but most were interested in something good besides sport. The visiting luminary came to the
memorable dinner for Langdell and sat with the dean, Chief
Justice Fuller, Associate Justice Horace Gray, Judge Holmes,
Professors Ames and Thayer, the Japanese Ambassador
Shinichiro Kurino, and many others of rank. Holmes remarked—his swirling mustachios turned iron gray—"I see that
we have a good many here who have graduated within the
last twenty-five years and therefore know that I am in the
presence of very learned men."

Holmes' brief talk was, with a bow to Sir Frederick, the
dessert of the evening. He alluded to his martial past, as
was his wont, and stressed the duty of the law to move away
from tradition and draw its postulates and legislative justification from science. He said:

> Our forms of contract, instead of being made once for
> all, like a yacht, on lines of least resistance, are acciden-
> tal relics of early notions, concerning which the learned
> dispute. And at times my friend Mr. Ames pitches into
> me, and at times I have thought perhaps I had in my
> boot a *skean dhu* or short-knife for the ribs of Mr.
> Ames.

The friendship with Holmes was a vibrant one. Brandeis
dined at his Beacon Street home and they reviewed the
judge's decisions in intimate discussion. Holmes valued the

younger man's appreciation and hoped there would be many years ahead in which he might have the pleasure and advantage of seeing him and hearing his "good, wise and suggestive talk." To Mrs. Holmes the judge would say when their visitor left, "A really good man." Brandeis struck him, however, as one who idealized the world.

The idealist was growing richer— by about twenty thousand dollars a year, the income from investments taking care of expenses. As the returns from his practice mounted he shared them with his employees: William H. Dunbar, George R. Nutter, D. Blakely Hoar, and his secretary E. Louise Malloch, each receiving a percentage of the increase in net profits. He made a place in his office for Professor Thayer's son, Ezra, and in a short time put him on a ten percent basis plus one hundred and fifty dollars' monthly salary.

Many of the clients were corporations trying to get their bearings in another period of depression. An entirely different kind of client was Mrs. Alice N. Lincoln, a friend of Mrs. Evans. A wealthy woman interested in the poor, she was so distressed by the conditions in Boston's pauper institutions that she formally laid charges before the commissioners and set the town talking by a letter in the *Transcript*. The buildings on the islands in the harbor were in a horrible state, and a herd of drunkards, paupers, criminals, and mental weaklings were huddled together. The city apparently had no thought but to keep them there at a minimum of expense. The mayor appointed Mrs. Evans to the visiting board; she confirmed the repulsive picture. After three years of agitation the board of aldermen called a hearing in '94 to thrash out the whole subject, and Mrs. Lincoln appeared to present her testimony. Some of the aldermen at first objected to her bringing counsel along—such eloquent counsel, at that.

Brandeis was impressed with her devotion to the cause of those human wrecks. He saw for himself the ugly barrenness of the buildings, the idleness and sinking stupor of the inmates, the atmosphere of listlessness and doom. There was

no classification, no facilities for studying them, no determination of who could work and should be given work. In
short, nothing was done to help them return to the world.
These people should not be treated as if they were machines,
but given something to interest them, to hope for, to do.

Brandeis saw Mrs. Lincoln through this fight in fifty-seven
public hearings stretching over nine months. He used witnesses as opportunities to declaim against the ruinously expensive economy of the management, whose main occupation was turning paupers into criminals.

"They are all deserving of your pity and the best study
and thought which Boston and the world affords," he told
the aldermen.

As a result the aldermanic board enacted a complete reorganization of the department of public institutions.

Mrs. Lincoln gave him three thousand dollars for his services. But he did not keep the money. After crediting his
colleagues with their customary percentages he sent checks
of five hundred dollars to the Municipal League of Boston,
five hundred dollars to the Associated Charities, one hundred dollars to the United Hebrew Charities, one hundred
and fifty dollars to the National Municipal League, and two
hundred dollars to John Graham Brooks for civil service
reform.

In those days he joined societies as they sprang up: the
Citizens' Association, the Public School Association, the Election Laws League, the Aldermanic Association, and others.
Acting on a thought which disturbed him long—that franchises should not be granted without a return to the public—
and representing no group, he appeared at a committee hearing at the State House in opposition to the long lease with
which the West End Street Railway sought complete control of a proposed subway. He compared the terms with
franchises obtaining in Canadian cities and managed to delay
legislative action. The newspapers gave columns to arguments in favor of the lease; if they mentioned Brandeis it was

only in a line saying he objected. But an agent of the company approached him with terms better than those he had in mind. This made him wiser.

With the sharp awareness that comes from the impact of experience he realized how easy it was for powerful corporations, hiring most able counsel while the public went unrepresented, to win privileges from the state. Moreover, the fat fees of these skilful lawyers were finally paid by the unprotected public. He made a resolution: to draw a line between private and public cases. Although his conduct in Mrs. Lincoln's cause may have been commendable, he should not have accepted her money in the first place. Hereafter, in entering controversies which appealed to him as opportunities for public service, he would fight for the Commonwealth—no retainer to encumber him.

The subway was just such an issue. He stepped into it despite the fact that the West End Company's promoters and stockholders included Back Bay's best families. The business section of Boston was a small area hemmed in by the sea, the river, the Common, and Beacon Hill. It had become a traffic snarl. The narrow streets, the creeping lines of trolley cars, the furore of exasperated teamsters, cried out for air and elbow room. The pedestrian was Sumner's "forgotten man." After the city built a subway under Tremont Street the politico-financial pains attendant upon such an event occurred. The West End offered to run the subway but demanded a fifty-year lease, for how else could the necessary capital be attracted? The average Bostonian, who wanted his subway, saw nothing wrong. The newspapers cheered on the enterprise. Brandeis went before the legislative committee on metropolitan affairs in '96 and argued, this time on behalf of the Municipal League, for a shorter lease and compensation to the city on the cost of construction.

Although the franchise was cut down to twenty years and the company was obliged to pay an annual rental of four and seven-eighths percent on the cost and agreed to the removal of the tracks on Tremont Street, the fight had merely begun. A financial net was being laid around the city's transportation system. Next year a group of New York capitalists backed by J. Pierpont Morgan took hold of the Boston Elevated Railway and arranged with the West End for a ninety-nine-year lease of the latter's lines. This deal, contrived through the good offices of the banking house of Kidder, Peabody & Company, would have drawn the strings of surface, elevated and underground traffic into one grip. But the eagerness of financiers to capitalize on Boston's transit problem was matched by watchful opposition.

It did not take much in Boston to be called a radical. To oppose the banking interests involved in the scheme and insist that control remain vested in the people was enough to earn this stamp. Brandeis got his first taste of newspaper hostility and some of his friends cut him. Not all the local bankers saw him in the light of an enemy. Lee, Higginson & Company, having no share in the deal, were happy. The new lease was reduced to twenty-five years. Brandeis had again talked to the legislature in his calm, hand-in-pocket style, with such an air of self-assurance that his adversaries feared he had damaging figures in that pocket, whereas he kept them in his head.

A whisper went round the financial district and newspaper offices that Francis Higginson had retained him. Two editors told him that the statement was given them in confidence. He pried further and after ten days learned from a friend who knew Albert E. Pillsbury, attorney for the other side, that Pillsbury had spread the tale. He straightway told his fellow-member of the bar that it was a lie. No one had retained him; he had acted only as a matter of duty. Since Pillsbury undoubtedly desired to fight fairly out of court as well as in, would Pillsbury take the trouble to tell him the source of his erroneous information? To Colonel W. A. Bancroft, who also repeated the intimation, he said he opposed the elevated company's bill because it would result in great injustice to the people and eventually to the capitalist classes with whom they were both in close connection.

By stepping out of line a man might witness a glacial drift. Boston's better people, unable to understand how one of their own could challenge society's charming etiquette, froze up to Mr. and Mrs. Brandeis. If he wanted to play the game and substitute teacup chatter for true talk he could easily rid himself of heresy and suspicion. But he now had enough social experience.

Chapter IV

THE TACTICS OF ATTACK

BRANDEIS worshipped personal freedom. One might be rich and yet not free. Social obligations consumed time and brought complications. He was now worth more than two hundred thousand dollars, making money faster than ever, but he carried his independence with him as a mariner courts the company of the North Star. In Brandeis' phrase, nothing must deflect the magnetic needle. To hold to a course of self-abnegation it was not necessary to be a born ascetic. Like Thoreau, a man might arrive at it rationally; you simply gave up one thing for another and exercised your will.

In his law work he had reached the enviable position of being able to treat cases as opportunities for mental growth. When a case began to drain his energy, he learned to avoid nervous crises by fleeing the office. When a man became obsessed with the belief that he could not leave his work, it was a sure sign of an imminent breakdown; one's judgment in business could not be trusted in such a condition. Ordinarily Brandeis approached Devonshire Street with brimming energy—looking to another day of progress; but if he lacked eagerness of a morning he knew something was wrong and he had better not go.

Ever ready for a holiday, he took his family to Louisville for a grand reunion on his father's seventy-third birthday. All the children and grandchildren were there. Adolf Brandeis was especially proud of the honor Harvard had bestowed

*The only portrait for which Brandeis posed, painted by
Frank H. Tompkins in 1888*

upon Louis in making him an honorary member of Phi Beta Kappa.

Louis and Alice had two daughters: Susan, who was four years old, and Elizabeth, the newcomer, named for Mrs. Evans. They continued to spend weekends at Dedham; summer found them at Newport or elsewhere on the coast. In preparation for a summer at Block Island he took charge of the arrangements, writing specifications to cottage managers—he needed two small cribs with mattresses, a stove in the rear bedroom, a large foot tub; in the sitting room a lounge, three rockers, an open stove for a wood fire, two reading lamps with shades, and a round center table which must be quite large.

As a man of affairs the niceties of personal relationships did not escape him. When one of his office force remained away a long time because of illness and offered to renounce his salary, Brandeis answered, "I like to think of our office as a league defensive as well as offensive, and that when one falls wounded in the ranks his fellows will bear him on to glory."

At the beginning of '97 the name Warren & Brandeis was dropped, for Sam no longer expected to return. It was changed to Brandeis, Dunbar & Nutter, and in place of guaranteed compensation a partnership was formed whereby profits (or losses) were payable monthly. The profits of their first year were fifty-five thousand dollars; Brandeis' share was two-thirds. As the century closed, his wealth expanded into almost half a million dollars, and he increased the percentage of his partners.

He followed a rule regarding investments which he expressed when a relative asked about buying Wisconsin Central stock— never to invest where he was advising professionally; but he committed a technical violation of the rule when he ordered four hundred shares of United Shoe Machinery pfd. The United was a merger of five firms manufacturing different kinds of machinery. Brandeis had been counsel and a director of one of the combining companies and purchased the stock just before the consolidation in '99. His firm was not general counsel for the United, but acted for it now and then, the matters being handled sometimes by Dunbar and sometimes by his new associate, Edward F. McClennen. He became a director in the United as the representative of a Chicago family which held a substantial interest. Later, with rights going along with preferred stock, he bought a few shares of common. At any rate, he was not an adviser to the German Empire and so felt free to buy a few thousand dollars' worth of that nation's bonds. But he dropped them soon in a revulsion from Prussianism and withdrew later from the Germanic Museum at Harvard in a disagreement with Professor Hugo Münsterberg.

As a substantial citizen he stood on cordial footing with many men in public life who could open channels for his ideas. Before Governor Josiah Quincy—"dear Quincy" to him—wrote the inaugural address, Brandeis laid out a plan for reorganizing the state department of public institutions; the governor's recommendations followed these lines. And if the incumbent governor happened to be one he did not know personally or had even voted against, Brandeis was quick to praise him for some courageous veto.

While at City Hall on Mrs. Lincoln's retainer he accidentally picked up in the aldermanic chamber some blank forms to be addressed to franchise corporations in recommending men for jobs. The forms bore a facsimile of the city's seal and were the best evidence of the prevalence of bribery. He approached a friend in the legislature who was a leader in the civil service reform movement and suggested the introduction of a bill making it a penal offence for office-holders to seek such favors. Brandeis drew up the bill himself and astutely limited it to aldermen and councilmen; passage would be made easier by omitting reference to members of the legislature. Besides, the evil lay largely in the city council.

The Municipal League, aiming at the proper functioning of the city government, was a small group consisting of representatives of other organizations; it was based on Benjamin Franklin's junto. Brandeis felt that each member should be given some specific and laborious task to perform and he contrived a comprehensive scheme for watching the workings of the hundred separate city offices and departments. When the Public School Association was formed he advised against attempting radical changes in the machinery for governing the schools—this would divert public attention; the Municipal League had dissipated its force by concentrating on changes instead of on knowledge. Once intelligent interest and knowledge were developed, even the present machinery could work fairly well. The framing of changes should wait until the public was sufficiently informed.

The press was an ideal vehicle for popular education and it seemed to Brandeis that a reform newspaper like the *Post* was neglecting its duty in calling attention only to new revelations of evil. The abuses suffered so patiently by the American people were due less perhaps to indifference than to forgetfulness. Today's manifestation of the abuse would be forgotten in tomorrow's swirl of interests. A newspaper ought not merely to tell what was new—he counselled the editor of the *Post*—but to keep reminding its readers of the old.

The weakness of protest usually lay in its being an emotional splutter. Saying "gosh darn!" did not get far. Viewing with alarm still lacked vision. One must determine on an objective—and on the method. Brandeis was often consulted for the right technique.

In '97 Brandeis went to Washington on the tariff question. The McKinley Tariff Act of 1890 had boosted the average duty almost to fifty percent; a slight downward revision was achieved during Cleveland's second term, and now, after McKinley's election, a special session of Congress was called to raise new revenues. Hordes of manufacturers stampeded the

Capitol to get what they could. Brandeis arranged with two Democratic members of the House to be heard.

"I desire to speak in behalf of those who, I believe, form a far larger part of the people of the United States than any who have found representation here," he addressed the ways and means committee. "I speak for the men who want to be left alone, those who do not come to Congress and seek the aid of the sovereign powers of government to bring them prosperity."

Chairman Dingley asked if he had any information to present. It was this: that the merchants doing the great bulk of the country's business and the great mass of laboring men "have not come before you and will not come before you, because they want to be let alone."

But what did he represent? The New England Free Trade League. There was jeering laughter.—

> The members of the executive committee of the League are large carpet and woolen manufacturers. Other members are paper manufacturers, and a great many are mere consumers....I ask you to remember in considering the evidence and claims before you that these men who are telling you the piteous tales of their suffering have suffered because the foreign importations during the year 1896 were $120,000,000 less than they were the year before, and these goods would have been a boon—

A bystander wanted to know if the gentleman was in order. Brandeis' friend on the committee supposed that one spokesman for the consumer might be allowed. The chairman said this was not the place to make a speech on free trade. Brandeis replied that he was simply objecting to a change in "the condition which we are in, which is very far from free trade."

"What I make an argument for," he continued, "is in behalf of the business men and laboring men and the consumers, that business may be left in peace in order that it may recover."

But wasn't he aware that additional revenue must be raised? This could be done without affecting the tariff, he answered, by putting a dollar tax on every barrel of beer.— "We would not disturb business. The only result would be a little more froth in every glass of beer a man was called upon to drink." His heckler asked how the government was going to exist during the time business was recovering. Then one indulgent congressman remarked, "Oh, let him run down." And Brandeis put in another observation to the effect that if Congress let business alone imports would increase and provide revenue—"but these gentlemen who have appeared here are arguing for protection regardless of revenue."

His ten minutes expired, and a member of the House desired to be heard for a moment on the subject of jewelry.

A man in the chamois industry asked protection but admitted he could supply only one-tenth of the amount of chamois used in the country. "Yet he desired to tax 70,000,000 people for that one small factory," Brandeis told a meeting of the League.—

> This asking for help from the government for everything should be deprecated. It destroys the old and worthy, sturdy principle of American life which existed in the beginning when men succeeded by their own efforts. That is what has led to the evils of the protective tariff and other laws to that end, by which men seek to protect themselves from competition. Never before did I realize the rightfulness of the movement we stand for and to which all must flock if they will save themselves and save American civilization. What we need is peace, business peace. Let us have it and the people will work out their own salvation.

The Dingley tariff bill passed after scant notice of the contention of the minority report that the inevitability of higher prices was a sufficient condemnation; the tariff would foster trusts; it was a gross perversion of the sovereign power of taxation, employed to enable favored classes to levy unjust charges on the great body of the people.

Anti-trust legislation had been lulled somewhat by the passage of the Sherman Law, but industrialists ignored both the agitation and the lull and proceeded with their gigantic enterprises. Henry Demarest Lloyd created a considerable stir when his *Wealth Against Commonwealth* was published by Harper on Howells' recommendation. The book deeply impressed Brandeis, but he thought it should have been written in a more popular style; shorter, naming names. The chief trouble with efforts directed against the trusts was the lack of popular support. Americans must be educated to an awareness of the conditions under which they were living. They still admired the captains of industry but would be less likely to do so if the facts collected by Lloyd were put before them. We could not make progress against the trusts unless we overcame the admiration of the American people for the individuals who were the leaders of the trusts.

William Jennings Bryan, in his own eloquent way, was educating the public and winning the support of more than five million voters, Democrats and Populists. Their campaign for an income tax law was checkmated by the Supreme Court; their assault on the high tariff was repulsed by the triumph of McKinley; their advocacy of free silver split the party and resulted in a distinct body of gold Democrats. They condemned the labor injunction; it was used against Eugene V. Debs for organizing a strike against the Pullman Palace Car Company in Chicago. Bryan appealed to the disowned children of the new industrialism. He led embattled farmers against Wall Street—but their pitchforks were unavailing against the tridents of the demons of capital. And Bryan was weak in economics.

While declamations against predatory plutocracy were shouted across the prairies the phalanx of aggregate capital

marched into Boston to establish a transit trust. Its recent
setbacks were no discouragement, merely untoward incidents in a career of habitual acquisition. In '99 the city's
traffic snarl needed further untangling and a new subway was
required under Washington Street parallel to Tremont, the
two streets constituting the ganglions of the business district.
This subway the Elevated Company offered to build but also
own in perpetuity, or at least till Plymouth Rock should split.
To strengthen its hand and make that the upperhand the
company sought to restore car tracks on Tremont Street in
violation of the old agreement. The new subway would link
the transportation system from one end of Boston to the
other, but if the company could join its lines by replacing
the surface tracks it would be in a position to dictate terms.
Instead of a tenant of the city it would become a monopolistic landlord.

The company's bill had the endorsement of the respected
names in the Citizen's Association (with which Brandeis was
no longer connected). But the sponsors did not count on
Edward A. Filene, a bantam fighting cock, whose father
owned one of Boston's most progressive department stores.
He insisted on the public's right to determine whether the
tracks should be laid down. He turned to one lawyer after
another in quest of a man unafraid to meet the powerful traction interests, someone, in fact, who shared his dream of an
unrelenting war on the encroachments of all public service
corporations. It did not occur to him at first to ask Brandeis,
who had served the store in a legal capacity from time to
time, and he was surprised to find that this businessmen's
lawyer was not only willing but already aroused by the Elevated Company's breach of faith. But Filene also found
himself answering many questions which seemed to be pry-
ing into his purpose. Brandeis was simply being thorough,
not mistrustful. They agreed to work together to save the
city from surrendering control of its transportation facilities
to the financial clique.

Filene busily organized a group to counteract the influence of the Elevated. Some of the men assembled were B. F. Keith, the theatre owner; Dr. Morton Prince, son of a former mayor; Laurence Minot, trustee for large real estate holdings; Charles M. Cox, of the Chamber of Commerce, Robert Treat Paine, Jr., Richard Henry Dana (Brandeis' classmate at Harvard), and Edward R. Warren (not related to Sam). They brought pressure on the governor and induced him to force a referendum on the track issue.

The group worked against the odds of opposition from almost every newspaper in town. Some refused to run its advertisements. Circulars were resorted to—New York printers being used to avoid treachery. The essential points of the transit problem were reduced to simple language. The man on the street must be told and convinced. The referendum was injected into meetings of the Central Labor Union, the Building Trades Council, the Fruit & Produce Exchange, the Associated Board of Trade. Although the support of these bodies was won, the general forecast was that restoration of the tracks would surely be authorized. But a tidal vote rejected it.

A modified bill came before the legislature in 1900 to permit the Elevated to operate the Washington Street subway for forty years without compensation to the city other than absorption of the cost of construction. Brandeis spoke up in the name of the Board of Trade and undermined Pillsbury's contention that it would be unprofitable to take on another subway at a rental of four and seven-eighths percent. Brandeis produced figures showing that every passenger gave the company a profit of one and one-half cent, and traffic had increased fifty-nine percent in five years. Moreover, he knew parties who stood ready to take the lease on the rental basis (Sam Warren, Higginson, Keith, Prince, etc.—but he did not mention names).

While the company delayed on general principles or in the hope of getting a legislature the next year more to its liking, the Filene-Brandeis group organized on a permanent footing as the Public Franchise League. Their immediate object was to press legislation for a city-built subway to be leased for a short term. Brandeis drafted a bill which the Board of Trade introduced.

Filene was dashing about with publicity and Brandeis was giving him pointers. Success depended on the thoroughness with which Filene accomplished the following: Get editorials and notices advocating the Board of Trade bill into various papers, to appear Sunday, Monday, or Tuesday, the earlier in the week the better; have labor organizations repeat their protests against the Elevated Company's bill and see that copies were sent by special delivery to each member of the legislature from the metropolitan district on Monday morning; induce people to write their representatives for seats in the House during the debate; get more and more letters into Boston papers. The greatest danger was from the Boston members; it could be overcome by a strong showing from their constituents.

"We rely upon you for this work," Brandeis told him.

Filene developed a technique of his own. On a dull Sunday night he dropped in at a newspaper office, one of the few friendly papers, and offered the night city editor a choice bit of news. He found this fellow avid and grateful, and as they sat around waiting for the story to be set Filene smoothly persuaded the editor to pay him in galley proofs. As soon as the proofs came up Filene rushed to the other newspapers and flashed the story their rival was going to publish.

But the legislature responded to its master's voice. By vast majorities in both houses it adopted the Elevated Company's proposal. Forty-six of Boston's fifty members in the House voted for the lease. Governor W. Murray Crane considered it an extraordinary and reckless proposition and vetoed it so sharply that popular opinion obliged the legislature to reverse itself. The mayoralty candidates, Republican and Democratic, both declared themselves for a city-built, city-owned, short-lease subway. Brandeis sent Governor Crane a letter: "You have performed a great service for the Commonwealth. You have not only defeated a bad measure, but you have done it in such a way as to teach the people what to strive for, and what to expect."

Again the traction interests went into hibernation. It would be good to wait until Crane was out of the way; until the transit situation became unbearable to a clamoring citizenry. In 1902 they preferred not to ask for legislation. But the Public Franchise League was bent on action, and for this a most determined effort had to be made to arouse opinion. Brandeis prodded Filene: "I commit the work to your hands, convinced that you can achieve success." His own contribution towards molding public opinion was to persuade Mayor Patrick A. Collins to appear at a hearing.

The League and the Board of Trade again joined forces, and again Pillsbury pleaded that the conditions were impossible. Brandeis analyzed his statements to find them misleading or incorrect; Elevated stock had risen from 150 to 170 and paid $600,000 in dividends in one year; the actual ratio of cost of operation to gross receipts had declined, and in anticipation of the subway lease the company had increased its dividend from four percent to six percent, thus putting a charge upon itself of $200,000 which was equal to four and seven-eighths percent of the estimated cost of the new subway.

Pillsbury put in: "Shows how much you know of the subject."

Ignoring this, Brandeis went on to criticize the company's attempt to secure permanent tenure of the tunnel as it had of elevated locations.

Pillsbury: "Do you call that an offensive provision?"

Brandeis: "Your company tried to get that which would give it absolute control of the situation while the control ought to rest with the people, with the community and not with any corporation, whether domestic or foreign. A provision for getting such control I deem to be offensive."

After the hearing the company got in touch with Mayor Collins. Capitulation was the word. Brandeis informed Governor Crane of the terms of the proposed agreement but refused to commit the League and the Board unless the directors of the company passed a vote of assent and delivered a certified copy to the mayor. The concession of a four and one-half percent rental would otherwise be withdrawn and the fight for the measure in its original form would be renewed. Brandeis took no chances; after Pillsbury went through the draft he made a point of reading it over with the mayor.

Talking in New York at a convention on municipal ownership, Brandeis summed up the victory:

> Boston will own all the subways which are the connecting links in both the elevated and surface systems through the heart of the city. Without these subways no practical elevated system is possible and no surface system could be successfully operated. So long as Boston retains this ownership and the right to revoke surface locations the city will control the transportation system and will have power to compel the corporations to pay adequate compensation for the use of the streets.

Several times during that three-year fight Filene asked him to send a bill for his work. Now that it was over Filene insisted, asserting that he would no more think of taking his services for nothing than Brandeis would think of going into the Filene store and walking off with a suit without paying. At last the lawyer relented.

"I'll take," he told the merchant, "half of what you got out of it."

They understood each other and went on to their next problem—municipal misgovernment. On the authority of a former alderman they learned that when a resolution favoring public ownership of the subway came up the Board of

Aldermen voted against it on the pain of being punished
by the Elevated through loss of patronage. One clever member had managed to get as many as two hundred cronies and
campaign workers on the utilities' payrolls. Brandeis drafted
measures to combat this form of corruption and submitted
them to the Public Franchise League for discussion. The
League conducted some little agitation on the subject and
then decided not to complicate its specific subway battle
with a general attack on this practice. Now they were
ready for it.

Someone else introduced a similar bill but the League did
not support it, partly because of the sponsor's reputation,
partly because it would be better to educate the public to
demand properly framed legislation. Upon Governor John
L. Bates' election Brandeis suggested that the League hoped
he would feel disposed to write a strong recommendation in
his inaugural. The new governor said he was open to suggestions and invited Brandeis for a talk on all matters that
interested the League. After these backstage preparations
the League announced its anti-patronage bill and Brandeis
instructed the secretary to make it appear in the papers that
it was being presented to carry out the governor's recommendations. The statute was enacted in 1903, prohibiting
persons in public office from soliciting employment from a
public service corporation and subjecting the companies to
the same penalty ($200) for giving it.

At the time Brandeis was chairman of the Aldermanic Association other cities also had a rotten core of corruption and
Lincoln Steffens was writing "The Shame of the Cities" for
McClure's Magazine. Brandeis regarded the moral tone of
the aldermen as being pretty low; they would go into secret
sessions under the title of committee on public improvements
and emerge with huge appropriations. The expenditures of
the street department, for example, had increased 82%.
Only payroll padding could account for it. Boston was
spending $21,000,000 a year.

"We cannot submit to the dishonor of being represented by these men," Brandeis said at a dinner of the Boot & Shoe Club. "We should not allow ourselves to be represented by thieves and convicts. It is needed that good, honest, honorable men be drafted into service as officeholders."

He wrote to several people for data on flagrant real-estate deals and other information for use in a speech at the Unitarian Club.

"The conviction has come to many minds that misgovernment in Boston has reached the danger point," he told the next meeting. "Fortunately Mayor Collins has blazed the path to good government. Recognizing, as Cherbuliez says, that 'arithmetic is the first of the sciences and the mother of safety', Mayor Collins immediately upon his inauguration ordered an investigation into the financial condition and operation of the various departments."

An intelligent public opinion was the first requirement. The fundamental cause of municipal misrule was ignorance. A complete cure could come only by substituting knowledge. Spasmodic indignation at wrong would not suffice. Light must be thrown on the government day by day. If the people knew the facts they could not help thinking about them, and good men would run for office. His assertion that the best men could be had any time they were wanted led the *Traveler* to observe that the reason he was so busily engaged in leading the star-eyed goddess of reform by the hand was now evident: "Mr. Brandeis is a reform candidate for mayor of Boston this year, or any other year when the reformers can control the election."

As a reflection on his efforts "to make the world revolve his way," the *Traveler* editorially recalled that years back he appeared for the Museum of Fine Arts (which was Sam Warren's absorbing interest) to get restrictions removed from land on Copley Square donated to the museum by the city; the purpose was to mortgage the property and buy other land for an annex. The editorial said, "They got all they

asked for after something of a struggle, a notable victory for
Brandeis. But the annex has not been built and it is reported
that the land has been sold at a good price, without the restrictions."

He replied that the *Traveler's* account of his City Hall
activities was incorrect as far as stated and not exhaustive.
His main experience there seemed to have been forgotten, he
said, recalling the investigation of public institutions which
resulted in a complete reorganization.

"Nothing could be farther from my thoughts than to be a
candidate for mayor or for any other public office," he said
in the *Record*. "What I have desired to do is to make the
people of Boston realize that the most important office and
the one which all of us can and should fill is that of private
citizen. The duties of the office of private citizen cannot
under a republican form of government be neglected without serious injury to the public."

These duties did not exempt him from the shafts of rebuttal. Alderman Bromberg rose to a question of personal privilege to resent his remarks on the Board.

"I have many reasons to be attracted to Mr. Brandeis," he
began. "He is a man of remarkable legal and literary ability,
a great scholar, a very influential person and, I am told, he is,
or was, my coreligionist.

"But on the other hand, his education has been neglected.
His entire life as a counsel for wealthy clients and as an associate of wealthy men is colored by the greenish-golden light
of finance. He has pleaded the cause of capitalists so long
that that part of his brain which is not used in such work has
shrunk, and therefore when he attempts to discuss a question
in a broad and manly spirit he becomes pitifully weak and
unconvincing."

The alderman continued:

"I tell you, Mr. Brandeis, there are more poor men than
rich men in this city and that before the rich man can sit in
this hall he must convince the voters that he has a heart as

well as a brain and must come before the people with clean hands."

The nomination of a candidate three months after conviction of conspiracy to defraud the federal government gave Brandeis another occasion to denounce criminal representatives. He saw Boston slipping from the noble heritage "handed down to us by our fathers," the Boston round which clustered sacred memories of American history. He told the Good Government Association that as men of honor they could not permit immigrants—future fellow-citizens and perhaps rulers—coming to this country for liberty and opportunity, to be taught that in Boston liberty meant license to loot the public treasury, and opportunity meant graft.

In 1904, just before the Democratic state convention, the political gossip was that William L. Douglas, the shoe manufacturer, and Brandeis were seriously being considered for the gubernatorial nomination. Brandeis said it was all news to him and parried reporters' questions.

"Isn't it quite probable that you will allow your name to be used?"

"I cannot say anything about it as I have never given the matter a thought."

Douglas won the nomination and the election. Since the Democrats had taken a strong position in the campaign regarding contributions from corporations seeking favors from incoming administrations, Brandeis sent the governor-elect the draft of a bill covering the subject and asked Douglas to make an inaugural recommendation. In national affairs such contributions were likely to be made by protected industries and the trusts. In state and municipal campaigns their source was often the utilities. The bill passed.

Brandeis' appetite for banquets—for addressing them—became keener. He talked to the Massachusetts Medical Society on the relation between municipal graft and medicine, urging physicians to use their political weight by organizing; they were now dealing with public health, society as a whole were their patients, success would be possible only through good government. Did they not realize that a million dollars had been spent on contracts for work in the Back Bay Fens while the promised hospital for consumptives was still a mere promise?

"The reason is this: you physicians are of no political importance."

As against nineteen hundred doctors in Boston there were thirty-five hundred men employed in the street department. Join forces with the Good Government Association, as the bar and business groups had done, he urged the physicians.

In the next mayoralty campaign he stumped for a Republican and attended rallies in various parts of the city. He was supporting Louis A. Frothingham, who as speaker of the House had introduced the subway bill and was one of the four Boston members to resist the Elevated Company; on the other hand, Frothingham's opponents had done the company's bidding. There was no such thing as a Republican or Democratic principle in city administration. The only question to ask a candidate was, Will he devote himself to the honor and best interests of the community?

The Public School Association, over which Brandeis presided and which included Eliot and Lowell, concerned itself with politics only to the extent of helping to select members of the school committee; in nearly every year since its formation men and women of its choice were elected, and twice its nominees were in control. Not the strength of the opposition but the failure of so-called friends of good government to vote accounted for the association's occasional failures.

"We have little to fear except from indifference or ignorance," he told a meeting at Tremont Temple, "and if the indifference of our citizens is removed most of the ignorance will vanish, too."

The pressure of other public interests prevented him from keeping up with the Free Trade League. But when the

League planned to hold a meeting to advocate free coal and free beef he gave advice. In the first place, the protest should be limited to coal. Secondly, the League should not hold the meeting under its own auspices but should get the full advantage of the community's demand for free coal; by asking for it as a Free Trade League objective general support would be lost and old prejudices strengthened. The League should keep itself in the background while trying to get the authorities of the coast cities to join in a demand for repeal of the coal duty. A good opportunity would be lost if the meeting was going to be held as proposed.

He had occasional odd-jobs to perform, such as introducing Abraham Flexner, who conducted a preparatory school in Louisville, to Bliss Perry, now editing the *Atlantic*; Flexner had written a paper on the relations of colleges and secondary schools. Then there was Nissim Behar, of the Alliance Isréalite Universelle, who was trying to remove discrimination in Russia against American Jews; he wanted an introduction to Richard Olney, former Secretary of State under Cleveland. (In 1904 Brandeis supported Olney as against William Randolph Hearst for the presidential nomination.)

Again Brandeis walked up the hill to the State House to stop the legislature from acting blindly in the matter of incorporating a company which proposed to construct freight tunnels in Boston, Cambridge and Somerville. The financiers seeking the charter wanted perpetual rights with it.

"But," he interposed, "the legislature is called upon to deal with this proposition without the possession of adequate information bearing upon it. It almost escaped the attention of the ever-vigilant press." No public discussion had taken place. But come what may, the people must reserve absolute control over rights in the streets and under them. "I shall submit on behalf of the Public Franchise League and its associates a bill providing for an investigation by a joint committee."

Soon a new crusade was in swing—against the gas companies. Eight of them were consolidating and planning to water their capitalization. Boston had had a bitter taste of high finance and high rates in gas; for twenty years the situation had been one of the financial and political scandals of the land, the chief actors being at various times J. Edward Addicks, Henry W. Rogers, Thomas W. Lawson, and Henry M. Whitney. One of Addicks' tricks was to give his company a $4,500,000 note by means of which he milked it—in other words, the public. The dark brown memory of Addicks was easy to revive, and the gas service was still unsatisfactory and oppressive. The lowest price in Boston was one dollar per 1,000 cubic feet. One company was charging $1.25 and paying enormous dividends. With consolidation came the prospect of dizzy rates.

The combined outstanding securities of the eight companies totaled $15,124,121; that is, $9,309,600 was stock and the balance was funded debt. But the Boston Consolidated Gas Company—organized with the help of Kidder, Peabody & Company and New York interests—contended that the properties cost more than $24,000,000 to the new owners, who asked that the capitalization be fixed only at $20,000,000. The Public Franchise League took the position that any excess in value over $15,124,121 represented not contributions by stockholders but accumulations from excessive payments exacted from consumers, which should not be capitalized. It was of fundamental importance to retain the original amount because a high dividend rate paid on a small capital issue would tend to keep the public vigilant.

From the first the question of capitalization caused dissention in the League. Dr. Prince and Laurence Minot in their public appearances did not oppose the Consolidated on that ground. Edward R. Warren complained to Brandeis that the League was not concerning itself with the gas situation as it should, and if it was not disposed to insist on a fair capitalization he himself felt disposed to interest a new set of men. Brandeis told him it was inadvisable to make a quixotic attempt to repeal or amend the law in order to prevent the capitalization of property which was in part an accumulation of past earnings. He agreed it was the League's duty to stick to the gas fight. He did not feel it had outlived its usefulness, but ought to strengthen its membership with younger men. To form a separate organization would be a mistake, losing the influence justly earned by the League; and, by the way, who were the new men Warren had in mind?

One of the latest recruits was a young lawyer named George W. Anderson, who would steal time from his office to attend to League affairs. At the gas hearings he represented the League while Brandeis spoke in the name of the Massachusetts State Board of Trade. Anderson attacked the consolidation act and accused the promoters of using financial methods comparable to those of old Addicks. Counsel for the gas company, Frederick E. Snow, denied that it lacked the right to consolidate with capital greater than the sum of the uniting firms; the League pamphlet implying that the debts of the properties purchased by the Consolidated were open to suspicion was a mean innuendo. Anderson retorted that Snow and Kidder-Peabody were unwittingly hastening the doubtful remedy of municipal ownership; the Consolidated's real motive was to capitalize excess earnings not proposed to be used in the gas business; to fool the people by paying six percent on $20,000,000 instead of twelve on its $10,000,000 of gas assets, and by getting a big capitalization on which to argue price before a state commission that always dealt with gas companies on the basis of capital and not assets.

The petition Brandeis presented sought general legislation providing that the total capital stock and the total debt of the consolidating companies should not be increased by reason of merger. This was to prevent stock-watering, in line with the established policy of the Commonwealth. To the argument that the attempt to enforce this policy was communistic or socialistic he answered:

> The greatest factors making for communism, socialism or anarchy among a free people are the excesses of capital; because, as Lincoln said of slavery, "Every drop of blood drawn with the lash shall be requited by another drawn with the sword." It is certain that among a free people every excess of capital must in time be repaid by the excessive demands of those who have not the capital. Every act of injustice on the part of the rich will be met by another act or many acts of injustice on the part of the people.
>
> If the capitalists are wise they will aid us in the effort to prevent injustice. They should welcome anti-stock-watering legislation as tending to protect them from the temptation to do injustice.

He argued that while capital originally invested should be allowed a dividend commensurate with the risk, surplus should not be allowed dividends of any larger percentage than the money could be borrowed at, say four or five percent. There would be no justice, on the other hand, in confiscating the property; it should have a fair return. If the Consolidated wished to issue stock to pay off its debt it should apply to the gas commission which would decide the market value of the stock, and the new stock should be issued at that figure.

Sorry to disagree with Brandeis, Dr. Prince said that the League opposed any dividend on past earnings; the companies had this surplus property and were distinctly benefited to that extent; the consumer should also be allowed to benefit.

Brandeis observed that there was in the community such a thing as vested wrongs as well as vested rights. The community was wrong in allowing the surplus to pile up. There should be some return on the surplus—that fund was one in which the community had an equitable interest, but it had no right to confiscate it.

"The conservative classes are not those who wish to leave unrestricted the power of wealth, but those who in economic relations are working for justice to capitalist and the public alike," he said.

Warren complained to him for taking a stand not held by the League. He felt that the League's counsel, although unpaid, should represent its views.

Brandeis turned to Filene and told him his organizing power, judgment and influence were essential to the success of the gas fight; Filene should take it up vigorously with Warren, Prince, and Edwin L. Sprague of the Board of Trade.

Filene in the course of his publicity duties learned a business lesson from General Charles H. Taylor, owner of the *Globe*.

"Why doesn't the *Globe* give its readers our side of the gas hearings?" Filene asked him.

"I'm in business, Mr. Filene. I'm a merchant, just like you, Mr. Filene. I sell my merchandise at a dollar a line."

The Filene brains were competing with a publicity genius in the gas company who sent out a story to the country papers with instructions to run on page one at the highest advertising rate. The story was to the effect that the Consolidated and the League had reached an agreement. By mistake one of these letters was sent to the *Springfield Republican*, which exposed the scheme. Hearst's *Boston American*, lately come into the field and blowing hot and cold on the League, clipped the item as it appeared in many papers and ran a layout of them.

The president of the Consolidated came to call on Brandeis in Devonshire Street. He was James L. Richards, formerly in the tobacco business, quite a successful man; and having sold out he had a great deal of money and no occupation. Because he possessed a good reputation Kidder-Peabody got hold of him to head the gas enterprise. President Richards wanted to become acquainted with his adversary

and found him a moralist. Disarmed by Brandeis' quiet
sincerity, he listened to an exposition of the immorality of
stock-watering and there he sat, convinced.

Gaily ridiculing the League, a magazine calling itself *Practical Politics* took a fling at "high-toned members of invisible
reform organizations" and directly at Brandeis, who had, "of
course, no selfish interest." The periodical said:

> Mr. Brandeis can argue plausibly and he obtains large
> fees for arguing plausibly. Retained by the gas com-
> panies or promoters of consolidation, he would have
> argued still more plausibly and with still greater recog-
> nition of exact conditions now existing. That Mr.
> Brandeis was not retained by those who are trying to
> bring about the consolidation shows that they believed
> in the uprightness of their aim rather than in the neces-
> sity of employing counsel whose words are winged with
> eloquence.

The League and the Board of Trade came to an agreement. And so did Richards. In 1905 after a two-year campaign the capital was set at $15,124,121 representing the ag-
gregate par value of the outstanding stock and funded indebtedness of the Consolidated companies, and the price
of gas was to be reduced to ninety cents within a year. There
were congratulatory advertisements by Thomas W. Lawson,
who recently bobbed into fame with his series, "Frenzied
Finance," in *Everybody's Magazine*. Lawson had attended
some of the meetings of the League and in his ad he thanked
"those sterling citizens who so persistently and ably have
aided me in my long battle against corruption." At lunch
one day Dr. Prince asked if it would not be possible to reopen the question of capitalization, and Brandeis said, "Don't
cry, baby."

Richards immediately reduced the price to ninety-five
cents and discontinued charges for connecting ranges, an
added saving to consumers of $25,000 a year; he was break-

ing in a new tradition—for a utility company to recognize
that its best asset was the public's goodwill. Brandeis felt
that the gas business in Boston would become a source of
pride to the city instead of its long-standing disgrace. With
economies incident to consolidation and the increased use
of gas, which efficient management under Richards promised,
there would be such a reduction in the cost of production
as to enable the company to sell more cheaply and still leave
a liberal reward for investment and managing ability.

There was a new angle. In London a sliding-scale was
used whereby dividends were adjusted to price. The Boston
corporation counsel brought it to the notice of the legislature, which authorized a report on the expediency of adopting a similar system. The Public Franchise League showed
no interest when five investigators were appointed to make
the study. Three of them (gas commissioners) reported in
favor of the existing system of regulation as against a contract between the public and the company. The two others
(appointed by the governor) championed a sliding scale and
recommended that the standard price of gas be fixed at ninety
cents and the dividend at seven percent with an increase
of one percent for every five cents' reduction. The Consolidated was paying eight percent.

Brandeis realized, after poring over London's experience,
that a law enacting a sliding scale would be good government and good business. He convinced Richards, and
Richards agreed to call off his lobbyists. The principle was
accepted by the Consolidated but on condition that the scale
start at eight percent. And in the League discord broke
out again—Warren opposed. At a stormy meeting of the
League's executive committee Brandeis cooly carried his
points; Warren held out as a minority of one. Anderson as
junior counsel sided with Warren but soon after wrote
Brandeis a letter admitting that his senior was right. This
was the first time anyone who had differed with him acknowledged the error.

At hearings in 1906 Anderson spoke first, followed by
Brandeis endorsing his views. Behind the scenes Brandeis
was negotiating with Richards, who committed himself in
writing to the plan. Richards thought it wiser that a bill
be introduced not by the company but by the League and
without specifying that the Consolidated favored the terms;
if it passed in this form the company would accept, but if
it did not pass the Consolidated was not to be quoted as
having assented to seven percent. Thereupon Brandeis went
before the legislature with a measure providing for a ninety-
cent rate, a seven-percent dividend (to be increased at one-
fifth of one percent for every cent of reduction), publicity
as to costs, a method of accounting, and a limit on the reserves of one percent a year; excess profits beyond this were
to be paid to the cities and towns in proportion; and after
ten years the standard price was to be subject to revision
according to changes in the general conditions.

This time Brandeis had the support of the pampered press.
It feared municipal ownership, which the vociferous *American* was dangling before its readers as a much more desirable
alternative. Opposition to the sliding-scale bill came mainly
from those who would hate to see the company declare,
after successive price-reductions, very large dividends. Brandeis believed that under proper conditions a reasonable assurance of the undisturbed enjoyment of large dividends might
be the best method of attaining cheap gas. In this case the
possibility of a large return on capital should be regarded
as an incentive for the gas business to secure the best kind
of management. Had not America always advanced along
the lines of intelligent self-interest?

The *American* played up Edward Warren's resignation
from the League and the alleged betrayal of principles.
Robert Treat Paine, Jr., protested that consolidation meant
economies anyway, and a guarantee of dividend increases
was unwarranted; that eighty cents might be as remunerative
next year as ninety cents this year. A gas commissioner

argued against giving the company ten years' immunity from interference. The League said in a circular: "The lobby is opposed to it....the lobby will make no more money out of Boston gas consumers."

In the strenuous struggle against alarmists and demagogs the League now had Anderson on the executive committee and a new secretary, Joseph B. Eastman, who had come from Amherst to do settlement work. The League contrasted the thirty years' operation of the sliding scale in England with twenty-one years of administration by the gas commission without peace, public confidence or low prices—"a constant row....the lobby and speculators have profited; the gas consumers and the investors have paid the bill." Echoing the Brandeis argument on liquor licensing in '91 another League circular declared, "The sliding scale will put gas managers out of politics and politicians out of gas management."

Handbills were part of the technique of going to the masses for backing. Brandeis paid for the hiring of halls and spoke on gas in one section of the city after another. Complicated issues were always reduced to simple reasoning and plain speech.

The bill passed both houses by wide margins. Ten days after Governor Curtis Guild, Jr., signed it the Consolidated reduced the price to eighty-five cents.

Here was another triumph for the League—that civic irritant—proving its value as a constructive force. It could restrain, conserve, and build. It had become a powerful organization. When the League spoke the voice of thousands seemed to rise. Hardly an outsider knew that the twelve men on the executive committee just about constituted the entire membership.

Next year gas went down to eighty cents and Richards ascribed his success to the fact that he and his associates were free of the eyestrain of watching State House and City Hall. Brandeis wrote an article for the *Review of Reviews*

on how Boston solved the gas problem and he accepted a
fifty-dollar check for it.

This repressor of capitalism's excesses spoke of socialism
as a spectre. Beacon Hill and Back Bay might not be discerning enough to differentiate among critics, but his trend
of thought was never in the direction of socialism. Mazzini's
program when the Republic of Rome was established expressed his own:

> No war of classes, no hostility to existing wealth, no
> wanton or unjust violation of the rights of property;
> but a constant disposition to ameliorate the material
> condition of the classes least favored by fortune.

He considered this a noble ideal, well attainable within
the American form of government. The legislatures had
ample powers, limited by the Constitution; laws which over-
stepped the limits were unconstitutional. The province of
courts to declare acts invalid was as old as the colonies—
"the natural, almost necessary, form of government itself,"
he used to tell his classes at the Institute of Technology. If
asked what he thought of the Constitution he replied that
it was "pretty good" and even the Fourteenth Amendment
was "all right" if properly construed. While Bryan and
Debs inveighed against the entrenchment of Mammon in
the Supreme Court, President Theodore Roosevelt named
Holmes to fill the place of Horace Gray. Brandeis admired
Holmes as a good example of the type of judge to whom the
law could be entrusted.

But the administration of justice was under reproach because of the general unresponsiveness of courts to the changing world. Radical criticism went to caustic lengths. It
was characteristic of Brandeis to believe that the first step
in reform should be to raise the requirements for admission
to the bar. The evil effects of a lack of integrity and intelligence were obvious. The only practical way of increasing
the moral standard of lawyers was by increasing the educa-

tional. This judgment and his work for Harvard Law School were of a piece.

Of course, the political struggle undertaken by the Socialists served a useful purpose in publicizing the plight of the workingman. Debs, as the spearhead first of the Social Democratic Party and later of the Socialist Party, was a warm-hearted apostle whose cry was justice. The noise was disproportionate to their numbers—the only similarity to the Public Franchise League—and it was effective both in influencing platform-makers of the major parties and in awakening union leaders to their duties.

Brandeis' nature was less hospitable to the theory of the class struggle than to the philosophy of new lamps for old. Where Karl Marx failed, H. G. Wells impressed him immensely. A new book by Wells appeared, and after Brandeis and his wife had finished reading it they gave it to Mrs. Evans and spoke of their interest in Fabian socialism. They sent her to England to make inquiries about the movement.

Studying labor since the Homestead strike, he kept thinking in terms of the community as a whole. Industrial ills not only affected laborers but made society suffer. Correctives must be conducive to the general welfare. Since strikes and lockouts were evils, industry must strive to avert them, and strong unions were essential in this democratic striving.

He reasoned that manufacturers had come to stand in a relation to their employees as associates. The world had passed through the stages of master and slave, master and servant, employer and employee; now these parties were partners to a contract. Conciliation and arbitration were indispensable in this period. Manufacturers in difficulties with their help must eventually consent to the power of arbitration, which was no more an improper interference with their business than ordinary police regulations restricting men in the conduct of their affairs or courts undertaking to enforce contractual obligations.

Whenever he supported the labor side, as in the Haverhill shoe strike of '94, he made it a point to clarify the grounds. On that occasion he told social workers he stood with the strikers because the employers were resisting arbitration; the men, on the other hand, were not striking for arbitration, but against a system of individual contracts whereby part of the wages was to be held back to secure due performance and prevent the workers' quitting without notice. He considered the system desirable, for the employers were not dealing with a corporate union but with individual help, usually financially irresponsible. His conviction that unions should incorporate led him into a debate at Tremont Temple in 1902 with Samuel Gompers, president of the American Federation of Labor.

"Pardon me," said Gompers, "if I may use an old phrase that we should fear the Greeks even when they bear gifts."

Brandeis spoke with slow, conversational tranquility, kept his left hand in his trouser pocket and the other on the desk, and calmly built up his case. Unions would not alienate the sympathy of the American people if they curbed their own recklessness. By making their funds difficult to reach they achieved a practical immunity from legal liability but they opened the door to government by injunction. Courts dealing with a responsible union instead of with irresponsible defendants would doubtless refuse to grant writs of injunction, and issues would be resolved by trial on oral testimony and with full opportunity of cross-examination. If the trial established the union's innocence the gain would be immense. If the union were found guilty of wrongdoing and had to dip into its sick-benefit funds to pay damages, no better expenditure could be made; the officers would be restrained from making future transgressions and the union would be strengthened in the eyes of the people as a dependable body, ready to abide by the law. Where court decisions were unjust the way to correct them was not to evade the law but to amend it.

Gompers asked what chance did labor have for fair play when the whole history of jurisprudence showed the legal mind to be against the workingmen. "There never was a tyrant in the history of the world but who found some judge to clothe in judicial form the tyranny exercised and the cruelty imposed on the people."

Brandeis called this argument emotional. Gompers answered that even if he was emotional he was emphatic as well, and a recent denial of the right of assembly proved it was the courts that transgressed—"so please excuse us if we decline to step into your parlor."

Gompers' attitude stung Brandeis into something close to acerbity.—"Who is this man to take it upon himself to say that a judge or a jury returned the decision erroneous upon the facts?"

Although the defender of the legal process had faith in his remedy, he looked for the cause in the economic process. Labor trouble could not be diagnosed by a simplification of the contest into overlord versus underdog. In the anthracite coal strike in Pennsylvania that year he put his finger on the railroads' extortionate charge for freight as compared with the rates for bituminous coal; on the economic as well as legal wrong of combining mining and transportation in the same hands; on the relation of overcapitalization to low wages. He made this analysis at the instance of his neighbor, Henry Demarest Lloyd, who was then helping John Mitchell of the United Mine Workers' Union with funds and advice. Lloyd asked Brandeis to get in touch with Mitchell and with Clarence S. Darrow, a fiery Chicago rebel who was one of the workers' counsel in an investigation being held by President Roosevelt's strike commission.

Darrow expected him to argue the economic side of the case before the commission and wrote from Scranton, offering pay. Brandeis was willing to give him a list of disbursements but wanted no compensation other than the satisfaction of aiding a good cause. He prepared a brief and sent

it on to Scranton, being unable to go himself because of a
long case assigned for trial. As a line for rebuttal he suggested that Darrow point out the Erie Railroad's acquisition
of the Pennsylvania Coal Company as being a direct violation of the state constitution. A pertinent reply to charges
of lawlessness on the part of the strikers would be to bring
out the open defiance of the operators to the fundamental
law of Pennsylvania.

But the prime cause of strife, he told Darrow, was the lack
of continuous employment: emphasize the spasmodic character of production and work strongly for some recommendation of changes in methods of doing business so as to secure a regular output. A way could be found to run the
mines continuously with a practically average output each
day. A somewhat lessened market price, a provision for
storage yards, a quest for special markets in the lean periods
of the year might help. He was certain the change was
possible and should be worked for. Coal mining was pre-
eminently a business in which steady employment was an
industrial possibility.

Irregularity of employment was a cross borne by shoe
workers, among others. It was absurd that men who were
willing to work should be content to remain idle from ten
to fifteen weeks a year. It was outrageous that a great industry like shoe manufacturing should periodically shut down
its plants. Seasonal conditions was not a sufficient answer.
Leather and shoes were not perishable products. He approached McElwain, for whose ability he had high respect,
and pointed out the economic waste as well as the misery
and demoralization which irregularity inflicted upon workers.
He urged McElwain to devise new marketing methods—
which the shoe man proceeded to do—and he advanced the
idea that a superior article turned out by steady workmen
would increase demand. Soon McElwain was launched on
a system of all-year employment. The theory worked.

Brandeis took it up with another client, the Rand-Avery

Supply Company, printers of timetables, who had a strike on their hands every spring when the peak season came. He concluded it was irregularity of work that prompted the employees to assert themselves. To his client he said, "Get your orders in advance. The railroads know what their schedules are going to be and there is no reason why they should all delay their orders until spring. First go to the customer who is most likely to see the light. After you get one the second will be easier, and so on." Railroads had no particular love for labor, anyway, and eleven of them were won over. Thus the presswork was done in what ordinarily was a slack season. In spring the client came to him with rumors of a strike. Brandeis told him to go out of town and have the workers referred to him. They saw Brandeis and from force of habit laid down an ultimatum; they would strike in an hour. The hour struck. But a few days later, when they realized that the stoppage was not affecting the company, they came back.

Labor was slow to understand that irregularity was the root of economic distress and not the evil flower of it. Steadiness of work should be foremost in the unions' demands, Brandeis said. Manufacturers were lazily accepting seasons as inevitable and angrily fighting the chaotic consequences; they should give their customers some inducement, whether of price or improved product or punctual delivery, to ensure a steady flow of business.

He tried to get statistics from government agencies bearing on regularity of employment but found that no one had taken the trouble to investigate the subject, and rarely was any reference made to it. Obviously it was as important as the rate of wages; perhaps more important. He witnessed the foolhardiness of the Boston Typographical Union in calling a wasteful strike of compositors for an increase in wages of one dollar a week; and saw how dynastic union leaders destroyed the workers' strength. Brandeis was counsel for the employers' association in the struggle, which involved a sympathetic walkout of pressmen and other violations of contract; McClennen obtained an injunction against the union. But Brandeis told the master printers, celebrating their victory at a banquet, not to forget the merits of unionism in their indignation against abuses. Peace and prosperity could not be attained by attempting to weaken the unions. Hope lay in their growing strength and stability. Neither side should stand at the mercy of the other; the sense of unrestricted power was equally demoralizing for both. Industrial despotism must be avoided, but industrial liberty must rest on reasonableness.

"We gain nothing by exchanging the tyranny of capital for the tyranny of labor," he said. "Arbitrary demands must be met by determined refusals."

A number of employers in various lines organized an Anti-Boycott Association "in defence of individual initiative and liberty," to brook no interference from workers' groups and "to see that the laws are enforced." When the secretary of the Typographical Union objected to it, at a meeting of the Economic Club, there was only one other speaker sharing his view; Brandeis ridiculed the notion of the anti-boycott adherents that industry was like an army, subject to the command of the masters. Leaders, not masters, were needed. The goal was liberty of all, not of employers to do as they pleased. Despite occasional lawlessness trade unionism expressed a high ideal and was the best school of American citizenship.

Filene and his brother Lincoln and some others formed the Industrial League in 1903 to promote investigation and education in economic and industrial questions and aid in improving labor relations. Brandeis, unanimously elected president, met many important businessmen in this way and found the activity instructive. He clashed with Edward Filene, advocate of mass production, on the desirability of introducing labor-saving machinery. Correlation of accumulated business facts sharpened insight and shaped conclusions.

The following year a cut in wages brought a strike at the textile mills in Fall River. As Brandeis analyzed it, Massachusetts had a surplus of labor-creating goods and a dearth of labor-supplying service (as on farms and in homes). While cotton manufacturing was an undesirable occupation for any class that had reached a higher standard of living, it offered a marked advance in the scale for immigrant Italian, Portuguese and Armenian girls, and attracted Russian and Roumanian Jews as a temporary occupation. Nothing could be done except to help people like Mary Kenney find positions for the girls in other employments away from Fall River. Any effort to better conditions would have to be in the direction of supplying communities with their needs.

Because he believed that the interests of employers and employees were not basically hostile, any more than were those of dealers and customers, he was attracted to the National Civic Federation, which had entered on the idyllic adventure of harmonizing capital and labor. As second vice-president of the New England branch he addressed the Central Labor Union and congratulated them on the stand of the American Federation of Labor in clearing the atmosphere of socialism.

He figured that on the principle of the greatest good of the greatest number, the employees—being the greatest number—should get as much as possible of the fruits of industry. Before a division could be made the business must be profitable. Unless profits were tempting, capitalists would not risk their money but would place it in safe investments. Unions should not seek to restrict the output of a worker but increase the earnings of the business so that the aggregate fund available for paying the men, the managers and the capitalists would be large. Wasted effort would increase costs, and higher prices without larger incomes would reduce consumption; thus restriction of output meant not more work for more people but less goods to the people for their money. But if the unions concentrated on steady work in-

stead of higher wages, factories could be run full time,
owners would be satisfied with a smaller rate of profit, and
the lowered price would increase consumption. More men
would be employed; each man's means of comfort improved.

The question for workers to consider was not how high
were their wages when they worked but how much they
earned in a year. In the anthracite coal inquiry it appeared
that the men worked only 181 days. Lack of earnings and
lessened purchasing power were only a small part of the
consequences; irregularity took further toll in the bad habits
and wastefulness of the workers' lives. The unions should
demand steady work, but their leaders should have a knowledge of the needs and possibilities of the business. The reason
John Mitchell was successful was that he understood the
technical conditions of the coal business and the employers
did not comprehend the workingmen's side.

Brandeis was pleased to see this speech create more comment than he had anticipated. But he was denounced by
the head of the Employers' Association as a revolutionary.—
"Does Mr. Brandeis believe that the hour has come when
mind-power, with all its acquisitions, is to be subject to the
demands of hand-power? The peril of the workingman
today is not that he is deprived of rights but that he has
come into possession of so many, his spirit is becoming tyran-
nical." Brandeis' language was an affront to the American
employer; his policy would result in the destruction of the
state. And at about this time Dr. Eliot was calling the industrial scab "a good type of American hero."

Brandeis repeated the speech with variations in Providence
and Portland. At a Civic Federation meeting in New York,
August Belmont presiding, he again spoke from the same
platform with Gompers. The cause of industrial liberty,
he said, was ordinarily best served by an open shop in which
a strong union had a predominating influence; but often, as
a weapon against the discriminating employer, a closed shop
must temporarily be adopted by a union to secure strength

necessary to exert that predominating influence in the trade. Speaking to the staff of the Filene store, who were organized in a partnership experiment as the Filene Cooperative Association under a plan worked out by him, he said they had an unusual opportunity in their little world of self-government to help solve the greatest problem before the American people—how to reconcile the industrial system with political democracy.

Essential to the solution was free thinking—"Democracy is possible only among people who think." And they must have time to think. A full dinner pail was not enough. A ten-hour day meant about twenty-one hours for subsistence and a small fraction for living. Citizens must be in a physical and mental condition to grasp the difficult problems of industry, commerce and finance, which necessarily became political questions. Without time for education they would become the prey of financial schemers and ambitious demagogues. An eight-hour day in most occupations and for most people was not too short.

If he seemed to be developing into a champion of the common man it was not because he was a special pleader. Neither camp could claim him; neither could readily understand him. Deep in his marrow he was an old-fashioned Jeffersonian democrat. In the modern world such a man must prove his practicality.

Chapter V

HIS "GREATEST ACHIEVEMENT"

B RANDEIS pursued his law career as though it were the
poet's long brown path, wherever it might lead. The
easy, paved roads of an ordinary practice could take him
only to conventional destinations—to a large fee, a moderate
or a small one; to victory, defeat, or settlement. But an
untraveled, difficult, winding road excited Brandeis; so that
when Edwin H. Abbot brought in a few large policyholders
to see him after the Equitable scandal broke in 1905 he knew
he was going to have an adventure in insurance.

The men had no grievance against the Equitable Life
Assurance Society and no desire to take sides in a controversy arising from the disclosure that a vice-president had
formed a syndicate with several other directors and bought
securities with treasury money for their private profit.
Abbot, William Whitman, head of the Arlington Cotton
Mills, and two other men represented nearly a million dollars
in premium payments to the company and wanted to organize as a precautionary measure. Thus was born the
Policyholders' Protective Committee, with Brandeis advising
a non-partisan stand. His firm handled local law work for
the Equitable and he told them so. This did not preclude
setting up committee headquarters at the Brandeis address.

He sent out a circular calling upon cooperating policyholders to pay one-fifteenth of one percent of the face value
of their policies to defray expenses. A few replies were received; not enough to provide a fee. To the moving spirits

94

he said, "Yes, you can retain me, but you must pay me nothing. I must be free to act according to my conscience." They wanted to stop him, but he continued, "This matter is not private but public, and I don't care to be paid for public service. Accept my services gratis or leave them."

In New York fresh evidence of scandal revealed the dangerous condition of the company and nine directors made a rush to avoid contamination by resigning. No mere change of executives would put the Equitable on a satisfactory basis, Brandeis told the press; the funds must be protected, radical economies introduced in the management, the competitive scramble for business discontinued, and the methods of savings banks followed more closely. While the committee was conducting an investigation and preparing recommendations it immediately took up the cause of cheaper rates. The reference Brandeis made to savings banks sprang from knowledge once gained in representing a bank association at the suggestion of Governor Crane.

Brandeis and Whitman called on Grover Cleveland, to whom the majority of Equitable stock had just been turned over in trust, and they were deeply impressed with his character. (Brandeis thought Cleveland had been one of the greatest Presidents.) They outlined their plan of reform looking to a complete mutualization of the business and control by the policyholders. The sole aim of the company should be to furnish insurance of absolute safety at the lowest possible cost; a mere increase in the volume of business could give no benefit to policyholders; an insurance company was not like a railroad, whose fixed charges could be distributed against total earnings, or a private concern where a larger volume might induce the owners to accept a smaller margin of profit. No one should be lured into taking insurance he could not afford to keep up; there had been 33,354 lapses in 1904, a year of general prosperity. Insurance funds were held for purposes similar to those of savings banks, yet safeguards such as were applied to savings bank investments were lacking. The day after this meeting with Cleveland, Whitman was put on the board of directors.

So insistent was the demand in New York for a legislative investigation of life insurance companies operating there that reluctant Governor Higgins at last called an extra session in a message saying, "The state cannot permit the subjects of its supervision to exist as licensed prodigals of other people's money without becoming an accomplice to the offence." Senator Armstrong of Rochester was given a resolution to introduce; the Armstrong committee was created. In Brandeis' opinion the first thing for it to expose was contributions made to political parties as well as financial graft.

The relation of the insurance companies to Wall Street, the investment of huge funds belonging to the people in securities almost wholly of corporations in which Equitable directors were interested, the dangerous accumulations of capital in the grip of a few people having a community of interests—these things were tolerated by pillars of society. Thanks to the heyday of muckraking in the newspapers and periodical press the public was no longer mistaking graft for evidence of extraordinary ability. Estimable citizens were no longer esteemed for stalking off with valuable franchises. Brandeis proposed that on every occasion where acts of corruption were attributed to a corporation a list of its directors should be published.

"The very satisfactory solution of the gas troubles before our legislature last year was due in large measure to the publication by the *Springfield Republican* and the *Boston American* of the fake news items which were sent to the papers for insertion as reading matter at cash advertising rates," he said in a Sunday article in the *American*.

The Armstrong committee selected as counsel a studious and forceful lawyer named Charles Evans Hughes, for whose firm, Carter, Hughes & Dwight, the Boston correspondents had been Brandeis, Dunbar & Nutter. Hearings began in the fall— headlines screamed their revelations— preachers

shook the needle's eye at bloated camels. The Reverend
Charles H. Parkhurst declaimed against graft. Felix Adler
in Carnegie Hall decried the pursuit of wealth as an end
instead of a means. Hughes uncovered the fact that George
W. Perkins of J. P. Morgan & Company had contributed,
as chairman of the finance committee of the New York Life
Insurance Company, $48,702.50 to Roosevelt's campaign
fund; also that Perkins turned over $4,000,000 of insurance
money to the House of Morgan for bonds of the International Mercantile Marine, a huge shipping trust of Atlantic
freight lines.

Brandeis went through the records of the Equitable, the
New York Life, the Mutual Life—the Big Three—and other
companies, and found them charging twenty percent more
than when they began business. Success merely made insurance more expensive, and the poor man had to pay more
for his policy than the rich. Although the billion dollars in
assets held by the three Wall Street companies was a trifling
fraction of the nation's wealth, most of the assets was quick
capital. Money talked—with special fluency. The Steel
Trust and other trusts were recognized as menaces to the
people's welfare, but the insurance companies were their
creditors and thereby wielded monstrous power.

Federal licensing was offered as a panacea by Senator John
F. Dryden of New Jersey, who happened to be president
of the Prudential Life Insurance Company. The proposal
was supported by James M. Beck, then counsel for the
Mutual Life. Brandeis in his private campaign of education
denounced it as an attempt to free the companies from state
scrutiny and rob the states of the power to protect their own
citizens. Supervision would not suffice by itself, whether
federal or state.

"Federal supervision would serve only to centralize still
further the power of our government and to increase still
further the powers of the corporations," Brandeis said.
"Under the decisions rendered by the Supreme Court of the

United States an act providing for federal supervision would appear to be clearly unconstitutional. But it is apparently believed that the Supreme Court can be induced to reverse itself."

He brought his ideas to the Commercial Club of Boston and stripped the insurance business of its mysteries. The state could very easily go into it. There were simply three elements: the initial medical examination, the calculation of the net premium of insurance and mortality reserve (which was a mere matter of arithmetic worked out by the actuary), and the proper investment of funds, which in Massachusetts could be taken up by state and municipal loans. State insurance was the only alternative to the high rates of the corrupt, dominating private companies if corrective measures were not taken.

"In my opinion, the extension of the functions of the state to life insurance is at the present time highly undesirable," he told his audience. "Our government does not yet grapple successfully with the duties which it has assumed and should not extend its operations at least until it does." He said the talk of the agitator alone did not advance socialism a step; it was being hastened by the formation of trusts with the attendant rapacity of their potent managers and their frequent corruption of legislatures. "The great captains of industry and of finance, who profess the greatest horror of the extension of governmental functions, are the chief makers of socialism. Socialistic thinkers smile approvingly at the operations of Morgan, Perkins and Rockefeller."

The compelling comparison of savings banks with insurance plunged him into an examination of bank figures and he proved that the insurance companies' cost of management was seventeen times higher. These companies, with all their fancy financial expertness, earned less on their investments than the obscure but conscientious treasurers of the modest saving banks.

"Life insurance is but a method of saving," he said and

drew out the analogy. "How many wage-earners would insure in these companies if they were told that for every dollar they pay, forty cents will go to the stockholders, officers' and agents' salaries, or for other running expenses? How many wage-earners would assume the burden of premiums if they knew that there is but one chance in twelve that they will carry their policies to maturity? How idle is the boast sometimes made by these companies that they have returned to the policyholder the whole of his premiums. It is as if the savings bank should boast of returning to the depositor all of his deposit, but without any interest." The plain English of his figures was that the companies took as compensation for the care of the money all that the money earned.

He continued to advise Whitman and through advertisements, circulars and pronouncements in the committee's name hammered at the facts. Few knew how large the committee's membership was; it was somewhat more than ten. He informed Governor Guild—"dear Curtis"—that the committee was very desirous that the governor insert in his inaugural certain recommendations on life insurance to pave the way for corrective legislation. In New York the Armstrong report closely resembled the lines laid out by Brandeis to Cleveland.

Brandeis was following through his own thinking about savings banks. The companies had said they could not afford to lower the premiums or liberalize the terms. He turned to his office assistant and said, "Miss Grady, let's take them at their word. They can't give cheaper insurance. Very well, we'll devise a means of getting it." Why not authorize savings banks to issue insurance? In November, 1905, he communicated the idea to Walter C. Wright, a consulting actuary who had offered his professional services to the committee and who was the son of Elizur Wright, pioneer insurance commissioner of the state. Brandeis employed him to array the necessary statistics, having in mind a law to permit these banks to open life insurance departments. It was Wright's opinion that Brandeis was wasting money in paying him; such a bill would never pass. But Brandeis had a vision. He took home suitcases filled with bank and in-surance reports, to his new house in Otis Place or to Dedham, and for a year he worked until satisfied with his draft of the bill. He would peer at huge sheets spread over the broad table, and Mrs. Brandeis and Mrs. Evans would marvel at his passionate attachment to them.

The old Brandeisian formula of stirring up public dis-cussion and demand was now brought into play. This time he had a new vehicle in *Collier's Weekly*, edited by Norman Hapgood. Brandeis met him through John Graham Brooks and in his eagerness for making the acquaintance broke the rule of staying out at Dedham on Saturday afternoons to have lunch with them in town. Hapgood, just as keen on meeting Brandeis, was fascinated by his civic accomplish-ments and regarded him as "a conservative and sound lawyer." Brandeis decided to use *Collier's*, with its national circula-tion, for the first announcement of the bill he intended to have introduced at the next session of the Massachusetts legis-lature. His signed article appeared in the fall of 1906 and described the wastes of industrial or weekly-premium insur-ance; it proposed a new attitude: that the function was not to induce working people to take out policies regardless of their desire or ability but to supply insurance on proper terms to people who did want and could carry it. Savings banks could serve this purpose by a slight enlargement of their powers, with little extra expense, and no peril to their present safety. The article was published in time to present copies to the legislature's recess committee on insurance.

The publicity received was splendid. The *Transcript* observed that some change was inevitable and conservative people should favor a plan like this for securing reform by retaining the advantages of private initiative rather than seek a remedy in a form of state socialism. The *Traveler* said his suggestion was not in the least radical. The *Republican* said it merited favorable attention and would be heard from in public agitation and "it is in order meantime for those who object to it as too radical or 'Socialistic' to present a better plan." The *New York Evening Post* said, "The new legislature should take decisive steps to introduce this reform. It means the saving of tens of millions of dollars to the workingmen of Massachusetts."

When the bill was ready—after submission to manufacturers, trade unionists, and others for criticism—he sent a copy to George L. Barnes of the recess committee (and another to Hughes) and appeared before the committee with his new project. There were two months in which to work before the session opened. The Massachusetts Savings Bank Insurance League burst upon the scene. Filene, Brooks, Frothingham, and Bishop William Lawrence were among the leaders. Dr. Eliot joined. Ex-Governor Douglas joined. Newspaper publicity was generous and constant. Brandeis found his old rostrums hospitable—the Unitarian Club and the Boot & Shoe Club—and he wrote other magazine articles. The state branch of the A. F. of L. threw in its support. Labor understood the argument that in fifteen years Massachusetts workingmen had paid $61,294,887 to the industrial life insurance companies and received back $21,819,606, whereas if the money had been paid into savings banks and the twenty-one-odd million withdrawn, within those fifteen years the balance in the banks would have come, with accumulated interest, to $49,931,548.

All this time Brandeis' firm continued to take on cases for the Equitable. No remonstrance was made by the company because of his pamphlets or speeches or Protective Committee work. A local policyholder sued the Equitable for an accounting, charging dishonesty; Brandeis, Dunbar & Nutter filed answer. The suitor amended his petition and adopted language almost identical to that used by Brandeis in his Commercial Club speech; Brandeis himself argued against a motion to remand the case to the Federal Court. But patronage from the Equitable did not impede his hammering demands for radical reforms.

As soon as the session began, on January 1, 1907, the bill was filed to permit savings banks to establish insurance departments. It was not a mere wisp of grain in the legislative hopper. It had been nurtured too well to pass through unnoticed. And that meant a vigorous fight against it. Where some bank trustees were quoted in favor, others were opposed. Brandeis dropped all social engagements and went on a stump speech tour—to Brockton, Worcester, Melrose, Gloucester, Quincy, and all over Boston—twice a week, six times a week, before unions, boards of trade, church groups. He admitted that two of the largest savings banks in the state were against the bill but of course no support could be expected from trustees affiliated with insurance companies or interrelated banking interests. The recess committee unanimously recommended it; he was able to relax a bit and do a chore for President Roosevelt.

The President asked him for an opinion on a measure before Congress aiming at a model insurance law for the District of Columbia to serve as a basis for uniform legislation in the states. In a few days Brandeis dispatched his recommendations, which Roosevelt in turn transmitted to Congress. Standard-form policies were necessary for a comparison of costs in the various companies and for protection against the insertion of improper provisions. Of more immediate importance than the further liberalization of terms was the reduction of costs.

His new League was receiving tens of thousands of endorsements from members of unions and other organizations, and he went out after more. He talked before the Congregationalists of A. A. Berle's church in Salem, before Methodists in Beverly, to others in Pittsfield, Springfield, and elsewhere. A minor rival appeared in Erving Winslow, advocating state insurance. When the legislature's regular

insurance committee met in March, Brandeis drew a crowd
larger than the room could hold. He did not have to be
eloquent: his figures were. Half of the amounts paid by
workingmen in premiums was absorbed by the companies in
expense. The wastefulness of the system was due largely
to the fact that it was conducted for the benefit of individuals other than policyholders. The needs and financial
inexperience of wage-earners were being exploited for the
sake of stockholders and officials. He spoke for three hours.
When adjournment was taken he said he would need another
day to complete his presentation. To one of the senators
asking him to conclude he replied that this bill was the most
important one before the legislature. At this point Haley
Fiske, a vice-president of the Metropolitan who had come
up from New York to protect its interests, asserted that the
insurance companies did not intend to oppose the bill but
to correct his misstatements. An officer of the John Hancock company said the same. In an aside Fiske remarked,
"In fact, I'd like to see it passed. I think we can have
some fun with you fellows over it."

Thirty-four treasurers of savings banks appeared in opposition. The tenor of their argument was that nothing should
be done which might in the slightest degree shake confidence
in the Massachusetts savings bank system; avoid the experi-
mental; the petitioners were not practical men in this particular field and knew nothing of the details of banking or
insurance. They warned against departing from safe conservatism.

"This is absolutely conservative," Brandeis assured the
committee.

He said the companies' agents would probably begin to
attack the savings banks, and this sniping would assume large
proportions if fostered by the companies; but an automatic
campaign of education would start as soon as the people
found out that policies were being bought cheaply, and this
would offset the defamation. Besides, for every depositor

who gave up his account twenty-five new depositors would be obtained through the necessity of going to the bank to make policy payments.

Page ads appeared in the papers in the form of a signed statement by Haley Fiske, saying: "We do not know where Mr. Brandeis gets these figures and we do not know as to their accuracy."

The League marched on with Ex-Governor Douglas as president, Ex-Governor Bates as first vice-president, and Alice H. Grady as financial secretary. More than 100,000 names of supporters were gathered and attached to a petition. Approved in committee, the bill passed the House by a vote of 126 to 46; an amendment requiring a majority vote of the depositors in any bank intending to open an insurance department was killed. Intact as Brandeis drew it up, the bill was delivered to the Senate, and there he was obliged to combat savings bank officials who maintained that there was no demand for it; that the banks would be injured. He said the law would be permissive and no bank would be forced into the movement. He was really not desirous that a large number should take part at the start. Meyer Bloomfield of Civic Service House said no one had argued that the plan would be bad for the poor people, and John Golden, head of the United Textile Workers, said it had the backing of the six thousand members of the union in Fall River.

On the third reading in the Senate the bill passed by 23 to 3, one of the dissenting Senators admitting that it had been "drawn by a master hand, by a man who left no loopholes." On June 26, 1907, Governor Guild signed it. The voice of Erving Winslow was raised in the papers, decrying "the scheme of a doctrinaire," "the crude experiment" propagandized at a considerable expenditure; he foresaw failure through the natural opposition of savings banks and the deliberate defiance of all experience which obviously proved that the business of small insurance must be conducted by canvassers.

Brandeis regarded it as his "greatest achievement."

A year later the system got under way. It was slow in starting because novelty begot timidity. One of Brandeis' clients, Charles H. Jones, president of the Commonwealth Shoe & Leather Company, had influence in the Whitman Savings Bank and persuaded other shoe manufacturers with plants in Whitman to share in providing the guaranty funds required by law. This bank, in June, 1908, opened the first insurance department and Jones took out the first policy. Richard W. Hale, a Boston lawyer and close friend of Holmes, was Policyholder No. 2. Before the year closed Ex-Governor Douglas, president of the People's Savings Bank in Brockton, advanced the funds for this bank's department. And now the question was, how well would the public respond in the absence of solicitors. The League took on the task of helping the baby grow up, with Miss Grady as governess. The father of savings bank life insurance continued on his speaking tour.

He wanted his invention to be a success for more than the manifest reasons. Beyond cheaper and more liberal policies for the people of his state, beyond Massachusetts, beyond insurance, was the establishment of a new principle of social economy—a public enterprise undertaken not by the state but by the people themselves to compete with private interests, break up their domination, and press them into parallel service.

With the detachment of a man who could assay his own work he viewed it as an example to others who might take up a specific problem and concentrate on it with exclusive devotion. "Not consistency but persistence is the jewel," he said. True, conditions were ripe for the insurance idea but a great deal of work had to be done—perfecting it, working on the legislature, getting in touch with people who had influence and with those who thought they knew much; invading a field where the most practical fellows held sway and daring to do that because he believed their whole system was wrong; taking hold of one of the oldest institutions in the state and endowing it with a brand-new function; giving up all other activities to agitate in numerous localities, traveling when it was hard to get around from place to place; and after the bill became law, winning the banks and inducing the public to use them. The campaign of education must be continuous.

Antagonists painted his creation in the red letters of socialism. But mutual savings banks had appeared in Massachusetts before Marx was born. He considered his system as being the exact opposite of socialism.

Chapter VI

ENEMIES ARE BORN, NOT MADE

BRANDEIS' office was so well organized that Filene wondered why he did not take on more clients than he did. But Brandeis had no ambition for grandiose size and preferred to devote more time to public works. A millionaire by 1907, he was earning more than fifty thousand dollars a year from his practice and he had his investments placed where anxiety did not need to follow them. He could sleep as peacefully as an orphan, if not a widow. Businessmen would urge him to participate in their grand plans—especially tempting when he had formulated them himself. But he aimed to keep his judgment untrammeled by personal consideration—that much for the even-minded lawyer; and he steered clear of financial entanglement—so much for the independent publicist. His bare requirements could not plague him. Without a million-dollar grip on life he could still have practiced law in his peculiar way, looking not to the client's victory primarily, but to the community's larger gain which in turn would benefit the individual. But because he sought solutions with a judicial eye he created suspicion among the perplexed. They were accustomed to retaining lawyers for their own sweet uses.

Brandeis painfully reflected that his profession had deteriorated in the last generation and had become a business. The public was losing confidence. Lawyers were spoken of as belonging to this or that corporation, not as free men. To redeem himself a lawyer should exercise the moral courage in the face of financial loss and ill-will to stand for right and justice. These were Brandeis' thoughts, incomprehensible to tale-bearers, who might have understood better had they heard him describe to undergraduates at a meeting of the Harvard Ethical Society the immorality of advocating as a lawyer measures which one could not approve as a citizen.

He denounced able men who neglected the obligation to use their powers to protect the people; who failed to stay independent enough to check the excesses of either the wealthy or the masses. The leading lawyers of the country were hired out to evade or nullify crudely drawn laws designed to curb the grasping corporations. The highest order of legal ability was needed in such questions as the regulation of trusts, the fixing of railroad rates, the municipalization of public utilities, and relations between capital and labor, but thus far ability expended on these questions was almost wholly in opposition to the contentions of the people.

"We hear much of the 'corporation lawyer' and far too little of the 'people's lawyer,' " he said. And he gave this warning: "There will come a revolt of the people against the capitalists, unless the aspirations of the people are given some adequate legal expression. And to this end cooperation of the abler lawyers is essential."

Describing the private practice of the modern lawyer he pointed out that men of his profession had become advisers because their minds were trained to see both sides of a question and tended to be judicial. Financial and industrial matters coming before them were of a magnitude equal to questions of statesmanship. The relations between rival railroad systems were like those between neighboring kingdoms. The trusts were to the consumers or their employers as feudal lords to commoners or dependents. A lawyer's training equipped him to grapple with the problems of democracy.

Brandeis often found his opponents lacking in imagina-

*"St. Louis of Boston"— a derisive caricature
from "Truth," a Boston weekly,
December 14, 1912*

tion. They could not conceive of someone's acting impartially, of having no private interest to color one's judgment. Nature provided the wicked with a blindspot—which sometimes gave him a tactical advantage over those who suspected his motives and attributed to him their own.

A case which fed calumny (and eventually brought a fee of $200,000) was that of the Old Dominion Copper Mining & Smelting Company. A Boston stockbroker named William F. Fitzgerald, whose partner was a director in the company, interested Brandeis in a proxy fight against the original promoters, Adolph Lewisohn and A. S. Bigelow, who were supposed to have taken secret profits. Brandeis was retained in 1902 by Charles Sumner Smith, a minority stockholder, and obtained enough proxies to oust the management and put in Smith as president. For this he was paid five hundred dollars. The new board learned that the promoters had issued fifty thousand shares to themselves without making a disclosure to the other original stockholders; Brandeis was engaged to sue for the recovery of two million dollars. The suit against Lewisohn in New York was lost, Justice Holmes writing the final decision. The suit against Bigelow in Massachusetts was making favorable progress.

Meanwhile the new management of the mine properties was having its difficulties. In the first place, it was inexperienced; in addition, a flood cut off the revenues needed for financing improvements. The directors appealed to Brandeis to raise money, and the opportunity of combining with the Phelps-Dodge interests came up. Smith considered that the advantage of a partnership with this reputable concern was more valuable than the Phelps-Dodge mine itself. Brandeis figured that the merger would bring the Old Dominion what it needed most: efficient and honest management, financial strength, and unequalled facilities for securing low freight rates. The directors approved of the consolidation. But Fitzgerald opposed and went to Brandeis. Brandeis told him:

"Fitz, you had better come over on the other side. That's where the big money is." Fitzgerald went away swearing.

A mining engineer made a report on the Phelps-Dodge property for the Old Dominion. A holding company was devised, and stockholders were invited to exchange half their stock for an equal number of shares in the new company. Fitzgerald put on Brandeis the responsibility for withholding the engineer's report. He said Brandeis had double-crossed the stockholders and scuttled the thing they originally fought for—full and complete information. Brandeis retored that as counsel for the company he had no authority to issue any statement to the stockholders; the most he could do was to make recommendations to the directors; he was not influenced by the value of the other mine and had little information on it, but here was an unusually good bargain and the stockholders would have a chance of earning much more if they put up half of their stock than they could hope to get on the whole stock without the merger. And Brandeis wondered why Fitzgerald was so insistent.

The directors, including Fitzgerald's partner, had voted the suppression of the report, at Smith's suggestion; the relative values were of no particular use in determining on a partnership. They advertised to stockholders to come in and see the report and get an explanation. But a newspaper agitation for its release was inspired by Fitzgerald, and two weeks later it was published in the *Boston News Bureau*, a financial newspaper owned by Clarence W. Barron. The engineer had reported that a fair basis of consolidation would be one share of Old Dominion for three of Phelps-Dodge; the relative values of the properties were about three to two. What was Fitzgerald's game? Smith and Brandeis were both sure that he was bent on putting the Old Dominion into receivership to buy it up cheaply; that this was why he wanted Brandeis to stick with him.

The merger was effected and it prospered. The two-million-dollar suit against Bigelow also prospered. It was being prosecuted by the original company and any proceeds were to go into its funds; the directors decided to give Brandeis, besides his retainer, not more than ten percent of the amount that might be recovered. During the trial in 1906 Brandeis brought out that Barron, who had puffed the Old Dominion in the Bigelow days, had written to the promoter for "those fifty shares promised me." From the company's files a letter was produced in which Barron wrote that he had just got a new safe deposit box and wanted to put the securities in it and see what would grow atop of them. There was laughter in the courtroom. Brandeis did not make a friend of Barron.

Another man so lacking in imagination as to be unable to perceive honesty in an opponent, was Sidney W. Winslow, head of the United Shoe Machinery Company. Brandeis resigned from the board of directors at the end of 1906 after a disagreement over the oppressiveness of the leases under which shoe manufacturers could use the machinery. The legality of these leases had not been questioned until January of that year when a bill, aimed at the United, was introduced in the Massachusetts legislature to prohibit machinery companies from making the condition that lessees would not use the machinery of any other firm. Although a number of shoe manufacturers were clients of Brandeis none of them appeared to be interested in the bill; and he himself saw no legal or moral objection to the United's policies. He really believed the leasing system beneficial to the small manufacturer because the terms were alike to big and small and promoted competition. So after President Winslow asked Director Brandeis to represent the company at the hearing in April, he argued before the joint committee on the judiciary that the tying clauses of the leases enabled the United to do a large volume of business at a low price; removal of the tying clauses would necessarily ruin small shoe manufacturers.

Brandeis was reinforcing James J. Storrow, who appeared

as counsel for the United. Their adversary was an attorney
who supposedly represented shoe firms in Lynn and who
denounced the corporation as ruinous, heartless, the meanest
of all trusts, making helpless slaves of the manufacturers; he
said the arguments of Brandeis and Storrow did not touch
on the real point: the exclusion of independent makers of
shoe machinery.

A month later McElwain, Jones, whom he had served since
1890, and other shoe clients of Brandeis talked over the
leases with him but agreed that it would be better to have
their objections straightened out by amicable conference
rather than by the compulsion of legislation. Winslow
promised to consult with them if the bill were defeated.
With this understanding some of the manufacturers were
persuaded by the United, in a letter drafted by Brandeis, to
oppose the bill, and it was killed in the Senate.

Feeling an obligation toward these men, especially after
they gave him additional information on the workings of
the leases, in conflict with Winslow's assurances, Brandeis
tried to bring about the conference. Moreover, his doubt
about the constitutionality of the bill was removed by a
recent ruling in Washington, and in the fall another federal
court decision limiting patent monopolies made him question
the legality of the leases. Winslow went to Europe. There
was more delay.

Brandeis received a letter from Erving Winslow (the insurance antagonist, not related to Sidney W.) posing a question about a friend who wanted to invest in the United but
who extended moral scruples to business affairs. Was the
United, in its control of the essential shoe machinery, refusing to let manufacturers make use of other shoe machinery
inventions under the threat of revoking leases? Brandeis
answered he would be glad to know who the friend was;
the statement grossly misrepresented the facts.

When it became evident in December that the United
officials were not taking steps to remove the grievances of

McElwain and the others, Brandeis decided to rid himself of the responsibility for the leases which he had as a director. He might take his fight into the board, but he was one of nineteen; or he might resign. A fight with these men would be unpleasant and fruitless. He telephoned President Winslow and sent a polite letter of resignation which merely said that the established success of the company no longer required his representation of the Chicago family, that his own holdings were insignificant and "I feel therefore that I ought not to continue an exception to my general rule of not holding the office of director in any corporation for which I act as counsel." So he got out, as he said, in a perfectly quiet way without raising any trouble at all.

One of his partners remarked, "I suppose this means we lose a client?"

"I suppose that's so."

But it brought a new potential client, introduced by Jones as Thomas G. Plant, another manufacturer of shoes, who was developing a machinery system of his own. Brandeis declined to be his counsel. Next he was drawn into consultation again by Winslow when a new measure loomed in the legislature. McElwain and Jones were present. To the staring Winslow Brandeis argued, on facts produced by the others, that if the United did not abandon its policy of monopoly and modify its leases it would wreak havoc on the community and on the company itself. The conferences ended. Brandeis presented his last bill—for October 1, 1906 to January 7, 1907, to professional services, investigations into anti-trust laws, consultations, $750.

In June a law against machinery-tying clauses was enacted, but the United forestalled any attempt to enforce it by adding a rider to the leases reserving the company's right to cancel on thirty days' notice; in this way it could withdraw its machines from a manufacturer who dared to buy a single part outside and thus push that bold character into bank-

ruptcy since no competing system was available. Winslow
had resourceful associates; also he was a very patient man.
On one occasion Brandeis held him listening for five hours—
without the slightest impression. Incidentally the Department of Justice began to investigate and prepared to sue
the United as a combination in restraint of trade.

It was another panic year. A distressed tanner from Lynn,
accompanied by a creditor for a quarter of a million dollars, called on Brandeis for advice. In a short while James
T. Lennox added his name to the list of those who believed
Brandeis guilty of desertion. The imputation was made at
a bankruptcy hearing, where Lennox testified to having
engaged as counsel the man now ranged against him.

Lennox had come into his office one September day, desperate. Notes were falling due daily. He did not know
how to meet them and he owed about $1,500,000—wasn't
sure how much, the books were kept loosely. With him
came a New York creditor, Abe Stein, and Stein's lawyer,
Moses J. Stroock. Stein wanted to advance Lennox $100,-
000 additional, but his lawyer hoped to arrange an extension
with the Boston creditors (among whom were clients of
Brandeis).

With a stenographer taking down the conversation, Brandeis put Lennox through a thorough questioning. The business of P. Lennox & Son had been managed by the son for
the past ten years; Patrick Lennox was seventy-seven, inactive, at home, and unaware of the condition of the business. When Brandeis told James Lennox to discuss it with
his father, the son said the old man was gravely ill and the
shock might kill him. To Brandeis the situation was far
more serious than it seemed at first, and an assignment was
necessary. "Go out and talk the matter over with your
father and let's then have a talk together again, perhaps
early tomorrow. Your father may have some preference
in the matter of counsel."

Lennox came back with his friends the next day and said

his father did not think himself equal to offering suggestions but wanted to pay a hundred cents on the dollar.

"Of course he wants to pay," said Brandeis, "but do you think there is a chance there?"

The immediate question to decide was whether Brandeis should act for Lennox.

"The position that I should take if I remained in the case for Mr. Lennox would be to give everybody to the best of my ability a square deal."

Lennox wanted to know if Brandeis would be his counsel.

"Not altogether as your counsel but as a trustee of your property." And bearing the full force of admonition on the debtor, he continued: "My own feeling is that the best thing for you to do is not to be thinking of yourself, but thinking of your creditors. I feel that it is for your interests, as it is in accordance with good morals, that you and your father should be just as frank and fair in the present situation as it is possible to be and not to do anything which would incite any of the people who have been misled by statements which have been made to take actions which might prove a serious blow to you and would be a fearful blow to your father."

An assignment was made out and Lennox brought it back with his father's signature. Nutter became the assignee, and the law firm the assignee's attorney. Lennox and Nutter were soon in conflict—the books had not been balanced since 1902, auditors discovered that James' certificates of personal investments were missing, that money had disappeared; James laid himself open to criminal prosecution but later restored ten thousand dollars. The same day the assignment was filed a lawyer appeared, representing Patrick Lennox, and disagreed with Nutter about turning over large real estate holdings in Lynn. Both Lennoxes were relaxing as to assisting the assignee and were not willing to give information about assets or the means of laying hold of them. Patrick disclaimed being a partner in the company. Stroock wanted

Brandeis to represent Stein's rights especially, but Brandeis answered he was acting for the general interests (including Stein), with the reminder that the Lennoxes would not be allowed to grasp property from creditors and—"I have only gone into this upon assurance that they wanted to give the creditors all that they have."

The next phase was James Lennox' demand that he be kept on the payroll at five hundred dollars per week, and after Nutter refused to grant this James abstained from conferring with Nutter or Brandeis and gave no further assistance. For that matter, neither did Brandeis continue to take an active part in the case. Nutter sent a notice to creditors in November, telling of the difficulties in discovering assets; the Lennoxes were not cooperating; large creditors were agreed on filing a bankruptcy petition.

Sherman L. Whipple, one of Boston's great trial lawyers, was now brought in by James Lennox. Whipple was somewhat puzzled by the Brandeis firm's bringing bankruptcy proceedings, and was not sure whether Brandeis had been acting for the Lennoxes when advising an assignment to partner Nutter. Whipple disagreed on this procedure.

"I should say I was counsel for the situation," Brandeis told him. After all, Brandeis had not asked Lennox for a retainer nor sent him a bill.

Whipple thought at the time that Brandeis was going with the property as a covenant runs with land—likely to get, as counsel for the bankrupt, a modest fee, while as assignee's counsel the fee would be large. But when he was convinced by Brandeis that there was no mercenary thought in his head, Whipple realized that Brandeis regarded the Lennox difficulties simply as a problem in distribution. In the end the bankrupts took their licking but James Lennox kept his wound open.

Struggles and quarrels incident to corporate organization echoed down the hallways of Brandeis' office. In these civil wars of conflicting interests he was a fascinated student of the strategy of directors out on a raiding party. One such case concerned the Gillette Safety Razor Company, which Brandeis had helped organize in 1901 when an old client of his, King C. Gillette, came to him with a valuable patent but not much money. Five years later a stockholder brought suit, charging some of the directors with fraud. As Gillette was eager to be rid of them, Brandeis called the stockholder's lawyer to his office and outlined a plan to form a holding company. Through this attorney a number of people were influenced to cast their stock on Gillette's side; but after the successful contest the suing stockholder, who had been promised an $18,000 position as vice-president by the inventor, brought Brandeis his grievance. Gillette did not give him his plum, apparently having been blocked by the board, and Brandeis was obliged to tell the disappointee that the agreement could not be legally enforced. And so another man nourished disillusionment.

Unjust accusations were heaped on Brandeis in a proxy fight the next year over the management of the Illinois Central. Suspicious souls said he was upholding one theory in public and its opposite in practice. He played no particular part in this matter, much less than was supposed. What happened was that a representative of Sullivan & Cromwell, New York lawyers, for whom the Brandeis firm had been Boston correspondents for fifteen years, called on Nutter to direct proxy solicitors for Edward H. Harriman, a power-blind titan of the railway world. Nutter said Brandeis had to be convinced of the justness of Harriman's position before the case could be taken, and the New York man had the unusual experience of being made to explain. It took two hours of explaining. Brandeis wanted to know what arguments Harriman was using against Stuyvesant Fish, ex-president of the road, who had been ousted for misconduct and was now trying to stage a comeback.

Nutter's caution was well-founded, for at this time Brandeis was opposing a merger attempted by the New York,

New Haven & Hartford. Harriman (the dominant force in
the Southern Pacific and the Union Pacific) had the majority
of the Illinois Central board with him. Fish said they were
his puppets. In the presence of the Sullivan & Cromwell man
Nutter asked Brandeis if the principles at stake in the New
Haven fight would be compromised. Was there anything in
it to prevent Nutter's supervision of the proxy gatherers?

"Nothing whatever."

The campaign for proxies was conducted openly and the
solicitors applied, among others, to men known to be opposed to Brandeis on the New Haven merger. One of the
prospects was Francis Peabody, a lawyer specializing in trust
estates; he was a friend of Sam Warren and a member of the
Dedham Polo Club, and daily met Brandeis on the bridle
path. Peabody favored Fish, and the young solicitor who
could not win him over probably used Brandeis' name too
freely, with the result that Peabody suspected Brandeis was
not altogether sincere in attacking the New Haven, but was
acting under cover for Harriman.

It was inconceivable that anyone should take great pains
to expose the New Haven, depress the value of its stock,
offend Kidder-Peabody, Lee-Higginson, and the First National Bank, incense the many Boston lawyers who were
mindful of widows and orphans, and 176 out of Massachusetts' 189 savings banks which held New Haven securities—
to do all this without a sinister motive. And he put himself
forward as a public-spirited citizen.

The New Haven story began in 1905 when Brandeis was
making speeches on the gas company consolidation and incidentally opposing a bill to permit Massachusetts railroads to
buy up competing trolley lines (which carried freight). The
established policy of the state was to forbid such acquisitions without the legislature's consent, but the New Haven—
a Connecticut corporation—had defiantly absorbed one-quar-
ter of the trolley mileage of Massachusetts, and now the Boston & Maine Railroad was asking for similar authority. Bran-

deis took the stand at a legislative committee hearing that the question before them was not whether the B. & M. was entitled to compete with the New Haven on a fair basis but whether steam railroads should be allowed to combine with trolley lines and put the transportation business of the state virtually under monopolistic control.

The bill was defeated, and when another measure came up designed to put the two roads on an equal footing, Brandeis revealed its defects; saw that it legalized the New Haven's already acquired trolley system, and pointed to the New Haven's contention that it was beyond the reach of Massachusetts law because it had not purchased trolley stock but held stock in another corporation which held stock in the street-car companies. The *Boston Post* was clamoring, "Arrest the Trolley Kidnapers!" and otherwise demanding that the New Haven, "this persistent and chronic foreign lawbreaker," be brought to book.

Representative Robert Luce of Somerville, in the closing days of the session of 1906, introduced a new bill giving railroads two years in which to dispose of their trolley holdings. He said Brandeis had drafted it. To still the fear of further absorption of trolley companies President Charles S. Mellen of the New Haven promised to add no new lines "until such time as the merger question has been settled." This was in a letter obtained by Representative Joseph H. Walker, a friend of Brandeis since the gas fight. On Mellen's assurance the legislature adjourned.

Up to this time Brandeis had appeared for the Public Franchise League. Into his office came William B. Lawrence, whose father owned about two million dollars' worth of Boston & Maine stock, and retained him to stave off a plan of the New Haven to obtain control of the B. & M. Local banking interests were arranging an exchange of stock and by the spring of 1907 succeeded in getting 109,948 B. & M. shares out of a total of 295,096 outstanding. Barron's *Boston News Bureau* observed that the New Haven, having recently merged its street-car holding company with the New England Navigation Company, now had more than $30,000,000 of stock, "which will suffice for the exchange of the entire capital stock of the Boston & Maine." Governor Guild, alarmed by the perils of merger, fearful of stock-watering and rate advances, summoned the legislature to take action. Shippers began to be worried. Several of the B. & M. directors became directors of the New Haven—including Richard Olney and Lewis Cass Ledyard. Mellen predicted ultimate union of the roads.

It meant a new fight for Brandeis. Representing Lawrence before the railroad committee he offered a bill to stop the proposed consolidation. "This legislature has power to prevent the control of one road by the other," he said. "And this legislature has just as much right to order the New Haven to give back stock already acquired in the Boston & Maine as it would have if this stock had been acquired contrary to existing laws. It is precisely this power that the New York legislature has already exercised with reference to the insurance companies."

A broader conception of police power had recently been adopted by the Supreme Court of the United States. Not only matters of health and public morals were encompassed, but also those affecting the general and financial public interest.

"If it is to the public interest that the two great railroad systems here under discussion should be separate, then the legislature should see to it that the separation is as complete as possible," Brandeis said.

As for common talk that the legislature might as well sanction the merger, since the promoters could effect it by stock purchase, he was certain that a stockholder in one of the companies could be prohibited from holding stock in the other. The idea that the Great and General Court of Massachusetts was powerless in cases where stock was held outside the state was exploded by the decision in the Northern Se-

curities case. "If you determine that it is not for the interest
of the people of this Commonwealth to have the same people
who hold stock in the New Haven hold the stock of the Boston & Maine, you have only to say so; it will be as you determine."

The chairman asked him whether he believed in mergers,
generally speaking.

"There is for a community a given limit where efficiency
can be reached by consolidation," he answered. "To that
point I am in favor of it, but I am now and always have been
directly opposed to a distinct monopoly. The matter we are
considering here is an attempt to consolidate the entire railroad transportation of the community."

But would he favor this merger if properly safeguarded?

"I do not believe it is possible to create a power strong
enough to 'properly safeguard' it."

But wouldn't he be willing to leave it to a majority vote
of the Boston & Maine stockholders? Couldn't they, the
owners of the road, be trusted to look after their own interests?

"They could be trusted to look after their own interests,
I have no doubt," Brandeis said, smiling, "but I doubt
whether their interests and the interests of the public would
always be identical."

Lawrence pointed to inaccuracies or misleading statements
made by the New Haven in its last financial report to the
railroad commissioners. Another speaker said the road had
concealed or failed to state thousands of dollars of operating
expenses; the cash-boxes of public service corporations were
opened every fall to help elect friendly candidates; the Connecticut legislature was under the domination of the New
Haven and would let the octopus rob the people; the road
was recklessly and criminally overcapitalized.

The learned *Transcript* observed that Brandeis was an intelligent student of corporation and franchise questions, but
the Northern Securities decision, dissolving the merger of

Northwestern lines, had probably not changed rates one iota; it was difficult to get persons to maintain competition when they could do better by cooperative action, and compulsory competition was next to impossible. The *Transcript* catered to Back Bay. Brandeis was living in Back Bay, but apparently did not belong.

On the day of the hearing the newspapers carried a story that the New Haven had acquired another trolley system and with it the ownership of all lines between Worcester and Providence. When he reached home his daughter, young Susan, exclaimed: "But father, where's the competition?"

Mellen's breach of faith intensified Brandeis' fighting spirit. True, in exchange for the real, solid, heavy-rail roadbed B. & M. stock the New Haven was going to palm off some puddle stock. But beyond this bad bargain and Lawrence's personal concern was the question of public policy. Brandeis saw it as the most important question in Massachusetts since the Civil War. The financiered New Haven must be stopped. A vigorous anti-merger campaign must begin. He gave up his retainer.

The next day Mellen appeared at the hearing. He had a beaming, honest expression, bald head, white mustache and a wing collar affording ample room for his double chin. He told the committee that if the New Haven had not gained control of the B. & M. a few weeks back the New York Central would have got it.

Brandeis arose, slim and limber in contrast, and crisply said that Mellen had broken his promise to the legislature, and then turned to him. There was a question he wanted to ask, but Mellen walked away, saying he was ready to furnish information for the committee but would not provide material for vindictive opponents. Brandeis called after him, "I want to ask you something—I want to tell you something." Mellen suavely remarked that he would read it in the papers, and left the chamber.

The chairman said, "Mr. Mellen does not wish to answer

the question and the committee does not wish to compel him to."

Brandeis said, "I assume that."

He was keeping one eye on the flippant Mr. Mellen and another on the alternative measures which were being considered with his own. The Speaker of the House had drawn one of the bills, seemingly to prevent the New Haven from controlling the B. & M., but Brandeis showed that it provided no penalties. It would permit the New Haven to sit tight till July 1, 1908. It said nothing against a holding company or about disposition of stock already acquired. It empowered the railroad commission to draft a law for consolidation (if demanded by the public interest), but did not authorize the drafting of a law to protect the public interest if the commission deemed consolidation undesirable.

The question of committing Massachusetts' entire transportation to a single corporation, controlled and managed "by foreigners who have in the past defied and evaded our laws," transcended the proper province of the railroad commissioners, Brandeis announced in the *American*. It was not a matter of the adequacy of facilities but the prosperity and policy of the Commonwealth.

"No system of regulation can safely be substituted for the operation of individual liberty as expressed in competition," he said. "It would be like attempting to substitute a regulated monarchy for our republic. Human nature is such that monopolies, however well intentioned and however well regulated, inevitably become oppressive, arbitrary, unprogressive and inefficient."

He used the phrase "regulated monarchy" again and again.

A composite of a dozen bills was made and the Speaker's name was appended. Mellen, serious, called on the Speaker. A clause providing for a fine was dropped with the help of United States Senator Henry Cabot Lodge, leader of the Republican state machine. The prohibition of consolidation was not made clear. Brandeis hammered away in the two friendly papers, the *Post* and the *American*.

"What's happened to the press of Massachusetts?" asked the *Lawrence Leader*. "Is it hypnotism or paralysis?" The papers were colorlessly neutral on the "gobbling up of New England's only railroad by the New Yorkers . . . there is not a line of criticism or objection. Strange!"

The *Transcript* reprinted a *Springfield Republican* editorial to the effect that "we already live under railroad monopoly and no substantial factor of competition exists which will be suppressed by the merger. . . . If public control is our protection against railroad monopoly as now existing, may it not be made so against a more unified railroad monopoly? If not, why not? This is for the political gentlemen manoeuvering for position behind the curious antimerger bill to answer."

The *Herald* recalled that Brandeis had lamented "the decline of the standing and influence of lawyers" and—

> Without instituting any comparisons, is it not strange that there is a popular impression that lawyers can be hired to "say anything and do anything" in their line of advocacy or defence for a big enough retainer or a chance to gain a notoriety that can be capitalized in legal fees or public offices, when a man of Mr. Brandeis' standing . . . sets up this scarecrow of "monopoly" borrowed from the yellow and catch-penny press. . . . Would Mr. Brandeis advise that the Boston & Maine system be dissolved and the one hundred and twenty-five different roads which were consolidated to create it receive back their charters and begin to exercise again their "individual liberty as expressed in competition," which he says is essential to the protection of the people? . . . Simply to ask these questions is to shatter Mr. Brandeis' disingenuous pleas, which in the mouth of some other men would be called demagogic.

The Speaker's bill passed, holding up the merger until 1908. Mellen promised to abide by the law to the letter, and in the meantime the matter of trolley acquisitions was pending in the Supreme Judicial Court. But the railroad did not let grass grow between its ties; the Connecticut legislature empowered the New Haven to merge with any transportation company wherever organized. Thereupon Brandeis wrote to the *Republican* that the New Haven was contending it could exercise its power without being bound by the limitations of Massachusetts laws. Governor Guild appointed a commission to ponder the merger question during recess.

Brandeis did not spend his summer writing letters to the editor. Studying the annual reports of the New Haven, he concluded that the prices paid for the trolley lines and for other subsidiaries were suicidal. He compared the reports the railroad made to the state with others it made to the stockholders and the New York Stock Exchange, and found discrepancies. The company's current liabilities were listed as $21,139,552 in its statement to stockholders, $26,509,548 to the Massachusetts railroad commissioners, and $17,624,318 in *Poor's Manual*—all as of June 30, 1906. With assistants at the office he worked on the figures, often till midnight.

Autumn found him still grappling with the reports, trying to discover the New Haven's actual financial condition and operations. One obstacle was the road's suppression of data bearing on most of its seventy-nine subsidiaries. The commissioners were satisfied with information given by the New Haven and they had to be prodded to obtain more; even so, they were lax. He looked for some real fun ahead in bringing out the facts. Before he got through the estimable men who scrambled for the chance of exchanging their B. & M. stock for New Haven would feel they had received gold bricks. It seemed to him that Mellen was joyously plunging, like other Napoleons of finance, as long as borrowing was easy, and that he would run against a stone wall as soon as borrowing capacity ended. Mellen was resorting to all sorts of devices to get money, but what had he done with the huge amounts previously raised? Brandeis would not be surprised if it turned out that some had already gone into dividends.

In Washington it was said that President Roosevelt was taking a personal interest in the situation involving his friend Mellen. The Department of Justice instructed its Boston district attorney to investigate. Mellen paid a visit to the White House, and the New Haven set up a bureau near the Capitol, putting one of its vice-presidents in charge to look after its interests "and cooperate with the government."

In Boston the commission appointed by Governor Guild was supposed to be preparing a report for presentation to the 1908 session. Thomas W. Lawson was advertising the sensational advice: "Sell New Haven—Buy Boston & Maine." The condition of the New Haven made "even my hair stand on end, and I am used to corporation rottenness." Lawson warned savings banks and trust companies to look to their loans on New Haven debentures. More frenzied finance. He intimated he knew "buried things" that would make the insurance and Standard Oil scandals "resemble cats playing with yarn balls compared with tigers tossing raw meat." Massachusetts savings banks had $12,500,000 invested in New Haven bonds.

From New York came a report that J. Pierpont Morgan, the largest individual stockholder in the road, had acquired the Consolidated Steamship Company and merged it with the New Haven.

In the city of New Haven the annual meeting, on Morgan's motion, voted to increase the capital stock by 431,219 shares. The capital now stood at $165,000,000, almost double that of the year before. Then, instead of issuing the new stock, the directors decided to substitute an issue of six percent bonds.

Brandeis had a chance for the mayoralty of Boston in 1907, when the Republican City Committee urged him to run as the candidate of their party and of the Good Government Association. The Republicans thought his success in securing the savings bank insurance law would constitute a great source of popular strength. But he wanted nothing to interfere with his anti-merger work. Of course, the New Haven and some of the local public service corporations would have combined against him. The prospects for a really good fight were not too bright. His course in knocking heads right and left was not precisely a policy to make him a popular political figure. His main reason for declining was that a finance commission of the legislature, investigating city affairs, would report in 1909, and it was better to have a thorough job done than to palliate present ills.

As the new session was about to open, Barron's *Boston News Bureau* carried a rumor that the New York Central or a Canadian line was making an offer to the New Haven for its B. & M. stock. Mellen at first let it go unanswered, preferring the public to think that his pet project—the development of the port of Boston by great improvements in its railroad and shipping facilities—would be abandoned with the stock. Then he announced—through Barron again—that the offer was not from the Canadian Pacific but that negotiations were in progress with two other parties. The bogies of Harriman and Vanderbilt were intended to put the anti-mergerites in a dilemma. High officials in Washington would look upon a sale to a Canadian road as a national calamity, it was said; and axe-grinding politicians and selfish interests would see a new light and choose the New Haven as the least wicked of a half-dozen evils. Mellen's strategy became transparent in the hands of Barron.

Lawrence publicly called it a hoax and focused attention on the peril ahead. As a result of the merger Boston merchants would have to pay millions more a year in advanced freight rates. Mellen's trolley lines were not making money, his steamships were losing money, the whole system was going to fall behind expenses in another year. Fixed charges of the New Haven had jumped from $9,752,000 in 1906 to $15,187,000 in 1907 and would exceed $19,000,000 the next year. As the road never earned more than $17,000,000, Mellen's strenuous efforts to get the B. & M. were not surprising. With competition stifled and rates increased, the New Haven could avoid a deficit. Mellen continued to hint at outside negotiations and Barron resumed the song.

Brandeis arose from his studies to debate at the Boston City Club. His adversary said that opposition to the proposed merger was based on an antiquated fear of monopoly; if Boston and Massachusetts would keep abreast of the age they should depart from the provincial policy of separation and advance the policy of concentration; in the United States there were now ten railroad groups embracing two-thirds of the country's railroad mileage; this was in accord with the economic trend of the times; if the legislature sanctioned the merger, material progress would flow.

Brandeis' reply was that he could not be content to see Boston and Massachusetts abreast of other cities and states; they should lead as they had in the past. The New Haven was not in a position to assume additional burdens. Its reputation for progressiveness was unwarranted, since it was gained by extravagant expenditures. Under Mellen's administration the road's credit no longer rested on its oldtime firm foundation:

"It has been compelled to offer to its stockholders forty-year six percent gold bonds at par. How has this come about? It has come about, gentlemen, through progressive greed, through their desire to own everything. This progressive New Haven management brought it to the point where, if they are to continue their dividends, they must discontinue the good honest policy of paying as they go, and that is what they have done."

The fear of monopoly was no more antiquated than the fear of absolute monarchy, Brandeis continued:

"If we have monopoly we are bound to have the evils of monopoly and cut off every other possible avenue of escape except government ownership. Every man who wants government ownership will join in supporting the merger with the socialists, who with rare political acumen made it their great plank."

To the argument that consolidation meant economy he replied: "That seems to me extremely unsound, although in it there are certain elements of truth, for it is just as possible to have a unit too large as too small."

The New Haven's publicity forces renewed activity. An editorial in the *Herald* said:

> Brandeis speaks, and the gaunt world should, but does not, hang quivering in space, suspending its customary functions. . . . When Brandeis speaks Sirius turns red and ten million cubic yards fall into Culebra Cut. . . . Brave Brandeis! The people are not helpless while he lives. To them he gives himself freely and without stint. There is nothing in it for him, he says.

The railroad sent clippings of this editorial to the newspapers of the state with the ingratiating remark that reproduction would be deemed a favor. The results clearly showed which papers were currying favor—quite a few. It took the honest old *Springfield Republican* to tell the inside story: "We might be doing a favor to this press agent to reprint the article entire, but it would be no favor to the New Haven road." Some of the dailies using the editorial added as a seeming conclusion of their own, in identical language: "Brandeis' enthusiasm for certain 'reforms' is, it is sometimes suggested, tempered by a 'quid pro quo' like that of other men."

With the opening of the 1908 legislature Brandeis released a seventy-seven page pamphlet, the fruit of his study of the New Haven's finances. It was more a bombshell than fruit. It exploded the theory of the railroad's sound condition.—

> The New Haven's credit is strained to the uttermost. The heavy fixed charges and dividend balance leave it no appreciable borrowing capacity. For years to come the closest attention to the development of the properties already acquired and wise economy in operation

and administration will be essential in order that this company may carry the financial burdens unwisely assumed and ultimately recover from the excesses of recent years. Its officers have no surplus of time or ability to give to the problems of the Boston & Maine system.

In six years the New Haven's outstanding stock had increased 122.8%, its liabilities 366%. With the additional $30,029,600 bonds about to be issued, the liability increase would be 434%. If the company's customary charge for maintenance had been made in the last year, the net income from all sources would have failed by more than $1,000,000 to provide for its eight percent dividend. A large reduction in the dividend rate was inevitable.

The pamphlet carrying this warning was sent to the legislators and the security holders. Barron's *Boston News Bureau* called it a savage arraignment of the road; the *American*, a powerful analysis. The *Transcript* gave seven columns to a condensation of the pamphlet and offered space to any equally authoritative statement from the other side. The *Traveler* said the next move was up to Mellen; the best financial authorities had endorsed Mellen as a railroad manager and approved his financial administration, and the state authorities had not discovered that the New Haven was a bankrupt institution; but here was an outside lawyer who said he was working strictly *pro bono publico*. The *American* challenged Mellen to meet Brandeis in Tremont Temple or Faneuil Hall.

Barron quoted an anonymous but "leading New England banker" as saying that Brandeis never had real experience in railroading, while Mellen had made an enviable mark; did Brandeis really believe that J. Pierpont Morgan, William Rockefeller and other prominent men on the New Haven board shared Mellen's so-called poor judgment? One of the Connecticut papers said that the motive behind Brandeis' savage assault was to scare off the merger for the sake of a client; that Brandeis smelled carrion where no other noses could detect it.

Annoyed by the charge in Barron's paper that he was "generally supposed to be acting on behalf of certain Boston & Maine stockholders," Brandeis replied that he was doing precisely as he had done for the Public Franchise League, the Board of Trade, the Massachusetts Savings Bank Insurance League, and the Policyholders' Protective Committee—always without accepting compensation because these matters were of a public nature. And he warned Barron to be very careful about what he said in the future. The organized effort to discredit Brandeis continued, but he decided not to let these attacks hamper him. It had once taken him three weeks to track down a lie. The enemy could make up enough lies in a day to keep him busy answering ten years. So while they attacked he was going to saw wood.

He sawed at luncheons and banquets and church meetings. To the Credit Men's Association he described the New Haven's relentless policy of suppressing coastwise steamship competition at cost. The credit men had invited Mellen; Mellen's refusal, Brandeis said, was part of the policy of the New Haven to settle everything for itself secretly. To the Real Estate Exchange he repeated his dictum that fear of monopoly would never become antiquated. To the New England Dry Goods Association he repeated that the merger question was the most important one that had arisen in the Commonwealth since the Civil War.

"The very size of the proposed consolidated system and the diversity of its interests would be such as to impair its efficiency," he said. "Man's works have overrun the capacity of the individual man. No matter what the organization, the capacity of the individual man must determine the success of a particular enterprise, not only financially to its owners but in service to the community.

"For every business concern there must be a limit of greatest efficiency. What that limit is differs under varying condi-

tions, but it is clear that an organization may be too large
for efficiency and economical management, as well as too
small. The disadvantages attendant upon size may outweigh
the advantages."

He drove home his point by reminding audiences of the
wretched service on the Boston & Albany since its absorption
by the New York Central. Moreover, the political dangers
surrounding a monster transportation monopoly were "too
obvious to require comment, particularly in the case of a
corporation having the political traditions of the New
Haven."

The pamphlet containing his financial study met with an
abject hush from the three thousand bankers in New England and New York who dealt in the New Haven's securities. In Brandeis' opinion they lacked the courage to speak
up. Ordinarily a controversial issue could be counted upon
to bring out a fifty-fifty alignment, but not this one. A friend
asked him to tell the facts to one of the bankers; this gentleman listened to a recapitulation of the analysis and then went
out to sell his own five hundred shares at 165 but uttered
nary a word to his customers. Thus numerous trustees for
estates failed to get advice from those on whom they relied.
Morgan was taking personal care of everything.

The news from Washington was not encouraging. Although the Department of Justice had received its report
from Boston and a White House conference had been held,
the document was to be kept from the public. The New
Haven's vice-president, on the job, was granted two weeks
in which to submit a statement for the road. Mellen paid a
visit to Roosevelt—purely personal, said the railroad man.

Brandeis went before the legislative railroad committee
with a request that they get the Massachusetts commissioners'
report in their hands before hearings were resumed. The
commission was delaying with one postponement after
another, and Mellen was cheerfully leaving the matter to the
legislature "and the good sense of the people concerned" but

without staying or relaxing his press agent's poison pen. Brandeis was ready with a number of bills to make the New Haven give up its B. & M. stock, void stock issued by the New Haven for the exchange, prevent future acquisitions, and punish violations by fine and imprisonment; another bill to tax New Haven stock, then tax-exempt, as being of a foreign corporation; another to prevent savings banks from investing in bonds or notes of the New Haven as not being a railroad company within the meaning of the law.

Consistent with his theory of educating the public so as to provide a leavening for legislative action, Brandeis fostered the formation of the Anti-Merger League. Jones was president; Joseph B. Eastman, one of the members; but Filene did not side with them. The League planned to secure prominent citizens as speakers in all parts of the state. Boards of trade, businessmen's associations, and various kinds of clubs applied. The League started with five hundred members and reached thirty thousand in less than a month. Considerable help was given by the *American* by appending membership blanks to its editorials.

Brandeis spoke at the Fruit & Produce Exchange at noon-hour to men in white coats, and complimenting them on knowing more about eggs than anybody else in New England he suggested that they knew better than to put all their eggs in one basket. That basket would demand higher freight rates. The meeting was well organized. Copies of his Dry Goods Association speech were given to people as they walked in, along with membership blanks. Brandeis spoke also in Dr. Berle's church in Salem and another Congregational church in Somerville. He relished opportunities to talk on the moral aspects of this crusade. But one night, when scheduled to speak, he was absent in Washington to argue the Oregon ten-hour law for women before the Supreme Court.

Lines were forming, and in the other trench a Businessmen's Merger League appeared. What distressed Brandeis

was not that men held an opinion opposite to his but that all
State Street and all Wall Street clamored for merger and
some did so under duress. Finance stuck out its fangs and
businessmen were paralyzed. He needed support from substantial persons to reinforce the protests of the so-called radical element, and he was glad when one of the officers of the
Boston Chamber of Commerce publicly declared himself
against the New Haven's plan. Brandeis won a promise from
him to speak at Faneuil Hall, the customary place for protest
meetings, but at noon on the day of the scheduled event this
man telephoned that he had changed his mind; he was part-
owner of an investment banking firm and was accustomed to
getting large loans from certain interests behind the merger.
Brandeis said he would not press him under such circumstances and admired the frankness of the man, who might
have begged off by inventing a sudden engagement in New
York. But Brandeis was disgusted to see him trotted out by
the New Haven at a later hearing to make a speech to the
effect that he did not have a full understanding of the situation when he opposed the merger.

Here was a shameful example of a man not free.

CHAPTER VII

FREE TO FIGHT THE NEW HAVEN

TO LEAP from the anti-merger fight to oral argument on a labor law before the Supreme Court did not require seven-league boots. Both moves were in the direction of an economic ideal. Not even a casual newspaper reader could help being confronted with the labor issue and forced into reflection, what with Gompers building up the A. F. of L. to one and a half-million members and Debs polling half a million challenges to capitalism. Labor's demands, dignified to some extent in statutes but often throttled by the judiciary, insisted on attention. Brandeis belonged to the American Association for Labor Legislation and followed the work of the International Labor Office at Basle. His sociological background was adequate.

Twenty states had laws in force regulating the working hours of women, and this much progress seemed secure until employer interests in Oregon assailed the constitutionality of the state's ten-hour law. They asserted their right of liberty under the Fourteenth Amendment as against the health of an overworked woman in a Portland laundry. The case they carried to the highest court involved more than the welfare of every female factory hand in Oregon; it threatened to tear down similar legislation in the other states.

The National Consumers' League stepped in. Mrs. Florence Kelley, its leading spirit, and Mrs. Brandeis' sister, Josephine Goldmark, who was her close associate, called on Joseph H. Choate, as one of the foremost members of the

American bar, to bid him defend the Oregon act on the invitation of the state's attorney general. Choate saw no reason why he should; and why shouldn't a big husky Irishwoman work more than ten hours a day in a laundry if her employer wanted her to? No, Choate was not the type; in arguing against the income tax law he had described it as a "communist march on private property." Mrs. Kelley and Miss Goldmark thought of Brandeis.

He accepted at once. The League had informally consulted with him on other matters, in particular a recent New York case where the court held there was nothing to show that night work bore a relation to health. He thought this could be demonstrated. In his new role as counsel for the State of Oregon he found very little legal argument available. He must prove that the statute lay within the scope of the state's police power and that health or general welfare would be endangered if the hours were not curtailed. The Supreme Court had already invalidated a New York law limiting hours of work in bakeries as a violation of the principle of freedom of contract (Holmes dissenting). Brandeis was obliged to turn from law to life; from abstractions to realities.

His idea was to prepare a brief summarizing society's experience on which this kind of legislation was based. He directed Miss Goldmark in the assembling of the material; she did the research and collation, going into reports of legislative committees, factory inspectors, commissioners of hygiene, physicians and social workers, citing and quoting from more than ninety sources. Evidence was amassed to show that the female organism suffered under strain, fatigue contributed to chronic ailments and accidents, overwork caused moral laxity, deterioration inevitably made the entire community suffer. Shorter hours afforded the only protection; moreover, they produced a beneficial economic effect in heightened efficiency and a more equal distribution of work through the year. Ten hours was a reasonable limit, though it probably should be less. Here was a unique brief: fifteen

pages given over to a review of American and foreign legislation; ninety-five pages to "the facts of common knowledge
of which the court may take judicial notice"—and two pages
to law.

In January, 1908, he appeared for oral argument. Chief
Justice Fuller still presided, flanked by associates Brewer,
Harlan, White, Peckham, McKenna, Day, Moody and
Holmes. This was an intellectual gathering to his taste, but
he listened sadly as opposing counsel contended that women
were endowed, equally with men, with the fundamental right
of liberty; that their right to contract with employers could
not be impaired. In the silence of this solemn chamber the
dry bones of legalism rattled; a dead hand tried to shut the
court against the living world. Brandeis swept aside these
archaisms and produced a picture of the hazards of modern
industrialism. This might be the time and place for pure
thought, but also for moral fervor. A month later the court
unanimously upheld the Oregon statute. The opinion delivered by Mr. Justice David Josiah Brewer took judicial cog-
nizance of the facts of life, mentioning Brandeis by name as
having filed "a very copious collection of all these matters"
and referring to his able argument.

On the night following the decision Brandeis addressed
the Sheet Metal Workers' Union in Boston to win more members for the Anti-Merger League.

A hundred or more converts were all to the good, but it
was necessary to swing them in by the thousand. On previous
occasions, when the financial community was divided, Brandeis found the sledding not so rough. Here was James J. Storrow, now of Lee-Higginson. A man of high ideals but not
of high courage, he joined the Businessmen's Merger League.
William Whitman, whom Brandeis had helped in the Equitable matter, also went pro-merger. Although Whitman said
he owned no securities in either of the roads, the *American*
exposed him as a fellow-director with Mellen in the First
National Bank of Boston. Kidder-Peabody and the National

Shawmut Bank, with other banking interests, completed the ring forged in New York by J. P. Morgan & Company. On the other hand, Edward Filene, who believed in the principle of merger, abstained from taking sides—he was working on an idea for a national chamber of commerce.

If Brandeis could persuade public figures, each with a large following, to give their energy or lend their names, progress would be quickened. He dictated long, detailed letters to men of standing, asking them regardless of their belief in the economic aspects of consolidation not to remain silent in the face of the New Haven's defiance of Massachusetts law and policy. A typical reply came from Bishop Lawrence: he was overloaded with work and could not take up the subject thoroughly.

More of Brandeis' social connections dissolved—without annoyance to him. It mattered, at first, to Alice, who did not have the compensating exhilaration of battle. To say he sacrificed friendship for principle would be inaccurate. He made a choice. He chose to fight. Most important, he was free to fight.

While his Anti-Merger League was circulating petitions and gathering names and winning so valuable an adherent as Filene's brother Lincoln, who contributed toward expenses, Brandeis kept up a daily onslaught, using every available line of approach. He warned unions that the creation of a monopoly of transportation would strike a tremendous blow at organized labor, as witness the Steel Trust. He lectured on the false analogy between railroads and local public service corporations. When the governor's special commission reported three-to-two in favor of the New Haven he fought its findings. And he spoke at a hearing on a bill to remove the road's securities from the list of legal investments for savings banks. Just once the tension snapped his self-restraint. In the question period after a speech at the Central Labor Union, when a carpenter declared that the real fight was between Harriman and Mellen for control of the B. & M., Brandeis shouted from the platform, "I believe that to be a confounded lie!"

To the legislative railroad committee he described the New Haven's misleading bookkeeping methods which failed to show its actual financial condition. A new system of accounting had been adopted in 1906, so that in the company's report for 1907 ordinary accounts which had hitherto appeared were omitted for the first time; $12,000,000 of liabilities were not disclosed, and the account of net earnings showed $10,-000,000 of equipment depreciation which should have been charged to operating expenses and which would have decreased the road's earnings by that amount. Had the same bookkeeping system been retained as in previous years, there would be a million-dollar deficit. He argued all morning and did not finish by adjournment.

The governor's commission recommended that the best form of merger would be to allow the New Haven to hold B. & M. stock already acquired, the state to have the right to buy it back after five years if dissatisfied. The recommendation was signed by Joseph B. Warner, who owned twenty-two shares of New Haven; George G. Crocker, who owned 717, and Charles Francis Adams 2d, who held 217 as trustee and 418 for Harvard University. Crocker's family holdings totaled 1,250 shares.

Neither of the minority of the commission held any. One of them, Ex-Governor Douglas, maintained that monopoly invariably led to economic apathy and was apt to end in moral degeneracy; he opposed it in every form; no safeguards by the state could protect the people from such a power.

Brandeis criticized the commission for its secrecy and its refusal to let him examine statements Mellen made to it. The commission had engaged an accountant in the employ of Lee-Higginson (the firm had aided the New Haven in buying a large block of stock) and this expert might as well have been in the New Haven's employ. The figures Brandeis com-

piled after months of special study pointed to conclusions
radically different from those presented by the commission.
Here was a case of high financiering with no purpose other
than to conceal the actual conditions. Brandeis said he tried
to get from Mellen reports on the road's subsidiaries. One of
the missing reports concerned the New England Navigation
Company.

"It was this company," he said with a smile, "which took
over the Boston & Maine stock and turned over its steamships
to the New Haven road for $20,000,000 when they were not
worth over $10,000,000—an exquisite illustration of carrying
water to the second power."

In a Brockton church he riddled the majority's proposal
of safeguards against rate increases and the reduction of facilities; the Interstate Commerce Commission, not the Massachusetts railroad commissioners, had the power of regulation.
The majority repeated the glittering promises of improvements, electrification, tunnels, and four-tracking which the
New Haven had been holding out as bait to induce the community to swallow the merger, but at the same time expressly
said that none of these was to be required as a condition of
the merger; and they said nothing about the New Haven's
defiance of Massachusetts law and the violation of its pledge.

Mellen's breach of faith was a favorite theme with Brandeis. In a series of debates with Timothy E. Byrnes, vice-
president of the New Haven, he never forgot to mention
it—often with vehemence, sometimes with that quiet play of
sarcasm which he knew how to use.

"Gentlemen," said Byrnes, "I have as much respect for
the law of Massachusetts as Mr. Brandeis has. Mr. Brandeis
speaks of Mr. Mellen as an alien. Why, he was born in the
city of Lowell, and it seems to me has just as much right to
claim Massachusetts as his home as any of us. Nearly forty
percent of our interests are owned in Massachusetts. Doesn't
that make our company a Massachusetts corporation? Are we
aliens because we were not born in Kentucky?"

Professor William Z. Ripley of Harvard said monopoly was essential to good service and the New Haven was a friend indeed. President Jacob Gould Schurman of Cornell said railroad monopolies were a development of modern industry and to fight consolidation was to set oneself against the trend of the times. But Brooks Adams pointed out how the railroads were exercising the attributes of sovereignty belonging to the government, and the people were in abject subjection to them, much as the French peasantry had been under the nobles.

Answering Byrnes, Brandeis said Massachusetts had but two men on the New Haven's board of directors. Answering Ripley and Byrnes, he said a consolidation might be a good thing or a bad thing; the Boston & Albany, formerly acknowledged as one of the best roads in the country, had now reached such a degree of degradation that few men in Massachusetts did not suffer by it. The merger would involve such grave evils that government ownership would be the only alternative.

"My friend Brandeis makes a lot of trouble for me," said Byrnes. "He is the most persistent worker I ever got up against."

In one of the debates Byrnes offered as a solution the idea that the state should buy the B. & M. stock from the New Haven. There was a little colloquy on this in Cambridge, and a few days later, when they unsheathed their swords again in Fitchburg, Brandeis asked if the New Haven had authorized the offer.

Byrnes said, "Are you authorized by the state to ask the question?"

"No, I ask you as a citizen who has a right to know."

"Then my answer to you is no."

Day after day Brandeis spread his anti-merger doctrine, insisting that the railroad wanted to kill off the only remaining competition and fix rates to make the public pay for its management's mistakes in securing such burdens as trolley

lines at exorbitant prices. The New Haven was forced out
of its shell of silence and not only let Byrnes continue the
debates but put ads in the papers saying, "The cry of monopoly is an appeal to prejudice, not to experience or judgment."

In the midst of Brandeis' continued argument before the
railroad committee a senator inquired what motives prompted
him to make his investigation.

"I did not at first have the large doubt of the financial
stability of the New Haven road," he answered. "I said not
a word six months ago but subsequently I investigated the
New Haven's acquisitions to determine if in my judgment
they did not constitute an infringement of the anti-trust laws,
and the thought came to me that while any one purchase
could have been made without loss or detriment to the interests of the stockholders, the aggregate purchases must be
tremendous and even perilous in their magnitude." Mellen's
withholding of information about the subsidiaries obviously
had a reason. "The only motive for my presence here is in
making it a part of the campaign I have made to prevent the
merger, and I come here retained by no one. I appear as a
citizen."

The obligations of the New Haven, he found, were three
times the amount of its capital stock; savings banks should
not be permitted to invest in its securities because the Massachusetts law limited the issue of bonds to the amount of capital stock. The chairman intimated that he would be pleased
if the speech were cut short, but Brandeis replied he would
need at least two or three more hearings. On the next occasion he put in new memoranda to the effect that the road's
funded indebtedness of $309,383,675 was over eleven times
greater than in 1896 and almost two and one-half times the
then market value of stock outstanding.

The New Haven's attorney at these hearings, Charles F.
Choate, Jr., denied Brandeis' charges of concealment and de-
ception and called him "a self-appointed representative of an

undefined public, who appeared to be allied with persons interested in attacking the New Haven road."

The Chamber of Commerce took a card-poll of its members, and a large majority voted against the merger. Whitman declared, "I take exception to nearly every argument that has been advanced by Mr. Brandeis, the man who is the brain for the opposition." The president of the Chamber contended at a hearing that state regulation would be impossible. The Anti-Merger League gathered twenty thousand signatures. The Businessmen's Merger League next presented a bill providing for legislative safeguards. And finally Choate submitted one to permit the New Haven to hold and vote its B. & M. stock. Some action had to be taken by July 1 under the legislation which held up the merger the year before, so that now, in May, plans were crystallizing.

Debating with Byrnes in Worcester, Brandeis was pressed to tell what he would have the New Haven do with the stock. He suggested a sale to an authenticated syndicate of Massachusetts business and financial men pending a solution of the state's railroad problem, or a direct purchase by the Commonwealth. Byrnes asserted that the road would be perfectly willing to sell to the state.

"This is farther than I've heard you go before," said Brandeis, beaming.

But the railroad man explained the next day that he was willing for the state to hold the stock provided his company obtained first option at a reasonable rate.

In the midst of these unofficial exchanges two things happened. The Department of Justice in Washington dealt a body blow to the octopus. The Supreme Judicial Court of Massachusetts gave it another.

Brandeis had consulted Roosevelt on various congressional matters as a member of the executive committee of the People's Lobby, a group including Lincoln Steffens, William Allen White, John Mitchell, Judge Ben Lindsey, Robert J. Collier, Mark Sullivan, Brand Whitlock, and others. In this

connection Roosevelt asked him to draft a bill regulating
stock transfers and another to prevent the use of the mails
in bucketshop speculation. In April the President invited him
to call at the White House on his next trip to Washington,
and the occasion came when the Supreme Court scheduled
the Old Dominion Case for argument. Brandeis used the visit
to talk about the New Haven.

He did not feel sure about Roosevelt. T. R. struck him
as being self-centered, not objective in his thinking. And
only a fortnight before in a message to Congress the President
had urged modification of the Sherman Law, which he
thought the courts were construing too sweepingly: combinations were absolutely necessary in the modern industrial
world, and while some were among the most powerful of all
instruments for wrongdoing others offered the only effective
means of meeting actual business needs. But Brandeis prodded
him to instruct Attorney General Charles J. Bonaparte to
file a general suit against the New Haven under the anti-trust
law for its holdings of B. & M. stock and ownership of trolley
and steamship lines. Two days later the news came out that
Roosevelt was directing a plan of action against the road.

The New Haven's other worry was a decision handed
down by the full bench of the Supreme Judicial Court in
May, ordering an injunction against the road's engaging in
the street railway business. Brandeis was quick to emphasize
the lessons to be drawn—first, the Massachusetts law prohibiting a railroad from acquiring the stock of another corporation
without the legislature's consent should be supplemented by
an adequate penalty. The New Haven would not have undertaken to buy B. & M. while a proceeding was pending
against it for taking trolley stock if there had been the likelihood of a large fine and the imprisonment of guilty officials.

Choate at the next hearing said the New Haven would
promptly obey the decree and, as the principle enunciated
by the court applied also to the holding of B. & M. stock, this
must likewise be disposed of, unless the legislature decided

it should be retained. A committee member asked Brandeis if he would still oppose unification should the committee think it worth while.

"Yes, and I'll tell you why: because a thing more vital to the Commonwealth is the maintenance of the supremacy of the law!"

He said that nothing could stir up social uprisings more readily than to let the people believe that a big corporation like the New Haven could depend on favorable action by a law-making body when it directly and arrogantly disregarded the law. The New Haven's procedure was of the kind that strangled individual enterprise and shut out small business-men, who were the source of real progress. Even if the uni-fication of the railroad system North and South of Boston should some day be desirable, the question of not seeming to condone a violation was too important to be controlled by the question of economic value.

A speaker for the Merger League said the agitation was created by one paid attorney.

"Do you mean me?"

"I do."

Brandeis told the committee he was not in the employ of Lawrence or anyone else but was acting in the public in-terest, even as the pro-merger speaker was active. The latter remarked that he knew Brandeis too well not to accept his word.

But the poison of imputation had been well planted. It spread from State Street to Wall Street. Finally the rash broke out at a hearing. Warner, of the special commission, stood near Brandeis and turned toward him again and again with bitterness in his voice. In a long address Warner said the commission refused Brandeis advance information because it did not feel like feeding fuel to a public controversy when there was financial unrest in the country and Massachusetts savings banks held $17,000,000 in New Haven bonds; Bran-deis' report on the financial condition of the road was radically wrong, it was a wilful perversion of the figures. Then came Warner's assertion that Harriman was vying with the New Haven for the Boston & Maine and that Brandeis was acting and had acted for Harriman. At that point the hearing was adjourned.

The next day newspapers carried a letter Brandeis sent to the committee, calling Warner's statements groundless and inaccurate; he had never represented Harriman directly or indirectly, but his partner Nutter had solicited proxies in the Illinois Central matter. Yet Barron published a story of rumors persisting in financial quarters that Harriman had hired Brandeis to defeat the New Haven's plans and that this accounted for his anti-merger activities; more than this, the Brandeis pamphlet analyzing the New Haven's condition was in reality prepared in Harriman's office, at 120 Broadway, New York; Harriman wanted the B. & M. supposedly for his Delaware & Hudson. The rumors overlooked the fact that Brandeis was sponsoring a bill to prohibit foreign corporations from controlling the stock of any Massachusetts road.

Edward Filene hastened to defend his friend. He wrote a long letter to the papers comparing himself with a spectator at a football game who could not bear to see a player knifed in the back by an opponent; the murder of the reputation of an honest fighter would be a national calamity. He said the idea of giving one's service without pay to a public cause was less common and therefore less believed than giving money for that cause; if a man donated fifty thousand dollars a year to philanthropies it was not astonishing, while if he gave that much in time he was suspect. Filene related his experiences with Brandeis. The subway fight, in which Filene thought he had engaged him, was waged without pay, Brandeis explaining it was a rule of his to give up some part of each day to public work and that if he devoted an unusually large amount of time to this struggle it was because he had determined to devote a greater part as soon as he could do so in justice to his family and partners. Filene, as treasurer of the

Public Franchise League, was in a position to say that Brandeis not only gave his time continuously for seven years without pay but also contributed liberally in cash to the League's expenses. In the past few weeks the newspapers of the country had been rejoicing at the great fundamental victory in the Oregon laundry case—again won without pay. And then there were his unstinting labors for savings bank life insurance.

"Let men who disagree with him on this merger question assail and disprove his arguments if they can," Filene concluded, "but let them beware of assailing by innuendo or by unprovable statements, wholly unsupported by facts, the character and motives of Mr. Brandeis or any other public servant of his kind."

Filene's irritation was nothing like the shock to Wall Street's nerve center. The market slumped on the news that the government had filed a petition in the United States Circuit Court in Boston to prevent the New Haven from exercising control over its B. & M. stock and to make it surrender trolley lines in Massachusetts, Rhode Island and Connecticut. (No reference to steamships.) Rumors from Washington had it that the action was forced by Bonaparte against Roosevelt's disinclination. Less than an hour after the news of the suit was released the Department of Justice, on instructions from the White House, telephoned the press associations to kill the statement. Bonaparte then threatened to resign, whereupon the President sent word to the department to disregard the kill order. It was said also that Byrnes had called on Roosevelt the day before and received assurance that no suit would be filed.

The New Haven continued to manoeuver in the Massachusetts legislature, but Acting Governor Eben S. Draper intimated that he would not sanction consolidation. The Anti-Merger League advocated the sale of the B. & M. stock within two years. The Senate, however, passed a bill to put the stock in escrow and await a report from the railroad commissioners. A story emanating from "railroad circles" in New Haven said that the road was not satisfied with the bill and would be content to wait until the case was carried over to a new federal administration. When the bill went to the House, Draper urged a "shall sell" provision, but the House turned it down and eventually also killed the Senate bill, leaving the railroad to battle with the courts.

In the middle of June the session was in its dying days. Under the act of 1907 the New Haven was prohibited from voting its acquired stock or acquiring new stock before July 1, 1908. Now that the court had pronounced the holdings illegal the state's attorney general could proceed and ask for a mandamus to compel the road to sell, but he must do this before July 1 or the wily and defiant railroad might steam ahead.

On June 30, to avoid litigation, the New Haven sold its 109,981 shares of B. & M. to a lumber dealer in Meriden, Connecticut, named John L. Billard. Brandeis assumed it was a sincere sale. If it was not, so much the worse for the road later on. Brandeis would not have been unhappy to learn that J. P. Morgan was a large owner in the B. & M., because personal owners were essentially temporary factors whereas a corporation was impersonal and permanent, and corporations once merged were almost indissoluble. The public fought against a merger into one corporation, and now the suits were made unnecessary because it got what it sued for without waiting for a judgment. When the legislature adjourned without taking action, the merger was dead. It was getting a decent burial. Choate, his adversary, who had been resisting the rôle of undertaker, received a fee of $19,018 for his strenuous objection.

But the state's attorney general said the New Haven must give proof of the genuineness of the sale. Lawrence with characteristic fury called it a transparent trick. And Asa P. French, federal district attorney, announced that even if the sale were valid it would not bar anti-trust prosecution for violation of past holdings and for a restraining order against the future. The *New Haven Register* observed: "Brandeis may be happy, but how about Boston? It wouldn't improve the case to change the name to the 'Meriden & Maine,' for literary Boston shudders at the cheap alliteration."

During the summer of 1908, while the New Haven was dipping into its bag of tricks, Brandeis handled a labor problem for the W. L. Douglas Shoe Company in Brockton. Douglas had rearranged his factories to produce a cheaper line; the union objected; the State Board of Arbitration and Conciliation found no violation of contract. Negotiations for renewal of the agreement were held in Brandeis' office, but the union insisted on a restoration of wages in effect before the factory changes and also demanded back pay. Brandeis told Tobin, the union president, that it would be a misfortune to organized labor if Douglas had to sever the ten years' relations which had strengthened the cause of unionism. Internal dissension in the locals complicated the situation and Douglas gave up the union stamp with regret, saying he would continue to pay the highest wages in the shoe trade.

This manufacturer had thirty-two hundred employees in his three Brockton factories and proceeded to discharge large numbers of them and open new plants in Marlboro and Haverhill and in New Hampshire and Maine. Brandeis obtained full authority from him and offered arbitration to the edgemakers and stitchers remaining in Brockton. Although they rejected it he acceded to their demands to avoid a strike. But he warned them against following an arbitrary course which would drive the shoe business out of the city and destroy the principle of mutual trust. Seven other manufacturers left Brockton to be able to compete with out-of-town plants. Local merchants were distressed. A citizens' committee was formed to look into the causes of the city's depression. Gompers tendered the good offices of the A. F. of L., but the union made no request for them. Finally agreements affecting the eight hundred remaining workers were

reached in Brandeis' office. What a wasteful controversy, he
thought, simply over a question of interpretation!

Another labor case concerned the ladies' garment workers
in Boston. A shop strike for union recognition spread through
the local industry when the employers joined with fourteen
other manufacturers in an association to blacklist union members. Smaller firms came to terms, but not the members of
the association. The strikers were given the use of Civic
Service House, where Meyer Bloomfield was head worker.
Bloomfield and others of the Civic Federation tried to bring
capital and labor together and at these conferences Brandeis
appeared as attorney for the employers' group.

The hitch in the negotiations was a demand for a closed
shop. Brandeis suggested the compromise of union recognition without closing the doors to non-union labor. His friend
McElwain, incidentally, who had succeeded in finding the
way to keep thousands of workers on the job three hundred
and five days in the year, wanted them all to join the union
on the theory that non-members should contribute for advantages shared, but left the question to their own volition.
This was a satisfactory setup. Brandeis' compromise offer to
the garment workers was rejected. The strike continued.
Brandeis' partner, McClennen, obtained an injunction against
the union leaders and after a four-month struggle the strike
was called off.

In the garment experience Brandeis did not get a chance
to come to grips with the industrial facts and he passed over
the aspect of irregular employment; nor did he pierce the
skin of the union organizers. But he made the acquaintance
of a skirt manufacturer, Maxwell Copelof, a man with considerable public spirit, from whom he learned much. A little
later, when a strike of longshoremen was imminent, he pointed
out to shippers that the intermittent and casual nature of
longshoremen's employment imposed an unnecessarily heavy
cost on shipping; a system could be developed which would
assure practically constant work at fixed wages and result in

a material lessening of the friction at the port of Boston. An investigation in England had clearly established that irregularity was a much greater factor in producing pauperism and other social demoralization than low rates of wages.

Concern for the upbuilding of the city of his adoption took him into a crusade hatched by Edward Filene and Lincoln Steffens. Richards and Storrow were in it, and gradually almost every Bostonian of note. "Boston—1915" it was called. Boston was to be the first city in the land in that millennial year. Brandeis saw the possibilities of social regeneration and contributed five hundred dollars. He suggested that they interest Gillette, a man of strong idealistic tendencies. He reported dissatisfaction with the placing of Mellen on the transportation committee. To Paul U. Kellogg, on the staff of *The Survey*, which was about to publish an article on the movement, he proposed as a motto lines from one of his favorite authors, Euripides:

> *Thou hast heard men scorn thy city, call her wild*
> * * *   *Go forth, my son, and help.*

To Steffens he sent another keynote from Euripides:

> *The simple nameless herd of Humanity*
> *Hath deeds and faith that are truth enough for me!*

The movement seemed promising at first. But the backers were looking for bigness.

The nation was now living under a new dispensation, the Taft administration. The Commonwealth had a new governor, Draper, who had resigned his directorship in the National Shawmut Bank (popularly known as Morgan's New England bank) on becoming a candidate. The New Haven declared its usual quarterly dividend of two percent although the annual report showed a deficit of more than two and a half-million dollars. Brandeis was in Washington conferring with the Interstate Commerce Commission. And his anti-merger ally in the Massachusetts legislature, Norman H.

White, was demanding an accounting from the road on the disposition of its B. & M. stock.

Interest now shifted to the purchaser, Billard, who turned out to be a director of the National Bank of New Haven, which was a depository of the company. Mellen and four other members of the New Haven board were also directors of this bank. In answer to White the road denied having any agreement or understanding with Billard but admitted that the securities had been sold to individuals whose attitude toward the New Haven was believed to be friendly. Billard, in turn, was incorporating a company to buy, hold, and sell B. & M.

Brandeis called him "clever John." The Meriden man gave the impression that he was going to do as he pleased with the stock. Governor Draper put through a bill creating a holding company to take over the stock. Higginson spoke for it, Brandeis and Eastman against it. Brandeis contended that the state could take the stock by eminent domain, whereas the Draper bill attempted to solve the merger problem by compounding a felony. Draper's excuse was that the Billard stock might not be brought into Massachusetts. Brandeis derided the bugaboo of alien ownership. "If that stock ever turns up in the hands of Harriman or the Canadian Pacific or anybody else it will be solely because the New Haven turns it over. The New Haven took it, they said, because they wished to prevent it from falling into other hands. So long as they want it they will continue to prevent it. Has Mr. Billard been here to consult with the governor on this bill? Has anybody been here other than President Mellen and Vice-President Byrnes? Has the bargain ever been made with anybody else?"

He raised the objection that the holding company bill would conflict with the federal suit against the New Haven. But he was answered by a quotation from Holmes' dissenting opinion in the Northern Securities case to show that the Sherman Law was not to be construed to mean "the univer-

sal disintegration of society into single atoms." Passed by the
Senate, the bill met with some resistance in the House, but
Henry Cabot Lodge whipped the doubtful legislators into
line by wiring them from Washington. During the debate
one of the members, a confidant of the governor, said that
the Department of Justice did not intend to press its case. A
week after Draper signed the bill Attorney General George
W. Wickersham dropped the suit. The principal reason, he
said, was the passage of this bill—"the community most directly affected is the State of Massachusetts, whose laws now
expressly authorize such consolidation."

"Clever John" now announced: "If the holding company
wants my stock it will have to pay the price I want."

The next development was obvious. The New Haven
entered into an agreement to buy all the holding company's
securities which would be issued in payment for the B. & M.
stock. The result, said the New Haven's next annual report,
would be "indirect control of a stock interest in the Boston
& Maine railroad through your ownership of all the outstanding capital of the Boston Railroad Holding Company."
A special meeting of directors was held and J. P. Morgan
moved the issue of five hundred thousand additional shares,
increasing the capitalization from $121,000,000 to $171,000,-
000. Mellen publicly explained: because of a Massachusetts
law providing that bonds could not be issued in excess of
capital stock it was found necessary to issue more stock.

"How safe are the $30,000,000 securities held by savings
banks?" asked the *American*.

"Who influenced Taft to withdraw this suit?" the same
paper wondered.

While the defeated anti-mergerites in Boston were asking
one another questions the gentleman from Wisconsin, Robert
M. La Follette, took the Senate floor and thundered the replies.

"The mask is off!" the insurgent said in April, 1910. "We
have all of us done injustice to Mr. Mellen." He said as much

for Byrnes. "Both of these men and others of their kind are but hired megaphones through which a beefy, red-faced, thick-necked financial bully, drunk with wealth and power bawls his orders to stock markets, courts, governments and nations.

"We have been listening to Mr. Morgan."

La Follette's fire set the whole course of the New Haven ablaze. Senator Lodge deprecated the agitation of a subject by one not familiar with the situation. But the insurgent flung fact upon fact at the administration's supporters. He was furious with Wickersham for dismissing the suit before coming to trial:

> A railroad company, engaged in interstate commerce, violates the common law against monopoly—violates the state law against acquiring other corporate property— violates the federal law against combination and monopoly to suppress competition in interstate commerce— is sued in the Massachusetts Supreme Court and judgment is rendered against it—is sued in the federal court and delays the case until a new administration is installed —seeks and secures state legislation which pretends to authorize it to combine common carriers engaged in interstate commerce in violation of the federal law—and then secures dismissal of the federal suit, which the federal court had sustained at every point in a running fight of thirteen months....
>
> In other words, a state legislature, at the behest of an interstate railroad corporation, presumes to repeal a federal law and license an act which Congress, in the exercise of its constitutional authority to regulate interstate commerce, has declared to be a crime against the people.

This was what Wickersham, with the lamest of excuses, tolerated. The government, if it had a mind to prosecute, might have amended its petition and reached out after the New Haven's steamship lines. Wickersham could have made this case the strongest ever presented under the Sherman Law, La Follette said.

It was a speech after Brandeis' own heart. It transferred the arena of the anti-merger fight to Washington.

Lodge's deprecation found a satiric echo in the Republican *New York Tribune*, which characterized La Follette and Brandeis as birds of a feather. The *Tribune* said this was the invariable comment of senators who had observed the growing intimacy of the two since Brandeis came to Washington. Quiet investigation by senators, the newspaper continued, showed that Brandeis had furnished La Follette with all the data for the speech; that La Follette, in his search for yellow material for his weekly, found Brandeis an invaluable asset.

What the quiet investigators did not know was that something more than intimacy had grown up. It was affection.

CHAPTER VIII

THE TILT WITH TAFT

IT WAS NOT the New Haven issue which gave Brandeis his first prominence in Washington. That fight was lying dormant while he turned to the Interstate Commerce Commission for a new line of attack. Another issue arose for Brandeis' attention. It was conservation.

The insurgent Western Republicans in Congress were embittered against Taft for his easy-going abnegation to the oligarchs of the East, for the Payne-Aldrich tariff, and for his departures from the program at least professed by Roosevelt. A scandal in the Department of the Interior under Secretary Richard Achilles Ballinger drove another wedge into the party. The sledge was put into Brandeis' hands by an odd chain of circumstances. Brandeis knew Hapgood of *Collier's;* and Robert Collier was a close friend of Chief Forester Gifford Pinchot, who had taught Roosevelt conservation; and *Collier's* published accusations by Louis R. Glavis, who had been dismissed from government service by Ballinger at Taft's direction.

On the eve of a congressional investigation Brandeis was absorbed in a suit arising from a Warren family quarrel. He received an urgent telegram from Hapgood to come to New York. In the law office of Winthrop & Stimson he found a conclave of legal talent: Henry L. Stimson, George Wharton Pepper, and Joseph P. Cotton, Jr. As Pinchot had originated the attacks on Ballinger's policies and would be a leading witness at the hearings, it was obvious that he, like young

Glavis, would need counsel. Since the reputation of *Collier's* was at stake, the magazine must have a good lawyer to protect itself. Stimson agreed to represent Pinchot. Cotton was brought in by a wealthy Chicago friend of Glavis, John Bass, active conservationist. There was much talk, but Brandeis returned to Boston not knowing where he was to fit.

Apart from a defence of conservation and the prospect of a fee there were serious implications in the discharge of a government employee for daring to be loyal to the people of the United States. Brandeis was impressed by the sincerity of Glavis. The young man, as Seattle field agent of the General Land Office, had tried two years before to prevent the patenting of fraudulent claims and charged that entries for more than five thousand acres of valuable coal and timber land in Alaska had been made for the benefit of a Morgan-Guggenheim syndicate. Glavis was in his early twenties; Ballinger was then commissioner of the Land Office and clear-listed the entries as the next step toward patenting. After resigning his commissionership Ballinger accepted employment as counsel for the claimants. The cases were still pending when he went back to the department as Secretary. Glavis, still heading off the claims, despite the obstructive tactics of the Interior, submitted a huge mass of documents to Taft on September 6, 1909, on Pinchot's advice. (First he took the precaution of making copies of important papers and sending them to the Forest Service; and two of its men aided him in preparing the charges.) The President was at Beverly, Massachusetts, making the game of golf nationally famous.

On September 13 Taft authorized Ballinger to dismiss Glavis. "I have examined the whole record most carefully," the President wrote, and concluded that the insinuations and innuendoes charging the Secretary with knowingly helping fraudulent claims and interfering with Glavis' efforts to defeat them embraced "only spectres of suspicions." Glavis was disloyal to his superior officers and unjustly impeached their official integrity; his charge that Ballinger was not sympathetic to the conservation program initiated by Roosevelt was baseless.

Two months after dismissal Glavis and his manuscript were introduced to *Collier's* by Bass; the magazine had already raised doubts as to the authorship of the Taft letter exonerating Ballinger. Glavis left his story with Hapgood on condition that there was to be no payment, for he did not want to commercialize his convictions. Once the articles were published the storm broke and the insurgents in Congress demanded an investigation.

The Senate put in a call for the documents on which the President had based his letter. On January 6, 1910, papers were delivered, including the sixty-thousand-word Glavis report and a voluminous memorandum by Attorney General Wickersham (dated September 11). Wickersham took up the accusations and denied them one by one; he said Glavis was animated chiefly by an exaggerated sense of his own importance and a species of megalomania resulting in charges warranting his immediate separation from the service. On the same January 6, while the conference in Stimson's office was taking place, Senator Jonathan P. Dolliver of Iowa read a letter from Pinchot on the floor, justifying the conduct of his two aids who had helped Glavis and thus risked their jobs rather than the loss of their country's land. Pinchot declared the issue to be broader than the immediate question—it was the conservation of popular government. Until this time Taft had attempted to soothe Pinchot and keep him from resigning.

On the next day the situation was changed. Taft dismissed Pinchot. Senator Elihu Root advised Stimson, his former partner, to step out. Stimson dispatched a clerk to the post office to retrieve his letter of acceptance to Pinchot but he offered the assistance of a bright young man named Felix Frankfurter. Pinchot engaged Pepper. *Collier's*, determined to get the best available man to support its side, yielded to

Hapgood and summoned Brandeis again. Then Stimson, with queasy caution, withdrew his promise of Frankfurter on the ground that he could not afford to let a protégé of his be associated with a radical like Brandeis.

Glavis found Brandeis so gentle that he hesitated to entrust his important case to so unassuming a lawyer. He thought also that Brandeis might be unacquainted with the law of conspiracies and wanted to tell him what constituted an overt act. After all, a great principle was involved—Glavis had given his article to *Collier's* for nothing when another magazine offered four thousand dollars and he needed the money. Cotton said Brandeis was the man. But while it was true the Bostonian knew conspiracies he had to sit down and learn public land law. He secluded himself for two weeks at the Harvard Club in New York and in that monastic retreat learned to distinguish a land location from an entry. He studied the complicated practices of the Interior, and absorbed an amazing myriad of names, dates and figures on a diet of grapes, shredded wheat, mutton chops and hot chocolate.

The resolution for an investigation provided for a joint committee, half to be appointed by the Vice-President, half by the Speaker of the House. Among those who suspected that the resolution really had been drawn by Ballinger was Representative George W. Norris of Nebraska, who planned a revolt against the iron rule of Speaker Cannon, Republican potentate, so that a real investigation would be assured and not a whitewash. By a ruse, waiting for the rules chairman to go out to lunch, Norris succeeded in having the House elect its own investigators. The well-organized insurgents met in caucus and agreed on Norris' choice for the committee, Edward H. Madison of Kansas, and arranged with the Democrats to keep out certain members of the administration wing. The Senate had already named four Republicans: Knute Nelson of Minnesota, George Sutherland of Utah, Frank P. Flint of California, and Root of New York;

and two Democrats: Duncan U. Fletcher of Florida and William E. Purcell of North Dakota. The Democrats of the House selected two men who were friendly to Madison: Ollie M. James of Kentucky and James M. Graham of Illinois; the Republicans were Samuel W. McCall of Massachusetts, Marlin E. Olmstead of Pennsylvania, Edwin Denby of Michigan. On January 26 the hearings opened, with Brandeis and Cotton appearing for Glavis.

"Mr. Brandeis," said Senator Sutherland, "I do not like to interrupt you, but it seems to me you ought to abridge your statement of the ultimate facts which you expect to prove here. You constantly state a fact and then characterize it, argue about it. The time for argument will come hereafter."

"Mr. Brandeis," said Chairman Nelson, "I wish you would confine yourself as much as possible to a statement of what you want to prove and not indulge in too much argument."

The interruptions came when he was answering questions. Although Glavis was on the stand the members of the committee were putting their questions to Brandeis. They wanted to know the specific charges. But Brandeis said he did not desire to make any charges of corruption—let the facts be brought out and the committee determine whether the great trust of holding this land for present and future generations was in safe hands. But first the committee should obtain certain documents and communications which were beyond his reach, and he submitted a list of them.

The political significance of the impending battle began to take shape when Senator Root implied that Glavis' motive was an attack on the Taft administration and when a letter from Ballinger was read, intimating that the pernicious activity of certain officials of the Forest Service was the inspiration for the charges.

After making further requests for missing documents Brandeis sought an adjournment so that he might proceed to Springfield, Illinois, and argue on the constitutionality of that state's ten-hour law for women. An earlier law had been invalidated before the Oregon decision, and the employer interests were challenging the new one.

On returning to Washington he again asked for papers which the Interior was apparently withholding. Some were presented with the explanation that they had been found only recently in a box in Seattle.

"Now that is the statement of the case as the chair understands it," said Nelson.

"No, as is alleged. Not as is proved, but as is alleged," said Brandeis. He objected to the route by which papers went to Ballinger for sifting before being passed on to the committee.

"I do not think that is a proper statement to make," Root told him.

Brandeis renewed his daily request. Counsel for Ballinger also came on the scene— John J. Vertrees—and complained; in cross-examining Glavis he got answers with "a string to it," qualifications not called for by the questions. "He comes here with an array of facts and statements and states them and itemizes them and details them."

Glavis possessed a remarkable memory. Brandeis had often been complimented on his own accurate memory, which he considered simply a process of concentration. But when he went over the ground with Glavis at the Harvard Club he was astonished to find a mind that registered automatically every detail in its proper relation to the whole.

On the other hand, some doubt regarding Wickersham's agility disturbed him. The long Wickersham memorandum of September 11 encompassed the massive Glavis report and made such accurate references to complicated documents that the Attorney General could not possibly have accomplished this feat in so short a time. The Wickersham report must have been finished long after September 11 and then predated to give the appearance of a thorough study on the part of the President.

But if Taft did not have it when he wrote his exoneration of Ballinger on September 13, where then did Taft get his information? From Ballinger? How could this be proved?

He examined the Wickersham report again for clues and kept thinking about it; there must be a slip somewhere to betray the actual date. Then one night in February at Pinchot's home in Washington, he heard an amazing confession. Ballinger's stenographer, Frederick M. Kerby, was on a visit to James R. Garfield, the Pinchots' house-guest. Garfield had been Secretary of the Interior in the Roosevelt Cabinet, and gossip had it that he bore animus towards Taft for failing of reappointment; but his friends knew this to be untrue. His former private secretary learned from conscience-stricken Kerby the real story of the President's vindication of Ballinger; and now Kerby, in fear of being called to testify and of being dismissed, asked Garfield how his information could be brought to light without these risks.

Garfield told Kerby to repeat the story to Brandeis, who happened to be under the same roof. The upshot was that Brandeis requested Chairman Nelson to direct Ballinger and Oscar Lawler, the assistant attorney general assigned to the Interior, to produce all papers or memoranda submitted by them to Wickersham or to the President. Brandeis did not let up. Some were produced, but he called attention to omissions. Days elapsed, and Ballinger resented a further demand for the records, saying it was obviously a mere fishing expedition. The calls continued to be made in monotonous fashion, with no hint of dynamite.

Meanwhile a host of witnesses had to be examined. Senator Fletcher said he enjoyed Brandeis' performance every day. It was a treat to watch this quiet but emphatic man reveal powers of memory, coordination and analysis, actually conducting the hearings by himself, as Cotton had dropped out. Polished but ineffectual, Pepper rarely came to grips with facts. He fought valiantly for points of order. There was a little amusement over the fact that Brandeis brought a green flannel bag to court while other lawyers carried leather briefcases; the bag was a holdover from his campus days. His notion of a successful cross-examiner was one who possessed a knowledge of the case greater than the sum-total of what all the witnesses knew. Their combined knowledge was like a cluster of dots; one witness might know a dot on the edge, another a dot in the middle, and each knew the lines connecting his own set of dots. But the cross-examiner must be able to draw a circle around them all so that when a witness attempted to connect a dot within the circle to another on the periphery he could be tripped up.

Brandeis did just that with Ballinger's general utility man, Edward C. Finney, the expert of the department, when questioning him about the Wickersham report. In Wickersham's summary of replies to Glavis' charges there was a paragraph on the unsoundness of the suggestion that it was unlawful for Ballinger to have a professional relation with the coal-land claimants because of his immediately previous incumbency as Land Office commissioner. Glavis had never made this charge to Taft. Finney nevertheless testified to having given Wickersham a memorandum on this phase of the law sometime in September—couldn't remember the date. Brandeis pointed out that the first time Glavis ever referred to this law was in his *Collier's* article in November.

"I would like to ask you one other question, Mr. Finney. Is it not a fact that this summary of the Attorney General, which purports to have been made September 11, 1909, bearing the date September 11, 1909, was, as a matter of fact, not completed for more than two months after that time?"

"I do not know when it was written, Mr. Brandeis."

The significance of the day's testimony was pointed out by Brandeis to the Washington correspondents who would gather in his room at Hotel Gordon of an evening. When the time came for Pinchot to testify, Pepper advised against a direct attack, but Brandeis cornered Pinchot in the New Willard Hotel and cited examples from American history to prove that open criticism would be in the best tradition. Pinchot characterized Ballinger as a dangerous enemy to

conservation who entered office with the clear determination
to make short work of the previous administration's policy
and who gave Taft an absolutely false statement on the coal
cases, who wilfully deceived Taft and was disloyal to him.
At the end of two days of cross-examination Pinchot was
asked, "When did you first conclude that the defence of
those policies required that some sort of movement should be
made to remove Mr. Ballinger?" He denied such a plan
ever existed.

The great issue in the case, Brandeis told the committee,
was whether Ballinger was unfit; did he lack truthfulness and
directness, as Pinchot distinctly charged? Ballinger should
be called at once. Root, Sutherland and Denby rushed into
the breach. The committee went into executive session and
voted to deny Brandeis' request and let Ballinger appear
whenever he desired.

In Kentucky, Ollie James observed, the defendant went on
the stand first or not at all, instead of following his witnesses.

"Now," said Brandeis, "I desire to know when Secretary
Ballinger will come and testify before this committee."

"Whenever we see fit to put him on," said Vertrees, the
opposing counsel.

"Now is this witness going to be allowed to withhold his
testimony in order that he may frame it so as to reconcile it
with that testimony which has previously been put in by one
and another of the witnesses, or is this witness going to be
treated as any other witness, to be called when the exigencies
of the inquiry in the interests of truth, and truth alone, demand that he shall answer the questions which have been put?
See that position, Mr. Chairman."

Sutherland said, "Mr. Brandeis, let me suggest to you that
this is an investigation and not an inquisition. You are discussing a proposition that is not before the committee. It is
entirely out of place and entirely out of order, and I think the
chairman should direct that you proceed with the investigation."

Vertrees passed a remark about people coming to the hearing with lips protesting they had no charges, yet their tongues were leprous with most defamatory insinuations. Imperturbable, Brandeis once more called for Ballinger, and Root again moved for an executive session. The request that the other side open its case with Ballinger was denied. Vertrees then made a statement promising to show that conservation had no steadier supporter than Ballinger, who held that "those who have already been born and now breathe have rights as well as those yet to be born and to breathe, and that development ought not to be exiled by theorists and doctrinaires."

"Glavis, suspicious by nature," Vertrees said, "became perverted by detective service until, apparently, he has become incapable of fair judgment. Mr. Pinchot, vain, and flattered as chief of the Forest Service by his own publicity bureau, had come to regard himself as the most important personality in the Department of Agriculture. Mr. Ballinger committed the unpardonable sin of defeating the ambition of a self-exaggerated man."

In May the Secretary took the stand, and it seemed to Brandeis as he listened to the testimony that while the Ballinger side maintained they were for conservation they did not have the honesty to say they wanted to conserve for themselves. Brandeis proceeded from what he called the inconsistencies in the Secretary's testimony to the moral issues. He reminded him that after Glavis had gone to Taft, Ballinger told newspapermen that he was going to kill some snakes.

"Well, now, did it ever occur to you, Mr. Secretary, that this supposed lack of loyalty, or, putting it another way, that the personal loyalty of one in public service to a superior or to an associate might involve disloyalty to 99,000,000 people?"

"I will not argue that question with you," Ballinger answered. And nobody was warranted "in accusing me of any irregularity or impropriety in public office." Several times he asked the stenographer to repeat Brandeis' questions "in order to eliminate the intonations of counsel."

Brandeis minutely traced the Secretary's movements of the past summer on returning from the West to Washington and going up to Beverly. He asked Ballinger question after question to build up a continuous picture of his activities, and Ballinger admitted each detail.

"Mr. Brandeis, I am merely curious to know, but did you have a detective shadowing Mr. Ballinger?" asked Root.

"No. I will be very glad later, or now if you like, to tell you the source from which I received my information."

"No, your word is enough."

Ballinger's answers were not enough. He neglected to say that he took Lawler with him to Beverly; did not think it material or important. But, persisted Brandeis, in view of the part Lawler played later—

"What part do you refer to?" the witness asked.

"Well, any part within your knowledge that he subsequently played."

"My answer is no."

His cross-examiner established that Ballinger arrived at Hotel Touraine in Boston on the morning of September 6, found Taft on the golf links with Governor Draper, and did not deliver documents to him until the evening; that the President went to a baseball game on the 7th and Ballinger did not see him again until the evening of that day. Root thought Brandeis was wasting time fixing dates and hours. Brandeis continued, pointing out that Taft spent a busy week of speeches, yacht races, a reception to the Mikado's grandson, a review of the Beverly firemen. Ballinger and Lawler returned to Washington on the 9th; Lawler saw Taft again in Beverly on the 12th.

"What did Mr. Lawler take with him when he went to Beverly the latter part of the week?"

" A grip with some clothes in it. I do not know what else he took."

The cross-examiner connected the dot of the grip with the dot of a memorandum. The witness admitted also that he went over the memorandum with Lawler beforehand, but denied knowing where any copies might be. At one point Ballinger said, "Your question implies an insult....I appeal to this committee for protection against the insolence of this man." At another point, when Ballinger was recounting something, Brandeis put in a "Why?"

"Wait a moment," said the Secretary.

"I beg your pardon."

"Just be calm a moment."

"I am calm always, I think."

"I do not think so."

"Not patient, perhaps, but calm."

On the evidence, a memorandum was taken to Taft, but Taft did not include it with the documents he forwarded to the Senate. Brandeis therefore asked that Lawler send a copy to the committee or, if unable to do so, that the President be requested to send the original. A few days later word came from Lawler that he did prepare a memorandum of the facts in the record at Taft's request and delivered it to the Attorney General. Brandeis then reminded the committee that Wickersham had been called upon to transmit all documents; Wickersham said he had sent all, so there must be a misapprehension on someone's part.

"I believe that everybody will realize, and must realize, that under the circumstances that memorandum is an extremely important one in the consideration of the case," Brandeis said.

"You must except me, Mr. Brandeis," said Root. "I consider it of no importance whatever."

While the divisions of the committee stood pat on the decision that the President's actions were beyond their jurisdiction, Brandeis did not relax in his effort to prove that Taft was too busy during that week in September not to rely on outside help for his letter. Kerby, torn by guilty knowledge and the futility of the requests, arranged to see Brandeis a second time and asked whether he should release his story. The United Press wanted it. Brandeis knew it would be improper to give such advice. The tenseness of the situation drove Brandeis to Nelson's office to demand that the paper be produced. And when the Senator summoned his entire force as witnesses to this scene, Brandeis turned the tables and browbeat him in front of them all.

The nation was beginning to suspect a conspiracy of suppression. Wickersham was forced into speech by a resolution of the House. He admitted that his long report to the President was not written on September 11, which was instead the date his rough notes were placed before Taft. But he reverently added that "due regard for the constitutional authority of the Executive forbids that the action of the President and his advisers shall be called into question by a coordinate branch of the government."

Brandeis gazed up and saw the air was clearing. It was pleasant May weather. Newspapers said that when he returned home he would leave behind the finest collection of enemies he ever made. They described him as having wearied Root, Sutherland and Nelson of efforts to squelch him. "After each attempt," said the *New York Telegram*, "Mr. Brandeis bobs up to the surface with a smile that is the most exasperating expression ever encountered by a discontented body of men. Instead of smoothing the ruffled feelings of the men before whom he is trying his case, Brandeis deliberately continues to rub the fur the wrong way until the spectators are constantly on the alert for an explosion." The *New York Sun* asked why was he staying on in Washington. He was supposed to be only Glavis' attorney and Glavis had long since finished testifying. "Who is Brandeis?" the *New York Tribune* demanded; Glavis was a man of very moderate means and Brandeis was certainly not a cheap lawyer, so there must be a large fee coming from *Collier's*.

Brandeis had already received five thousand dollars on account. It was commonly known in Washington that the magazine retained him, and *Collier's* had indicated it editorially more than once. The *Tribune* probably did not like him and called attention to a faculty for injecting "an uglier insinuation and deeper insult into a question framed in perfectly parliamentary language than any man recently observed in Congress." As for his knowledge of human nature—

He finds the weakness of an opposing witness with unerring accuracy and plays upon it. With some he uses a robust voice, shouting his questions in tones which completely upset the unfortunate on the witness stand. With others, not to be discomfited by thunderous tones, he puts his questions in an oily insinuating tone calculated to arouse the anger of the witness and cause rage to blind him to the purpose of the questions. And, finally, Brandeis possesses the rare sense of knowing when to stop . . . when he has exasperated the members of the committee to the extreme limit of their endurance he grows gentler than a suckling dove and more persuasive than a second-hand clothes dealer trying to sacrifice himself to give you a bargain.

The croaking was ill-timed. Kerby's news broke. After Wickersham's cavalier disposition of the call from the committee Kerby gave the newspapers a statement declaring that Lawler, the Ballinger attorney, dictated to him the draft letter obviously intended for the President's use, as "I" appeared throughout. "You" was used for Ballinger. Glavis was said to have "called upon me at my home in Beverly," and whole paragraphs were adopted in Taft's letter. The same afternoon, immediately after publication, Wickersham sent in the memorandum, saying it had just been found.

So a little lying on the part of high officials gave the administration an uncomely black eye. Taft lied when he pretended that his clearing of Ballinger was based on a report by Wickersham not then in existence. The Attorney General

lied (and the President with him) by antedating the report.
There was another lie in the hiding of the fact that the exoneration was actually based on the Lawler memorandum. And
—if this was not deceit it was at least a scandal—the whitewash was supplied by Ballinger's own department.

Unaware of Wickersham's latest move, the White House
announced that Kerby's statement was "absolutely without
foundation." The next day Taft sent a more considered message to Senator Nelson, explaining that Wickersham came
to him on September 12 with Lawler's draft, which was then
used as part of the material on which was based his letter of
the 13th.

Here was the finale. Nelson, excited, wanted Kerby to be
subpoenaed. Kerby was in the room and stepped forward.
He was twenty-four years old, he said; he had been discharged the day before, but the Scripps-McRae newspapers
promised him a job. "I considered that my position was under
the government of the United States," he said, "and not as a
private and confidential secretary to the Secretary of the Interior." He told how Lawler's notes were burned in the grate,
how the memorandum was read in Ballinger's presence before
it was given to Taft, how he feared dismissal and sought his
wife's approval before releasing his story, and how he removed the original stenographic notebook to photograph the
pages and reconstruct the dictation.

Lawler came next to testify, completely unnerved. He was
positive he had been followed by gumshoe men, despicable
scoundrels; and the record of the hearings showed "absolutely
that my suspicions were more than well-founded." Asked
who they were, he pointed to Brandeis: "There is one. The
man Hapgood, who has been sitting next to him for weeks,
is another one." He was reminded that he said his trail was
followed in September. Brandeis, he said, "is a subsequent development and is simply the flower of this foul flock." Kerby
was corrupted. Who was the corrupter? he was asked.

"I do not know, but I believe that James R. Garfield, Mr.

Gifford Pinchot and Mr. Brandeis are the parties." (Hisses from the audience.) "Geese and snakes make noises like that."

When Ollie James asked Lawler why he thought detectives tagged him, Sutherland said, "I want to remind Mr. James that during the cross-examination of the Secretary, Mr. Brandeis disclosed a surprising knowledge of the movements of Mr. Lawler and of everybody else, giving the time and place and train and almost everything else connected with the movements of Mr. Lawler."

"Senator Root said he was satisfied with Mr. Brandeis' statement, but Senator Sutherland seems not to be," James observed.

Sutherland, noting James' willingness to get an explanation from Brandeis, said that while he believed Brandeis' denial, someone else must have done the shadowing. Brandeis answered that this did not necessarily follow. "Every step of it came from sources so simple that they were open to every member of this committee if they had resorted to them," he said. Over the assertion of another Republican member that the matter was of no importance Brandeis cheerfully related how he pieced together the actions of the characters in the drama from letters and telegrams in the record and from the daily papers.

"Now, Mr. Brandeis, do you not think that sufficiently illustrates it without taking up any further time?" asked Sutherland.

But Brandeis went on to tell about the collation of items from Washington, New York and Boston papers, which covered every step in the period considered except a few facts appearing on the hotel register at the Touraine, which he gathered by telegraphing Miss Malloch to check up Ballinger's arrival and departure.

"It is a perfectly simple way," he said, "but when you put those in sequence, one upon the other, you have what appears to be a very extraordinary intimate knowledge—"

"Of gumshoeing?" Senator Purcell suggested.

"Yes, of gumshoeing."

Hearings closed on May 20, 1910, after five laborious but lively months. Root packed his bags and sailed for The Hague to the peace tribunal. Roosevelt was coming home from his African safari, wild with joy at the mimic war the Kaiser had just staged for him. Brandeis was preparing a brief to be entitled, "Is the Department of the Interior in Safe Hands?" and a date for argument was set.

He recited the history of the efforts under Secretary Garfield to protect the public domain against the insidious aggressions of special interests. He outlined the record of Secretary Ballinger's stewardship. J. P. Morgan & Company and the Guggenheims—"probably the most ambitious, energetic, resourceful combination of capitalists in the world"—through their control of transportation in Alaska were rapidly attaining domination of the Territory. When Ballinger became Secretary he impressed upon his subordinates that he would have nothing to do with Alaskan coal lands.

"Now, I ask you, Mr. Chairman and gentlemen, viewing the evidence as it is, was that a determination to avoid evil, or was it a determination to avoid the appearance of evil?

"I have been told," Brandeis continued, "that it is the common thing in clubs where they expect to do a lot of gambling to have as the first rule of the club that 'card playing for money is not permitted in this club.' Certainly this is the sort of order the Secretary issued."

He told how Ballinger yielded to the influences of Miles C. Moore, former governor of Washington, and his friend, Charles J. Smith, "the capitalist and Senator-maker, a man who seems to have here had extraordinary power over Mr. Ballinger and over all things in the State of Washington."

"Wherever there is pressure," Brandeis said, "there you will find him yielding. The only cases when there can be any doubt as to what Mr. Ballinger will do is where there is pressure from both sides at the same time."

For this position the nation needed a man of the character

of Stonewall Jackson—"but I do not believe anybody would ever think of calling this man Stonewall Ballinger." Garfield and Ballinger differed from one another "as Hyperion from a satyr." The employees in the department worked with equal loyalty for both.

"Now, that is not loyalty," he said. "The loyalty that you want is loyalty to the real employer, to the people of the United States. This idea that loyalty to an immediate superior is something commendable when it goes to a forgetfulness of one's country involves a strange misconception of our government and a strange misconception of what democracy is. It is a revival—a relic—of the slave status, a relic of the time when 'the king could no wrong,' and when everybody owed allegiance to the king."

In an investigation devoted to the ascertainment of the truth Ballinger's answers were inconsistent with the truth, and the committee barred the opportunity of forcing the introduction of facts which should have been developed by the production of the documents called for.

"Should Mr. Kerby, like the bookkeeper of the defaulting treasurer, have stood by in his selfish, blind loyalty to that man?"

Brandeis pointed out that the danger in America was not of insubordination, but of too complacent obedience to the will of superiors. With the creation of new governmental functions and an increasing number of employees attending to the people's business "the one thing we need is men in subordinate places who think for themselves and who will think and act in full recognition of their obligations as a part of the governing body."

Rounding out his argument to a roomful of spellbound spectators he said, "We are not dealing here with a question of the conservation of natural resources merely; it is the conservation and development of democracy; it is the conservation of manhood. That is what this fight into which Glavis entered most unwillingly means. That is what the disclosure which Kerby made most unwillingly means. It proves that America has among its young men, happily, men of courage and men in whom the heavy burden of official life has not been able to suppress manliness."

After recess Pepper followed with his opening argument, and Sutherland asked, "Mr. Pinchot does not regard it to be insubordinate, does he, to be in an attitude of insubordination to his superior officer?"

Pepper answered, "I do not believe that Mr. Pinchot would for a moment take issue with the clear and, it seems to me, unanswerable statement of principle that we heard from Mr. Brandeis this morning."

Vertrees in his argument called "the Pinchot brand of conservationists the thirty-third degree conservationists, who have run off with this as a fad." He said that reclamation meant development not only for posterity but for posterity's ancestry.

Brandeis called attention to statements of evidence which showed Vertrees to be as unfamiliar with the record as with the principles of conservation. There was little good in conservation if it meant that resources were to be preserved for the rich to make them richer, leaving the great mass of people "dependent upon certain large capitalists, dependent upon the very limited number of the rich."

"We insist upon new methods," he said, "because the old method of distributing and developing the great resources of the country is creating a huge privileged class that is endangering liberty. There can not be liberty without financial independence, and the greatest danger to the people of the United States today is in becoming, as they are gradually more and more, a class of employees."

From the concept of the claims of privilege came "the desire to give the public domain to the Guggenheims and Morgans in order that they may develop our resources, perhaps in a paternal and benevolent way, and out of their millions create Rockefeller, Carnegie and Russell Sage foundations.

But for the courage and public spirit of *Collier's* and the independent press of the country, and of men like Garfield and Pinchot, Ballinger and Lawler would have sacrificed Glavis and "there would have been done in this country an act of injustice as great as that done Alfred Dreyfus in the Republic of France, and for very similar reasons. The reason here is that the men in exalted station must be protected at all hazards, and if they can not be protected by truth then suppression and lies must be resorted to."

The brief, signed by Brandeis, Cotton and George Rublee, called on the committee to determine from the conduct of Glavis, Pinchot and their associates whether these were honest men or snakes to be killed and traitors to be shamed.— "If any one of them has told the truth, the Secretary of the Interior is dishonored and unfit for his public office."

At South Yarmouth that summer, for rest and meditation, he dwelt on the idea that Ballinger represented privilege, the power of the Morgans, while Glavis represented the small man. There was no difference between the small man in government service and the small man in business. The question was whether the small man should be a free man or merely one of millions who were going to work for a few masters.

Thinking of the educational function of the press, Brandeis sent copies of his brief to various newspapermen. Frankfurter, serving in the United States District Attorney's office in New York, where Stimson had placed him, asked for the brief and congratulated him on his victory in the Illinois Supreme Court. Pinchot heaped praise on him and served notice he would heap more work.

Brandeis regretted leaving behind in Washington the glowing warmth of the La Follette family. The entire insurgent group interested him, but La Follette was a man close to his heart and vision, who buttressed his assaults with facts and figures. La Follette felt about Wickersham in the New Haven matter as Brandeis did and was glad to get the material. Very

soon they were on terms of "Dear Louis" and "Dear Bob."
Mrs. La Follette, a truly inspiring wife, let him know they
were happy that the year had brought him to them. Bob, Jr.,
said, "Mother, I believe I like Mr. Brandeis the best of anyone we know." Then he qualified it, "Of course, not better
than Mr. Steffens, but better than almost anyone else." The
La Follettes admired his philosophy, his temperament and
capacity for hard work. They knew he would always keep
himself busy in the public interest and felt he could accomplish more as a free lance than as a holder of office. But Mrs.
La Follette thought how fine it would be to have Brandeis
instead of Lodge in the Senate. "Fighting Bob" was in Wisconsin, suffering from an attack of gallstones and was grappling with the Stalwart Republican organization there, which
the administration was backing. Bob thanked him for doing
a great piece of work.

The *Boston News Bureau* and other harbingers were pre-
dicting a committee vote of seven-to-five in vindication of
Ballinger. There was hardly any doubt how the seven regular
Republicans would vote, but a suspicion lingered that they
might delay until after the elections. At Nelson's suggestion
the committee adjourned to meet again in Minneapolis in
September and try to reach a conclusion. Fletcher traveled
all the way from Florida and found Nelson adopting stalling
tactics. The full committee was not there; Root was due back
from The Hague any day, Flint and others had not yet
arrived. On the first day Nelson took the committee to the
fair in St. Paul. On the next day he convoyed them to an
old soldiers' home. Fletcher and Graham, impatient, sat up
nights preparing their report. Purcell and James were on their
side, and so was insurgent Madison, who was writing a separate report (Norris coaching). That made five. Only three of
the regular Republicans were in town: Nelson, Sutherland
and McCall.

Demanding a meeting, Fletcher and Graham plagued Nelson, who had no choice but to relent. They gathered in a

hotel room. Sutherland and McCall were missing. Nelson insisted no quorum was present. The Democrats said they had a right to do business. Fletcher made a motion to the effect that Ballinger was an unfaithful public servant and should be removed. Madison offered a substitute resolution that the charges brought by Pinchot and Glavis should be sustained. James proposed an amendment providing for Ballinger's removal; Madison accepted it. Nelson said he was going out to the toilet.

A half-hour later someone knocked. A messenger brought in a note from Nelson saying the session was adjourned, to meet in Chicago in a week. The five members in the room took a vote on Madison's resolution and released the news to the reporters downstairs. It was big news, politically significant. It was flashed to the State of Washington, where Miles Poindexter, insurgent, won the Republican primaries for the Senate nomination. In Chicago the Republican members (Root was back) denounced the Minneapolis action as being in the worst form of ward politics, and they still delayed voting. But they could not stem the course of events. The next Congress went Democratic.

The majority report, not filed until December, held that Ballinger honestly and faithfully performed the duties of his high office with an eye single to the public interest. The minority report by Graham, summing up the evidence, called on him to quit. Graham expected a vigorous attack on the floor. None came. The Democrats tried to keep the issue alive, Fletcher demanding resignation and Graham making a carefully constructed speech, again in expectation of rebuttal. Thus the shameful facts were disclosed to the public, although Congress lifted no finger. Moreover, the elections had demonstrated that the Republican administration was discredited. (Incidentally, Brandeis' St. Louis brother-in-law, Charles Nagel, was in Taft's Cabinet as Secretary of Commerce and Labor.)

On the very day of the Fletcher speech Richard Achilles

Ballinger wrote his own political epitaph and took to his heel. Taft held back the letter of resignation, which pleaded ill-health, until the session had closed. It was evident, the President said, that "I was and am the ultimate object of the attack."

However, Brandeis applauded Taft's choice of a successor, Walter L. Fisher of Chicago. A short time later the Alaska claims which had been the bubbles in this cauldron, were officially burst. The precedent was set for disallowing hundreds of similar claims and the valuable lands were restored to the public domain. Taft stepped into hot water again by throwing open to private entry a large tract bordering Controller Bay, Alaska. There was talk of favoritism, and the Democratic House placed a new investigation in Brandeis' hands. He studied the case dispassionately and reported that no action was required. Taft was cleared.

But with Roosevelt pushing Pinchot, and vice versa, the rift in the Republican Party cracked wider.

Chapter IX

A NATIONAL FIGURE IN 1910

THE YEAR which brought Brandeis to the La Follettes had its sad aspects. Sam Warren died in the pain of a trial which exposed him to the same malevolent spirit in Boston that had closed in on Brandeis. Sam's younger brother, Ned, in a dispute over their father's estate, sued for breach of trust and for six years Sam's sensitive fibre was torn by the publicity. During a recess in the trial in February, while Brandeis was in Washington, an untimely death overtook him in Dedham. He was a brilliant man and only fifty-eight. After a settlement was reached and the other heirs bought off Edward's claim, the *Boston News Bureau* suddenly said that Brandeis was the power behind the throne who had formulated "a cheating plot."

These were the facts. When the elder Warren died in '88 he left property worth two million dollars. Sam was the only one of the five children who had experience in the paper business and he drew up in his own hand a plan to lease the mills to an operating firm to safeguard the property against the obligations of the lessees. He asked Brandeis, as counsel for the executors, for a legal opinion. The business was then reorganized so that it passed through a conduit (Brandeis) to the lessees, consisting of Sam, his brother Fiske and the superintendent, Mr. Mason, who were to pay the estate six percent interest on the value of the real estate and receive half of the profits. Sam wrote Ned to come home. Ned was living in England, a graduate of Oxford, and spent his time collecting antique statuary. Sam wrote him not to get an inflated idea of his prospective earnings, as 1888 represented the high-water mark of the company's earnings and competition had set in. Ned remaining in England, Sam sent him an outline of the terms of the lease, transmitted the papers by which a trust was to be created, and again asked him to come home. Ned signed the deed conveying the property to the trustees and settled back to receive his annual income and buy more antiques. Brandeis was to be counsel for all parties concerned and received two thousand dollars a year from the beneficiaries and two thousand dollars a year from the lessees.

In 1903, when money was not coming in fast enough for Ned, he asked for an advance. His antique business was a source of friction between the brothers, and resulted in his retaining a Boston lawyer to look after his interest. The lawyer went over the books and saw that Sam was getting from $75,000 to $100,000 a year, while the most Edward received was $20,000 in any one year. He looked into the charges for additions and improvements and discovered that under the lease these were to be borne by the trustees, while the lessees paid for repairs. His report to Ned formed the basis of the suit. The antiquarian brother insisted that the lease had never been shown him; that Brandeis had never informed him; that the lease was unfair, contrived for Sam's personal benefit. As if to lessen the sting of fraternal animosity, the idea was advanced that Brandeis had chloroformed Sam's conscientious scruples over the scheme. In the trial McClennen represented Sam. Brandeis was in Washington exposing Ballinger.

Up until the last the friendship between Warren and Brandeis continued on a warm intellectual basis. It resembled another association of Harvard minds—that of Holmes and William James—but the loadstone here was not so much philosophy as the philosophy of the law. A few years before his death, harking back to their literary collaboration, Warren

*A Photograph of Mrs. Robert M. LaFollette, Sr.,
and Mrs. Brandeis taken in Washington
about 1929.*

supposed that their article on the right of privacy, in the *Harvard Law Review*, had been inspired by an article of Godkin's in *The Nation*, but Brandeis reminded Sam that it stemmed from his own deep-seated abhorrence of invasion. Sam rekindled an interest in the subject and wanted him to draw up a statute to meet the chief forms of invasion "without covering more ground than considered public opinion would sustain." According to Warren no greater service could be rendered to the community; the courts lacked initiative and flexibility to meet new conditions—the remedy lay in the legislature.

Brandeis was less subjective. He drew his concerns from the common man's struggle for existence. While working on the Ballinger case he heard that Mellen put his foot down on the pension plan which he had evolved as counsel for a committee of B. & M. employees in conference with sympathetic officials of the railroad. This was the first cooperative scheme in the field. The New Haven was tinkering with a plan much like the Pennsylvania's, which tended to make the men dependent on the company, the road bearing the entire expense and the employees having no hand in creation or administration. The bill which Brandeis drew up for the 27,000 B. & M. employees provided for contributions from both sides, with cooperative management; it established the pension as an inalienable right and placed it under the same state supervision as applied to insurance. An elective obligatory clause made the contributions compulsory on the vote of the railroad and two-thirds of the workers.

When the bill went before the legislative committee the chairman, mindful that the B. & M. had changed its stand on the merger, evoked merriment when he asked, "Don't you think, Mr. Brandeis, from your knowledge of the matters before this committee last year that we would be justified in shrinking from reporting this bill?"

Brandeis smiled broadly. "I think the railroad committee would not only not shrink from this obligation but would rejoice at the opportunity of pressing this bill to the House."

Immediately after Draper signed it the author sent out an expository letter to his magazine friends: Hapgood of *Collier's*, Lawrence F. Abbott of *The Outlook*, Hamilton Holt of *The Independent*, Oswald Garrison Villard of *The Nation*, Arthur Kellogg of *The Survey*, and also Samuel Bowles of the *Springfield Republican*. The new plan supplemented savings bank insurance and marked a step in developing an American system of workers' insurance and pensions. The broad purpose underlying it was to make men financially independent so they could be free citizens. The great defect in the pension plans of railroads and other large corporations was that they created a body of dependents; the pension, not being a legal right, often proved delusive and more frequently was used to limit the worker's freedom. Brandeis believed the new scheme was an important sociological advance, but thought possibly that he overrated it because he had framed it.

He had no doubts about savings bank insurance. After its first year a dividend of 8⅓% was declared; after the second, 12½%. Only two banks had opened insurance departments, but six others were receiving stations and forty-seven agencies were operating in factories, unions, stores and welfare institutions. In 1910 a total of $1,367,000 insurance was in force, covering thirty-three hundred policies. And the by-product was decidedly pleasing: the old-line companies were obliged to reduce premium costs by twenty percent. Banks were slow to identify themselves with the experiment but the community was coming to adopt the view that life insurance was another form of saving. Brandeis stressed the point that no wage was a living wage unless it permitted the worker to set part of it aside against the future.

Propaganda for a minimum wage law was brought to the United States by Florence Kelley from an international congress in Switzerland. The concept of state interference with wages met with the same conservative reliance on the country's political traditions as in the case of maximum hours, but within two years the new legislation was adopted in nine states.

The battle for regulation of hours for women had not been completely won in the Oregon case, and after the decision Brandeis felt that a better brief should be kept on tap. With the aid of a large corps of readers working for several months Josephine Goldmark compiled more recent and reliable data, so that when the Illinois case came up Brandeis presented a brief of six hundred pages of medical and social experience. There were still only a few pages of law. Though straining under a heavy load in the Ballinger investigation he made the trip to Springfield for the oral argument and swayed the judges of the Illinois Supreme Court into overruling the earlier decision of their court.

His contact with women doing effective work in a man's world converted him to equal suffrage. By 1904 he believed women would ultimately help redeem municipal political conditions and were rapidly fitting themselves for the vote; but even so, it was not wise to hasten the extension of suffrage— the work of preparation should proceed further. Mrs. Brandeis and Mrs. Evans came to realize that their anti-suffrage stand was a vote against women and agreed it was worth the risk to try for more democracy. Mrs. Kelley and Jane Addams took up suffrage because they felt it was the only way to achieve reforms for women and children. And now Brandeis became convinced society had grown so complex that it was necessary to have women participate; not merely for democracy but for the insight women had shown into social problems. Men needed them to have the ballot. Mostly he was influenced by the close examples of Miss Goldmark, his secretary Miss Malloch, and Alice Grady.

Someone was always leading him into one cause or another; or so it seemed to him. Lincoln Filene came to his week-end house in Dedham late in July, 1910, to interest him in the New York cloakmakers' struggle. It had developed from a strike into a war. The Boston merchant said he was going to take a look at it and wanted Brandeis to come along. The answer was: "I'll have nothing to do with any settlement involving the closed shop." Unions were essential for equalizing bargaining power, but a closed shop was repugnant to the ideal of liberty and would lead to overweening power and a monopoly of labor. Brandeis was unwilling for workers to be coerced into joining a union. He objected to compulsion in any case (although he was not above exerting pressure).

As for Filene, the strike situation hurt his business less than it troubled his conscience. He was in a position, as one of the country's largest retailers, to obtain merchandise despite the stoppage, but he did not want to buy goods made under the repulsive conditions complained of by the workers. Retailers bore a responsibility towards them, but none was lending a hand. Apparently nobody cared except the parties in deadlock and their respective attorneys who were firing pronunciamentos at each other. Filene called in Bloomfield, at whose settlement house workers used to fall asleep in classes on citizenship. (Americanism could not be taught to people half-dead from overwork.) Having helped form the International Ladies' Garment Workers' Union, Bloomfield was a good man to send to New York.

Filene, too, had been active in union organizing, and many a meeting was held in his house when workers had no place but saloons in which to congregate. His sympathies earned him the trust of the strike leaders. With Bloomfield as emissary something might be achieved. The mission in New York was to persuade both sides to invite Brandeis in writing to act as mediator.

Sweatshop conditions in the garment industry had reached the point of sub-sub-contracting. In the fever of cut-throat competition manufacturers slashed their labor costs by paying contractors a lump sum for the work; these men parceled it out to inside contractors, men in their own shops, who in turn hired cutters, operators and pressers to meet the specifications.

Sometimes the hair was so finely split that a presser would hire other pressers and make a profit on their labor. This long chain of bosses left the worker helpless, and reduced wages to a pittance. The evils of the system were many: long hours, nightwork, homework, irregularity of payment, charges for thread and electricity, disregard of Sundays and holidays, unsanitary conditions, blacklisting of active union men. A common sight was a worker in the evening carrying a sewing machine and a bundle to his tenement for the few additional cents he could make in overtime, often with the help of wife and children.

In this sad condition the workers were not, however, supine. For twenty-five years outbursts of shop strikes kept throwing the industry into turmoil; a resort to gangsterism further demoralized it. The unrecognized union maintained a Joint Board of locals, but only a small portion of the fifty thousand workers were members. Agitation for a general strike had been going on for two years when the International, holding its 1910 convention in Boston, authorized preparations. The strike was skillfully organized. When the call came, shears, needles, treadles, irons were laid aside on an afternoon in July, and every worker marched to his designated strike-hall. From headquarters came a list of demands. To this the newly-formed Cloak, Suit & Skirt Manufacturers' Protective Association replied that they would not enter a conference unless the union waived its demand for recognition, a closed shop, and a collective agreement.

Bloomfield approached both sides and found them skeptical. Filene, also in New York, felt sure the impasse could be overcome and called to Brandeis. On July 24, acting for the Joint Board, Brandeis sat down with the manufacturers. It was useless. Some members of the union's strike committee objected to hushing up the question of the closed shop and refused to participate. Out of his store of proverbial wisdom he quoted, "The wise man yields." They retorted, "Let the other fellow be the wise man."

He returned to Boston. The workers' confidence in him was somewhat shaken as a result of the manufacturers' press-release which made it appear that the strikers had retained him as counsel and thereby waived their most important demand. But on July 27 Meyer London, attorney for the union, and Julius Henry Cohen, attorney for the employers' group, telegraphed Brandeis that they were willing for him to be chairman at settlement negotiations. They sent him in writing the express understanding that the closed shop would not be brought up, and he came back on that assurance. At a three-day session in the Metropolitan Tower, in an atmosphere tense with animosity, Brandeis held the scales of dispassion. Twelve items were on the agenda, and the skillful negotiator put the easiest things first.

"Gentlemen, we have come together in a matter which we must all recognize as a very serious and important business, not only to settle the strike but to create a relation which will prevent similar strikes in the future."

The grievances were taken up in turn. The question designedly left for the last was, How were agreements to be enforced? The union's simple answer was that the manufacturers should agree to employ only union labor. It was rejected at once. Brandeis quietly reminded the conferees that they had come together on the condition that the closed shop would not be discussed, and he must insist on the observance of this condition. Then he broached his own device —an invention, he called it, whereby the union would be so strengthened that in time it would enroll practically all the workers as members. The manufacturers were to be a party to this growth (and a strong union maintaining union conditions would inure to their benefit also) by giving preference, when hiring, to union men, provided they were equal in ability to non-union applicants. The employer would retain the right to decide between them as to competence, and complaints of discrimination against union workers would be adjusted by arbitrators.

Despite the wrangling Brandeis was impressed with the general good temper of the twenty men in the room and their amenability to parliamentary procedure. It was a delight to witness the understanding Jewish bosses and Jewish workers displayed of each other's problems. In all his previous labor activity he had not encountered such tolerance flavored with a moral quality. "Yes," said a member of the manufacturers' association, "I would think that way if I were a worker." Brandeis enjoyed sitting down with them to a glass of beer of a hot evening. (In Washington his one dissipation was ice cream.) They plied him with questions about the Ballinger case and he gleefully told them how Senator Root suspected him of using a detective.

The idea of a preferential union shop was not acceptable to Cohen, but Brandeis' won over Cohen's clients. To the mass of workers it sounded like a sell-out. Abe Cahan, of the *Forward*, the East Side's great champion, derided it as "an open shop with honey." When the proposal was rendered to the strikers at Beethoven Hall by the treasurer of the American Federation of Labor they howled it down—so ferociously that he had to sneak out by the fire escape. Gompers was wise enough not to administer a public rebuke to them. The negotiations were broken off, and for three weeks longer this issue prevented settlement. The Jewish community was in turmoil. Jacob H. Schiff, financier and philanthropist, lent his lawyer, Louis Marshall, but he made no progress. Picketing was reinforced and Acting Mayor John Purroy Mitchel instructed the police not to interfere. The destitution of thousands of families taxed the facilities of the public charities. On the East Side the word "preferential" slipped into the Yiddish vocabulary; bearded old men used it in excited discussions after synagogue services and in coffee shops.

Filene, Bloomfield and Henry Moskowitz of Madison House strove for harmony and found that the Brandeis idea was beginning to be understood. The hitch lay in the phrase used in the agreement, "a man of equal ability to do the job."

Now the strike committee came forward with a counter-proposal; the bosses should agree to employ union men as long as union men were obtainable and could retain the right to discharge for incompetence. The manufacturers rejected it as being a surrender of control, but the workers demanded it as a protection against the ousting of union men and, ultimately, of the union. Cohen obtained an injunction against picketing on the ground that the main purpose of the strike was a closed shop and therefore even peaceful picketing was illegal. But many individual settlements and a tax on the earnings of re-employed workers fortified the strikers' resistance. The strike was prolonged into its ninth week.

Filene worried over the likelihood of the union's losing public support and, with it, the strike; if that were lost the union would be destroyed. Marshall, Cohen and London consulted together until they arrived at a modified plan in September, acceptable to the association and to the shop chairman.

This was the protocol of peace, based on Brandeis' negotiations, abolishing inside sub-contracting and charges for electricity, establishing maximum hours, minimum wages, holidays and a Joint Board of Sanitary Control, and providing for price committees to fix piece-work rates. The protocol was to endure without time-limit. The protocol introduced the preferential union shop in this form:

> Each member of the manufacturers' association is to maintain a union shop, a union shop being understood to refer to a shop where union standards as to working conditions, hours of labor and rates of wages prevail, and where, when hiring help, union men are preferred; it being recognized that, since there are differences of degrees of skill, employers shall have the freedom of selection as between one union man and another, and

shall not be confined to any list, nor bound to follow any prescribed order whatever.

The protocol also established a permanent Board of Arbitration (with a representative of the public) to which important disputes would be appealed from the committee on grievances. Brandeis was hailed as "the father of protocolism." The prospect of peace instead of devastating seasonal strikes hovered over an industry which for the first time in its history was blessed with a collective agreement. Brandeis was surprised and delighted that the preferential union shop had been adopted; mostly surprised. It would be infinitely more effective than a closed-shop agreement entered into under duress with a mental reservation that it would be evaded or broken at first opportunity. As with the solution of other public problems evolved in the laboratory of his experience, he hoped his invention would be adopted elsewhere. Jane Addams asked him to come to Chicago when the garment workers there went out on strike. She had in mind a public meeting where he might arouse support for the new principle. At this time, in November, he was engaged in a fight against a ten percent freight rate increase proposed by the Eastern railroads. Besides, the idea of the preferential union shop was too new to be urged first in public; educational work with Chicago's leading manufacturers and union men was necessary, and he advised Miss Addams to obtain the teamwork of Filene, Bloomfield and Moskowitz.

In New York the Board of Arbitration was set up: the manufacturers designated Hamilton Holt, the union Morris Hillquit, and both parties agreed on Brandeis as chairman, representing the public. The success of the plan would depend on absolute good faith; employers and employees must carry out the letter and spirit of the protocol—this was the way to industrial peace and industrial democracy. The interdependence of society had reached a state where no man could stand apart and be judged solely by his own action.

Many manufacturers were innocent of the abuses that led up to the strike, but it was impossible to escape the responsibility of being one's brother's keeper.

"What good did it do them?" Brandeis was addressing the cloak and suit buyers' association. "It rained alike on the just and the unjust. I found that no matter how just these manufacturers tried to be it did not help them any."

To a trade paper reporter he looked "all the world like those early pictures of Abraham Lincoln."

The Board of Arbitration held its first session in March, 1911. To the auditorium in the Bar Association Building came manufacturers and workers to watch—pompous but industrious Cohen, books laid out before him, acting as though this were a court; London, demonstrative, speaking with the fever of a people's advocate; Brandeis, the quiet chairman, imparting a calming dignity to the proceedings. The employees had charged the union with violations of the protocol; the union brought counter-charges. Some cloak men were operating out-of-town shops to evade the agreement. The Board, sitting for two days, ruled against this, handed down other decisions, and provided machinery for adjusting disputes. Grievances thereafter would be handled by clerks of both sides; if the deputy clerks failed to reach a decision the matter would be taken up by the chief clerks; then it might pass to a committee on grievances; in case of deadlock it would go before the Board of Arbitration, the final tribunal. By means of the elaborate rules and procedure thus formulated Brandeis hoped to make recourse to the Board an infrequent and even rare occurrence.

After a year of the protocol the preferential union shop was in reality becoming a union shop. The development was automatic, without a change in the protocol. The manufacturers, encouraged by their clerk, Paul Abelson, fell into the habit of requiring union cards. In the ladies' tailoring trade a strike was settled on a similar basis and several thousand more workers were brought under the aegis of protocolism.

Brandeis cited this new success to Garfield, who was trying to solve a garment strike situation in Cleveland, but counseled against interference by New Yorkers as something which the manufacturers would resent. Brandeis was sure, however, that a publicity campaign on a national basis would effectively reach the employers. The Cleveland strike broke down under the manufacturers' organized opposition. But the industry in New York was so elated over its period of peace that it hailed the protocol as a beacon for the rest of the country and took pride in the fact that the experiment began in an "immigrant industry" consisting mostly of Jews. The old guerrilla warfare was past.

By no means was this the final solution of the labor problem. To Brandeis the experience disclosed the possibilities of advancing beyond the point they had attained. The open shop was definitely disposed of. The way for improving conditions did not lie in splitting differences but in adopting constructive measures to remove grievances. The same Board of Arbitration was continued for another year, and London and Cohen privately agreed not to bring up cases except on vital issues.

The garment strike of 1910 influenced Brandeis' life profoundly. He discovered during those hot days in August that he was a Jew. He recognized his own passion for justice as an identical spirit in the two camps. Before that he had regarded his heritage simply as a historical fact, like blue eyes or straight hair. He had never taken an interest in what was called the Jewish Question. He had spoken in 1905 at a celebration of the 250th anniversary of the settling of Jews in the United States, but that was merely from the standpoint of Americanism. Now he was beginning to think in terms of world Jewry and was ripe for the visit paid him one day by Jacob de Haas, editor of a Boston weekly, *The Jewish Advocate*. De Haas came to discuss savings bank life insurance and stayed to convert him to Zionism.

Before being led into that field he was drawn into a new

battle by David O. Ives of the Boston Chamber of Commerce. Railroad shippers were joining forces to resist an advance in freight rates. But the issue, at bottom, was one affecting consumers—they would have to bear the increased costs—and the consumers, as usual, lacked organization to present their side. The railroads, sure to be represented by able and expensive counsel, contended that higher expenses, especially wage rises, warranted a horizontal advance of ten percent in justice to investors in their securities. Ives shared Brandeis' views on the New Haven, knew his public spirit and had confidence in his knowledge of railroading; as chairman of the traffic committee of a group of Eastern commercial bodies, Ives arranged that Brandeis appear as counsel for the shippers at hearings before the Interstate Commerce Commission.

Brandeis remembered having read a book on scientific management by Harrington Emerson which told how savings were effected on the Santa Fé Railroad by efficiency methods. When the rate case came up he tapped his mental reservoir. It was not so much his memory that stood him in good stead as his faculty for coordination. Congressman Graham had noticed it in the Ballinger case and called it the skill to fit details into a great mosaic. Brandeis realized that the principle of scientific management could apply here and he talked it over with Emerson, who agreed to testify at the hearings. They went through the names of other industrial engineers: Frank B. Gilbreth, who applied efficiency to motion studies; H. L. Gantt, to labor relations, and Frederick Winslow Taylor, the father of the efficiency movement. Emerson was not on good terms with Taylor but was willing for Brandeis to use his office telephone to make an appointment with Taylor and integrate his ideas.

The conclusion he reached was this: that the country needed cooperation to reduce production costs in place of combinations to increase prices. "The results of the application of efficiency methods in many departments of industry have shown that in the United States we have been shockingly prodigal of our resources of labor and material, and we are now facing a situation where the indefinite continuation of the theory of increasing prices every time there comes a demand for more revenue must be checked."

The new case brought Brandeis back to New York only a few days after the garment strike settlement. He had not seen much of Devonshire Street that year. The Ballinger investigation, which brought a fee of twenty-five thousand dollars, was so prolonged that he was not able to spend his first full day in the office until the middle of June. Vacation and the novel experience among the cloak-and-suiters brought the year into September. La Follette bade him come to Madison for a visit; he had no time. Pinchot wrote of having spoken to "the Chief" at Sagamore Hill about enlisting Brandeis in a new project; nothing came of it.

The I.C.C. hearings at the Waldorf-Astoria were being held under a recent amendment to the interstate commerce law putting upon the carriers the burden of proof that they were unable to earn a fair and reasonable return. The railroads presented their sets of figures before a special examiner and put their experts on the stand. A self-possessed man with black hair streaked with gray—it stubbornly stayed tousled—cross-examined them and drew out admissions that they did not know how the figures were arrived at. He asked an officer of the New York Central the reasons for the advance—and were shoe shippers consulted beforehand?

"I just want to say," the official answered, "that your boot and shoe shipper does not ask the consumer when he is going to raise the price of his commodities."

"No," said Brandeis, "but the boot and shoe shipper, the manufacturer, is governed by the law of competition. He is not a public-service corporation, and there has not been provided any tribunal which, because of the public service and quasi-monopoly or actual monopoly features, is to guard against that improper exercise of judgment which you speak of, and which must be deemed to be arbitrary if no reason is given for its exercise." The witness had no answer to offer.

After eight days, during which Brandeis tried to pry into the railroads' expenses and discover economies of operation, the hearings were adjourned at the request of the roads to October, when their presidents would testify before the I.C.C. as a whole in Washington.

In the interval Brandeis heard the sickening news about the shoe machinery monopoly. Thomas G. Plant, working out a system to rival the United, was ready to market it. Jones and other shoe manufacturers had pronounced it good and asked Brandeis if their leases with the United were legal and enforceable against them. Brandeis was of the opinion that under a recent Supreme Court decision the leases would be held invalid and the way was open to restore competition. Plant went so far as to publish this opinion in advertisements in Boston newspapers in July. But late in September, with notes totaling $1,500,000 falling due October 1, he was told by his brokers that this time the notes would not be renewed. Plant was in a panic. The brokers admitted they had been selling them to the United. The banks were closed to him; the financially powerful United had stopped his credit. He saw no alternative but to sell his patents to the trust.

For Brandeis this was the turning point. He decided he could no longer properly remain passive in the shoe machinery controversy; if called upon he ought to fight the monopoly policy of the United. (In *Hampton's Magazine* an article on President Winslow said that the United, closely associated with Morgan interests, had earned more than seven million dollars for the year; as an instance of its ability to make profits the writer cited a welt-sewing machine which cost two hundred and fifty dollars to manufacture and reaped more than six hundred dollars annually in royalties; at the end of the seventeen-year lease it would earn $10,200 and be returned to the company).

In October the railroads pleaded poverty to the I. C. C. Brandeis, cross-examining James McCrea, president of the

Pennsylvania, brought out the fact that the road's stockholders had received fourteen percent in dividends within the past twelve months.

"I assume, Mr. McCrea, that this proposed increase of freight rates was the result of conferences and an understanding among the leading financiers who had to be consulted and whom you referred to as those whom it was necessary to satisfy in order to raise more money. Isn't that a fact?"

"I do not think I made any such statement that it was necessary to satisfy any financiers."

But as to the presidents—"was there any consideration on their part of concerted action to secure a reduction of expense by securing a reduction of price in any part of the articles which the railroads are compelled to buy—for instance, steel?"

"None that I know of at all, sir."

Daniel Willard, president of the Baltimore & Ohio, took up the argument that the credit of the roads would suffer if denied the advance. His company was faced with a wage increase of $2,000,000.

"Now," said Brandeis, "assuming that you need more income, there are several ways possible in which to get it. One is by a rate increase. Another is to keep the rates as they are and to increase the efficiency of operation. Your problem is to manufacture transportation more cheaply. Now, I ask you whether it is not a fact that approximately a three percent cheaper manufacture of transportation would not meet your need, or this need, just as well as an increase of rate?"

"I think you have shown that it would."

Willard said he had in mind, though, the necessity confronting the B. & O. for raising new money—"and I doubt very much if such an argument as you have advanced would help us materially in our efforts to get money if we did not show a sufficient surplus to justify it."

Brandeis passed over the money question; just then he

wanted to take up efficiency and show that the roads were lax.

"My study of this subject," he said, "has led me to believe that that is really at the root of the matter, more than anything else. As we find in every other realm of human effort this difference of efficiency between men and in the same man under different conditions, is it not reasonable to suppose that if the mind of man is addressed to securing greater efficiency with the same equipment that greater efficiency will be attained?"

"Well, that is assuming that proper efficiency has not previously been attained."

Brandeis alluded to the possibilities of improvement in method and the saving of labor through scientific management. Going back to the question of credit—wasn't there concerted action on the part of "those eminent financiers, very few in number, who actually control the operations of the financial world and of the railroads" to make it appear that unless the roads got what the financiers wanted they could not obtain money for the desired improvements?

"Oh no," said Willard, "I saw no evidence of that."

The next witness for the carriers was W. C. Brown, a vice-president of the New York Central. Brandeis used his presence to expose the interlocking position of J. P. Morgan as a member of the executive committee of this road's board of directors and as head of the firm which was its financial adviser and the medium of floating its bond issues.

"Did you, in considering the means of increasing the net income from the operation of your properties, take up with Mr. Morgan, as an influential officer and director of the United States Steel Corporation, the question of the railroads securing a reduction in the price of rails and other steel products?"

"No," Brown answered. "Of course, Mr. Morgan does not sell steel rails. We do not buy them of him. We do not negotiate with him. We buy steel rails of the people in immediate charge."

"Precisely. But Mr. Morgan is an influential director and Mr. Morgan—"

The chairman cut him short.

Brandeis showed that the road had increased its dividend that year from five percent to six percent with the approval of Morgan and in spite of the employees' demand for a rise in wages.

"So that with full knowledge of this wage increase pending, and with knowledge of the other facts that have been testified to as to the financial condition of the company, this company of which the greatest banker of the world was a member, increased the rate of dividend," he continued. "Is it not a fact that by increasing that rate of dividend you disabled yourself to the extent of $1,786,000 a year from laying by that surplus from which betterments and improvements may be made, which you deemed and you say the bankers deemed to be a proper and necessary incident of a railroad which should deserve good credit?"

In presenting the case for the shippers he again aired his economic views. The railroads were suffering from a strain resulting from the administration of units of extraordinary size, from the absence of the stimulus of competition, and from the interference of the great financial powers. Systems like the New Haven, the New York Central, and to a lesser extent the B. & O., had burdened themselves with financial obligations by overexpansion; the error should be borne by the stockholders and not by the community. If higher costs were to be met by higher costs—as Willard said, the tendency of rates was continuing upward—where would be the limit? In businesses where scientific management was adopted the fundamental principle manifested was that higher wages meant lower costs. The railroads' inability to deal with increased operating expenses was due to the failure to use the new science.

"What is this science of management? It is a complete reversal, in the first place, of the principles under which work

is done." Instead of a military system of putting it up to the
employee to get work done and using pressure on him to do
it, there was the process of aiding the worker to greatest
achievement.

"We shall show you, may it please your honors," Brandeis
said, "that the estimate which has been made that in the railroad operations of this country an economy of a million dollars a day is possible, is an estimate which is by no means extravagant."

This startling statement was headlined across the country.
It caught the imagination of telegraph editors, make-up editors, and the hordes of newspaper readers. It made a sensa-
tion.

One million dollars a day! Brandeis became a national
figure. The reputation of the Ballinger investigator was
meagre compared with his new fame. In one breath he had
popularized efficiency.

Gilbreth went on the stand and said, "I am here, brought
by Mr. Brandeis, to tell you that this thing will solve the industrial warfare between capital and labor. It is the one thing
that will enable you to raise the pay of the workmen and get
down production costs, and there is no question about it."

Gantt told how he learned scientific management from
Frederick W. Taylor in the Midvale Steel Works; how sys-
tematized plants effected savings by making the management
and not the man responsible.

Emerson spoke of his experience with the Santa Fé. He was
Brandeis' star witness.

"You have been quoted, Mr. Emerson, as stating that in
your opinion, by the introduction of proper efficiency system, or scientific management, the railroads of the United
States could effect an economy of perhaps $300,000,000 a
year, or not less than one million dollars a day."

"That is correct—that is, I have been quoted as saying
that."

"Is it your opinion that that is the fact?"

"At least that."

"And in which of the departments of railroad operation is it that large economies can be effected, in your opinion?"

"In all of the departments except traffic. The efficiency of the traffic by my standards is very high."

The carriers contended that they had reached the maximum of efficiency in operating their lines. Brandeis, finishing with his experts, declared he had produced evidence that the roads had not adopted scientific management; the burden was on them to show that they had attained the possible economies in maintenance of way, maintenance of equipment, and handling of freight, transportation and terminal.

So much stir was made by the million-dollar-a-day assertion that a telegram was sent to Brandeis from Chicago in the name of the presidents of Western railroads offering him employment—he could name his salary—if he showed a practical way of saving a substantial portion of this amount. Their proposition, they said, was made in the same spirit of sincerity in which he had made his statement to the Commission.

He accepted. They thought they could put him in a hole. He was willing to arrange a conference at an early date, with the Eastern presidents, too.

"I must decline," he added, "to accept any salary or other compensation for the same reason that I have declined compensation from the shipping organizations whom I represent, namely, that the burden of increased rates, while primarily affecting the Eastern manufacturers and merchants, will ultimately be borne in large part by the consumer through the increased cost of living, mainly of those least able to bear added burdens. I desire that any aid I can render in preventing added burdens shall be unpaid service. Kindly suggest date and place of conference."

The correspondence was dropped. Later one of the railroad heads called on Brandeis in Boston and said he had not authorized the telegram.

Public interest in the lawyer who was shocking other mem-

bers of the profession by his habit of giving service gratis
was evidenced by newspaper and magazine articles on "this
altruistic type of Jew." He minimized the habit as being a
little hobby—

> Some men buy diamonds and rare works of art.
> Others delight in autos and yachts. My luxury is to
> invest my surplus effort, beyond that required for the
> proper support of my family, to the pleasure of taking
> up a public problem and solving, or helping to solve, it
> for the people without receiving any compensation.
> Your yachtsman or automobilist would lose much of his
> enjoyment if he were obliged to do for pay what he is
> doing for the love of the thing itself. So I should lose
> much of my satisfaction if I were paid in connection
> with public services of this kind.

The Brandeises were living on no higher scale than when
they married almost twenty years before. They still had
their original furniture, mostly wedding presents. Indeed,
their personal expenses were lower; formerly they had wine
on the table, keeping up with the Joneses and/or the Cabots,
but as their circle of friends changed they found they could
get on without elegance. And long after the automobile
came into vogue Brandeis continued to drive to his office in
his buggy.

Newspapers pressed him for his private opinions. They
learned that he believed in property rights but that the courts
often made them an end instead of a means.

"Correct that error, put property back into its right place,
and the whole social-legal conception becomes at once consistent," he said. Life was short. "Why waste it on things I
don't want most? I don't want money or property most. I
want to be free."

He made efficiency a household word. He also gave currency to the line from Euripides: "Go forth, my son, and
help!"

Some of his detractors apparently did not believe he could follow the advice. "Brandeis? Why, he's a joke. He doesn't know what he's talking about. He's a fool!" said a vice-president of the Illinois Central. The head of the Erie said something about self-advertising. Chauncey M. Depew, chairman of the board of the New York Central, observed, "When it comes to railroad experience, I fear Mr. Brandeis is somewhat lacking." After all, a ten percent increase in rates was at stake; it would mean $27,000,000 more revenue a year.

In his brief Brandeis blamed the roads themselves for putting a strain on their credit by their mistaken publicity campaign for higher rates; and, among other things, by their immoderate ambition for size. Mellen for example, expanded the New Haven by stock acquisitions and thereby diminished the margin of safety, i.e., the proportion of net income available for dividends to the fixed charges.

"There is obviously in all human institutions," he said, "a limit of greatest efficiency. A railroad may be too large, as it may be too small, to be managed and operated with the best results. There is strong reason to believe that a number of the American railroad systems have far exceeded the limit of greatest efficiency."

As to questionable practices, there were many. The undue influence of the Steel Trust explained why rail prices were high and freight rates for steel low. The power of the Standard Oil, as directors of the roads and as bankers supplying money, accounted for the exclusion of other oil companies in supplying the carriers—and at twice the proper price.

In his oral argument in January, 1911, he warned the carriers that if they did not embrace the opportunity to follow in the steps of James L. Richards, who had raised the Boston gas business from scandalous inefficiency to a model for the country (and lowered the price to eighty cents) the time would soon come "when the government will take over, of necessity and in answer to an irresistible popular clamor, the ownership and the operation of the railroads of the United States."

The I.C.C. report was thick with exhibits and tabular matter. But there was one small nugget: "*Held*. That there is no evidence before the commission which establishes the necessity for higher rates." How much the commissioners were impressed with scientific management was not clear. "Something should be expected from the introduction of additional economies," the decision read, "but perhaps not to the same extent as in the past."

When congratulations came to Brandeis he answered, "The railroads are really the ones to be most congratulated. We saved them from themselves."

Chapter X

GIRDING AGAINST THE TRUSTS

INSURGENCY—the revolt against privilege and the fight for popular government and progressive legislation—beckoned "Uncle Louis" of the La Follette household. Soon after Congress convened in December, 1910, the senator told him of a plan to get "men of our stamp" to work together. Economic forces were destroying the promise of American life, but under the Capitol dome lay the means of resurrection. Only a handful of men in Congress were mindful of it; they were compact and persistent and they rejected Taft's bidding to make peace with the party. La Follette proposed to unite them with others in public life—Roosevelt, Pinchot, Garfield, William Allen White, Judge Ben Lindsey, Rudolph Spreckels and Charles R. Crane of Chicago—about thirty leading progressives, to start a National Progressive Republican League and arouse the nation. After the initial announcement two or three hundred others would be invited and another instalment of publicity would be gained, thus showing their growing strength.

Many reforms were needed. Labor laws could be introduced and campaigned for. The movement for the initiative, referendum and recall could be crystallized, the machinery of government simplified. Citizens were entitled to vote for the direct election of senators. Attention must be given to the Supreme Court, which would in the next few years pass on questions involving the income tax, the extent of federal regulation of railroads, the control of corporations.

When Justice Rufus W. Peckham died, Taft was caustically criticized for appointing in his place Horace H. Lurton, regarded as a "property rights man." Peckham had written opinions in some of the leading Sherman Law cases—and bungled them, it was commonly said. (Someone once asked Holmes whether he thought his associate intelligent or simply profane. Holmes replied that Peckham's major premise was always "God damn!") On Taft fell the grave duty of filling three more vacancies in the court in 1910. He raised Edward Douglass White to Chief Justice on Fuller's death and nominated Charles Evans Hughes, whose insurance fame had brought him a governorship, Joseph R. Lamar of Georgia, and Willis Van Devanter of Wyoming. Senator Sutherland had been mentioned as a possibility, but he was disqualified in the eyes of insurgent senators for opposing the income tax.

The following January the League was organized. It was to bring government back to the people. The word Republican was retained because some of the senators and representatives felt that the semblance of a third-party movement would spell their defeat at the coming elections. Brandeis found himself in the company of Hiram Johnson of California and five other governors, Albert J. Beveridge of Indiana and eight other senators, Representative Charles A. Lindbergh of Minnesota, Norris, the brothers Gifford and Amos Pinchot, Crane, White, and a number of others, but not Roosevelt. Senator Jonathan Bourne, Jr., of Oregon was president; Frederic C. Howe, secretary. The first task given to Brandeis was to help win supporters in Massachusetts. He contributed a list of names and two hundred and fifty dollars.

At times the progressives foregathered in the Washington home of the Pinchots, whose mother was lavish of hospitality. Gifford soon became melancholy over the project—Bourne and Howe seemed to him not to know what each other had in mind; the whole thing, he felt, was desultory, ineffective, useless. In a few months Howe resigned over a personal difference with Bourne, who was the big money man. Gifford busied himself with writing an article to prove Taft unworthy and undeserving of renomination, and Brandeis encouraged him to refresh the public's memory of the deceit practiced by Taft and Wickersham.

Brandeis did not blame particular men. Few were wicked but many were weak; conditions existed which taxed their character too much—they were given opportunities for wrongdoing. J. P. Morgan, for example, was no worse than the rest; he simply had greater ability. The function of government was to create such favorable conditions as to avert evil and enable people to evolve social solutions. Brandeis had little faith in what passed for good government, the paternalistic hand which stunted growth. Ancient history was studded with instances of the demoralizing effect of benevolence; in Rome, after a period of benevolent emperors, the populace stagnated. America's need was not more government but a greater development of her citizens. Business enterprises should receive incentives to efficiency rather than an opening to shift burdens on the state.

Brandeis thought he ought to work with the progressives because they, like himself, did not feel obliged to choose between the predatory and the socialistic; nor did their course lie in the middle of the road—it was in the opposite direction from both. Still aloof from politics, he looked at his country with the eyes of an economist and discerned the paramount struggle as being economic liberty against financial servitude.

"We have no place in the American democracy for the money king, not even for the merchant prince," he said. "We are confronted in the twentieth century, as we were in the nineteenth century, with an irreconcilable conflict. Our democracy cannot endure half free and half slave. The essence of the trust is a combination of the capitalist, by the capitalist, for the capitalist."

He proceeded from the general to the particular when the officers of the Shoe Manufacturers' Alliance, a Mid-Western group, came to ask him to be their legal adviser in an

effort to make competition possible in shoe machinery. He
attended their meeting in Cincinnati and laid out the program
for which he would serve: not to fight the United Shoe Machinery Company as such, but to free shoe manufacturers
from the necessity of using only United machines.

This monopoly incensed La Follette as hotly as the New
Haven combination and in his crusading weekly he called
upon Wickersham to investigate the United, which was protected by a forty-five percent tariff. As he put it, the American people were paying tribute to a trust every time they
bought a pair of shoes. The senator was wroth at the emascu-
lation of the Sherman Law by the constructions the Supreme
Court put upon it. The "rule of reason" enunciated by the
court was a clear usurpation of power; Congress should declare how far reasonable restraints might be permitted and
should put the burden of proof upon combiners to show that
their combination was not unreasonable. Immediately after
the court ordered the dissolution of the Tobacco Trust he
telegraphed Brandeis to come to Washington and help draft
bills to amend the law. Brandeis was more than willing. He
had in mind a deterrent to strengthen the preventive purpose
of anti-trust legislation. The penalty of a breakup of large
units, if effectuated, was not sufficient; violations of the
Sherman Law should be followed by the payment of damages
to all firms victimized by illegal restraints.

Brandeis' contacts at the capital inevitably gave him a
greater sense of mastery in handling his private cases. Having
sold his shares in the United he sat down with President
Winslow and other directors of the company as spokesman
for their opponents. He reminded them of the shoe manufacturers' grievances over the leases in 1906, the United's do-
nothing attitude, his resignation, the Massachusetts law and
the company's evasion of it. He repeated a remark he had
made, before the purchase of the Plant system, that such a
course would be a flagrant and impertinent violation of the
Sherman Law, deserving of a jail sentence. He related that

when the Alliance men approached him he said he would not be interested if their purpose was simply to get reductions in terms from the United; it was a question of business freedom and the stifling of progress by a monopoly. "I did not care a rap if what they sought was to get an advantage over other people," he said. "They said the policy I outlined was the policy that they believed in; that if they had freedom they could take care of their interest and the excessive charges. What they wanted was freedom, and they wanted freedom to use a machine which would best do the job."

He told the United directors that the Alliance men spoke of them with the greatest friendliness and showed no hostility either at the Cincinnati meeting or at the present time.

A few days after this conference with his former colleagues Governor Eugene N. Foss sent a message to the legislature calling for an investigation of the shoe machinery trust to prevent the further throttling of one of the state's principal industries. The joint committee on rules replied that no legislation was necessary; an anti-trust law existed. The Governor sent a second message saying that the law was either insufficient or not properly enforced. He denied being inspired by a political motive or a desire for revenge on Storrow, who had put him off the board of the First National Bank.

The rules committee met again. Jones described how the United overcame the 1907 law by inserting a cancellation clause, and he read a bill, drawn by Brandeis at the request of the state's attorney general, to prevent discrimination against users of the machinery. The hearing room was crowded. Charles F. Choate, Jr., now representing the United, appealed to local patriotism by declaring that the source of the attack on the company was an association of Western shoe men.

"Is it right for the legislature to let a lot of people from west of the Mississippi dictate business in Massachusetts?" Choate asked.

And then, to the surprise of many in the room, judging

by the dramatic gasps, he announced that none other than Brandeis, late defender of the United, was the Westerners' attorney. The committee voted to put the inquiry over to the next session.

Meanwhile a federal grand jury heard evidence gathered on Wickersham's instructions and returned indictments against six United officers for criminal conspiracy in restraint of trade.

This was something in the nature of amends for Wickersham's discontinuance of the New Haven suit, which was Brandeis' solitary failure to date. The New Haven question was kept alive, however, on the home grounds. After the road's securities received the blessing of a validation commission the *Boston News Bureau* announced that its magnificent credit was higher than ever—

> . . . it is instructive to recall the reckless onslaught upon the finances of that company and the integrity of its management made a little over three years ago by Louis D. Brandeis, Esq., of Boston. This remarkable concoction is practically forgotten. Even its author might now blush to read it. The public has a short memory. But Mr. Brandeis now holds the stage as a national figure and poses as an economic messiah.

"Mere guesswork," was Eastman's opinion of the validation report. Writing in the *Boston Common*, a weekly which Brandeis supported financially, Eastman said the report furnished no evidence on the road's financial condition; the commission's experts did not have sufficient time to make an original appraisal of its physical property nor to audit the accounts of its controlled companies; the New Haven was an unsupervised holding company, having securities of fifty separate corporations, some of which were likewise unsupervised holding companies, including steamship, electric light, gas, water power and construction firms, hotels, newspapers, quarries and a button company; the intricacy of their transactions and accounting was so great, within and between, as to justify the conclusion that it did not arise from any demands of legitimate business.

Brandeis' old revelation of the New Haven's exchange of securities with its subsidiaries was revived by the *Boston Journal*, which recalled how the road "made a swap with itself" and credited itself with "a profit of $8,521,000 of stage money." When Mellen accused him of hiring a detective Brandeis said, "Cuvier, the great French naturalist, could take a single bone of a prehistoric animal and construct a complete skeleton. He could do this because of his special knowledge of anatomy. My special field of knowledge is figures. And so I was able to take a few published figures of the New Haven road, and working backward, build up their complete system of bookkeeping."

Despite a steady decrease in net earnings the New Haven voted its usual quarterly dividend of two percent. Mellen faced a need for drastic retrenchment; not getting the ten percent rate advance in Washington, he cut down the working days of a large number of men. New Haven stock was selling at its lowest price in several years, within twelve points of the level struck in the 1907 panic. The Pennsylvania Railroad increased its investment and became New Haven's largest stockholder. Mellen could not be enjoying dreamless sleep —his system would be obliged to refund almost $51,000,000 within the next year. But Morgan's fine financial hand deftly postponed a reckoning; the issue of short-term notes of $11,000,000, dictated by the House of Morgan, would be covered by a new bond issue. Mellen was reported to be chafing.

Brandeis went off to Manchester at the request of the governor of New Hampshire to block the attempt of the Boston & Maine to get an increase. He served without pay, and was only partially handicapped by the coincidence that the owner of the *Manchester Union*, which was antagonistic to the knight errant from Boston, was chairman of the railroad rate committee. Accounts of the hearing published in the *Union* quoted the railroad lawyers but suppressed Brandeis' rebuttals. A reader, asking the newspaper's business manager (the right person) for an explanation, was told that the material was furnished by counsel for the road and paid for at so much per line, and if counsel for the state wished their matter published they should avail themselves of the same opportunity. The rate rise was refused.

Brandeis absented himself from Massachusetts so frequently that he participated little in local affairs. He encouraged the *Boston Common* as an organ of progressive thinking, considered the time ripe for a state branch of the National Progressive Republican League, and presided at a meeting of the Boston Equal Suffrage Association, introducing Jane Addams. Greatly impressed with Eastman's work as secretary of the Public Franchise League for the past six years, he proposed a higher salary. Eastman was one of the finest fruits of the League, a man utterly devoted to public service. Originally the sponsors employed him for half-time work during the legislative session at a nominal salary; in their preoccupation and own comfortable circumstances they overlooked the fact that he was giving his full time and using the pay not for himself but for a stenographer and telephone expense. On realizing this after a year and a half they doubled his pay; it was still meagre. Once when labor trouble broke out on the Boston Elevated and both sides sought out Brandeis to arbitrate their differences, he suggested Eastman in his stead; but knowing Eastman would ask too little, Brandeis stipulated that they must let him fix the compensation. The arbitration was arranged skillfully, satisfactorily. Then Brandeis learned that Eastman put in a bill only for time spent at hearings and did not count preparatory and other work.

In July he paid a visit to his brother in Louisville. The oaks, the maples, the broad lawns at Ladless Hill Farm were restful. Congressman Ollie James of the Ballinger committee came to call. Local railroad officials, eager to talk to the sensational figure of the rate case, turned up the winding path. All day long there was a pilgrimage from town to see the national celebrity. Several hundred local lights arrived—bankers, lawyers, doctors, editors, manufacturers. Some had known him as a boy. His soft Southern accent, they noticed, had become modified by his residence among the Yankees.

That summer the Democrats in Massachusetts offered him the nomination for attorney general. He told the party leaders that he did not expect to be a candidate for political honors, "at least, not in the immediate future, for my private business and other plans will occupy my time. Though I have always voted the Democratic ticket and firmly believed in the principles of the party, I have a strong La Follette tendency." Governor Foss and others of the party who counted on him to help in the elections were dismayed by the transfer of Brandeis' interest to the division in the Republican camp.

After the President had made a speech upholding the Sherman Law as a model of perfection Brandeis gave the United Press a statement contrasting Taft, the mere lawyer, with La Follette, the constructive statesman. Taft was ignoring twenty years' experience with the Sherman Law while the insurgent was using it to improve the law. At present violators were left in possession of their spoils, and the crushed competitors and the public were left without a remedy. As interpreted by the Supreme Court, the law put the question of reasonable restraint in vast uncertainty and necessitated the government's proving that the restraint was unreasonable. The amendments introduced by La Follette would enable the victims of a trust to prove damages in the same proceedings. They specified acts which in practice had been shown to be destructive of competition. They provided that where a combination in restraint obtained the burden of proof that it was reasonable should rest on the defendants, paralleling the requirement put on railroads seeking a rate advance.

La Follette was out to wrest the nomination from Taft, and the energies of the National Progressive Republican

League were bent his way. Brandeis quickly announced to the press: "There is nothing like him in the country"—one of the safest, ablest, wisest men in public life. Taft, if nominated, would certainly be defeated. Medill McCormick and Rudolph Spreckels of Chicago came to Boston to persuade Brandeis to take charge of the fight for La Follette delegates from New England, but he told them he was not a political man; short of assuming such a responsibility he was ready to cooperate in every way. Born a Republican, he had been a Democrat twenty-five years, and now identified himself as a progressive or a Democratic progressive. The country was divided between progressives and reactionaries and would vote thereafter for principle and not for party. Nevertheless, he contributed to the Democratic State Committee's campaign fund.

And now a private case against the Tobacco Trust came into his hands. As attorney for independent manufacturers he opposed the reorganization plan submitted by Thomas Fortune Ryan and his associates in the American Tobacco Company, proposing to split the trust in three. While Taft was praising the Supreme Court for its Standard Oil and Tobacco decisions, and denouncing detractors like Bryan (and saying at Pocatello, Idaho: "I love judges and I love courts. They are my ideals on earth that typify what we shall meet afterward in heaven under a just God") the plan for disintegration was condemned also by James C. McReynolds, who had prosecuted the Tobacco Trust. Having won the suit, McReynolds quarreled with Wickersham for accepting a scheme which was merely a subterfuge. Four states filed protests, Wisconsin designating Brandeis as special counsel.

At a hearing on the plan, held by the Circuit Court in New York, Brandeis said the court had no power to approve it if it did not restore real competition. In his opinion the reorganization was a sham, substituting for a trust owned by one group of men a monopoly divided into three parts, owned by the same men. He proffered an alternative proposal for breaking up the company into thirty parts; either that or a receivership. The decree of the Circuit Court approved the company's plan and rejected the modifications proposed by the independents, saying: "No time need be given to the consideration of these as long as there is no suggestion that the defendants will adopt them. On the contrary, counsel for the defendants expressly stated on argument that they would not undertake to carry them out."

To Brandeis this was a nullification of both the Sherman Law and the Supreme Court decision. It was an amazing misapprehension of the intent of the Supreme Court, which had committed to the Circuit Court the duty of withholding approval unless the plan restored conditions essential to fair competition. The lower court failed to insist on a lawful plan and thought it was obliged to take the best plan offered by the trust. The court's assumption seemed to be that the offer which the trust said was their best was really the most the court could get.

Wickersham was so sure the plan would recreate lawful conditions that he blocked the efforts "of outsiders to inject themselves into the situation and to delay or prevent the carrying out of the plan." The independents appealed, but the Supreme Court denied their petition to intervene. With no chance of review, their only hope was in Congress. The three-part trust was to be owned and controlled by the same owners in the same proportion as before, except that Ryan sold all his stock to Morgan banks. Brandeis observed that the lawyers on the other side appeared to have discovered in the Constitution a new implied prohibition: "What man has illegally joined together, let no court put asunder."

A body greater than Congress had to be reached: the American public. There was a widespread notion that competition had proved an economic failure; that monopoly made cheaper and better production possible. It was a popular fallacy. The book-paper business, for example, was competitive, and despite a diminishing supply of raw material the

price-tendency was lower than in the monopolistic field of
petroleum products with its increasing supply. The manufacture of shoes was competitive and it had brought about
higher wages, better quality and only a slightly higher price.

"These results," Brandeis told a reporter in Washington,
"cannot be secured by monopoly and price-regulation. It is
utterly impossible. Progress, advance in methods, invention
—all these stand still when competition's spur no longer
pricks. That is industrial history."

He was at the Capitol for hearings by the Senate interstate
commerce committee on anti-trust bills. The measures poured
in despite Taft's assurance that the Sherman Law needed no
improvement, and among them were La Follette's amendments. Brandeis listened for a whole day to the testimony
of George W. Perkins, the servant of Steel and of Morgan,
and his temperature ran high when Perkins asserted that an
increase in size brought an increase in efficiency.

But there was no fever in his manner when he took the
floor the next day. He was armed with facts. In his armory
was first-hand knowledge of the Shoe Machinery Trust, the
Tobacco Trust, and labor unrest; a study of the Steel Trust
by John A. Fitch, the recent confession of the McNamara
brothers, and other items in the news. Back in '97, when he
came down to Washington for his first congressional encounter, he did not command so much attention.

"Anyone who critically analyzes a business learns this:
that success or failure of an enterprise depends usually upon
one man, upon the quality of one man's judgment and, above
all things, his capacity to see what is needed and his capacity
to direct others," Brandeis said. "There is a limit to what one
man could do well."

In huge organizations demoralization set in. Unless they
dominated the field or controlled prices they failed or showed
no marked success. Their profits could be ascribed to monopolistic power, not to efficiency in management. He cited
Morgan's creation, the International Mercantile Marine—a

failure; the Sugar Trust steals, and other instances. He took up Perkins' praise of the Steel Trust's profit-sharing system— in ten years the corporation distributed $12,000,000 to its workers. The employees numbered two hundred thousand, which meant an average of six dollars a year or fifty cents a month for each worker. On the other hand, Mr. Perkins' firm, J. P. Morgan & Company, received a commission of twenty percent or $12,500,000 for managing the syndicate which promoted the United States Steel Corporation and more than $7,000,000 as members of the syndicate.

"Is that Mr. Perkins' idea of justice to be attained through these great corporations by applying profit-sharing?"

Wages in the steel industry were lower than in 1892. Hours had shockingly increased. But the profits of the trust totaled $650,000,000.

"The steel companies in their might were able in the years following the Homestead strike to destroy the only protection which labor has, namely, the trades union." Destruction of unionism appeared to be a cardinal principle with trust-builders. There were no unions under the Standard Oil, Tobacco, or Shoe Machinery trusts, which had stabbed industrial liberty in the back. The real trouble with business was social unrest. The McNamara bombing of the *Los Angeles Times* building was the horrible criminal expression of a sense of injustice. Men like the McNamaras were led to believe that dynamite was their only recourse for improving the workers' condition. There was a causal connection between the development of huge, indomitable trusts and such crimes.

"Is it not irony to speak of equality of opportunity in a country cursed with their bigness?"

Before the advent of trusts the money power of Wall Street was practically confined to railroad securities. Mobilizing huge capital in the formation of trusts was like pouring oil into the rising flame of the Money Trust. Property formerly owned locally and controlled in different parts of the country had now become subject to the money kings. With the conversion of American capital into stock-exchange securities a condition of irresponsible absentee landlordism was created. Wealth without responsibility was dangerous to society. Remote from the workers, the owners had one desire—dividends.

"Large dividends are the bribes which the managers tender the small investor for the power conferred to use other people's money."

He cited the Shoe Machinery trust, as much a financial power as an industrial power. Its managers controlled the First National Bank of Boston and had an important influence in the Hanover National Bank and other banks in New York. The allegiance of the shoe manufacturers in Massachusetts to this trust was due in many cases to its financial might. The United might be very helpful in securing credit and it might also cause credit to be withheld. There was the case of Mr. Plant, whose assets were such as to entitle him to any reasonable amount of credit, but men disposed to lend him money withdrew. One of them told Plant that he was unwilling to oppose the important financial interests which had intimated to him that they did not want Plant to have credit.

Turning to the provisions of the La Follette bills, Brandeis said that the Supreme Court in declaring the practices of the Standard Oil illegal confirmed what anybody ought to have known since Lloyd wrote *Wealth Against Commonwealth* in '94, but still there was no redress for those who had been crushed by Standard Oil, one after another. The Sherman Law offered only a paper remedy against oppression. The decision against the Tobacco Trust was another futile victory. In both cases the securities of the companies had been given an immunity bath.

The trust problem can never be settled right for the American people by looking at it through the spectacles of bonds and stocks. You must study it through the spectacles of people's rights and people's interests; must consider the effect upon the development of the American democracy. When you do that you will realize the extraordinary perils to our institutions which attend the trust; you will realize the danger of letting the people learn that our sacred Constitution protects not only vested rights but vested wrongs. The situation is a very serious one; unless wise legislation is enacted we shall have as a result of that social unrest a condition which will be more serious than that produced by the fall of a few points in stock-exchange quotations.

After recess, Brandeis resumed his testimony. He referred to the advance rate hearing at which railroad heads admitted they made no effort to secure a reduction in the cost of steel rails. He said the directors of the Steel Trust were directors in most of the large railroads, and the railroads were controlled by these steel men.

That is one of the incidents of this big business. We risk our whole system, judicial, political, and industrial, by creating a power which we cannot control, as happened when the United States Steel Corporation was formed ten years ago.

Trusts acquired their position largely through methods in themselves reprehensible.

No huge corporations would be created today if corporations were made to act according to rules of fair competition. I am so convinced of the economic fallacy in the huge unit that if we make competition possible, if we create conditions where there could be reasonable competition, these monsters would fall to the ground.

In the creation of trusts the commanding cause was not a desire for greater efficiency, but for avoidance of annoying competition, a desire on the part of promoters and bankers for huge commissions, a desire to capitalize an inability to compete. The steel men paid Carnegie many times the real value of his business, practically bribing him to retire, the bribe being paid by the American people in order that these less efficient businesses might not be destroyed.

Senator Albert B. Cummins, Iowa insurgent, remarked that the words "restraint of trade" should be made to mean what the people believe they ought to mean; there was no such thing as reasonable restraint.

Brandeis replied, "That is my belief, decidedly."

Senator Francis G. Newlands of Nevada, who had introduced a bill for an interstate trade commission as a curb on trusts, asked what limit should be put on corporations.

Brandeis did not suppose it would be unconstitutional to limit size. Congress had the power to confine the privilege of interstate commerce to corporations of a particular character, but he was not able to say at the time which administrative bureau or provision could be invoked. He was clear that the maximum could not be properly fixed in dollars uniformly, but the La Follette bill provided that where a combination in restraint of trade was found, controlling forty percent or more of the market, this would create a presumption of unreasonableness.

Senator Thomas P. Gore of Oklahoma asked about the shoe manufacturers. Brandeis said they were going to suffer a good deal more from the machinery monopoly if it were not broken. The monopoly was held not by virtue of the patents but by the tying clauses. The United Shoe Machinery exercised an extraordinary strength of position, the equal of which he did not know in the whole realm of industry. Criminal proceedings had been instituted against its officers, and just recently a civil suit against the corporation alleging ninety-eight percent control.

As the afternoon lengthened he dwelt on the Money Trust. A few men controlled a large part of the quick capital of the country. Practically no great enterprise could be undertaken without their consent. The industrial trust was the greatest contributor of power to the Money Trust, and further ex-

tension of the industrial trust would put that power far beyond the reach of Congress or anyone else.

The moment you are able to reduce the favored position of the industrial trust you will have made some advance, however, small, toward grappling with that most
difficult subject, the control of capital.

He did not approve of licensing concerns engaged in interstate commerce but favored a commission having broad
powers of investigation to determine the facts in any trade,
with ample publicity and an opportunity for competitors and
the public to be heard. In the tobacco case, because of a lack
of knowledge, the courts had shown themselves unable to
cope with a commercial question. He deprecated the kind
of action pursued by the Circuit Court judges in holding conferences with Wickersham and the Trust's counsel and determining the general lines of dismemberment in private without information to the public until the plan was agreed upon.
Brandeis took this occasion to praise McReynolds for his
admirable professional performance. The La Follette bill set
forth that the court had the power which the judges assumed
they lacked—to place restrictions on the divided parts of a
trust.

He picked up a Washington newspaper and after telling
about the twelve-hour day, seven-day week, and eighteen-
cents-an-hour wage in the steel mills, read to the committee
the news that Elbert H. Gary, head of the steel corporation,
was intending to give his wife a half-million-dollar string of
pearls for Christmas.

I have referred to that because it seems to me an extremely serious matter in the time of our present discontent. Here is what would seem to me a perfect sham of
profit-sharing which has been paraded a great deal over
this country. See what that means to the social unrest.
Isn't it the same sort of thing that brought on the French

Revolution, and which may suggest to everyone in this particular connection the damage which the queen's necklace did in those days? That seems to me to be one of the horrible manifestations, the by-products, of this aggregation of capital . . . unearned wealth, unearned by those who are enjoying it and taken out of the lives of the people who are toiling for them.

Gary issued to the press a sad statement:

"I am grieved that he has come down to such cheap talk. I had hoped his efforts to help solve the industrial and economic problems of the country would be maintained on the high intellectual plane which I had thought he occupied. I feel his exhibition at Washington today will disappoint the whole country."

Most of the senators were sympathetic in their questions, but now a Pennsylvania member was aroused and took a defensive stand for the steel industry. Brandeis answered all thrusts with precise information. He continued talking all of the next day.

Senators Gore and Cummins were still interested in licensing. Brandeis said a license might be construed as an immunity from prosecution; revocation would not be a deterrent because it was easy to dissolve a corporation and form another. The question was how to distribute the property of a trust to prevent its renewed use for destroying competition.

Reorganization plans should depend largely upon detailed questions of fact. If a federal trade commission were formed its first step should be to accumulate data; the power to make decisions, at this stage, would lead into erroneous paths. To investigate, to hear complaints, to disclose results to everyone interested—this should be its province. Later it might be safe to take the next step of giving the commission judicial scope. It was extraordinary how little knowledge was available at this time to the men in business.

There used to be a certain glamor about big things.

Anything big, simply because it was big, seemed to be good and great. We are now coming to see that big things may be very bad and mean.

At the end of his two and a half days of testifying he sang the praises of cooperatives as the proper regulator of excessive profits from competitive businesses. Consumers' cooperatives on one side, free competition on the other, would give the community all the protection it needed.

At one point Senator Charles E. Townsend of Michigan referred to the La Follette bill as "your bill." Brandeis said it embodied most of his ideas as to what should be done with the Sherman Law.

All in all he had a great time, he told his friends, and believed he put a dent into the steel corporation's armor which they would find difficulty in hammering out. While in Washington he was deep in insurgent counsels and his admiration for La Follette grew. No man in public office expressed the ideals of American democracy so fully. La Follette had vision, deep convictions, indomitable will; he was straightforward, able, hardworking, persistent, courageous. Some people called the Wisconsinite a radical, chiefly those who were unable to realize that nothing is abiding save only change. The National Progressive Republican League endorsed him as its choice for president, and Gifford Pinchot—on Roosevelt's assurance that his campaign hat was on his head and not in the ring—launched the boom. Pinchot spoke at Tremont Temple and broke the Massachusetts ice. Brandeis was ready to help the younger men who were starting the progressive movement there, with money and advice.

When he was home in Boston of a Sunday evening he would invite students over from Cambridge to discuss social-economic themes. The living room was dimly lit, as he always protected his eyes from glare. Most of the talk came from Brandeis' corner. The man of the world, rich in experience, clear in analysis, optimistic in spirit, was the teacher. On one

of those nights he dwelt on the developing rate of unemployment following the introduction of labor-saving devices and
said labor should demand a large share in the saving rather
than resist technological advance. This idea fastened its fila-
ments upon Marlen E. Pew, watching the shadowed profile
of his host. Pew, whose policy as editor of the *Boston Traveler*
had attracted Brandeis, saw that the workers needed the light
of long-range thinking and he straightway persuaded Brandeis to speak before the Central Labor Union.

Labor had the fault of not looking beyond its immediate
controversies. Brandeis' espousal of scientific management
perplexed those who were so color-blinded by their passions
that they perceived only black and white or *pro* and *con*.
Union leaders did not understand why this friend of labor
legislation and arbitration should advocate a system which,
in John Mitchell's words, meant specialization of work, speed-
ing up and ultimate insanity. Gompers asserted that the promise of high wages was baseless talk. Upton Sinclair also took
a fling at scientific management. Brandeis' consistency was
overlooked.

He contended that scientific management offered not only
social gain—the ultimate solvent—but conservation of human
energy and development of the worker's self-respect and
satisfaction with his work. The purpose was not to speed
up the worker but to teach managers to use their brains.
Labor demanded high wages but management countered by
importing cheap foreign workmen. Far better would it be if
industry were able to increase the productivity of the individual and if the union cooperated toward that end.

"There is absolutely nothing in scientific management opposed to organized labor," he told the Central Labor Union
audience.

"We have got to have the union fix the rate of day
labor and see that when profit is made from the introduction
of the new method it is divided with both views properly
presented."

A woman shouted, "You can call it scientific management if you want to, but I call it scientific driving."

"There is nothing scientific in what you say," he retorted. "Nobody who knows anything about it calls the bonus system scientific."

He was against the bonus system as applied in ordinary business, and he did not think scientific management had "to shake hands with the piece system and not absolutely with the bonus system." Efficiency methods brought larger production not by increasing speed but by removing obstacles which exhausted workmen and providing the best possible way of doing a job. It led to shorter hours and regularity of employment. Lower costs made price-reductions inevitable, except in the case of monopolies, and even with wages remaining the same more goods would be bought.

But if wages rose without a compensating gain in efficiency the cost of living would mount. To follow each wage-increase with an increase in the price of the product to the public, as the railroads sought to do, was working on the principle of the endless chain. Labor should welcome scientific management for its resultant lowering of prices and steady work.

The audience seemed unimpressed, dreaming doggedly of high wages. Brandeis was trying to make them see problems as a whole. The margin for improvement of the worker's condition could not be measured by the amount of the present available profit. Given an unjust system of distributing the harvest of industry, there was low efficiency. Given a more just system, recognizing the workers' rights and introducing scientific management, there would result greater efficiency and therefore a larger divisable profit.

Henry George had once complimented the Boston typographical union on their intelligence in not bucking against the introduction of the linotype machine. But labor did not get its rightful share of the profits that came with the introduction of machinery. Here, said Brandeis, was a second chance. The workers should tell the manufacturer: "We will join with you and make just as much money as possible, but when it is made we are going to have the lion's share of it." The rest should go to capital and to the community.

Why fear overproduction? "There is no such thing as overproduction. There is such a thing—and it is permanent with us—as underconsumption. As long as the ability to secure and consume exists, we want things cheaper so we can buy more." The demand for labor grew because the demands of the people grew with the ability to supply them.

The application of the principle of industrial democracy to the reality of industrial conditions necessitated social invention. American legislators must be inventors. Businessmen must be inventors to cope with the ravages of rapidly advancing industrialization.

Brandeis sometimes would visit his social-minded friend, Lincoln Filene at Weston, Massachusetts, and spend Sunday afternoon in the woods, talking about such things. Worth a million and a half himself, and having a practice which yielded one hundred thousand dollars in 1911, Brandeis was bothered by the question of irregularity of employment, the most sinful waste of all. The country was growing more and more profligate.

The right to steady work was coequal with the right to regularity in the payment of interest on bonds. It should be regarded as a fixed charge, taking precedence over dividends. A reserve to ensure regular employment was as imperative as a reserve for depreciation. He discussed this thought with Filene and Bloomfield and then worked out a plan for them to consider. Knowing human nature's weakness for incentives, he proposed that employers be induced to reorganize their businesses and be stimulated into enterprise by the adoption of a sliding scale of wages.

His plan called for the depositing in a trust company of a certain part of each week's wages. The average number of days' employment would be determined, and at the end of the year an accounting would be made of the amount of em-

ployment exceeding the average, with a division between
employer and employee of the sum accumulated in the trust
fund. For each day's employment in excess of the standard
fixed the employer would be entitled to take back a portion
of the deposit; for each day he failed to give employment the
worker would be entitled to some part of the deposit. If the
employer provided a full year's work he would get back the
entire sum; if he did not exceed the average, the entire sum
would be paid over to the worker. Thus a reserve would
be stored up to relieve the worker from the evil of temporary
unemployment; and on the other hand the employer would
have, through a lower wage-unit, an incentive to make such
improvements as were necessary to obtain greater uniformity
of employment.   Brandeis did not offer this as a rigid plan.
The profit arising in case of full employment might be shared
equally by employer and employee. The point was that in
some way there should be divided, on an equitable basis, the
net gain resulting from eliminating the waste due to partial
idleness.

Brandeis believed unions should agitate for unemployment
insurance, not for the direct purpose of paying a man when
he was out of work, but to force industry, through the cost
of insurance, to find it cheaper to run regularly than spo-
radically.

Social workers came to him for advice on various plans,
and always he laid stress on adequate preparation. To one
who advocated pensions for widows with small children he
said a survey should precede a petition to the legislature; the
first step should be a careful diagnosis, and when the facts
were determined a basis would exist for deciding the need
and nature of a remedy. There was agitation for workmen's
compensation laws, but he cautioned against adopting make-
shifts which would congest the courts with wasteful and
demoralizing litigation. A system of compensation should
proceed on the basis of insurance with contributions from
both the employer and the employee, joint administration of

the fund and joint responsibility for the prevention of accidents. Compensation payments should be made not in lump but in instalments continued throughout the period of need, and every accident resulting in compensation should be investigated to determine its cause and avert its recurrence.

Social workers were taken aback by a decision of the New York Court of Appeals defeating the first workmen's compensation law in America. Economic and sociological arguments such as those used by Brandeis in the Oregon case had been presented, but the court did not let them subvert its conception of property and held the law requiring compulsory compensation "a deprivation of liberty and property under the federal and state constitutions." Louis Marshall's argument in behalf of the defendant railway had carried such weight and publicity that Julian W. Mack asked Brandeis for a statement to offset it. In *The Survey* Brandeis wrote: "I read the opinion some days ago and reached a very clear conviction that the decision is woefully wrong. I am inclined to think that we shall find legislatures of some of the other states undeterred by the decision of your Court of Appeals; and some other court will have the opportunity of soon making a more just decision." His prediction was soon borne out in the State of Washington, where the constitutionality of a similar law was upheld. But everyone knew that the question was not settled. It would yet come before the Supreme Court.

Massachusetts had led the movement to protect women workers from excessive hours. Now it was the first with a minimum wage commission to save women and the Commonwealth from the evil of inadequate wages. (Mrs. Evans was appointed to the commission.) The underlying principle of the new law was that every business or industry should be self-supporting; where wages were too low to maintain workers in health serious burdens were being developed which would fall on the state.

The other Massachusetts experiment on which Brandeis kept a close eye was insurance. As a pioneer institution it involved the meeting of difficulties as they arose day by day. In three years' experience the mechanism was constantly developed, and he was pleased with the steady progress. The Berkshire County Savings Bank in 1911 became the third bank to open an insurance department. Almost $2,000,000 of insurance was in force. Although he did not believe the system should be established in other states until perfected in all its details, he sought national publicity and kept supplying Hapgood with editorial suggestions for *Collier's*. When writing on the high cost of living Hapgood might tell how the Massachusetts movement brought about a twenty per cent reduction in wage earners' life insurance throughout the country. When commenting on the concentration of capital the editor might refer to this attempt to resist the piling up of reserves in the old-line companies, so huge as to menace the community. Incidentally, Brandeis thought this growing accumulation and concentration would afford a special reason for substituting government insurance for insurance by private concerns. If the government became the insurer the need of reserves could be wholly eliminated and payments would be made as on serial bonds, from taxes or other current receipts.

"We need a comprehensive system of workingmen's insurance," he told the National Congress of Charities and Correction, convening in Tremont Temple. Sickness, accident, invalidism, irregular employment and superannuation made men financially dependent upon the will of others. They were not free men. How then could political democracy function successfully? If the government permitted conditions to exist which converted large classes of citizens into dependents, the evil "should at least be minimized by the state's assuming, or causing to be assumed by others, in some form the burden incident to its own shortcomings." These social doctors assembled were amazed to see a layman seize their therapeutics and shake it into one strong solution: the dose of insurance.

But Brandeis did not mean a security program in the sense of a lapse into irresponsible laxity; he prescribed it rather as a preventive. He thought the social workers' intentions were good but they lacked business experience and the economic slant. He admonished them that the expense of obtaining indemnity should be recognized as part of the daily cost of living. Mere description of the misery unnecessarily entailed by inhuman conditions in industry would fail to remove them. But if society and industry were made to pay the cost from day to day—"consider how great would be the incentive to humanize" these conditions.

Chiefly he brought the awakening concept of a minimum standard of employment for America, leaving social forces free to work out progress beyond that. Consistently he advocated the principle of self-help; the government's rôle was that of an assistant. In the industrial contest the masses could use the strength of their numbers to meet the might of the privileged predatory forces. High financiers exercised control not so much by their wealth as by manipulation of the small savings of the people. "The masters of finance become the masters of the trusts and of the people's liberties by their use of other people's money." The British cooperatives showed the way to emancipation. By utilizing their power of production and their own purchasing power, workers and consumers proved that industrial democracy was practicable and successful in competing with capitalistic enterprises.

Here in America we faced the tyranny of the trusts—they cramped development in every respect.

Chapter XI

POLITICS: LA FOLLETTE AND WILSON

FOR BRANDEIS 1912 was going to be another anti-trust year. The solution of the trust problem became the most vital political issue before the country. Taft in a message to Congress criticized the critics of the tobacco decree and said the Sherman Law was not intended to prohibit mere bigness. Roosevelt, writing in *The Outlook*, wanted trusts to be retained but under rigid regulation—and this was acceptable to Perkins, Gary, many other big businessmen and much of the press. In another category were men like Bryan, La Follette and Cummins, demanding destruction of the trusts. Brandeis entered politics.

"This man," a magazine writer named Frederick W. Coburn said of Brandeis, "has for fifty years past been building up within himself a big mind trust." That was one way of putting it. He had been absorbing information, merging his lines of communication, consolidating his knowledge. But he did not sit at home and make a monopoly of it. The campaign committee of the progressive group in Washington arranged speaking dates for him. Unaccustomed to political campaigning, he preferred not to appear on the platform alone but in conjunction with others, and to speak after one or more of them in order to get the feel of an unfamiliar situation.

His first date was January 1 at Columbus, before a gathering of Ohio progressives. His theme was industrial liberty, the struggle for social justice. The new industrial conditions had

crushed freedom and there would be no deliverance until the
great corporations were curbed. If big business did not give
laboring men their rights it would let loose a flood of socialism and perhaps conflict. The progressives were engaged in
the most momentous struggle since the Revolutionary and
Civil wars; the greatest, because it was to be carried out along
the lines of peace, by the ballot and not by the sword. The
steel corporation was the worst offender; only Russia exceeded it in despotic methods. The country needed a man
with the mental grasp to see and the moral courage to cry
out, spare not, and lead the way. That man was La Follette.

The purpose of the meeting was to win endorsement from
delegates who were to go to the Republican national convention, but only their personal approval was won. Pinchot was
credited with preventing formal action. Brandeis planned on
this speaking tour to avoid politics and cling closely to the
trust problem. In Chicago two days later he regretted that
the recent Supreme Court opinions contained no suggestion
of redress to steel and tobacco independents wronged by the
illegal operations of the combines; the La Follette bill would
make reparations automatic. La Follette, he pointed out, was
an indefatigable worker who investigated and gathered facts
before proposing a remedy, who felt the brotherhood of the
American people as no man since Lincoln. In Minneapolis,
next day, when the temperature was eighteen degrees below
zero, Brandeis arrived to deliver a similar speech and made
several. Something of the politician's tact slipped into his
manner in spite of himself. He passed a complimentary remark about the Minnesota climate—"It's dry. That's why you
don't feel the cold." The chimes he struck were the same:
the court decisions, the Steel Trust's oppression of labor, the
greatness of La Follette. He added that the conservatism of
the East, where there was a greater diffusion of stocks and
bonds, was beginning to give way to an expression of anti-
Taft sentiment.

"My idea of the solution of the present-day economic

Attention Progressives!

Louis D. Brandeis

Will speak at Memorial Hall
COURT HOUSE
TO-NIGHT
8 o'clock

Mr. Brandeis is one of Boston's leading attorneys, popularly known as the "Attorney for the People". He represented the people in the Ballinger-Pinchot investigation; in some of the leading railway rate cases and in other cases involving public rights.

Mr. Brandeis is one of the leading Progressives of the country and an authority on all the big questions of the day. He will speak on

"Representative Government."

Senator J. M. Hackney of St. Paul will preside

TO-NIGHT---8 P. M.   **Go to Fourth Street Entrance**

A handbill in the LaFollette campaign, for a Progressive rally held in Minneapolis, January 4, 1912

trouble is not to stop competition and regulate monopoly but rather to stop monopoly and regulate competition," he said.

While he was on this tour United Shoe Machinery went on the war path. His too frequent use of its name made President Winslow bestir himself and publicly deny that the company had acquired Plant's patents through control of the money market. (At about the same time Congressman Lindbergh was trying to obtain an investigation of the Money Trust.) The United followed Brandeis' trail late in January to a hearing of the House committee on the judiciary, to which all anti-trust bills were being referred. Henry C. Clayton, of Alabama, was chairman.

Brandeis came to explain the bill introduced by Representative Irvine L. Lenroot of Wisconsin as the counterpart of the La Follette bill. The section which classified tying-clause contracts among unreasonable restraints was earmarked by the United's counsel. Brandeis said, "The importance of the shoe machinery corporation in this connection is, at most, by way of illustration of the necessity of certain legislation."

Chairman Clayton observed that Brandeis was practically the author of both bills.

"Our learned friend here," said the lawyer for the United, Charles E. Littlefield, "was a director of the company from 1899 to 1906." As there had been no change in the company's policy since, Littlefield assumed that the business was being carried on rightfully "because I do not think that Mr. Brandeis would be associated with such an institution that was proceeding in an unlawful, illegal manner."

After Jones testified on the workings of the leases Littlefield put in evidence the letter Brandeis had written in 1906 to Erving Winslow in defence of the United. Brandeis was glad to have it introduced as it showed that his present views in no sense arose from hostility. His relations with the officials were still, he said, extremely friendly; but it was incorrect to say that the situation of the company had not changed. The

United had violated the Sherman Law by putting an end to competition from Plant.

President Winslow wrote a letter to Senator Moses E. Clapp, chairman of the interstate commerce committee, and sent a copy to Clayton, telling how Brandeis appeared for the United at the Massachusetts State House in 1906 and did not dispose of his holdings of United stock "until after he had been retained by the Shoe Manufacturers' Alliance and after his clients had taken measures to bring about the prosecution of the company, the announcement of which would be likely to lower the value of his stock."

This exposure, this version of his dark past, was a blow to the insurgents, according to the *New York Tribune*.

Brandeis was convinced that his reiteration of the simple facts in regard to excessive hours and days of labor in the steel industry, to which Fitch had first called attention, was making a deep impression on the people. Seven-day weeks would soon be a horror of the past. Planning to go into the steel company's labor conditions more thoroughly at an investigation started by Representative August O. Stanley of Kentucky, he sought additional data from Fitch.

Brandeis appeared before the committee on January 29, two days after the Clayton session. Counsel for the company objected to his venturing into its labor policy as being beyond the scope of the inquiry, but Chairman Stanley ruled that labor cost was incident to production cost. Brandeis went on. What this corporation with its size and power did in respect to labor exercised great influence over the whole industrial policy of the country. Judge Gary had boasted of its treatment of employees, but Brandeis showed it to be incapable of forming a conception of human needs and human suffering. Thousands of workers were deteriorating, transmitting their weaknesses, and causing racial degeneration.

"I ask you, gentlemen, to remember that these persons, however they may differ from us in race or in their habits of living, are individuals," he said. "Imagine what would be our condition if we, seven days a week, undertook to work twelve hours a day."

The steel industry in making derelicts proved itself to be a parasitic industry, protected by a tariff supposed to be in the workers' interest and putting its burdens on the rest of the community, which had to support the paupers. Negro slavery had been socially and economically wrong but it was mitigated by the personal relations of the slaveholders to their dependents. Here was a terrible case of absentee landlordism, for all the company's strenuous advertising to the effect that its stocks were held widely throughout the country.

"To my mind that is one of the most serious problems of this whole question. Thousands upon thousands of individuals, with small amounts of stock, have absolutely no control and consequently cannot feel any responsibility for what is being done by the corporation, but are receiving the benefits of it," Brandeis said.

Irresponsible stockholders had no interest other than for a dividend.

"Every slave was regarded as a piece of valuable property. From a pure self-interest the slave-owner would not destroy his property any more than he would destroy his animals. We Kentuckians always had a great fondness for horses and we knew that one of the finest things to do to a horse was to take care of him."

A horse was a valuable asset. So was a slave.

"But these workmen are not valuable assets. They are paid as they go along and when they cease to be valuable . . . they have been turned off. They went upon the scrapheap, but without that penalty or cost which comes to the owner in turning a machine upon the scrapheap, because every machine was paid for its full value, and these men are not paid their full value. They have been paid for the value of their use—and the depreciation charge has not been paid."

He undermined the fallacy constructed by the company's publicity engineers that steel workers were getting fatherly protection. Referring to his brief on the Illinois ten-hour law he pointed out the economic result of shortening the work-period, the effect of fatigue, and the need for rest and recreation.

"There is no difference," he said, "between us and the iron-worker in that respect at all. His recreation may be different from ours, as his work is different from ours; but they are all and we are all equally men and brothers, and if we bear that in mind, and as long as men do bear that in mind, there will be no such thing as inhumanity in these steel workers' condition."

He was to resume his testimony the next morning. That night a conference at the progressive headquarters revealed the Teddy-lovers in the camp. The Rooseveltians wanted La Follette to withdraw in favor of T.R. La Follette did not recognize Roosevelt as standing for progressive principles. As a result Gifford and Amos Pinchot and Medill McCormick departed, while all the others assured La Follette they would go through with him to the end. For Brandeis it was easy enough to choose between Fighting Bob and a man who veered as the wind blew. When things were bad, Roosevelt was for La Follette, but when they went well he was all for Teddy. Public sentiment against Taft had become so obvious that it was translated by the champion of the strenuous life into a call to leave the quiet sanctuary of Oyster Bay.

In the morning the immediate fight against Steel was taken up again. Brandeis turned the Stanley committee's and the country's attention to the anomaly of tragic labor conditions in such a rich industry. How could they explain it?

> I take it there is only one explanation, and it is this: While this corporation is the greatest example of combination, the most conspicuous instance of combination of capital in the world, it has, as an incident of the power which it acquires through that combination and through its associations with railroads and the financial world,

undertaken—and undertaken successfully—to deny the
right of combination to the workingmen, and these horrible conditions, which are a disgrace to America, considering the wealth which has surrounded and flown out
of this industry, are the result of having killed and eliminated from the steel industry, unionism. All the power
of capital and all the ability and intelligence of the men
who wield and who serve capital have been used to make
practically slaves of these operatives.

Since the elimination of the union from the Carnegie plant
at Homestead there had been a marked reduction in the rate
of wages for skilled labor, a constant tendency to reduce the
number of skilled men, and a decrease in the purchasing power
of unskilled labor. The worst part of it was repression, espionage, and denial of the right of collective bargaining. The
pension fund with which the company tried hard to impress
the committee was in Brandeis' opinion only another chain
to rivet the workers to the corporation and deprive them of
the liberty of American cititzens. The pension plan of the
steel company, like that of other trusts, created a state of
peonage; the worker could draw benefits only if he remained
in the company's employ and stayed "loyal." The trusts used
it as strike insurance. A proper pension system would be one
like that authorized by the Massachusetts legislature for the
Boston & Maine employees—but which the New Haven frustrated upon acquiring the B. & M.

Leaving the hearing he hastened to Nebraska to continue
his speaking tour. At Fremont he urged businessmen to take
time off to think: "It is more important than private business
and the people must take hold of it. I have left a fairly good
private business to come West to talk. The East needs the
West as it never did before." He spoke highly of Norris, then
seeking the nomination for the Senate, and credited Norris'
fight against the old House rules with the naming of a committee which probed the Ballinger scandal to the bottom.

At Hastings, Nebraska, he was asked about the United.—
"My early life was placed where my prejudices would certainly be in their favor. My friends, my associates and my
companions were all of that class, and when I quit them it
was to quit a very profitable association. I am no theorist on
the subject of big business and trusts. I have had a large
experience and know what I am talking about, and they
know that, too. Most of those who are fighting abuses are
necessarily theorists; that is why big business is fighting me.
It explains the attempts to offset my work by reports of my
earlier association with them."

At Kansas City he admitted having put faith in Taft in
1906, but it was a mistake. Taft had no firm convictions, no
well-defined policy as befitted a president. He wobbled. He
lacked sympathy with the common people and their problems
because all his life had been in association with the rich and
exclusive; all his leanings were therefore aristocratic. Taft
was of a judicial temperament, not of the executive type.

A Kansas City reporter asked, "Do you think Taft would
make a good Supreme Court judge?"

"I did not say Taft would make a good judge. I said he
did not make a good president."

Brandeis in his speech extolled La Follette's Wisconsin as
a state which was leading the way in solving many questions
that were contributing to social unrest and cited its compensation law, industrial commission, and state insurance department. At this time a textile strike was raging in Lawrence,
Massachusetts. The violence of the clash with labor was
nothing less than what capital could expect, he said.

His next stop was St. Louis, the city he left in his youth.
In New York he addressed the Society for Ethical Culture.
On returning to Boston he sought out persons having contacts with the Lawrence strike and proposed to offer the
preferential union shop idea as a solution. Mary Kenney
O'Sullivan had been active in the strike from the very first
day, organizing relief for the workers' families and getting

rich New York women, such as Anne Morgan, J. Pierpont Morgan's daughter, to contribute food. Jack O'Sullivan was covering the story for the *Boston Globe*. Marlen E. Pew, then of the Scripps-McRae papers (Winslow had bought up the *Traveler*), was on the ground and in the confidence of the I. W. W. leaders conducting the strike.

Pew persuaded Senator Poindexter to come incognito and see for himself the beating of men, women and children, then go back to Washington and make a national issue of it. The senator was touched most keenly by a little girl, a workman's child, who sat in his lap, her head bandaged, and he asked her what had happened. "A cop hit me," she said.

But Poindexter hesitated about raising the question in the Senate. After a talk with Brandeis he felt prepared. Brandeis outlined the speech for him: denial of civil rights under the guise of enforcing the law; terrible dangers to the entire country from any weakening of respect for the law arising from its being wrested to suppress the strike; conditions of the workers in an industry where, as in the steel industry, the tariff and combinations protected the product and left the workers without protection; present situation as the natural result of denying workers the right to combine; necessity of unions for social justice. Either the Senate should institute a special inquiry or the situation should be made the basis for an appeal for the appointment of a Federal Commission on Industrial Relations. Poindexter considered the Senate the most discouraging place in the world to make an appeal for Lawrence strikers. He said his colleagues were "a lot of self-satisfied old fossils quibbling and pettifogging over forms and precedents, and chuckling over the unfortunate condition of these mill workers." The conditions were devilish, he acknowledged, and the public should be informed of them.

Pew reported to Brandeis that the I. W. W. leaders were reasonable men, who were striving to avoid violence, knew about the preferential union shop, and were willing to try for a strike settlement. They trusted Brandeis absolutely and wanted to talk to him. But Brandeis thought a conference would be undesirable. He told William Allen White and other publicist friends that the time was ripe for a great advance in unionism—the disclosure of the trusts' labor policies had made many Americans recognize that collective bargaining was essential to industrial liberty, and the rioting at Lawrence and the operations of the I. W. W. showed that conservative trade unionism was essential to the maintenance of law and order. The abuses of unionism would stop when public opinion was brought actively to the unions' support and their bitter struggle for existence was over; but the American people would not accept the closed shop any more than the unions could accept the open shop as an alternative.

In his own behalf Brandeis felt it was necessary to send Senator Clapp a letter answering Winslow. He said Winslow's purpose seemed to be rather to attack him than to aid the committee in determining important economic and social questions. Brandeis proceeded to tell when, how, and why he had become convinced that the policy and methods of the United were morally and legally objectionable. He admitted having been of the opinion early in 1906 that under some conditions monopoly in industry could operate beneficially to the public; in other words, that there were good trusts as well as bad trusts. The United treated all shoe manufacturers, big and little, alike. The big ones were not given discounts for quantity, the little ones could operate by the system of leasing on small capital and get equal service. The United thus promoted competition in shoe manufacturing although itself a trust.

Then he told how serious doubts were raised in his mind by McElwain's and Jones' protests against the tying clauses; how he resigned from the board and how his suggestion in 1907 that these be eliminated from the leases was rejected. He denied having any connection with the Massachusetts legislation of that year or advising the company on its constitutionality or serving the company in any way after his resignation. Not until 1911, when the Shoe Manufacturers' Alliance came to him, did he become active in opposing the United, and he then made his position clear to Winslow and other directors.

To this Winslow retorted with a second letter to Clapp which asserted "in spite of his quickened conscience Mr. Brandeis continued to act as counsel for the company and to accept its fees for three years after his resignation as a director and even up to a few months of the time when he appeared as its active assailant in the pay of those who are now trying to bring about its disruption." To discredit Brandeis the United inserted newspaper ads headed "Peculiar Practices of 'The People's Lawyer',", and distributed a pamphlet called "Brandeis and sɹǝpuɐɹq—The Reversible Mind of 'The People's Lawyer', As He Stands Revealed in His Public Utterances, Briefs and Correspondence." His reversed attitude was "open to but one interpretation."

Whatever the effect this scurrilous advertising may have had on the running reader, Brandeis was still a desirable ally in Roosevelt's eyes. T. R. announced his candidacy for the Republican nomination on a progressive platform but let it be understood that he did not intend to form a third party if he failed. The Pinchots tried to get Brandeis to use his influence with La Follette for the release of Hiram Johnson's pledge of support. La Follette was keeping out of communication with the Pinchots for fear the public might misconstrue their relations. George Rublee reported that the Colonel was speaking of Brandeis in the friendliest way and with a strong wish that Brandeis would pass a night at Oyster Bay and discuss social and industrial questions.

To see the Colonel at that juncture would be to destroy the possibility of bringing the progressives together. The immediate danger was a division in three: Taft progressives, La Follette progressives, and Roosevelt progressives. Later these discordant factions might be united, and Brandeis could help restore cooperation if he retained La Follette's confi-

dence in his loyalty. Fighting Bob felt a distrust of the Pinchots and others who had urged him in the fall of 1911 to become a candidate and who were now supporting Roosevelt.
As almost the only remaining member of the original progressive group which surrounded La Follette, Brandeis feared
that a conference with Roosevelt under these circumstances
would be mistaken by La Follette as a defection. Brandeis
believed that each man had honestly exercised his own judgment as to what was best for the cause, but insistence upon a
Roosevelt-Republican party would postpone the real realign-
ment.

In the Taft ranks were Secretary of the Interior Fisher and,
of course, Stimson, who had lately been appointed Secretary
of War. Frankfurter, taken by Stimson into the War Department, reported that Roosevelt was deeply stirred by the social problems at stake and had a lively emotional appreciation
of them. Frankfurter was anxious for T. R. to get an intellectual grasp of them from Brandeis.

As spring drew on a conference on the Lawrence strike
took place one evening at the Brandeis home. Steffens, Brooks,
Edward Filene, Bloomfield and Ray Stannard Baker were
there, consulting with the United States Commissioner of
Labor, who wanted to break the strike by arresting the
leaders. Brandeis had received private advices from Pew that
twelve thousand men and women were on the picket line,
that their leaders' arrest would cause an outburst of violence,
that the town was full of strong-arm men. Some way must
be found to avert the violent intentions of the manufacturers,
and "the I. W. W. fellows will make any sacrifice to prevent
bloodshed." In the end higher wages were granted. Brandeis
regarded the whole affair as a marvelous achievement for the
I. W. W.; but this was the beginning and not the end. The
country must realize that industrial democracy was the only
way out.

In this task the press had a holy mission. Brandeis always
found newspaper workers ready to cooperate, and those he

encountered in Washington covering the Ballinger case and the political arena constantly gave him valuable information and suggestions. Reporters were beginning to assume the political functions of French journalists, acquiring a sense of statesmanship. In the early days of the Boston battles the difficulty was with the newspaper owners. In the palm of the special interests, they suppressed news which the public should have known, and the Public Franchise League was obliged to stage demonstrations and make the news so dramatic that the papers were unable to ignore it. As the influence of the League increased the press grew more hospitable and Brandeis became more successful in using it.

The *Chicago Daily Socialist* observed in March, 1912, that it was puzzling to find Brandeis issuing statements that came so near the socialist analysis of industrial conditions, yet not making a flatfooted plea for socialism. "Mr. Brandeis is endeavoring to find a way by which capitalism can be saved. Perhaps he does so not so much out of a love for the capitalist class as in response to some inherent inclination to preserve the established order if possible. Mr. Brandeis' progress along these lines is interesting, especially as, if he is as sincere as may justly be supposed, he can only wind up in the Socialist ranks."

Brandeis gave five hundred dollars for the La Follette campaign in Massachusetts, but the number of adherents there was so slight as to make the situation unpromising. The Woodrow Wilson campaign committee appealed to him for a contribution, saying that Governor Wilson was a poor man with no great campaign fund. La Follette kept firing telegrams from the West. He needed Brandeis as a speaker, but though Brandeis' heart was with La Follette he could not go. From San Francisco La Follette sent out a Macedonian cry: "You must come and help carry California. You can do more here than any other man."

Brandeis issued statements in his behalf and promised to give the United Press an interview on the day after the Wisconsin primaries. It was impossible for him to take the trip.

At home he kept close watch on the New Haven, which was resorting to its old tricks. The latest development was a bill to dissolve the Boston Holding Company and effect a physical merger with the B. & M. Besides, the New Haven had been continuing the alarming policy of buying up more steamship lines. It sold $30,000,000 of notes to Morgan and Higginson to meet its maturing obligations. Mellen persuaded Governor Foss that he was ready to spend $50,000,000 for improvements, and the governor felt that the financing of improvements was difficult under the holding company. Brandeis denounced the offer of electrification as a bribe and a delusion which could not brace up the service outside of Boston. He urged the legislature to find out why the service was notoriously poor and broken down. To enact the bill would be like applying a quack medicine to a sick patient without even making a diagnosis.

Eastman pointed out to Foss that the state had the right to acquire stock control of the B. & M. The new plan of leasing that line to the New Haven would make the B. & M. an interstate road and put it beyond Massachusetts' reach. The Morgan interests had not demonstrated the advantages of unified management. Quite the contrary.

Brandeis said: "This renunciation by Massachusetts in favor of New York capitalists of the control of the railroad situation in northern New England, which it now possesses, is absolutely without justification." The bill imposed the conditions of electrification and a tunnel on a railroad which was suffering from inadequate net income. Huge fixed charges for improvement would not materially bolster up the operating revenues, if at all. "Let us learn whether the defect lies in the condition of the roadbed and of the equipment or whether in the practice of unwise economy or any other incompetency of management, or whether it is due to the control of our transportation system by New Haven and other interests alien to Massachusetts." Trains were being cut off and the number of employees cut down to meet the deficit. Money was being paid out in dividends which should be expended in proper service. Moreover, the people had an absolute right to compel electrification without making a trade with the railroads. Brandeis wanted the legislature to delay action until the Interstate Commerce Commission reported.

The bill was killed. The I. C. C. began hearings in Boston that summer, and Commissioner Charles A. Prouty of Vermont made it clear that he perceived "in this territory what is practically a railroad monopoly greater than that which exists in any other equal area in the United States." Brandeis appeared for the Boston Fruit & Produce Exchange, complaining about service. Ives appeared for the Chamber of Commerce and said the first step should be to determine the financial condition of the roads. Prouty announced that the hearing was not based on their complaints but on information obtained by the Commission's own agents; nevertheless Brandeis had borrowed Eastman from the Public Franchise League and put him to work at digging up the facts.

Before the I. C. C. resumed the inquest other affairs of national importance occupied Brandeis. First was the proposed revision of the patent laws. A majority of the Supreme Court had decided in the mimeograph case that the owner of a patent had unrestricted rights as to price and terms of use. Congress seemed to share the view of the dissenters. Brandeis went to Washington in May with a statement to make before the House committee on patents, which was planning legislation to overcome the court's construction of the law.

He argued that the power of the manufacturer to fix the resale price of a patented article was not dangerous to the community but beneficial, except where the manufacturer held a general trade monopoly. Price-maintenance on razors, for example, had not suppressed but developed competition because it enabled every small distributor to become a purveyor of the article and compete with department stores; it opened a field of comprehensive advertising and made a market for invention. As long as there was competition among manufacturers there did not need to be fear of exorbitant prices. If a maker fixed his price too high, other manufacturers would be incited to enter the market.

Chairman William A. Oldfield of Arkansas brought up the question of prescribing a "reasonable price." Brandeis said the doctrine of reasonable profit was applicable only to public service companies because they held monopolies "but where you are dealing with a business where there is ample opportunity to keep alive competition, what you want to do is not to cut down but to welcome a large profit and rely upon the opportunity that other men have, the intelligence, the genius, the enterprise of other men to step in and work through the laws of competition to see to it that we get not only a cheaper but a better article. And I believe we can, with the immense capital available, and with the greater capital that is in the brain of the American people, rely upon a reasonable price and a good article as long as the avenues of competition are kept open."

Where a monopoly existed the taxing power of the corporation was apt to become extortionate and there was a tendency to stop invention. Brandeis suggested that the committee report the present law injurious in operation only where patents were used "as an instrument of obtaining a commercial monopoly, such as is obtained by the United Shoe Machinery Company" and the Tobacco, Standard Oil, Harvester and other trusts.

He embarked on further criticism of the United, "a monopoly the like of which does not exist in the completeness of its control and in the dealing, as it does, with the absolutely essential parts of mechanical industry." Because of its tying clauses and clean sweep no one could enter the field without a complete system. He repeated the story of Plant and showed how the patent law permitted the United to suppress competition. What stood in the way of new invention was the absence of a market; the shoe manufacturer was tied hand and foot. What stood in Plant's way was the money trap of the trust.

"Take this matter of wireless telegraphy, which is in every-body's mind today," Brandeis said. "I happen to have per-sonal knowledge of it because I was counsel for the company when it started." A remarkable series of inventions had come to naught because the capital needed to put them into the field was lacking. In the razor business Gillette would have been wiped out but for capital coming through at the last moment. There was danger in creating a corporation so large and so rich that its alliance with the Money Trust crippled potential competitors. Great organizations were constitu-tionally unprogressive. Freedom of enterprise, freedom of capital, were essential.

The battle for freedom was a battle for life. Lawyers, he said, had a special obligation to make the law efficient and wipe out the disgrace that had come to the law. "We make rules and do not provide any machinery for enforcing them." The La Follette-Lenroot bill, then reposing with the judiciary committee, would make the Sherman Law effective, wipe out abuses, open the field of invention and commerce, and reduce the cost of living.

"I wish," said Chairman Oldfield, "I were a member of the judiciary committee so that I could help bring that about."

Lenroot, who was also on the patents committee, saw no likelihood of a report.

But Brandeis was optimistic. The patents committee could do as much as the judiciary committee; it could make a care-ful investigation and use it as an educational document throughout the country.

Discussing patent law in general, he regarded it as a de-lusive protection. Court proceedings were expensive, there were delays, and it was a question of wearing out the other fellow. Giant corporations could "spend anything" and defy the real owner of a patent. "In my own practice I have been

confronted with just that situation. A man comes with what
appears to be a most valuable invention; comes to a body of
men who are perfectly ready to invest in that invention a
reasonable sum of money—$50,000 or $100,000, or perhaps
$25,000 if the invention is small. I have had again and again
to say to them: 'This is an invention which will interfere
with the field that is controlled by one or the other of the
great concerns. Your $25,000, your $50,000, your $100,000
will all vanish. You may have the best thing in the world, but
as long as our patent law procedure, as long as our equity
procedure in the federal courts, is what it is, your money will
vanish in lawyers' and stenographers' fees, and then when you
get all through and perhaps get a decision in your favor in
our circuit, there are eight other circuits where you will be
fought.' "

This was a scandal to the legal profession. Only the big
fellow, with inexhaustible resources, was safe; the small man
was compelled to play into the hands of the trust. The public suffered. Its disrespect for the law grew. What was needed
was legal invention, machinery to enforce the rule embodied
in legislation.

Brandeis suggested that the committee's report would be
more readable than the bill under consideration, and editorial
writers would be able to pick it up and understand it where
they might find some difficulty in following the provisions of
the bill without careful study.

Returning to the subject of prices, he said he was stren-
uously opposed to the government's fixing prices in any competitive business. The public's protection against exorbitant
prices was its option to take another article. In the case of a
trust it had no chance to choose. Price-fixing on patented,
trademarked or copyrighted articles was an incentive to individual perfection, to a reduction in cost and improvement
of quality. The man who acquired a patent gave something to
the community in return. Combinations, on the other hand,
took away from the community its various avenues of ad-

vance, and the economies described in their prospectuses never came true. "On the contrary, when these fellows got power you had this condition arise: the prices go up, and what is more than that, the salaries go up in very large proportion as against the wages."

Brandeis liked this sort of participation in the fashioning of national policy, and even when bills died in committee ideas did not. He did not feel like a messiah, as the *Boston News Bureau* characterized him, but had an appreciation for discipleship. Oldfield embodied his suggestions in a report; in fact, Brandeis drafted it. The Stanley committee also adopted his anti-trust ideas in substance. He maintained an extensive correspondence with people in public life who sought him out for advice and influence. Newton D. Baker, mayor of Cleveland, asked him to endorse the coinage of a three-cent piece, and he authorized the use of his name in connection with a memorial which Wilson, Roosevelt and Mayor Gaynor of New York signed. With Senator Joseph L. Bristow of Kansas, who consulted him on the Alaska Railroad bill, he agreed on the wisdom of government ownership and operation of the road. To Frankfurter, who was looking for suggestions for the new Federal Industrial Relations Commission, he proposed the name of Mrs. Evans, recommended as the most active member of the Massachusetts Minimum Wage Board. Josephine Goldmark informed him of the appeal from the decision of the California Supreme Court against maximum-hour legislation, and he was ready to argue the case before the Supreme Court of the United States if she would prepare the brief as usual. Mary E. McDowell of the University of Chicago Settlement brought up the thought of attempting federal legislation for a minimum wage for women. He saw a grave constitutional difficulty, but aside from that the question of federal power ought not to be submitted to the courts until a great mass of data had been collected; it was better to work out social problems in the detached laboratories of the different states (as Holmes believed).

George W. Kirchwey of the Columbia Law School discussed with him the need of constructive work to restore respect for the law. This led to definite conclusions involving an extension of the functions of law schools, and he convinced the authorities at Harvard that legal education should be socialized; lawyers should not merely learn rules of law but their purpose and effect on the affairs of man. For this they must study the facts—human, industrial, social—to which laws were to be applied.

At the commencement exercises of Brown University that year he hailed the work of McElwain and the Filenes as examples of the constructive public service of which businessmen were capable and he urged the recognition of business as a profession. McElwain had succeeded in regularizing employment. The Filenes had recently moved into a new building affording nine acres of floor space, but their success was measurable more by their social attitude than by their size. Narrow-minded money-makers had hurled against these men the silly charge of being theorists, but their exceptional methods would some day become accepted methods. Big business would lose its sinister meaning and signify bigness in service.

"And as the profession of business develops," Brandeis said, "the great industrial and social problems expressed in the present social unrest will one by one find solution."

Mrs. La Follette renewed her campaign to induce Brandeis to run for the Senate. Her husband, discouraged and ill, dropped out of the race for the presidency. In the next session Senator Brandeis and Senator La Follette could be a team such as would capture the imagination and support of the country. Brandeis had been disposed to think the path of duty for him did not lead in the direction of office-holding and he saw no reason for changing that opinion. But it was very clear to him that he ought to utilize the insight gained from practical affairs to prevent well-meaning progressives from falling into the error of thinking that private monopoly was desirable if regulated. He welcomed the next turn of events. Bryan handled the Democratic convention in a masterly manner. Wilson was nominated. Brandeis had never met or seen him, but in following the New Jersey governor's discussion of economic problems he gathered that this candidate possessed qualities indispensable to their solution. To Senator Lodge, Wilson was a radical, too dangerous to be in the White House. To Brandeis' mind the Democrats had done everything that was then possible in purifying the party and in attempting "to drive the money lenders out of the temple"; the nomination of Wilson should have settled the doubts of all progressives.

Brandeis told La Follette, who admired both Bryan and Wilson, that the duty of progressives was not only to insure Wilson's election but to give him all the aid and comfort he would need in the very difficult task of carrying out his policies.

T. R.'s determination to proceed with his Progressive Party after the Republican convention stood by Taft, disturbed him; it would intensify the belief of many people that what Roosevelt was leading was a Roosevelt party. But if T. R. threw his weight on the side of Wilson there would be a chance of uniting progressives of every stamp.

Brandeis appealed to Gifford Pinchot. If the Republicans had named a progressive instead of the reactionary Taft and the Democrats had selected a reactionary instead of Wilson, there would be no question whom the progressives should favor. The situation now called for the fullest support of Wilson; otherwise progressive strength would be dissipated, Taft might be re-elected or the Wilson administration rendered impotent through lack of progressive support. Pinchot was sorry to hear that Brandeis had turned to Wilson; he had had a talk with T. R., whose position on industrial justice in the coming fight was going to be more nearly Brandeis' own than anybody else's platform.

Early in July Brandeis gave a statement to the press, calling upon all progressives to vote for Wilson:

> His nomination ranks among the most encouraging events in American history. Progressives, irrespective of party, should in my opinion support Woodrow Wilson for the presidency. He is thoroughly democratic in spirit. He recognizes that all of the people are entitled to equal opportunities and appreciates that the development of all of the people is essential to the attainment of American ideals.

When Wilson announced on August 1 a proposal to deal with the tariff problem by a gradual reduction at the rate of five percent a year Brandeis immediately wrote him that this was further evidence that the country might expect a wise administration from him; the simple plan was true statesmanship. It showed a thorough appreciation of the needs of business. Behind the scenes, several months before, Brandeis had discussed this plan with Congressman William C. Redfield of Brooklyn, a Wilson adviser. Ever since his appearance before the Dingley committee in 1897 Brandeis had been convinced there was no other method of dealing with the tariff properly. Wilson replied:

> Your letter of August first has given me a great deal of pleasure. I have been much cheered and reassured by the knowledge of your approval and support. I sincerely hope that the months to come will draw us together and give me the benefit of many conferences with you.

Teddy was angry. He thought he had seen eye to eye with Brandeis. According to a tale the *Transcript* carried he was now privately denouncing Brandeis for the use that had been made of Ballinger's secretary, Kerby.

"Instead of blaming Pinchot and Garfield for their part in this disreputable business," the newspaper said, "the Colonel is said to have condoned their part on the theory that they had been led astray by a tricky lawyer. His words about Brandeis are said to have been as strong as he could find. At any rate the Boston lawyer is for Wilson and the Colonel is said to be ready to score him publicly if he has aught to say in criticism of the third party." But after all, the chairman of the Bull Moose executive committee was Perkins.

Brandeis met Wilson for the first time at Sea Girt, New Jersey, on August 28. They had luncheon and talked about trusts. Wilson impressed him as having the qualities of an ideal president. The speed of Wilson's mental processes was astonishing. After the conference the news released was this: The Governor declared that Brandeis, more than any other man he knew, had studied "corporation business from the efficiency side to the political side."

The immediate result of the interview was discerned in an address Wilson delivered in Buffalo, disapproving of regulation of monopolies and approving of regulation of competition. This was followed by newspaper copy which Brandeis prepared, editorials in *Collier's* which he inspired (the weekly was not taking sides between Wilson and Roosevelt, but Hapgood favored the former), a campaign of letter-writing and a vigorous autumn of speech-making and working with William G. McAdoo of the National Committee. He contributed five hundred dollars to the fund. Cleveland H. Dodge, a close friend of Higginson, gave five thousand dollars.

The course Brandeis laid out for himself as a Wilson supporter was to attract voters who might be diverted by the call of the Bull Moose. The subject-matter of his talk would be the heresies of the new party's program. He planned to avoid Democratic rallies in favor of commercial bodies, clubs, labor groups, and the like. He was in politics only on the high plane of economics and industrial democracy.

This technique would not only preserve his independent character in the eyes of the public but would employ the strategy used by lawyers in court; given a short time for oral argument, they selected only the strongest points to drive home. The party which was calling itself Progressive was attempting under Perkins' leadership to perpetuate the most effective instrument for preventing the organization of labor. Perkins had been the chairman of the finance committee of the Steel Trust at its inception; Perkins was chairman of the Harvester Trust finance committee from the beginning; a director of the Shipping Trust, and before that vice-president of the New York Life Insurance Company in the golden days before Hughes investigated it. Perkins might almost have been called the father of trusts because as a partner in J. P. Morgan & Company he was especially active in organizing industrial combinations. And Perkins, with Frank A. Munsey, succeeded in eliminating a proposed Bull Moose plank to strengthen the Sherman Law.

Perkins and other advocates of legalized monopoly talked of unrestrained competition as though the only alternative were regulated monopoly. Brandeis pointed out that factory laws restricted the theoretical freedom of contract between employer and employee and thus protected the inequality of the individual worker's position. Similarly the right of competition must be limited in order to preserve it; excesses led to monopoly. The Standard Oil, practicing unrestricted competition, frequently destroyed weaker firms through a local price-cutting campaign. The Tobacco Trust had resorted to the same tactics. The Shoe Machinery Trust practiced another form.

The new party, instead of preserving competition, was prepared to put an end to it. Its purpose to retain monopoly but prevent harm-doing was an impossible task. Industrial absolutism might be reduced slightly but its deadening effect would remain. Monopoly meant death to incentive and progress. The true solution of the trust problem lay in the regulation of competition, the platform on which Wilson stood.

Brandeis' first speech was at a convention of the Massachusetts State Branch of the American Federation of Labor at Fitchburg. Never before had an outsider been permitted to discuss political subjects. But they hailed him as "the people's attorney" and they heard the lawyer pick the flaws in the new party's contract. Examine the Roosevelt platform not only for what it contained but what it omitted, he urged them. Although fourteen definite labor recommendations were listed there was no pledge to secure the right of labor to organize—without which all other concessions for the improvement of the worker's lot were futile. There was only a friendly approval of the practice. The platform promised industrial justice but not industrial democracy; justice of the sort which benevolent corporations were prone to administer through welfare departments—the justice of the trusts, which made the extermination of organized labor a cardinal principle. Strikes against trusts were vain; strike-breakers were backed by inexhaustible financial resources. If production happened to be curtailed higher prices were charged; the consumer lost, but not the trust.

"That cursed product of despotism, the New Party," promised legislation to protect labor, but would such laws be sustained by the courts? The Supreme Court had held invalid both the New York law limiting the hours of labor for bakers and the act of Congress preventing the discharge of workers for joining unions. No American court had yet held constitutional a law prohibiting night work for women or a general law limiting the hours of labor in private industry. Perkins could well promise laws and sit back for the slow march of legislation, court decision and constitutional amendment.

"Unless the right to organize is preserved and developed, all the laws advocated in the New Party platform, even if upheld by the courts, would be little better than dead letters."

Hiram Johnson, Roosevelt's running mate, came to Boston furious. He demanded a correction from Brandeis; the Progressive party was not silent on the right to organize; there

was a plank on organized labor and none other than John
Mitchell had written it.

In two signed articles in *Collier's* Brandeis continued his
microscopic analysis of the Rooseveltians' position by dis-
proving their thesis that trusts were needed for efficiency and
for maintaining the export trade. He wrote Clapp that he
was extremely troubled by the fact that the Progressive
Party had practically adopted the Perkins trust policy; on
the other hand, his confidence had grown in Wilson's straightforward and unflinching character. Later in September, when
Wilson came to Boston, riding through the streets in an open
automobile with Brandeis by his side, they talked over the
argument that the Democrats' trust policy would only continue the futile efforts of the past administration. Brandeis
explained. On returning to his office he received a telegram
from Wilson:

> Please set forth as explicitly as possible the actual
> measures by which competition can be efficiently regu-
> lated. The more explicit we are on this point, the more
> completely the enemy's guns will be spiked.

Brandeis had promised Hapgood material for an editorial covering this ground and mailed Wilson his notes for them, but
had to defer drawing up suggestions because of the I.C.C.
hearing on the New Haven in Washington the next day.

He had helped keep alive national interest in that particular
monopoly during the summer by means of a letter to Poindexter which was read in the Senate. In the course of debate
Lodge came to the New Haven's defence and Senator Henry
F. Lippitt of Rhode Island did likewise, calling Brandeis a
professional agitator who always turned up when there was
talk of monopolies. (Norris was doing his bit in the assault
on the trusts by clamoring against the secrecy shrouding the
government's case against the United Shoe Machinery).

At the I.C.C. hearing Brandeis showed that as soon as
Mellen stepped into the B. & M. he discharged many em-

ployees although business was rapidly improving. Vice-President Buckland of the New Haven interrupted to say that the roads were trying to approximate the million-dollar saving which Brandeis had declared possible not so long ago. Brandeis nailed the jest with a prompt denial; they had not followed his advice. Reading from the record of the advance-rate case he came to the assertion of the B. & M. that if it did the same business in 1911 as in 1910 its cost in wages would increase $2,663,000. Reading from its latest report, he showed that the road did $1,500,000 more business and its wages increased only $1,641,872.

"Where did that other million dollars go to?" he asked with a smile.

From another report of the road he read that its transportation expenses were steadily going down while the volume of business went up, and asked whether the explanation of the missing million was not that men had been forced out of their jobs.

As soon as the hearing was adjourned he dispatched to Wilson the suggestions requested: Remove the uncertainties of the Sherman Law, facilitate its enforcement by adequate machinery, and create a fact-finding commission to aid enforcement—and in a postscript he mentioned his authorship of the La Follette, Lenroot and Stanley bills. He told also of making arrangements to deliver speeches on the trust problem from Maine to Nebraska, but he could not heed Bryan's request that he go to California; the I.C.C. hearing would intervene.

In Brandeis' opinion the trusts were the fundamental issue of the presidential campaign. His protest was not so much against the Progressive Party's leader as against its prime minister. Was it not trying to serve both God and Mammon? Jane Addams on the one hand, George W. Perkins on the other: "two props of virtue for a Christian prince to stay him from the fall of vanity." In rapid succession he spoke before the Economic Club of Boston, the Economic Club of

Portland, the Twentieth Century Club of Boston, the Town Criers of Providence, the West Side Y.M.C.A. of New York, the City Lunch Club of Rochester, and he made two speeches in Cincinnati—all in ten days.

He punctured the theory that price-fixing by reducing trusts' profits could reduce prices: the lessened incentive to the trusts would diminish efficiency and increase costs. Fixing a maximum return on capital, like limiting the dividends of railroads, would be impotent as an attempt to secure low prices. The permissible dividends generally exhausted the profits.

In Rochester he told how he had become a keen advocate of woman's suffrage through his own efforts to bring about social and industrial reform:

> I came to the conclusion after a good deal of effort in that direction that if we were to improve the working condition of the people, it would have to be done by the people themselves, and in the effort to give the people this opportunity I found that the large part of those who needed it most were women workers, because they were less experienced, less protected by organization and because the demands of industry bore more heavily on them. I saw they needed not only protection but a knowledge of affairs. They needed much to uplift them out of the smallness and trivialities of life, and I saw that nothing would be more potent in that direction than the privilege of the ballot. Women often have greater opportunities than men to bring about social reform, for which all of us are working. They have the desire, enthusiasm and understanding. I learned much from them in my work. So from having been of the opinion that we would advance best by leaving the voting to the men, I became convinced that we needed all the forces of the community to bring about this advance.

In Cleveland he said that if respect for the law was desired the law must first be made respectable. He advocated absolute freedom of speech; the best way to handle dangerous ideas was to let them explode into words—the danger would thus be less remote. In Buffalo he told why a constructive statesman rather than a warrior was needed for the presidency; Wilson had manly virtues and would not stoop to unworthy means even to bring about worthy ends. He spoke in Canton, Toledo, Pittsburgh, Chicago. In Milwaukee he paid tribute to the University of Wisconsin and to La Follette. The Twin Cities completed his itinerary; he had to return to Washington. A talk to the Economic Club at Hotel Astor in New York was the finishing touch. It was November.

Several times during his tour the question of his political faith arose.

"I like to think I am an economist and not a politician," he said. "I don't know that anyone would call me a Republican"—with a smile—"I am a La Follette Republican or a La Follette Democrat or a La Follette Progressive." He did not even admit he was campaigning for Wilson. He said he represented himself.

One of the amusing aspects of the presidential fight was Roosevelt's conversion. T. R. had been thrusting his fierce energies into ripping Taft up the back, but Wilson's and Brandeis' criticism that he was aiming to legalize monopoly irritated him and in the last days he denied the charge with Big Stick vehemence. This was what he believed in, he said: the La Follette-Lenroot changes, damages for victims of the trusts, a definition between right and wrong, and he was against giving to the proposed federal trade commission the price-fixing power.

"It was a great victory," Brandeis said after November 5. He was well satisfied. To Wilson he wrote: "I feel that every American should be congratulated except possibly yourself. May strength be given to you to bear the heavy burden." And from Bermuda the President-elect replied: "You were yourself a great part of the victory; I know, therefore, how to thank you for your thought of me in sending me your gracious message of November 6. It now remains for us to devote all our strength to making good."

There was another victory that year for Brandeis. The City Savings Bank of Pittsfield opened a life insurance department. This was the fourth bank to adopt the system which he still regarded as his greatest achievement.

Chapter XII

PREOCCUPATIONS OF A PUBLICIST

IMMEDIATELY after the election newspapers carried reports that Brandeis was slated to be attorney general; but Wilson was considering trust-buster McReynolds, who had broken with Wickersham and who was the choice of Colonel Edward M. House. While Washington correspondents were embroidering with the thin thread of rumor, interests hostile to Brandeis mobilized for battle. In the middle of November, in House's New York apartment in East 35th Street, the President-elect went over a tentative Cabinet list and kept McReynolds' name for the post. The *Review of Reviews* observed that there was a greater need for Brandeis' talents in helping secure a proper law than in bringing suits under the existing statute. Colonel House took lunch with him and then reported to Wilson that their minds were in accord on the great questions of the day; that Brandeis was more than a lawyer—a publicist with an unusual facility for lucid expression. Although a large number of reputable people distrusted the man, this could be true of anyone holding advanced views. Then again, Brandeis came from the right part of the country. His name was put down as the likely secretary of commerce.

As soon as this became known protests were carried to Wilson. Charges of professional misconduct, brought together by the *Boston News Bureau*, cited the Old Dominion, the Lennox, the Warren and the United Shoe Machinery cases as evidence of Brandeis' character disqualifications. William F. Fitzgerald, his enemy of the Old Dominion days, fumed against him in Washington. The Massachusetts State Democratic Committee chairman, Thomas P. Riley, called at Trenton with a certified copy of Brandeis' enrollment as a Republican. The *Boston News Bureau* had dug up the astounding information that he registered from 6 Otis Place as a Democrat in 1909, failed to register in 1910, and appeared as a Republican in 1911. Democratic politicians from the New England states, headed by Ex-Governor Foss and abetted by William F. McCombs, Wilson's campaign manager, rushed in with every distortion provided for them. The Boston Bar Association was also enlisted. Wilson did not believe these tales. He had Hapgood, as a trained journalist, investigate the charges and bring him facts to use in refutation.

The opposition was not in its essence political. The Democratic machine leaders were sagaciously glad to have Brandeis identified with the party. But politics was a shield for privilege. The forces arrayed against Brandeis were the New Haven, the United, Kidder-Peabody, Lee-Higginson, Fitzgerald, and many other Wall Street interests. His name remained on the list until five days before the inauguration. The trick was turned by Cleveland H. Dodge, who was on the closest terms with Wilson, an intimate classmate at Princeton, and one of about four persons who addressed him as Woodrow. Dodge was also on friendly relations with Brandeis. Henry L. Higginson approached Dodge with a plea to save Wilson from a great mistake. He said a good many staunch Republicans had voted for Wilson and trusted him. Dodge went to Wilson on the grave mission and convinced him of the expediency of dropping the hot coal. Richard Olney, still high in Democratic party councils, also intervened.

Wilson decided not to begin his administration fighting another's battles and risk discord in the party. He gave the post to William C. Redfield. Really he was little interested in the Cabinet, but it was annoying to be balked and he determined to find a future place for Brandeis.

Although La Follette was furious, Brandeis took it in his stride. He asked nothing for himself; said he never had ambitions, for that would have diverted his judgment. He had been willing to enter the Cabinet only because Wilson wanted him. At no time was the invitation offered. Excluded by the financial phalanx, he did not lack abundant opportunity for work and growth. To McReynolds and Redfield he tendered congratulations. McReynolds was the wisest possible choice for attorney general; his record in trust prosecutions would assure the country that the President's trust policy would be carried out promptly and efficiently, and business would be freed at last. Brandeis planned to call on him soon and talk over New England's special needs.

To the slanders that kept him out of the Cabinet, Brandeis consistently paid no attention. Jones felt that an old friend should tell the truth about Fitzgerald's enmity, the effort to persuade the United to abandon its policy, and the facts in the Lennox case. Gossip flitted from one exclusive corner in Boston to another to the effect that Ezra Thayer, now dean of Harvard Law School, was spreading scandal about Brandeis. Thayer made a grieved denial.

A Cabinet post would have meant, in the last analysis, a reward—with perhaps the customary restrictions that go with office. If friends thought it might prove irksome to a free lance, to an attorney accustomed to full authority from his clients, Brandeis was sure he could work smoothly under Wilson and more so than under some other Presidents. But he did not need the reward. It was sufficient to know he had been useful and to believe that his exposure of Taft in the Ballinger case helped greatly in splitting the Republican Party.

Many sought his influence for jobs in the new administration. Pinchot was one of the first to pursue him, not for himself but for the national forests and waterpower sites. He pressed Brandeis to draw a statement out of Wilson at once

so as to offset a bipartisan combination of grabbers in the
Senate. Brandeis' policy with Wilson was to speak only if
spoken to. He had no doubt the President would be on the
right side of conservation when called upon to act but he saw
no likelihood of a statement before the occasion arose. Yet
he was willing to help Gifford by passing on information
to La Follette. Finally, indirectly, a conference with Wilson
was arranged for the conservation champion.

The man he was most anxious to serve at this period was
Hapgood, who had lost his place on *Collier's* for running
editorials during the campaign, opposing Roosevelt's trust
policy. The editorials had been written by Brandeis. After
Roosevelt was shot in Milwaukee a sentimental wave caught
up Robert J. Collier, who penned a paragraph in his praise
and then took a definite stand for his candidacy. In the issue
immediately preceding election day Roosevelt, given a page
to say his thanks, wrote that the magazine had been fla-
grantly unjust to him; that the Progressive Party suffered
from the dissemination of untruths through the editorial pages
of *Collier's* and the speeches of Wilson. T. R. did not spare
his opponents from the accusation of unscrupulous misrepre-
sentation of his position on trusts; but he did not mention
Brandeis. Collier himself did that. Collier, now his own editor,
wrote that the most important political editorials during the
campaign were not the work of Hapgood but of Brandeis,
for whom he had high respect but who was "one of Governor
Wilson's most powerful campaign orators" and in relations
with Wilson "somewhat too close" to be reconciled with the
impartial policy laid down by the magazine.

After setting Collier straight on the extent of his relations
with Wilson and informing him that the editorials had been
prepared at Hapgood's request, Brandeis went off to Hot
Springs with the late editor as a guest of Charles R. Crane.
They talked over the magazine field. (Collier hoped for
more articles and ideas from Brandeis and endorsed him for
the Cabinet.) Brandeis looked into *Leslie's Weekly* and *Mc-*

Clure's, hoping to find a suitable vehicle for Hapgood. As counsel for paper manufacturers for twenty-five years he had had occasion to learn much of the financial difficulties of publishing. The business was extremely hazardous and required large capital; it was better to avoid expensive properties and develop some publication whose initial cost would be low. *Harper's Weekly* offered a possibility although it had insignificant assets aside from its good name.

Brandeis loyally concerned himself with this quest and tried to interest Henry Morgenthau, Sr., and other Wilson supporters. Thomas W. Lamont was willing to sell *Harper's* for $100,000. In the spring Crane put up the money and installed Hapgood as editor, Brandeis having conducted the negotiations and handled the incorporation. The *Boston Common,* which he had backed three years before, failed to become self-supporting, and rather than feed it intermittent teaspoonfuls he dropped it.

Felix Frankfurter was another good man—so intelligent that Brandeis considered him a power for the right. Frankfurter was concerned with government and prepared a memorandum setting forth the difficulties confronting legislators and a method of affording aid. Brandeis had little faith in a plan for a small group of men to evolve a social system or even an important element of one. Reliance must be placed upon all America—and the rest of the world. In securing progress social legislation must be regarded as a field for discovery and invention. Advance in science was seldom one man's work, for it stemmed from a long line of experience, as in the evolution of the arts. Conscious collaborations were also rare. Just so, social invention must build upon the failures and successes of past endeavors, and it must meet the test of public discussion. But he agreed with Frankfurter on the value of a disinterested, well-equipped group who could give their time to threshing out legislative proposals and promoting those that appeared to be sound. This had been the principle behind the People's Lobby and the Progressive League. The trouble with the League was that it suffered from too many prima donnas.

In Frankfurter Brandeis saw an ally for the development of the Law School. Professor Roscoe Pound needed five thousand dollars for a criminal law library; Brandeis was ready to help raise the sum and asked Frankfurter if he knew some New York lawyers who might be willing to join in making this gift. Frankfurter said Judge Julian C. Mack had contacts with people who wanted to spend some of their money wisely. Later in the year, when Pound discussed the prospects of a professorship of administrative law for Frankfurter, Brandeis made suggestions for raising the endowment. He was convinced that Frankfurter could do worthy work at Harvard with the very qualities which Henry L. Stimson thought should be used for non-academic purposes.

The machinery for administering the law and the technical character of legislation both needed improvement. Close thought was required for devising methods which, in the light of social and industrial conditions, would make laws effective. A large part of the prevalent disrespect for the legal process was due not so much to the courts' failure to interpret legislation properly as to the carelessly constructed machinery provided by legislatures for carrying out the people's will. More and more Brandeis emphasized the quality of legal education. He differed with La Follette on the recall of judges. What good would be served to recall a judge who would probably be succeeded by one like him? In Germany there was a law school which encouraged its students, as part of their training, to go into factories and study the effects of Bismarck's social legislation; they became intelligent expounders of industrial law. More important than recall was the better preparation of judges.

Another man whom Brandeis befriended, in a way, was Mellen. He said it was unjust to put the whole blame on Mellen for the New Haven's many wrecks, its wretched freight service, and the depreciation of its stock from 225 to 133½. Mellen could not have persisted eight years in this fatal policy of monopoly and aggrandizement unless supported actively by the directors and supinely by the general run of stockholders. The horrifying succession of accidents on the road in those days was making the New Haven a ghastly household joke. Brandeis reasoned that the huge expenditures to suppress competition so weakened the financial structure that dangerous economies were resorted to in order to keep up the dividend rate. By reducing its operating force while its business was increasing the road put a strain on the men which recent wrecks showed they were unable to bear.

Mellen cavalierly gave his compliments to Brandeis and said to the *New York Times*, "And tell him I hope he'll be able to prove everything he says." But Brandeis persisted in pointing beyond Mellen. In a signed article in the *Boston Post*, he said:

> Whether J. Pierpont Morgan dominates the Boston & Maine directors it is certain that Mr. Morgan ordinarily votes the proxies at the annual meeting and of course Mr. Morgan may well be regarded as the father of monopoly for this country. . . . It is true that inasmuch as his business interests are vastly greater in New York and the West than they are in New England, New England has little to hope for so long as he controls the transportation system here. . . . J. P. Morgan & Company are bankers, their interest is to make money out of securities and particularly to make money out of securities which they sell. . . . The more securities the New Haven issues the greater the commissions.

Mellen asserted that Brandeis' attacks on the New Haven system were simply self-advertisement which brought enormous fees from corporate interests. Brandeis again preferred to ignore personal insinuations. If once he began to make denials or explanations it would easily be in the power of the other side to occupy him in that way eight hours a day and divert his attention from the more important business of attacking its policy. This was a struggle against measures, not against individuals. He said the people of New England were interested only in the merits of the question of transportation monopoly.

"We owe Mr. Mellen our gratitude," he told a group of business men in Providence, "because his restless, resourceful spirit has made it possible for every man to know what a monopoly does when it grips the transportation facilities of a people as the New Haven has gripped those of New England. Ordinarily such enterprises have their beginning in one generation and their development in the next, but we have seen the beginning of an error and its results.

"Private monopoly in business and industry is an exact analogy of political despotism. Liberty in industry as in politics leads to best results. Why is it that this bad service is complained of everywhere? It is because when you create a monopoly, you remove the stimulus, the incentive to all progress. Monopoly has a deadening effect because it undertakes to substitute a few minds for many minds."

He never tired of reiteration and never assumed that others were tired of listening.

Edward Filene, who believed in the merger in 1909, admitted at a Chamber of Commerce meeting that he had been slowly forced to take the opposite view; separation of the New Haven from its outside holdings was the only way out. Higginson, addressing the same group, said the attacks on the road prevented it from borrowing money; without money there could be no improvements; he had not advised anyone to buy the road's stock for the past two years. Eastman, fresh from an encounter with State Senator Calvin Coolidge on a bill to authorize the absorption of trolley lines, also spoke. Brandeis said, "Usually the order of a railroad finance is, first to look after operating expenses, then fixed charges, and last of all dividends. The New Haven has reversed this order. An eight percent dividend must be maintained." Coolidge was chairman of the railroad committee and after reading their speeches he tersely said, "Personally I feel that we have about exhausted the possibilities for good in a merely critical campaign."

New Haven and B. & M. stock kept falling. And the followers of Brandeis were held to blame. Brandeis told the *Transcript* that "the knockers have not brought about the reduction in market value any more than they have caused the accidents on the New Haven. The trouble is due to the New Haven methods. It's merely a matter of arithmetic, that's all. The New Haven has ignored the inexorable law of arithmetic and now it is getting the results to be expected." In a letter to Hapgood he predicted that Mellen, "obsessed with the delusion that two and two make five," would fall, at last, "a victim to the relentless rules of humble arithmetic."

The *Boston News Bureau*, by no means silent, observed in March that he was being considered as commissioner of Indian affairs:

> It is hoped that he will get this post and take his Indians from New England to Washington city. Our Puritan ancestors had to drive out the Indians from New England before they could be sure of a civilization in the New World, and their Puritan descendants, if there are enough of them left hereabouts, may have to rise a second time and drive out the Brandeis Indians before there can be any further advance in New England civilization. Fundamentally, civilization rests upon improving highways by improving business.

In April, on the resumption of the I.C.C. hearing in Boston before Commissioner Prouty, Brandeis was ready to deliver another blow to the New Haven. He had obtained permission to go through a trunkful of evidence gathered by the Commission's examiner and assigned to Eastman the task of sifting it. With the summaries Eastman provided him he was fortified to cross-examine the accountant and bring out sensational facts. Mellen was annoyed by the amount of publicity Brandeis obtained and substituted Charles F. Choate, Jr., for Vice-President Buckland as his personal attorney. Choate's strategy was to make objections and use the occasions for long speeches, thus getting equal attention and counteracting the points Brandeis publicized.

This came to light: how Billard bought the B. & M. stock held by the New Haven's subsidiary, the New England Navigation Company, for $14,850,000 with notes on the National City Bank which were unsecured; but they were liquidated by new notes of the Billard Company, secured by the B. & M. stock. Billard later resold the shares (bought at $116.50) to the Navigation Company for $150 per share, making a profit of $2,748,700 without having spent a cent of his own.

On another matter, bearing on the deceptive character of the New Haven's financial record, Brandeis showed that to conceal more than one million dollars in losses they were put on a subsidiary which made no public reports and the income was given to a company which had a deficit. He uncovered "a wonderful transmigration" of Old Colony stock, sold by the New Haven to the Navigation Company and delivered to Mellen for his personal note; nine days later the Navigation Company received the stock back from Mellen and sold it to the New Haven. Brandeis revealed that ninety-two thousand dollars of the New Haven's money was paid out to the *Boston News Bureau* in three months as advertising expense.

In the course of the hearing the Boston Fruit & Produce Exchange disowned Brandeis as its representative, but he continued to appear, with Prouty's blessing, as a citizen of Massachusetts. This meant nothing to his pocket because he had originally made the proviso to accept no compensation. Nor did he inquire who was responsible for the action, although general suspicion pinned it on Armour & Company.

"I, too, wish to appear as a citizen of Massachusetts," said Choate.

As Brandeis was demonstrating how a deficit of $7,500,000 in 1912 was transformed into a surplus of $12,500,000 by avoiding I.C.C. accounting practice, Choate put in: "That is very misleading. I——"

Brandeis: "I would like to raise a question whether we can have arguments here by Mr. Choate interrupting my examination."

When Prouty ruled that only explanations were permissible Mellen's man said, "It is explanation," and went further along.

"That seems like testimony by counsel," Brandeis said.

But Citizen Choate was equal to his part. A clash came every few minutes. And at last Brandeis asked, "Will you just give me a chance for five minutes without interrupting this examination?"

As the hearing ended pink-faced Mellen appeared as a voluntary witness. He was not sworn; that might have given him a claim of immunity in case the Department of Justice decided to prosecute him. He admitted contributing fifty thousand dollars to Republican campaign funds and being reimbursed by the New Haven, and—with hushed voice in alluding to J. P. Morgan, who had just died—told how he hesitated at paying a fancy price for the New York, Westchester & Boston Railroad but yielded to wisdom greater than his. To Prouty's suggestion that he let himself be cross-examined by Brandeis if he wished to enlighten the Commission, Mellen shook his head.

Brandeis would have made the pink face turn red. There was a new score to settle. Large advertisements signed by Mellen had recently appeared in all the Boston newspapers to discredit the New Haven's unrelenting foe. The first was entitled: "One Chapter in Brandeis's Career" and said the public ought to know his real character; he was not going to fool Commissioner Prouty—"The people of New England are asking who is the man higher up? Who will pay Mr. Brandeis for depressing New Haven stock at a cost of millions of dollars to New England stockholders? Who is behind

Brandeis? He has done this thing before." Mellen related in
the advertisement that in 1892, when he was general manager
of the New York & New England Railroad Company, Warren & Brandeis acted for Austin Corbin behind the name of
Goldsmith—the lawyer's "first appearance as a railroad
wrecker. . . . Who is the Corbin behind Mr. Brandeis's present activities?"

The second signed advertisement, "Another Chapter on
Brandeis," asserted that in many of his public appearances
some unpretentious client had been used to mask the real
party in interest; in the Ballinger case, purporting to represent a humble citizen, "he was paid by *Collier's Weekly* for
this work $30,000 as a fee with $20,000 additional for expense."

Are we not justified in suspecting in the present case
that his appearance as a private citizen is a humbug?

How much credit to be given to the evidence that
Mr. Brandeis brings out depends on whether he is seeking to elicit the truth, or to distort or suppress it. And
this may depend on whose retainer Mr. Brandeis is
holding.

He has not always represented the poor and unde-
fended.

When he was counsel for the United Shoe Machinery
Company he declared, publicly and privately, that its
business was legal, and its methods not only legal but
moral. When he was retained by the so-called "Shoe
Manufacturers' Alliance," an avowed enemy of the
United Shoe Machinery Company, he denounced that
company as an unlawful monopoly and its practices as
illegal restraints of trade.

Those who care to study Mr. Brandeis's career will
find other startling instances of the extent to which
his attitude is influenced by a retainer.

I shall still continue to inquire:

Who is the Corbin in this case?

Perhaps my grave error is that I did not retain Mr. Brandeis first.

I should recommend a long suffering public to await the submission of all evidence before giving adherence to Mr. Brandeis's view.

Inspired newspaper stories said that Brandeis' shoe machinery record was really what "threw him out of the Cabinet." A Wall Street rumor that McReynolds was going to engage him to prosecute the New Haven weakened the market, but McReynolds picked Thomas W. Gregory, a friend of Colonel House, as special assistant to investigate the system. In the oral arguments before the I.C.C. in Washington, Brandeis declared that wildcat management had ruined the road, swallowed millions and mulcted an unsuspecting public. He refused to put his name on the brief: Eastman had done all the work.

The Wilson administration fell heir to a number of antitrust cases including the shoe machinery. But the government lost its action against Winslow and other officers charged with conspiring to restrain trade when the Supreme Court ruled that the Sherman Law did not forbid the mere combining of competitors. Holmes, writing the opinion, said the organization of the United in 1899 was not in violation of the law, efficiency was the intent, monopoly was achieved only by holding patent rights, and the tying clause was not contemporaneous with combination or contemplated at the time. The case went back for trial on the single remaining indictment involving the tying clause.

Wilson was eager to introduce the reforms he had campaigned for and summoned Brandeis a week after moving into the White House. They had a long evening session together. It was Brandeis' third meeting with the champion of the New Freedom. He met the Cabinet officers and found them all anxious for good assistants, except Bryan. McAdoo sought his advice on an assistant secretary of the treasury and asked whether Edward Filene would take a customs post at Boston. McReynolds wanted his recommendation for a United States attorney for Massachusetts and an assistant attorney general for New England, but it was hard to find a good man who would be acceptable to the Democratic organization back home. Wilson called him in again for a talk on continuing the budget economy commission which ran over from the Taft administration.

In April Wilson tendered him the chairmanship of the Federal Commission on Industrial Relations. "Would you be generous enough," was the way the President expressed it.—

> There is no one in the United States who could preside over and direct such an inquiry so well as you could, and I wonder if it is possible for you to strengthen the whole thing by assuming direction of it. It would gratify me deeply if you could.

Brandeis deferred decision for a week because at that time the I.C.C. hearings were absorbing his whole attention. Then he declined. A month before, when Spreckels advised against accepting any other position after being dropped from the Cabinet list, he thought the judgment sound. Now he answered Wilson "that I ought not to accept the appointment you so kindly offered" and proposed in his stead Charles R. Van Hise, president of the University of Wisconsin. The two other members representing the public should be a sociologist and a social worker, one of them a woman. In a conference with Wilson he urged that one of the representatives of organized labor should be an I.W.W., a thought which was welcomed at first.

After consulting John Graham Brooks, Lincoln Steffens and Walter Lippmann, Brandeis favored Frank Bohn, a former instructor at Columbia University, but learned later that Bohn had resigned from the I.W.W. Frankfurter had some suggestions to make, La Follette recommended Mrs. Evans, and McAdoo wanted to know Brandeis' opinion of Frank P. Walsh of Kansas City for chairman. Wilson was weighing Van Hise and Walsh, and chose the latter. Brandeis did not propose Mrs. Evans as he had not been asked about a woman member.

Brandeis believed that the syndicalist aim of the I.W.W. was worthless from a practical point of view, but he felt the industrial unionists were exerting a valuable influence in putting the craft unions on their mettle and in promoting their growth. Also, the employers would recognize that while they could, and must, work with the A. F. of L., the I.W.W. represented in substance an irresponsible force, a menacing protest and not a helpmeet of industry. Yet in Lawrence they found waiting a piece of work that badly needed to be done, and full credit for that was no more than their due.

The question of currency reform brought Wilson to a crisis. There were difficulties with Carter Glass and Bryan, the Secretary insisting that control of the Federal Reserve System reside in the government, not in the banks. Wilson turned to Brandeis. They had a talk at the White House in which Brandeis supported Bryan's main contentions. The power to issue currency should be vested exclusively in government officials; the judgment of bankers might be biased by private interest and their function should be limited to that of an advisory council. Mere supervision by the government would not afford the public adequate protection. Although realizing the need of enacting a currency bill at an early date, Brandeis favored full and free discussion of any proposed measure as being essential to safety and confidence. Up to that time public opinion had been inspired only by the organized bankers. It would be unwise to adopt the bankers' plan on the ground that it could be passed at once to prevent panic conditions and that later the law might be modified when the public became educated to disregard the cry against the government's entering the banking business.

In a memorandum of their conversation Brandeis said the effect of immediate passage in allaying financial disturbances had been greatly exaggerated.

> The beneficent effect of the best conceivable currency bill will be relatively slight unless we are able to curb the money trust and to remove the uneasiness among businessmen due to its power. Nothing would go so far in establishing confidence among businessmen as the assurance that the Government will control the currency issues and the conviction that whatever money is available will be available for business generally, and not be subject to the control of a favored few. Any currency bill which is enacted should embody provisions framed so that the people may have some assurance that the change will enure to their benefit.

He added:

> The conflict between the policies of the Administration and the desires of the financiers and of big business is an irreconcilable one. Concessions to the big business interests must in the end prove futile. The Administration can at best have only their seeming or temporary cooperation. In essentials they must be hostile. While we must give the most careful consideration to their recommendations and avail ourselves of their expert knowledge, it is extremely dangerous to follow their advice even in a field technically their own.

The garment workers' union in New York also turned to Brandeis. He was their court of last resort under the peace protocol and controversies were brewing in abundance. The same industrial unrest which gave birth to the Federal Commission sowed dragon's teeth in the cloak trade. Shop conditions became worse and the union was torn by internal squabbles. Julius Henry Cohen, the manufacturers' attorney, described a condition of war; there was peace "on paper."

The trade was restive, waiting for the Board of Arbitration to meet.

What the union called a lockout in a shop the employers called a reorganization. The union sent its manager to Boston to plead for arbitration. Brandeis advised the use of the board of grievances; the issue should be straightened out by conciliation; arbitration should be resorted to as seldom as possible.

At last, in February, 1913, the Board of Arbitration met again—the second time since its creation. A vigorous, high-tensioned, new chief clerk for the union, Dr. Isaac A. Hourwich, who had been hailed by the East Side as the most intellectual Jew in America, fought with tooth and sharp nail. Although he won his point—that the protocol was an agreement of the manufacturers with the Joint Board of locals and not with the International Union—he asserted that the document was loosely drawn, defective in its statement of rights and principles.

There was a stoppage over a dispute in another shop, and as substitute workers were supplied during the lockout Hourwich declared that the union was being forced to act as a scab agency. He took the case to Brandeis, then in Washington, who again suggested conciliation. Hourwich demanded that the Board render a decision, but Brandeis could not be free for another month. Returning from the interview Hourwich announced to his comrades that conciliation as practiced by the board of grievances could not be successful without an impartial chairman, that Brandeis was hostile to them, and alternates should be chosen for the Board of Arbitration to make forty-eight-hour decisions possible. After the Board met in August and disapproved of the alternates plan Hourwich called Brandeis dictatorial and paternalistic. He wanted Brandeis to resign. But Meyer London, the union's attorney, persuaded the Joint Board to accept the decision.

The preferential union shop was gaining ground meanwhile in the shirtwaist and ladies' tailoring trades and, in

Boston, among the dress and waist makers, where Rose Schneiderman was the organizer. Gompers acclaimed it as a tremendous advance over the open shop. Lincoln Filene, handing out copies of the protocol like a Baptist minister with tracts, sent one to Dr. Eliot, who regarded it as "no real remedy" but a device worked out at the cost of the consumer. Eliot would never be converted to unionism despite his general openness of mind.

Although Brandeis was satisfied that the old distrust had gone, disaffection remained. Economic depression, the higher cost of living, the increase in complaints under the protocol, the recrudescence of outside contractors following the prohibition against out-of-town shops, the difficulty of fixing piece-rates, contributed to a sense of futility. Hourwich was blunt and insistent. At a Board session he said, "With all due respect to you gentlemen, I stated that our Board of Arbitration is something like the council of the Dalai-Lama of Tibet. It is too invisible. We have all the respect in the world for you gentlemen, but we have got to have a justice of the peace more often than a session of the supreme court, and unless we have it I do not see how this protocol can live."

Brandeis assumed responsibility for the infrequency of the meetings. But cases on which the board of grievances was generally deadlocked were those involving disputed questions of facts which should easily be settled by fair-minded, intelligent men. The arbitrators were to hear questions of policy and rulings as to matters of law. In respect to construction and interpretation of the protocol continuity of rulings was of paramount importance.

"You must have certainty," Brandeis said, "and you cannot have certainty unless it is practically the same body of men who are passing upon the ultimate rule to be laid down."

He recognized the right of the parties to the protocol to modify it as they saw fit. This was simply the Board's view.

Similarly in arbitration proceedings in the dress trade, where he acted as chairman, Brandeis said, "You have got to recognize that the protocol which you have made is not a final thing. It is like the Constitution of the United States or of the State of New York. It is like a good deal of our legislation. It expresses the greatest wisdom which the parties had at the time when it was drafted. But it isn't unchangeable. And just as you embodied in the protocol the best wisdom you had at the time, if experience shows that certain provisions are unwise, or if the instrument itself is inadequate in certain other respects, it is your duty to come together, consider carefully and absolutely dispassionately the facts in that respect and see what ought to be changed.

"The greatest progress will perhaps be made if all of you can give larger thought to your duties than to your rights."

But to Hourwich such abstractions were farfetched. He presented statistics as a basis for piece-rate increases (eighty percent of the men were piece-workers) and although the figures did not give a clear picture of earnings and the extent of employment, the Board granted a rise. Brandeis found the industry barren of adequate data and inspired a statistical investigation which was carried on by Walter E. Weyl, an editor of *The New Republic*. (Weyl succeeded to the ailing Hillquit's place on the Board.) Brandeis' suggestion that the industry seek some means of regularizing employment met with skepticism.

Hourwich bustled about, attacking the International Union as a machine and writing articles subverting faith in the protocol. His exacting nature was offensive to the Manufacturers' Protective Association, which insisted on dealing with the International only. But he had the following of the workers and managed to make each issue a personal one. The refusal of the Protective to sit down with Hourwich on the determination of grievances brought an impasse. Weyl understood he was going about discrediting the statistical study and charging that the figures had been doctored and reached in collusion with the Protective.

In Brandeis' private opinion Hourwich was an inveterate

trouble-maker. There would be no peace so long as he remained.

The acrimonious recriminations which beset the garment industry did not make Brandeis regret this contact with his fellow-Jews. The year 1913 in fact intensified his interest in the people with whom he at last identified himself. Although he had always been responsive to Jewish philanthropies and relief appeals, things intrinsically Jewish seemed foreign. The colonization of Palestine, which he read about in a magazine article while in Milwaukee in 1898, struck him as a plausible idea, but it touched no spiritual springs. He had not come under the influence of Uncle Lewis, who was learned in Jewish lore and an authority on certain phases of Jewish scholarship, because his uncle did not take up these studies until late in life. In Chicago in 1912 at a lecture on agriculture to which Crane had taken him, he met Aaron Aaronsohn, the discoverer of wild wheat, newly arrived from Palestine to develop an interest in dry farming. This young man possessed one of the finest minds he had ever encountered and unconsciously planted a seed of another culture. From a detached interest in the pioneer work of wrestling fertility from arid soil Brandeis grew into a staunch belief that the dream of a Jewish national state must be realized to give full effect to the social vision of his people.

Aaronsohn seemed to be more interested in Palestine than in Zionism. Later in the year Brandeis invited him to his house; Dr. Eliot and a few others were asked to meet him. The guests were thrilled and Brandeis beamed. But it was not wild wheat, it was Jacob de Haas, that drew him into Zionism.

On the day de Haas first came to him with a suggestion to make savings bank insurance enticing to the readers of the *Jewish Advocate* by introducing the idea of dowry and college tuition endowments, de Haas asked if Lewis Dembitz was Brandeis' relative. The nephew then learned of the esteem with which his uncle was held in the world of Zion-

ism, and from this it was a short step to the story of Theodore
Herzl, founder of the movement, which de Haas recounted
in further instalments many an evening. Prompted by this
fascinating talker, Brandeis read a great deal of Zionist literature and studied the implications.

In March, 1913, Brandeis made his first public confession
of Zionism at a reception at Plymouth Theatre, Boston, to
Nahum Sokolow of Warsaw, who was touring the country
for the cause. Brandeis presided at the reception and spoke
with brevity extraordinary in a convert. He seemed exalted
as he looked toward the eternal horizon—"the ideal of the
Jew for centuries—social righteousness, the war against
iniquity, relief for the burdens of the oppressed, and the lessening of the toil of the poor." The enthusiasm with which
Boston Jewry greeted his adherence was matched by the in-
credulity of his relatives in Louisville.

In April he sent one hundred dollars to the Federation of
American Zionists for its propaganda fund, joined the Zionist
Association of Greater Boston and the Menorah Society, and
became a member of the Hebrew Sheltering & Immigrant
Aid Society's advisory board. In May he spoke in Temple
Israel in Boston for the Federation of Jewish Charities as a
substitute for Edward Filene, and again at the Chelsea Young
Men's Hebrew Association. In August the Massachusetts
delegates to the Zionist Congress in Vienna pledged themselves to propose his name for the leadership of the world
organization.

He gave Sokolow a letter of introduction to Secretary
Bryan and urged Hapgood to get an article from Aaronsohn
on the high idealism developed by Zionism. The summer
vacation was spent at South Yarmouth; he could not attend
the Vienna congress with Sokolow but made suggestions for
his fellow-Zionists to consider. Palestine should be opened up
to the masses, large tracts of land should be obtained with
concessions from the Turkish government to assure freedom
of movement and security for investments necessary to the

development of the land. "While we need the land we need at the same time a large immigration of our people into Palestine. Numbers are necessary to rendering our position secure." He eagerly supported Sokolow's proposal for an American corporation to undertake the industrial development of Palestine. He was ready to contribute financial support and yet the thought that moved him was: "The greatest happiness in life is not to donate but to serve."

Chapter XIII

WASHINGTON AND THE HOUSE OF MORGAN

THE GREATER his stature, the more insidiously Brandeis' opponents tried to lay his reputation low. They had beaten him on the New Haven in Massachusetts, but he hit back through the Interstate Commerce Commission. They had succeeded in barring him from the Cabinet but not from the councils of the administration. There always remained the weapon of abuse. Supplementing the work which Barron hugely enjoyed and the performance of the *Boston Herald* (controlled by the United Shoe-New Haven group), a weekly magazine was started in Boston expressly to lampoon Brandeis. They called it *Truth*. A cartoonist artfully endowed Brandeis with mock-sanctity and adorned him with a halo. He was depicted also as a masked highwayman, stealing railroad stock and passing it on to a fellow-blackguard labelled, "New York Banking Interests." Another cartoon showed him receiving money from Jacob H. Schiff, the caption reading: "Master and Man." *Truth* linked the names Rothschild-Schiff-Untermyer-Brandeis in an Oriental plot for world domination.

Elbert Hubbard, whose pen had been used by the railroads in the ten percent advance rate propaganda, published in *The Philistine* an article echoing the lying lines of the Lennox and Warren attacks to prove him "a double-crosser like Judas Iscariot . . . by birth, education and parental tendency Brandeis represents the type of which Emma Goldman is our most distinguished example." He was compared with Gompers, Lefty Louie, Gyp the Blood—"all represent one common and particular type of mind." To well-wishers who resented the slanders Brandeis said he was inclined to think the best thing they could do about it was not to read *The Philistine*.

For Hapgood's first issue of *Harper's Weekly* he wrote an article on "The Failure of Banker-Management" (and returned a check for one hundred dollars because he did not want to take any pay for his writings until the magazine was on a dividend-paying basis.) Wherein lay the failure of banker-management? In the fact that a banker making loans to a corporation in which he was a director acted as his own client and passed judgment on himself. For a flagrant example, see the New Haven. There Morgan's will was law. Mellen had told the I.C.C. of having yielded to Morgan but "indeed, I don't know that it would have made much difference whether I yielded or not." Said Brandeis in *Harper's:*

> When a banker-director of a railroad decides as a railroad man that it shall issue securities, fixing the price at which they are to be taken, there is necessarily grave danger that the interests of the railroad may suffer—suffer both through issuing of securities which ought not to be issued and from selling them at a price less favorable to the company than should have been obtained.

Mellen resigned as president of the B. & M. in July, 1913, ostensibly to concentrate his energies on the New Haven. A stockholders' committee was organized to prevent further declines in New Haven stock and possible receivership, so that it seemed Kidder-Peabody was ranged against the Morgan-Mellen side. The *Transcript* turned against monopoly and the *Springfield Republican* spoke of "the fictitious appearance of financial strength." Although Commissioner Prouty's report for the I.C.C. saw in the financial status "no occasion for hysteria" it found demoralization, waste, and justification for the complaints against traffic conditions. "Had the stockholders of the New Haven, instead of vilifying the road's critics, given some attention to the charges made, their property today would be of great value and the problem would be an easier one." If the monopoly was to remain, Prouty held, there must be a power of regulation coextensive with the power of the monopoly. Brandeis was sorry over this conditional approval and urged La Follette to declaim in his weekly against attempting to make the situation tolerable by regulation. He conferred with Gregory (introduced by McAdoo's visiting card) and proposed dissolution into such units as would make New England transportation facilities easily financed and easily managed. "I am an optimist," he said.

Ten days after leaving the B. & M. Mellen quit the New Haven. To Brandeis, who had written his epitaph two years before, it meant that the Morgan scapegoat was sick of his part. To the head of the Travelers' Insurance Company, which owned New Haven stock, it meant that Mellen was "Brandeised" to death. *La Follette's Weekly* said: "The passing of Mellen is of no consequence. He was merely the agent of Morgan in the execution of plans operated on all of the big systems," and "With all competition suppressed no amount of government control, short of ownership itself, can make railroad monopoly a thing to be tolerated." It said that the Boston insurgents, led by Brandeis, had not been silenced by the specious plea that "this is an era of consolidation," that "the day of small things is past," that "monopoly means economy" and "competition means waste," that "the law should sanction monopoly and then regulate it." McReynolds and Gregory came to Boston.

The New Haven planned yet another bond issue through J. P. Morgan & Company— this time $67,000,000 of six percent debentures—subject to the approval of the Public Service Commission. Brandeis objected on the ground that the road could easily raise money to meet maturing notes by selling the securities of its affiliates. He also called for an itemized account for lobbying and publicity. He had a friend on the Commission, George W. Anderson, of the Public Franchise League. At a hearing it was charged that the stock-holders' protective committee was sheer humbug, the committee having been placated by the promise of a share in the $1,600,000 fee which J. P. Morgan, Jr., was to get for underwriting the issue. Lee-Higginson and Kidder-Peabody were both to participate.

Over the dissenting vote of Anderson the Public Service Commission allowed the new bond issue, but disclosures of payments made by the New Haven to the *Boston News Bureau* and State House reporters for "services, etc." requited the setback. It was shown that Barron's man covered the capitol also for the Associated Press, and on the payroll was Professor Bruce Wyman, who taught railroad regulation at Harvard Law School and lectured on railroad problems before trade groups throughout New England. The professor resigned. Further wrecks and deaths on the line shook public opinion more vigorously. A single wreck cost more than the thousands of dollars disbursed to cultivate that opinion.

Mellen, disconsolate, unbosomed himself. Thrown out, he said, as a sacrifice to public clamor, he wanted the world to understand the handicap he had labored under. Morgan, Sr., he told the *Boston Post*, had been absolute boss of the road. "I had no more to do with the financial policy of the New Haven than I had to do with the editorial policy of the *Post*."

New Haven stock fell to 71 ¾ and the dividend was passed. B. & M. fell to 44. Hundreds of Baptist ministers united in prayer in Tremont Temple for the widows and orphans.

Truth burst with the news that the new power in New England railroad finance was Schiff, the head of Kuhn, Loeb & Company, American representative of the Rothschilds, and "Brandeis' employer." As Samuel Untermyer was said to have been employed by Schiff to fight the so-called money trust in Washington, so Brandeis was the Untermyer of Boston, employed to destroy, "sailing under false colors—posing as the friend of the people, an eleemosynary advocate of the Common Good." The New England railroad fight was simply a part of a world movement—"the age-old struggle for supremacy between Jew and Gentile."

Another ominous rumbling came from Taft. He appealed to New Englanders to save the New Haven from destruction.

Untermyer had done admirable work as counsel for the Pujo committee, and most of its recommendations were commendable, but in some respects they were woefully inadequate and Brandeis felt that the committee should continue in action. There were meetings of the two lawyers and rumors about their acting together in a further investigation. Brandeis was disinclined. While preparing a series of articles for *Harper's* on "Breaking the Money Trust" he saw Untermyer again. He applied for information to various people, including McAdoo. Rublee worked with him, checking up facts and proofreading. With the accumulated data Brandeis planned also to draft new bills on trusts.

If there was any doubt that he considered J. P. Morgan & Company the nemesis of American business life and industrial liberty it was dispelled by his series in Hapgood's *Harper's*. In these articles he interpreted the findings of the Pujo committee and repeatedly cited Morgan in demonstrating how investment bankers dominated railroads, insurance companies, industrial corporations, banks and trust companies; how they controlled the nation's quick capital and rose to imperial power. Morgan, sitting in the middle of a spiderweb of interlocking directorates, made money with other people's money. With each transaction Morgan's power waxed. "The fetters which bind the people are forged from the people's own gold."

These banking magnates and their satellites, such as Lee-Higginson and Kidder-Peabody, tightened the concentration of power into a few hands. By their grip on credit they crushed competition, blighted small businessmen, and steadily strengthened their dictatorial might. The process was often simple. Morgan would buy securities of controlled corporations without expending anything of his own because he was their bank of deposit. The Armstrong insurance legislation in New York was circumvented neatly: the companies, ordered to sell their bank stock, sold it to Morgan associates, with the result that the direction of control was merely reversed.

Brandeis wrote of "the fatal entrance of Mr. Morgan" into the management of the once prosperous New Haven. "Was there ever a more be-bankered railroad than the New Haven?" New England's leading banking houses, instead of warning the public of impending disaster or protesting against continuous mismanagement, readily cooperated by taking generous commissions for marketing an endless supply of new securities. "Were these bankers blind? Or were they afraid to oppose the will of J. P. Morgan & Company?"

He showed that Morgan's statement, giving bankers credit for initiating economic development, was "entirely unfounded in fact." He told how bankers could be eliminated; he praised credit unions and cooperatives, pointed out that cities and towns could get together and make the state their common banker. The way to break the Money Trust was to attack its source of power, the industrial trusts. "Size, we are told, is not a crime. But size may, at least, become noxious by reason of the means through which it was attained or the uses to which it is put. And it is size attained by combination, instead of natural growth, which has contributed so largely to our financial concentration."

Wilson read these articles carefully, made marginal scorings, and preserved them. Later they appeared in book form under the title of *Other People's Money*. (The royalties were assigned to the magazine, which Brandeis otherwise helped by donating subscriptions to several hundred public libraries in New England.) The book opened with a quotation from a Wilson speech, abounded in references to Wilson's ideal, the New Freedom, and closed with another quotation from the President.

In Washington the main interest in Brandeis' summary of the Pujo investigation lay in his conclusion that the committee's recommendations would fail to break the Morgan vise. A comprehensive prohibition of interlocking directorates was essential to a realization of the New Freedom. Brandeis believed that Congress should reach into the states and by virtue of its regulation of the mails and the taxing power stop any business deemed by Congress to be injurious to the public welfare.

There must be a complete separation of industries from railroads and other utilities. He proposed amendments to the Hepburn railroad act to prohibit roads from owning stock in corporations whose products they transported, and vice versa. "But restrictive legislation alone will not suffice." Publicity must be used as a continuous remedial measure to free investors from the servility of their ignorance and expose the extent to which securities bought from bankers were diluted by excessive underwritings, commissions and profits.

With the decentralization of the Money Trust's power the emancipated smaller units would find no difficulty in financing their needs "without bending the knee to money lords. And a long step will have been taken toward the attainment of the New Freedom." Finally, when businessmen learned from farmers and workingmen the lesson of cooperatives "money kings will lose subjects and swollen fortunes may shrink, but industries will flourish, because the faculties of men will be liberated and developed." The New Freedom!

Wilson, goaded by Bryan, agreed to give anti-trust reform his next consideration after the currency question was out of the way. Early in 1914 he used Congressman Clayton as his intermediary and a message was sent to both houses to crystallize support. Among the Clayton bills one provided for a federal trade commission. The House interstate commerce committee quickly held a hearing on it and summoned Brandeis as the first witness. A variety of opinions obtained on the proper functions of such a commission. Clayton favored an investigating body which could present formal findings to the Department of Justice. Senator Newlands pressed for a quasi-judicial body to pass on reorganization plans of trusts. Untermyer and the National Civic Federation urged the power to approve trade agreements as to price and production. Wilson wanted a commission to serve as an auxiliary to the courts, a bureau of information without the power to grant immunity or regulate business.

Brandeis agreed with the underlying purpose of the bill as recommended by the President, but said he had not had time to study the measure. This much was needed: an administrative board to obtain a comprehensive knowledge of the details of business operations and to expose methods of destructive competition.

> The mere substitution of knowledge for ignorance, publicity for secrecy, will go far toward preventing monopoly. . . .
> The first essential of wise and just action is knowledge. And as a means of obtaining this knowledge we should secure uniform accounting. It was, as I remember, the great Colbert who said, "Accountancy—that is government."

The extraordinary diversity in accounting methods of railroads had been a stumbling block to the I.C.C. for twenty years. Facts must be ascertained comparatively. The ability to compare was a prerequisite to advance. The very basis of business was the determination of the cost of doing the business. The inequality between great corporations and small competitors would be lessened by the educational work which the trade commission could perform. Industrial business stood in no different position than railroading. There were no secrets in farming. The availability of medical knowledge did not prevent physicians from competing with one another, and in the practice of law the statute books and court decisions were open to all. To disseminate information on the best way to manufacture an article was a proper function of government in a democracy. "Why shouldn't we give the manufacturer or merchant a common-school education or, indeed, a university education in the business he wishes to pursue?"

Moreover, trade information would help the Department of Justice to deal intelligently with the intricate commercial problems involved in administering the Sherman Law.

At this time James H. Curley, newly elected mayor of Boston, tried to get him to take the office of city auditor. The municipal auditing system was antiquated, and Curley could use him for six months to clean it up.

Speaking of systems, Brandeis believed that industrial crime was not a cause but an effect; the effect of a bad system. If a good one were adopted there would be less industrial criminality. And this was the crux of the trust problem—instead of trying to deter corporations with punishment, why not prevent the rise of conditions leading to violations? The important thing in legislation was to prescribe the rule which would prevent, rather than punish, breaches of the law. The proposed federal trade commission could use the friendly powers instead of the hostile powers of the government to secure compliance with good trade practices.

The views which he and Wilson held on anti-trust legislation he expressed again at a convention of the Chamber of Commerce of the United States. The Chamber was antagonistic to the President's program. Big business was trying to scuttle it.

In Congress there was uncertainty and confusion on how best to frame the new laws; how far to go. The House interstate commerce committee abandoned its efforts, and work was started anew. The House judiciary committee (Clayton, chairman) called in Brandeis. He opened by giving unqualified approval to Wilson's recommendations, which included redress for injured competitors and definitions of undue restraints. Then he offered changes in the phraseology of Clayton's anti-trust bill to accord with the La Follette-Lenroot bill and suggested a section to cover the situation created by the United Shoe Machinery Company. The committee gave him a whole day and he delved into his trust experience—the tobacco case, the New Haven, and others, the overweening power of Morgan, the finality of Morgan, "the exaggerated respect for the correctness of his judgment."

> My objection to interlocking directorates is not on the assumption that men mean to do wrong. It is because it is humanly impossible for a man representing conflicting interests on two boards to do right by both, no matter how pure his purpose is.

Later the committee gave him another morning to explore this subject. "The greatest objection to this scheme of interlocking directorates," he said "is that by virtue of it it has become possible for a few men, like J. P. Morgan & Company, to acquire extraordinary power." Representative George S. Graham of Pennsylvania asked him on what theory Congress could legislate in regard to divorcing state banks from their industrial associations. Brandeis said there were several: "One possible theory is—although it has not yet been sustained by the Supreme Court—that banking is interstate commerce. It seems to me that it is, but that has not yet been adjudicated by the court and whether it is or not we do not know." His own opinion was that "the Supreme Court will eventually so hold when the question is put up to them." Graham thought the movement to expand the meaning of interstate commerce was a great mistake. He could not agree with Brandeis that a bank was as much an instrumentality of interstate commerce as a railroad, whereas Brandeis contended that every bank, including the smallest local institution, was being used as a means of conducting commerce between the states.

"I can feel no doubt in my own mind that the evils which we have suffered from the concentration of financial power would justify the exercise of any of these constitutional powers," he said.

It was not comfortable for the United to be used by Brandeis as an illustration of his points, so the company dispatched a letter to Clayton to expose the sinister purpose of this man who was posing as a public-spirited citizen; the very audacity of Brandeis' statements might naturally lead the committee to believe that his word could be relied upon, but it was for them to judge "whether he misrepresents intentionally or is merely careless of his facts." Clayton must not be blinded to the fact that Brandeis was counsel for a group of manufacturers who were attacking the United. The company pretended that he had helped draft the leases he was then opposing and had been retained by the other side "shortly after leaving our employ." His motives were "sordid and mercenary, as those who are most familiar with his professional record believe."

The anti-trust bills were riding a rocky road in Congress, and the lack of progress, coupled with stories trickling out of the White House, caused talk that Wilson was receding from his stand for New Freedom legislation. Brandeis went to see him. He found that the President simply had too much work to be able to keep track of everything and reported to his friends that Wilson was "all that we thought he was." Rublee got to work with Representative Raymond B. Stevens of New Hampshire, whom Brandeis had met in Manchester on the B. & M. matter, and devised a plan whereby the federal trade commission could issue cease-and-desist orders against unfair methods of competition. Brandeis at first was noncommittal; he let them work it out. Then he endorsed it and took it to Wilson, who publicly declared his approval. Congress followed suit.

When the Clayton bill came up in the Senate for debate Senator John W. Weeks of Massachusetts stepped up to defend the United's leasing system as a boon to small manufacturers. He charged this man Brandeis, instrumental in shaping the bill, with having been the very one to draw up the tying clause. The Clayton bill passed. Among the unlawful practices it defined were tying clauses whose effect was to lessen competition or create a monopoly. The measure had been called an omnibus bill but some of the passengers were half-awake (interlocking directorates were prohibited only in competing corporations) and some rightful occupants were crowded out (such as the section enabling victims to collect damages from monopolies). Brandeis accepted the partial victory philosophically.

In another phase of his rôle as unofficial adviser to Congress he objected to the form in which the Rayburn bill, passed by the House, embodied Wilson's proposal to regulate railroad securities. This bill authorized the I.C.C. to pass upon all future issues. Brandeis held up Senate action, although Senate leaders were in a hurry to carry through this part of the President's program, by demonstrating to its interstate commerce committee that approval of securities might be understood by the public as a government stamp on their soundness; such a grant of power should be deferred until the completion of the physical valuation of railroads which was then under way. The carriers favored the bill because approval would make their securities more marketable and jurisdiction would be taken from state railroad commissions. The I.C.C. would have to pass on about one thousand separate issues a year and become so overburdened with work as to function improperly, court discredit, and break the back of government supervision.

With Rublee he instructed the Senators in railroad economics. He offered an amendment to forbid carriers engaged in non-carrier business to issue securities except for the improvement of their railroad property. This was intended to curb the roads' ambition to go into coal mining, the hotel business, and other distractions. They must also be prevented from acquiring stock in other lines even for the extension of their system except after public notice of intention and after conditional approval of the I.C.C.

> We must keep in thought why we want these securities passed upon. The two chief evils to be corrected are expenditure of money by roads for purposes other than railroading and the unwise acquirement of other railroad properties. My bill prohibits the former and requires the commission to pass upon the latter. The roads should be permitted to raise money as they need it for legitimate purposes, without interference. . . .

The Senate committee listened, made a few concessions, but left too many loopholes. Brandeis next called on Wilson with Senator Hollis of New Hampshire and convinced the President that the bill as it stood would place the government in a position of practically guaranteeing railroad stock issues. Wilson accepted his substitute. But it came to nought. Action was deferred and, later in the year, numerous railroad defaults and consideration of the next year's maturities led the President to suggest to Congress abandonment of the effort.

However, there was activity in the New Haven sector in 1914. After Mellen's resignation Attorney General McReynolds negotiated with the new management for dissolution by consent instead of by suit. This did not pacify Senator Norris; he demanded a new investigation of the monopoly's financial deals. Impatiently he called for McReynolds to announce the status of the negotiations and he accused McReynolds of laxity. The Attorney General resented his interference, and Lodge, Weeks and other New England senators tried to quiet him. Taft made a speech deploring the severity of politicians and demagogues. But Norris was not a man to be hushed when he believed "a lot of pirates" had stolen millions of dollars from the stockholders. He did not oppose reorganization but he demanded punishment of guilty officials.

McReynolds enjoyed no peace. He went to Wilson and tried to convince him that Mellen would gain immunity if made to testify before the I.C.C. But the President supported the investigation ordered on Norris' resolution.

Billard, first witness, told of the help he got from Mellen, the New Haven, and the National City Bank; of the financial assistance which the Billard Company gave the *Boston Herald*. Then Vice-President Byrnes was asked to explain a $381 voucher "for 15,000 prayers."

"What did the New Haven want with fifteen thousand prayers?" the commission's counsel asked.

"It probably needed more than that," Byrnes said.

"This purports to be 'prayers from the hills.'"

Byrnes explained that the references was to a civic body, the Hilltown Association, whose support was sought against the separation of trolley lines from the railroad.

Then came Mellen for four days.

"After I get through there will be no feathers sticking to my claws," he said.

"There are many things I do not want to tell, but I am determined that I shall not be held responsible for things for which I was not responsible."

He told how he ventured to ask Morgan about the item of eleven million dollars spent for the Boston & Westchester. "Well, it was in the midst of the panic of 1907. Mr. Morgan was abrupt. I was humiliated by his words."

"What did Mr. Morgan say?"

"Mr. Morgan is dead. I was humiliated at the time. It was a humiliating scene. I would rather not repeat what he said. Suffice it to say that I received no information from him. I felt very badly, very cross. He was weighted down with probably more responsibility than any man in the world, more than the President of the United States."

Mellen said he was entitled to know "more about this and this . . . but I didn't learn anything. Mr. Morgan told me nothing."

He did not fear Morgan; he respected him. Pinned down, Mellen admitted he was too much of a coward to press Morgan for facts. Items went through meetings of the board of directors without discussion. After one meeting a director said to Mellen, "You've been flying pretty high, haven't you, spending eleven million dollars." Mellen replied that he knew as little about it as the other fellow. The director egged him to find out.

"I said, 'Here, Hemingway, I appoint you a committee of one to go to Morgan and get the information.' He threw up his hands."

The Boston & Westchester deal was put through by Tammany, Mellen testified; the necessary changes were made in the franchise by giving a police inspector $1,200,000 worth of due-bills to put in the hands of city officials.

The B. & M. deal, he said, was first suggested to him by a member of Lee, Higginson & Company. Mellen talked it over with his friend, President Roosevelt. "Roosevelt told me, as nearly as I can recall, that he was not a lawyer and he could not assure me that it was not in violation of the law, but that if there were no legal questions involved he, in my place, would be disposed to acquire the shares."

Mellen understood that Harriman also wanted the B. & M. "I called him the bogy man. I wanted the B. & M. and I used him as he used me."

He said Roosevelt had urged him not to sell the steamship lines because they might have fallen into the hands of Charles W. Morse, the deep-sea monopolist (later imprisoned) and Mellen thought that because of this advice no reference to steamships was made in Bonaparte's dissolution suit.

Trolley lines, he continued, would be purchased on a telephone order from Morgan. The New York law obtained by Governor Hughes required the Mutual Life Insurance Company to divest itself of the Worcester, Nashua & Rochester trolley line; Morgan of the Mutual sold it to Morgan of the New Haven.

Stockholders' meeting never discussed policies, Mellen said. He would have to get up and make speeches to fill in the time. Barely one hundred of the twenty-three thousand stockholders ever attended. "They are like sheep. While dividends come they are content to browse. When trouble comes they are still like sheep—all rush for the same hole in the fence and injure themselves trying to get out."

In the course of this hearing McReynolds was condemned by the *New York World* for inaction in criminal prosecution, *La Follette's Weekly* criticized him for not having dug up the facts unearthed by the I.C.C., and the *Boston American* called for his dismissal. Wilson had a talk with him. McReynolds then announced that he was ready to proceed with criminal actions against those responsible for the demoralization of the road. In the *New York American* the observation was made by B. C. Forbes that "the embittered Attorney General's belated activity" was intended to get a court ruling on whether the questioning of Mellen won him immunity.

McReynolds had originally planned, with Wilson's approval, on a board of trustees to take over the B. & M. stock and dispose of it judiciously. Brandeis was invited to serve as a trustee, but pleaded pressure of business. The government had to get the sanction of the Massachusetts legislature for this plan, and Coolidge, as president of the state Senate, read a protest sent in by New Haven directors. Coolidge mustered only four opposing votes but in the end, since the company rejected the arrangement, McReynolds filed a suit in equity under the Sherman Law for dissolution.

Next, the I.C.C. rendered its report. The directors of the road were criminally negligent in squandering funds to monopolize New England transportation. The downfall of the B. & M. was attributed to the Morgan and Rockefeller interests. The purchase of trolleys, steamships and the Boston & Westchester line was held a crime. Millions were made at the expense of the water thus added. The stockholders had lost $65,871,299. The Billard deal was a fraud. This, said

the Commission, was one of the worst instances of malad-
ministration in railroad history. New Haven stock fell below
50.

The management at last yielded to the government's insistence on dissolution. The civil suit was ended. The B. &
M. stock was trusteed. When a federal grand jury was im-
panelled in the criminal suit, of course Mellen claimed immunity, and while the jury named him as a conspirator he
was not indicted. Indictments were handed up against twenty
others.

Brandeis observed that the New Haven was on the right
track at last. He praised its new president for going about
his work "in the old-fashioned, frugally thrifty New England spirit" and bade stockholders to have patience. During
the long fight it was he who had been patient and persistent,
and everybody learned—friends and enemies alike—that Brandeis never gave up anything he started.

He was entitled to chuckle at the review of his book in
the *New York Times* which said he had not proved the misuse of bankers' vast power over other people's money. The
leading private banker (the review did not mention Morgan's
name once) could not possibly issue bad securities and defraud the public without being discovered; the harm done
was theoretical—"there being no complainants in court except the professional theorists." And, "It is safe to say that
those who avoided the security issues of the Money Trust
fared worse than those who followed their advice." The
Boston Evening Transcript treated his book in a mock-serious
vein; the bogy of the Money Trust interrupted Brandeis'
dreams and tortured his imagination: "He sees it everywhere.
His industrial world is filled with bankers and business men
hard at work robbing and despoiling rich and poor alike."
The sale of the book was not phenomenal.

A work of that type was like a seed catalog: the ideas
would always be available for someone's planting. Brandeis'
confidence in the progression of sowing and reaping showed

itself in a serene smile of optimism. He was happiest when a
good man reached a position of influence. Gregory, Anderson and Eastman were of that calibre. Wilson's nomination
of McReynolds to the Supreme Court when Mr. Justice
Lurton died was confirmed over the opposition of Norris
and other senators; Colonel House had advised the move to
make room for his friend Gregory. When Brandeis heard that
Anderson was being considered as district attorney for Massachusetts he told Gregory that the appointment would reflect
great credit on the administration. Congressmen from Massachusetts objected to Anderson, despite his having been nominated twice by the Democratic Party for state's attorney general, but Gregory was familiar with his excellent record and
appointed him.

When Anderson's place on the Public Service Commission was given to Eastman, Brandeis congratulated Governor
David I. Walsh and urged his magazine friends to publish
commendations, for the success of government regulation of
utilities would depend largely on the character of the men
named to the various commissions.

For the same reason he recommended Joseph P. Cotton
to Colonel House as suitable for the Federal Trade Commission. He asked Hapgood to write something by way of
introducing Eastman to the country. Only thirty-three years
old, getting a good salary, Eastman ought to be an encouragement to other young men seeking a career in public service.
Frankfurter was appointed professor of law at Harvard,
thanks to a contribution by Felix M. Warburg and Paul Warburg; and Dean Thayer acknowledged that gratitude was
owing to Brandeis.

He had tried, just before the I.C.C. investigation of the
New Haven, to get a place on the Commission for David
Ives, who knew so much about the situation. He worked
through Secretary McAdoo, Secretary Franklin K. Lane,
Senator Hollis and Representative Stevens. Wilson promised
"most earnest consideration" if a vacancy occurred. But Ives

was too well hated and could not survive the reputation which *Truth* and others gave him.

When the Commerce Court was about to be abolished, Brandeis felt it would be a calamity to lose Judge Julian W. Mack from public service and sought a new post for him. Mack was kept on the Circuit Court.

Nor was Brandeis unmindful of the duties of friendship. When he learned that Marlen Pew was in trouble with a political crew in Philadelphia managed by Boies Penrose, he did not wait to be asked. Pew was editing the *News-Post* in Philadelphia for Scripps-McRae and had been arrested in criminal libel suits for attacking the politicians. Brandeis left Washington for Philadelphia, called Pew to his hotel room, carefully went over the details and assured him he had nothing to worry about; they were bluff suits.

Chapter XIV

LIBERAL OR CONSERVATIVE?

BOTH friends and enemies had difficulty labeling Brandeis either as a liberal or a conservative. Some critics thought of him as the arch-enemy of the established order, and one wrote an anonymous letter saying, "You ought to be shot." On the other side of the firing line were people looking to a new order, their concept of justice wrapped up in some dogma, or their point of view sharpened by self-interest, who considered him a false messiah. A man who was not a doctrinaire had to make the best of being caught between opposite doctrines.

Brandeis was not bothered by his lack of a classification. Joseph Fels, the Single Tax advocate, believed he was wasting time with "philanthropically palliative work" and wanted him to fight for "actual basic reforms" such as the abolition of tariff, franchise and land monopoly privileges. Brandeis strongly approved of nationalization of land but he was certain this step would not bring the millennium. Moreover, to exaggerate the effectiveness of the Single Tax or any other remedy meant throwing discredit on arguments offered in favor of that remedy.

As for franchises, Brandeis thought charters should confer on cities the right of municipal ownership of public utilities; but when and to what extent the right should be exercised was a matter for consideration in the particular place, at the particular time, and with respect to the particular utility.

He went to New York for a wage-arbitration hearing for railroad firemen and found the arbitrators ignoring the principle of efficiency. If firemen could be educated not to waste coal the resultant saving of fifty million dollars a year would provide the money for wage increases and the necessity to discharge men might be avoided. Labor still suspected that scientific management was a disguise for the speed-up process. Machinists in the Boston Navy Yard cheered Franklin D. Roosevelt, Assistant Secretary of the Navy, for declaring his stand against "the Taylor system." Yet, figures issued by General Goethals on the operating costs of government railroads in the Panama Canal Zone showed that under scientific management in the past two years the government had succeeded in running them more cheaply and efficiently than any of the privately owned railroads were run in this country.

The characteristic in which Brandeis differed from most progressives in public life was the dispassion of his advocacy. A situation, not a philosophy, sent him into action. On another chore for the Wilson administration he again demonstrated his freedom from partisanship. And again he was misunderstood.

The Interstate Commerce Commission invited him to serve as its counsel in an investigation into the reasonableness of the five percent horizontal freight-rate advance which fifty Eastern railroads filed on the plea of the lowered purchasing power of the dollar. His first answer was no; it would embarrass the commission and himself to act in this official capacity because the roads would feel, in view of his opposition in the ten percent case, that the hearing would not be impartial.

Commissioner James S. Harlan, who had known Brandeis as a boy in Louisville, wrote that he had been instructed to take charge and see whether Brandeis would "undertake the task of seeing that all sides and angles of the case are presented of record, without advocating any particular theory for its disposition." On other occasions the I.C.C. had used special counsel in order to be advised of all the facts lest the issue be decided on a record made up largely in one interest. "You will be expected to emphasize any aspect of the case which in your judgment . . . may require emphasis," Harlan wrote. His own feeling was that Brandeis' participation would give the public at large assurance that the case would be fully presented.

His function being clearly set down, Brandeis accepted. This was in the summer of 1913. Harlan publicly announced that individual shippers were ill-equipped to enter the controversy and while some might have their own attorneys Brandeis would be the general channel through whom the views of the opposition might flow. The impression thus came about that this lone David was to stand against the titans of the railroad world.

A sample of the reception he received in the fearful press was an article in another of Elbert Hubbard's nicely printed magazines, *The Fra*, recalling with ridicule Brandeis' plan for saving a million dollars a day. Harlan reiterated that the commission had not retained him to advance or support any special theory, and just after the hearing opened in the fall Commissioner Edgar E. Clark made it explicit that Brandeis was not employed as an advocate for either side but to assist in analyzing the general question underlying the railroads' proposal.

Chief among the attorneys for the shippers was Clifford Thorne of Iowa, who had been on the same side of the table with Brandeis in the ten percent case. He represented his state's railroad commission and six other Mississippi Valley states. On behalf of two hundred thousand farmers and grain dealers he refuted the roads' contentions that their net revenues were steadily declining, that they were unable to maintain their properties, that their credit was seriously impaired and money for improvements was unobtainable. The carriers argued also that higher wages and the increased cost of materials and of new capital necessitated the advance.

"This case is very analogous to the one tried in 1910," said Thorne, professing that he would like to consider it, "as my brilliant Boston friend did in 1910, merely a friendly investigation as to expediency. It is true that on many, many matters the interests of the railroads and the people are absolutely in common," but this was primarily a contest between the roads and the consumers, he said.

Brandeis stated his position in his brief:

> Though a general need of greater revenues be shown, it seems clear that it should be provided in ways other than through the tariffs filed. The alleged horizontal increase would intensify existing injustice and discrimination in rates. It would give additional revenues where relief is not needed and would fail to give adequate revenues to carriers who are most in need of relief. It would burden some traffic already extremely remunerative to the carriers and exempt from contribution other which is unremunerative. The prosperous coal-carrying roads would have their revenues largely increased. Other roads, less prosperous, having a large passenger traffic, would get a much smaller addition to their revenues.

With the assistance of I.C.C. experts the facts which Brandeis thought pertinent were developed. He was able to fill the record with evidence that revenues could be increased by eliminating free services to favored interests and stopping other wastes.

But Thorne was disappointed and angry. On the day before arguments were to be made he learned indirectly that Brandeis was going to take a position at variance with his own. He regarded this as a betrayal.

The first sentence of Brandeis' address, following Thorne's argument, brought a chortle of glee from the railroad side and sorely discomfited Thorne. Brandeis maintained "that on the whole, the net income, the net operating revenues of the carriers in Official Classification Territory are smaller than is consistent with their assured prosperity and the welfare of the community . . ." Yet there were other ways of increasing the net "without resort to the unsound, illegal, and undesirable method of the alleged horizontal increase."

The next morning he resumed: "I have said, and I will say again, that whatever may be true of the rates, the net operating revenues and the net income of these properties are not such as to give assured prosperity to the railroads such as the welfare of the community demands. I say that because I believe that as long as our railroads are owned by private individuals we must be generous in the return which we allow." Capital invested by railroads, as in other business, yielded different returns according to the skill and honesty of management. Deserving roads must be given an opportunity to earn. "I myself care little for the laying down of any specific rule as to the percentage because I never would stick to any limit at all." If the percentage yielded just and reasonable rates the roads should earn it. They should also lay by a surplus for stability.

"The point made by Mr. Thorne is sound, that we ought not to be building up a surplus taken out of the community and then have the community pay for it again," Brandeis said. "I, for one, think it very much better to run the risk in court of protecting the community against injustice in respect to the surplus, when that comes up, rather than to deny the surplus which is essential to good business and essential to the retaining of capital at reasonable rates." He looked with hope to the ultimate solution of the problem by the Supreme Court.

Thorne said, "Did you understand me to deny any surplus?"

"I thought you were rather niggardly as to surplus."

"I allowed the same surplus that the commission did in 1910, and if your remark applies to my allowance it applies to the other," Thorne retorted.

Although the railroads had submitted elaborate charts

showing diminishing returns the data was insufficient. Brandeis drew up a questionnaire which the I.C.C. sent to the roads to determine the causes of the diminution. His seventy-eight exhaustive questions covered equipment purchases, financial history, financial interest of the directors in firms with which the roads did business, and many other phases. He was particularly eager to learn to what extent interlocking directorates prevailed and what influence they exerted in increasing costs.

It was nothing new for Brandeis to be baited in the midst of public work. The *Boston News Bureau* gave circulation to a new Hubbard article in *The Philistine* charging Brandeis with killing credit, "until America is no longer buying railroad bonds . . . The amount of misinformation which one man can pass out is almost past human belief. The persecution of the business interests of America by Mr. Brandeis has worked a hardship on a vast number of people . . . to make war on business is to paralyze payrolls." Another business organ said that the I.C.C. was "practically Brandeised." They did not like his exposé of an amazing system of special privileges to large shippers and pet warehouse companies.

In April, 1914, a blast at President Wilson was fired by La Follette, calling the appointment of Winthrop M. Daniels to the I.C.C. a reactionary step. The railroads were trying to get men on the commission who would adopt their view of valuation, he said; Wilson in backing water on the currency bill legalized the domination of the Money Power; and this was too much like the second year of the reign of Taft.

At the end of July the commission rendered its report denying the five percent advance but granting it to roads between Buffalo and Chicago, except on coal. A large part of the report followed Brandeis' brief in telling the railroads how they could save money by economies, financial reforms and the elimination of free services. Favors to the United States Steel Company cost them twenty-nine million dollars a year. The *Boston Herald* called it a "Brandeised decision."

Commissioners Daniels and McChord, dissenting, favored an advance for all the roads.

After the war broke out the carriers appealed to Wilson for a rehearing. They said they were facing a crisis and needed a higher rate to meet $563,000,000 of maturities. The foreign market for securities was cut off. Brandeis contended that all businesses were affected by the war, all must share the burden. The railroads should reduce their dividends. Engaged again as counsel by the I.C.C., at the reopened hearing he pitched into the questionable methods of railroad finance. If security-holders abroad were on the verge of dumping their holdings on the market the fault was the roads' own. He argued that the carriers had presented no new evidence since the decision which bore on the question of reasonable rates. They had failed to make a case. Moreover, the commission had no power to safeguard credit-funds. Again he recognized the need for increased net revenues.

Despite these arguments the I.C.C. granted the five per cent advance to the remaining lines, Commissioners Harlan and Clements dissenting.

All in the year's work was the task of solving problems for the New York garment industry. Brandeis would have been the last man in the world to think that his Washington activities overshadowed the mending he must do in the needle trades. But Dr. Hourwich, the union's fierce irreconcilable, denounced him for not understanding the duties of his office as arbitrator and not giving enough time to them. The Board of Arbitration had met only four times up to January, 1914. Demanding a salaried board which would sit as a court and decide individual disputes promptly, Hourwich was heedless of the disturbing effect of verdicts handed down right and left; and inattentive to the possibilities of conciliation and to the reason for reserving to the arbitrators only matters of protocol law.

From the very first time Brandeis listened to him he thought Hourwich had the wrong slant. Although keenly appreciative of his life-story— his bitter struggles in Russia, his membership in the first Duma, exile to Siberia and escape— Brandeis recognized from the points which Hourwich emphasized in his story that his view was distorted. And Brandeis remarked to Bloomfield, "This man is going to be a disrupter."

As if to challenge the manufacturers, the union's Joint Board not only sustained Hourwich but appointed him sole counsel. On a Sunday night in January the arbitrators met on the question of his staying in office. The life of the protocol was being threatened, Brandeis said, and the difference between the parties centered largely on one individual.

> The manufacturers have declared that it is their firm conviction that its purposes cannot be carried out so long as the union is represented by Dr. Hourwich. Whether this conviction of the manufacturers is well-founded we express no opinion, but beyond all question a crisis for the protocol has arisen on which Dr. Hourwich alone can supply relief. While the manufacturers have no power to compel his withdrawal he himself has the right to withdraw, and if in his loyalty to the union and to the protocol he voluntarily decides to do so, a continuance of the protocol would in our opinion be assured, and a dangerous and anomalous crisis, involving the certainty of great suffering for tens of thousands of men, women and children would be averted. Each side to the protocol has a right to terminate its existence at a moment's notice.

The Board suggested an eight-day truce.

Hourwich spoke: "My knowledge of the English language, Mr. Chairman, is imperfect, since I am only an immigrant from Eastern and Southern Europe, and I should like to know what is meant by 'truce,' because I should like to understand what should be considered as hostilities."

Both sides were to agree not to take any action terminating the protocol before noon January 26. Hourwich said he would ask the union to hold a referendum on his remaining—in other words, a vote whether to end the protocol. Cohen, the manufacturers' counsel, wanted to know whether the union accepted the truce and insisted upon an answer by noon the next day.

Hourwich replied with characteristic acidity:

> Under the rules of September 6, 1906, issued by the late Mr. Stolypin, the Premier of the Russian Empire, for the establishment of drumhead courts martial, for the trial of offenders caught in the act of committing terroristic outrages, the defendant was entitled to twenty-four hours' notice. We are given notice only until twelve o'clock tomorrow. This is a mockery. This is a mockery not at us; we can stand it. It is a mockery at the gentlemen styled here the Board of Arbitration . . .
>
> I personally will not stand in the way of peace. I shall submit this matter to the membership and it shall be for the membership to pass upon it.

Next day he submitted his resignation to the Joint Board, subject to a referendum. The situation was dangerous. The workers at large regarded him as their leader and deliverer. But the choice was between a strike and no strike. When his opponents in the union demanded an unconditional resignation, he at last yielded. Still the Joint Board hesitated. William O. Thompson, Clarence Darrow's law partner, told them that Brandeis promised a committee on immediate action with an impartial chairman if they would accept. After a fifteen-hour conclave the Joint Board consented, with tears. Their foremost concern was that peace might be preserved in the trade.

The whole experience impressed Brandeis with the capacity of these cloak men, both the workers and the employers, for growth after reaching maturity, and under such trying difficulties. They were made of good stuff. They reaffirmed his confidence in the possibility of improving industrial conditions. "I may say that nothing in all of my public experience has given me so much optimism."

That summer the largest wholesale drygoods concern in the world, H. B. Claflin Company, a holding company for twenty-seven department stores, failed. As a prophet derives no pleasure from his predicted calamities, he simply used the occasion as a springboard and in a signed article for a string of newspapers showed the parallel between this smashup and the wreck of the New Haven.

> It is an instance of the curse of mere bigness. It is another illustration of the failure of the Morgan methods of financing. In this instance we see John Claflin, the friend and protégé of Morgan, gathering together all these great stores until the organization came to a clear state of inefficiency. It is a sample of Morganized industry . . .
>
> What it is evidence of is the economic mistake of undertaking to link together a large number of businesses under a single financial management. Morgan sacrificed efficiency to monopoly in the New Haven railroad. The New Haven has been Morganized into physical and financial bankruptcy.

Returning to another favorite theme, scientific management as applied to labor, Brandeis gave ideas to Frank P. Walsh, who was entering on his new work as chairman of the United States Commission on Industrial Relations. A public hearing was held; Taylor, Emerson, Gantt and other engineers expounded their views. John Tobin of the shoe workers' international and John Golden of the textile workers' union raised the objections of organized labor. Brandeis thought it was folly for the unions to resist; scientific management would be adopted by non-union shops, which would then be in a position to keep unionism at bay. Labor should, instead, demand a voice in the application of the new system and use this opportunity for advance to get a very much

larger share in the increased production. The demands for shorter hours, higher wages, better conditions could not be met without an increase in the productivity of the individual worker.

> It seems to me that we are so far away in this country, and probably in any country, from satisfying the possible wants of the community, that there is no fear of over-production in its proper sense. It all comes to the question of what people can afford to buy . . . there is practically no such thing as there not being enough potential demand for all that we can produce.

Rather than rely upon individuals' kindness, society and labor should demand continuity of employment. When once workers were paid throughout the year, like a corporation's officers, no business could run profitably unless it was kept running— "because if you have to pay, whether your men are working or not, your men will work," Brandeis pointed out. Industry had been allowed to develop chaotically, mainly because irregularity of employment was accepted as something inevitable. "It is no more inevitable than insistence upon payment for a great many of the overhead charges in a business, whether the business is in daily operation or not."

The constitutional guaranty of the right to life was now being interpreted according to the requirements of social justice as the right to live, Brandeis wrote in an article for *The Independent*. In his opinion the basis for man's development was "leisure, which the Athenians called freedom or liberty." He put the Supreme Court to a fresh test in December after it had sustained him on the maximum hour laws of Oregon, Illinois and Ohio. Now he argued for Oregon's minimum wage legislation, again with Josephine Goldmark working on the brief. And he paid the court fees for the National Consumers' League as usual. This time the brief ran to four hundred pages and contained three hundred and sixty-nine extracts from scientific studies and official reports.

Counsel for the other side sought to prove that constitutional government would collapse if an employer were required to pay sixty-four cents more a week to a Portland factory girl. Mr. Justice Holmes punctured this specious appeal by remarking on the degeneracy of the working classes in England before factory acts put a curb on absolute freedom of contract.

When Brandeis spoke he held the justices in close attention—with facts. His delivery was quiet, conversational, deeply earnest. His style was narrative. He began with a history of minimum wage laws, since this was the first time the subject had come before the court. These laws were better described as prohibitory rather than compulsory. They prohibited the employment of women at less than a living wage. Wages insufficient to support women in health led to bad health and immorality, hence were detrimental to the interests of the state. Justification rested on facts ascertained through an investigation of conditions existing in Oregon and confirmed by numerous studies in other states and countries.

In Oregon a majority of the women had been found working for less than what was required for decent living. They scrimped on food and roomed under unwholesome conditions or were insufficiently clothed; or they supplied themselves with necessities by means of prostitution.

The Massachusetts law to which opposing counsel had referred with approval enforced minimum wages not by fine but by publicity and public scorn. Massachusetts believed that in its small, once homogeneous community of Puritan traditions the sense of duty could be relied upon if facts were publicly disclosed, Brandeis said, "But within the last decade, after our railroads had passed largely into the control of citizens of other states, doubts arose as to the efficacy of our law, and recently our Public Service Commission was given compulsory powers."

Oregon had concluded that legislation giving the commission only recommendatory powers would be ineffective, and the successful experiments in Australia, New Zealand and Great Britain were worthy of emulation. "Wise men" had contended that a minimum would become a maximum. The answer was that the predicted did not happen— experience showed that the more efficient received higher wages. Moreover, minimum wage acts tended to increase efficiency, regularize employment, and make industry more prosperous.

The step taken by the Oregon legislature was not a revolutionary one. Similar restrictions of liberty had been imposed among English-speaking people for one hundred and twelve years, beginning with the first child-labor law when five-year-olds worked fifteen hours a day in textile mills. British conservatism, exercised in the interest of manufacturers, took forty-five years to extend protection to women workers. Hours were gradually reduced. Later, laws were enacted to secure proper sanitary conditions. And now legislatures, finding further evils to be combatted, were entering upon the broad field of social insurance.

When Brandeis' time expired Chief Justice White told him it would be quite agreeable to the court to hear him through.

Brandeis, warming to his conclusion, declared: "How potent the forces of conservatism that could have prevented our learning that, like animals, men and women must be properly fed and properly housed if they are to be useful workers and survive!"

The only question to decide was whether the law had a reasonable relation to the end sought. The Oregon legislature knew the local conditions and was supported by the Supreme Court of the state. Was it so mistaken in its belief that the remedy would mitigate these conditions as to justify this court in holding that the restriction on liberty of contract could not be permitted?

Some may doubt whether this particular remedy is the best remedy . . . Even if you entertained a doubt well founded, you cannot interfere because you have doubts as to the wisdom of an act, provided that act is of such a character that it may conceivably produce the results sought to be attained. When we know— and on this point there is no room for doubt— when we know that the evil exists which it is sought to remedy, the legislature must be given latitude in experimentation . . .

This court is not burdened with the duty of passing upon the disputed question whether the legislature of Oregon was wise or unwise, or probably wise or unwise, in enacting this law.

There was a likelihood of economic and social error in all legislation. But social and industrial welfare demanded ample scope of invention.

It is a condition not only of progress but of conserving that which we have. Nothing could be more revolutionary than to close the door to social experimentation. The whole subject of woman's entry into industry is an experiment. And surely the federal Constitution— itself perhaps the greatest of human experiments— does not prohibit such modest attempts as the women's minimum wage act to reconcile the existing industrial system with our striving for social justice and the preservation of the race.

The justices gathered up their robes. At a Saturday conference they would discuss the case. Some Monday noon the Chief Justice would announce their decision.

"That fellow Brandeis," said a clerk of the court after adjournment, "has got the impudence of the devil to bring his socialism into the Supreme Court." A long period of waiting foloved.

Early in 1915 Brandeis went before a congressional committee with a new bill aimed at monopoly. In the method he chose for protecting the small businessman, the independent manufacturer and retailer, he was perplexing to people who thought he should advocate competition at any price instead of resale price-maintenance. Brandeis thought, however, that cut-throat prices were not a means of competition but a tool for suppressing it. The Supreme Court had consistently rendered decisions, in its ignorance of the operations of the commercial world, which aborted the purpose of the Sherman Law. Holmes was the only dissenter from an opinion written by Hughes holding invalid contracts by which makers of trademarked goods sought to prevent retailers from cutting an established price. "I cannot believe," Holmes wrote, "that in the long run the public will profit by this court permitting knaves to cut reasonable prices for some ulterior purpose of their own and thus to impair, if not to destroy, the production and sale of articles which it is assumed to be desirable that the public should be able to get."

The majority held price-fixing to be injurious to the public interest. They failed to distinguish between price-fixing, which was aimed at control of the market, and retail price-maintenance, an essential to independence. Their decisions were economically wrong. They played into the hands of capitalistic chain stores, such as the Riker-Hegeman chain, which combined retailing with manufacturing.

Back in 1911, when La Follette called him to Washington to confer with Lenroot, Clapp and others on anti-trust legislation, Brandeis took the position that "there must be reasonable restrictions put upon competition, else we shall see competition destroyed." A clear distinction had to be drawn between restrictions harmful to the competitive system and those which served it. One of the barriers needed against excess was a law to permit makers of branded articles to set uniform resale prices by contract. Since the Supreme Court rested its conclusions on grounds of public policy, Congress should proceed to declare the true policy and offset this judicial legislation.

Brandeis recommended to Secretary Redfield an investigation by the Department of Commerce into the extent to which the fixing of retail prices by manufacturers was beneficial or harmful. A comprehensive knowledge of the facts was needed to determine which so-called restraints of trade aided competition and which suppressed it. Such a study was needed also before legislation could intelligently be passed or Department of Justice action taken on trade agreements among competitors, for some agreements—like those concerning discounts, dating, reports on production and stock on hand—tended in the right direction.

Many businessmen thought that the way to achieve price-maintenance was to attack the Sherman Law. They mistook supporters of the act for opponents of their cause. William H. Ingersoll of the Ingersoll Watch Company, introduced himself at the Oldfield patent hearing in 1912 as a friend of Frank Gilbreth and invited Brandeis to talk before the Advertising Men's League of New York, having in mind a debate with a price-maintenance man. To Ingersoll's astonishment both speakers upheld the same side.

Brandeis went into this new campaign avidly, speaking before other advertising groups and their national convention in Baltimore. They must make clear to the public their reasons for asking the right to maintain prices. They must differentiate between rival manufacturers combining on a staple product and independents determining how best to market their goods. Toward the end of 1913, when he was preparing an article on cut-throat competition for *Harper's Weekly*, Ingersoll gathered data for him. Ingersoll wanted him to pitch into the government's pending case against Kellogg's cornflakes price-fixing and offered to round up retail organizations, each to subscribe a quota to meet his fee. Brandeis told him not to trouble about raising funds; if he should act as counsel he would regard the case as part of his general effort to help establish a proper understanding of the trust problem and undue restraint of trade.

He impressed McReynolds and Redfield with the desira-

bility of allowing the Kellogg case to remain inactive. When
the American Fair Trade League was organized by Ingersoll
and others to advocate price-maintenance, he advised them
on their course. They should not in their literature criticise
either the Department of Justice or Congressman Oldfield,
who had the highest motives but, like the majority of the
Supreme Court, lacked in this instance the necessary knowledge of business practice and conditions. Brandeis was
planning a bill for the League to sponsor. He called in Rublee
to draft it. The privilege of price-maintenance was not to
be given to producers having a monoply of the market nor
to anyone agreeing with competitors on selling prices, and
probably not to those who gave quantity discounts. Rublee
and Gilbert H. Montague did the work. Congressman
Stevens introduced it.

When the House interstate commerce committee held a
hearing on the bill Brandeis recalled to them the Democratic
Party's policy of coping with the trust problem by regulating
competition. This had led to the Clayton Act and the Federal Trade Commission. The Stevens bill would further
supplement the Sherman Law, as price-cutting was the worst
form of illegitimate competition and naturally resulted in
monopoly. He continued—

> The mere fact that the Supreme Court has rendered
> its decision does not foreclose the matter. Why? Be-
> cause it is Congress which must ultimately determine
> questions of economic policy in matters of interstate
> commerce.

The court was in error to suppose that Congress meant by
the Sherman Law to prohibit such agreements. Rich and
powerful producers could maintain standard prices by establishing agencies.

> The small man needs the protection of the law; but
> the law becomes the instrument by which he is de-

stroyed. The rule laid down by the Supreme Court is inconsistent with the business policy adopted by this country.... the court did not fully understand the practical application of these rules to the trade facts.

He was not asking for a privilege but for the restoration of a right commonly enjoyed in the leading commercial states and countries as a matter of course until the court's decisions abridged it— "the right which a man has by virtue of being a free businessman." Now retailers could take a branded article with a reputation for quality and value and use it as a loss-leader; cutting the price on something of known value ruined the reputation of the manufacturer. The customer thought he was overcharged and stopped buying. Other retailers, also discredited, stopped selling the goods. Consumers were frequently troubled by not being able to get an article and having to buy another for more than it was worth.

A member of the committee asked if he was appearing solely in behalf of consumers. Brandeis substituted "the public" for "consumers," as the broader term embraced all classes of people, including congressmen.

"I represent myself— nobody else," he said.

He was asked whether the Supreme Court would not invalidate a law embodying a practice it had already decided was against public policy.

"They would not have any right to," he said.

The court could pass on questions of public policy only in the absence of a declaration of the subject by Congress. Here no constitutional question was involved, the only question being: "What does the general interest of the community demand?"

It was still not clear to some of the congressmen that the measure did not play into the hands of monopolists. They asked Brandeis about such articles as the Ingersoll watch and Shredded Wheat. He answered that the ownership of a branded article did not give one a monopoly. "You may say

I have a monopoly of the Brandeis law practice because nobody else may use that name."

"Well, you are a monopolist," said a committee member.

"Every human being is a monopolist in that sense, but it isn't the proper sense of the word. Certainly not when you are speaking of the Sherman Law."

The real test of monopoly was whether the field remained open for competition. This bill would not drive anybody out of business; it would give a small manufacturer or dealer an incentive to improve quality so as to continue in business. True, Ingersoll and Kellog were not small, but they once were.

Talking about big department stores, he said it was a mistake to suppose they could do business more cheaply than small retailers. In large stores the expense of selling was more than twenty-five percent of the retail price and the percentage cost of doing business was constantly rising. The size of greatest efficiency was reached at a comparatively early stage. With growth came an increased cost of organization and administration. The small businessman brought all factors into their proper relation, often by "unconscious cerebration." The profits of department and chain stores came from their ability to get an inside price on goods.

> There is a limit on human capacity. As the Germans say, "Care is taken that the trees do not scrape the skies." . . . There is a point of saturation for every man's ability. Until that point of saturation he can gain constantly by increasing the field of his operations. But it does not follow that because I am making more money on a large volume that I am doing business at a less cost.

He admitted the tendency towards fewer and larger units. It was very regrettable but not inevitable. The very large unit would continue to remain socially objectionable. He opposed the practice of giving quantity discounts as menacing the little fellow. Take a leaf from the post office, where every customer, buying little or much, obtained equal terms.

Going back to the Supreme Court, he said it had inadvertently denied protection to small enterprises, and a congressman interposed: "We're not authorized to assume that the Supreme Court does anything inadvertently."

"Why not?"

Brandeis pointed out that the court in construing the Constitution was supposed to lay down the final law. "But we amended the Constitution in respect to the income tax because we believed that the rule laid down by the Supreme Court was not consistent with the public interest." The people, he said, were the supreme authority. On a question of public policy it was no disrespect to the Supreme Court to say that the majority of the court were mistaken.

> There is no reason why five gentlemen of the Supreme Court should know better what public policy demands than five gentlemen of Congress. In the absence of legislation by Congress the Supreme Court expresses its idea of public policy, but in the last analysis it is the function of the legislative branch of the government to declare the public policy of the United States. There are a great many rules which the Supreme Court lays down which may afterwards be changed, and are afterwards changed, by legislation. It is not disrespect to the Supreme Court to do it. Their interpretation of the law may be set aside by a new law.

If Congress did not agree with the Supreme Court in its interpretation of the intent of the Sherman Law, he said, "Congress should so declare by enacting the Stevens bill." As now interpreted, the law was working for the big units. "You certainly do not wish to crush the little men," Brandeis said, and they were the ones who needed this legislation.

Chapter XV

ZIONISM. . . . AND NEW WORK

THE BURST of war in 1914 projected a horizon far beyond immediate concerns of social and economic justice at home and it thrust Brandeis into international affairs. Till then, like La Follette, he had given little time to foreign relations. The size and the strength of the United States were too great for this country to venture abroad without danger of doing harm.

His only excursion was made back in 1900, when the business instinct of the nation was exalting the "white man's burden" and the manifest destiny of America in colonial conquest. He had strong doubts about the administration's Philippine policy, but his doubts became a conviction when he heard Taft defend it. Mrs Evans was the one who drew him into a movement to combat the government's program. Instead of sharing the abolitionist emotion of the New England Anti-Imperialist League he declined their invitation to join and subscribed to a private investigating committee which collated, sifted and published official documents and endeavored with difficulty to get the facts disseminated through the press. With characteristic detachment Brandeis associated himself with men who in the main had not expressed any pronounced attitude. The group included Professor Albert Bushnell Hart, an ardent adherent of President McKinley. Their Philippine Information Society did not get far, but neither did the anti-imperialists. After contributing sums for three years Brandeis closed the account. No international questions involved him thereafter. The wisest course was suggested by the German proverb: if everyone sweeps his own doorway the street will be kept clean.

But now the streets of Europe ran with blood.

Brandeis was thinking, while war raged, of peace. The economic causes were inescapable. But more fundamental, he thought, was political domination. Lasting peace must rest on acceptance of the idea of equal rights of all nations and races to live and develop their individuality.

> Whatever economic arrangement may be made, however perfect and comprehensive may become the machinery for enforcing the treaties of the nations, those peoples who are not accorded equality of opportunity for full development will prove a source of irritation; injustice will bring its inevitable penalty; and the peace of the world will be broken again and again, as those little nations of the Balkans have taught us in recent years.

He rejected the notion of a dominant race. In this he agreed with his brother-in-law, Felix Adler, who subordinated the practical devices of disarmament, world parliaments, and treaties to "reciprocity of cultural influence, favorable to the greatest possible variety of types and assuring to the different groups of mankind their integrity as distinct members, in order that they make may manifest the distinctive gifts with which nature has endowed them." Civilization would advance by extending the democratic doctrine of equality of opportunity for all persons and classes— to all peoples.

An opportunity for action in accordance with this creed came through the disruption of the Zionist movement. Its central bureau in Berlin broke down. Europe could no longer sustain its obligations to the Jewish colonists in Palestine whose fate now fell to the Zionists in America. But these supporters were scattered among many small societies. An emergency conference was called to organize a Provisional Executive Committee late in August at Hotel Marseilles in New York. Brandeis went, aware that the hope of Zionism for an autonomous country under the suzerainty of the Sultan of Turkey was blasted.

Newcomer though he was, the delegates unanimously chose Brandeis as chairman. The leaders expected him to be useful mainly as a name, and he himself doubted his qualifications, since he had been separated from Jews to a large extent in his fifty-eight years and had become ignorant of things Jewish. But recent public and professional experiences had taught him that the striving for justice and democracy was an ingrained quality in Jews. He said they had a deep moral feeling, a deep sense of the brotherhood of man, and a high intelligence, the fruit of three thousand years of civilization.

> These experiences have made me feel that the Jewish people have something which should be saved for the world; that the Jewish people should be preserved, and that it is our duty to pursue that method of saving which most promises success.

Brandeis' subscription of one thousand dollars started an emergency fund. He prepared to travel from city to city and arouse fellow American Jews to their responsibility. He studied Zionism as he had studied gas and insurance and railroading. In Baltimore he pleaded for contributions at a mass meeting held at the Lyric Theatre. In Boston the crowds at Symphony Hall hailed him with cries of, "The new Moses!" His friends marveled at the new Brandeis. To Mrs. Evans, who watched him rise on the platform, it seemed that his face "shone with an inner light that transformed his whole being."

As he swung into this work he thought about the few immigrants from Russia and Rumania who had gone to Palestine a generation ago— "these new Pilgrim Fathers"— to restore Jewish national life, protect it from the forces of disintegration, and help nurture their traditional spirit to full and natural development. They found the land treeless, arid, apparently sterile. And now oranges, grapes, olives, almonds, wheat and other cereals were growing in profusion. The export of oranges had increased in one generation from sixty thousand boxes to one million five hundred thousand a year. Statistics like these gave Brandeis great satisfaction.

In Boston he compared his appeal for money with the contributions the Irish had raised for the cause of home rule. In New York, addressing a meeting of the Menorah societies at Columbia University, he recalled that throughout the centuries of persecution the only life open to Jews which could give satisfaction was the intellectual and spiritual; thus were they protected from the temptations of material things and wordly ambitions. They developed faculties which became racial traits. The successful modern Jew was not a self-made man but the beneficiary of an inheritance, a treasure to be transmitted to posterity unimpaired if not augmented.

He identified that trust with the ideals of the early New Englanders and of American democracy. The kinship lay in the Jews' traditional sense of duty, in sympathy for one's fellows, which was the essence of social justice, and in a strong social feeling. He was fond of saying that his approach to Zionism was through Americanism and he did not hesitate to interest President Wilson in the Palestine situation.

In finding himself spiritually he came upon the words of a Hebrew philosopher, Ahad Ha'am, who gave beauty to the expression of his own rejoicing:

> I live for the sake of the perpetuation and happiness of the community of which I am a member; I die to make room for new individuals who will mould the community afresh and not allow it to stagnate and remain forever in one position. When the individual thus values the community as his own life and strives after its happiness as though it were his individual well-being, he finds satisfaction and no longer feels so keenly the bitterness

of his individual existence, because he sees the end for which he lives and suffers.

There were mass meetings that fall in Worcester, Springfield, Rochester, Buffalo, Philadelphia, Baltimore, Pittsburgh, Cleveland, Chicago, St. Louis. In each city Brandeis succeeded in raising enthusiasm and money. He tried to clear up misunderstandings about Zionism; it did not propose a wholesale hegira or plan to wrest the sovereignty of Palestine from the Turks. The aim was to establish a legally secured home, but the road must be cleared by acceptance after the war of the principle that no nation might expand in such a way as to abridge the equal rights of other nations to development. The clearing, he felt, would have to be done by the Allies. At least, in his hatred for kaiserism he counted on them to win and therefore consulted with the British ambassador, Sir Cecil Spring-Rice, who reported that his government was most eager to advance Zionist aspirations.

The opportunities opened for the Jews did not blind Brandeis to the disaster of war. Despite America's increased industrial activity and exports, the world was closely bound together and "ultimately we must share in the misfortune." The world as a whole had suffered by the Boer War in South Africa, the Russo-Japanese War, the Balkan wars. "In this war the effects of destruction will be felt all over the world."

Appeals for relief from the war zones and from terror-stricken Palestinian settlers fleeing into Egypt found the Provisional Committee alert and resourceful. In February, 1915, Brandeis called on Secretary Bryan with Rabbi Stephen S. Wise and Rabbi Judah L. Magnes and urged him to use his good offices. They arranged with the Department of State to have the American consulate at Alexandria act as a depository and distribution agency for Americans sending money to refugee relatives. From the British and French governments they obtained promises of protection for a food-ship. Through Secretary of the Navy Josephus Daniels they were granted space on the collier *Vulcan* for nine hundred tons of food supplies and medicines. Daniels told them that Wilson was much pleased to know that this could be done.

Brandeis' administration of Zionist activities was something novel in a realm of unsystematic goodness of heart. His stern injunction to observe order and precision discomfited old hands, unpracticed in putting idealism on a businesslike basis. And he antagonized the American Jewish Committee, a small group of dignified philanthropists, of which Louis Marshall was president. They held aloof from his proposal for united action. Brandeis and his associates wanted to call a congress representative of all organizations. The Marshall group preferred to deal with select bodies. Brandeis insisted on a democratic congress, a forthright policy eliminating indirection and reliance on influence. Magnes, a member of the American Jewish Committee, resigned from the Provisional Committee. Rabbi Wise, Judge Mack and Professor Frankfurter cooperated with Brandeis.

In April he opened the annual meeting of the Eastern Council of Reformed Rabbis at Temple Emanu-El in New York and pleaded for resurrection of the Jewish nation as a living nationality.

> The reason we must make common cause with all the small nations of the world is that the large nations will surely come to the day when they will see that it is not good national policy to suppress any one people and drive out of those people their national instincts. We have had much of that in Russia.

He spoke in Providence, Portland, New Haven, Atlantic City. At the end of June, when the Zionists held their annual convention at Ford Hall in Boston, he sat as chairman. Here the issue was drawn: a congress versus a conference; a congress to formulate demands for full civil rights for Jews in all lands. The Marshall committee was horrified at the prospect of an open assertion and discountenanced both the nationalist aim and the proposal for a self-governing body having responsibility equal to its authority. The convention supported Brandeis.

He spoke in Salem, Baltimore, Washington, Louisville—ignoring the strain of speech-making in the passion of a cause which commanded all his heart. In return he was warmed by the admiration of each Jewish community as it welcomed him as a great figure in Jewish life. He was glad he had not entered the Cabinet. This share in the struggle would otherwise have been denied to him. When someone suggested that the Cabinet might have served as a stepping stone to the Presidency, he said: "That would have been a greater misfortune."

Brandeis hastened to Baltimore before the presidents of Jewish organizations were to gather there to choose between a congress and a conference. Speaking at the Opera House he declared that the American Jews must have a hand in decisions affecting their brethren abroad when the war would end. There should be unity and a body with authority representing active, not acquiescent, adherents and deliberating after open discussion. In short, a democratic instrument for ascertaining the Jewish people's will and carrying it out.

> The decision must embody the wisdom, not of the few, however able and public-spirited, but the thought and judgment of the whole people. The support must be active; it must be financial as well as moral. It must be the support of the million, not of a few generous, philanthropic millionaires.

The conference proposed by the American Jewish Committee would be futile, he said, because it would lack both mandate and support. It would be dangerous— its secrecy would engender suspicion and possibly prejudice. It would discourage activity on the part of people assuming that the conference had relieved them of the obligation to do their part. Finally, as most of the organizations had already refused to participate in it, there would be no unity.

In time, as Brandeis expected, the congress was established.

A young man who had run away from anti-Semitism in Atlanta and obtained a municipal position in Philadelphia only to encounter the same prejudice blocking his advancement, inquired if he could get a law opening in Boston. Brandeis' observation taught that there was little difference among cities in this respect. The wise thing to do, he answered, was to meet that feeling, not seek to escape it and abandon the start already made in Philadelphia. Most men would be doomed to disappointment, he said, if they measured achievement by the degree of appreciation they received.

The war dramatized the perennial plight of the Jews and laid bare the causes which Brandeis thought could be removed only if the Jews emancipated themselves as a people. He took no interest in religion. He had never gone to synagogue. The only time he attended services was two years later in connection with a Baltimore convention.

Congress in Washington was preparing a barrier to the immigration from Europe which was expected to follow the war. Brandeis denounced the pending bill, disguised as a literacy test, as an exclusion bill which would result in more loss than gain to the country in thus departing from its fundamental principle. Taft had vetoed a literacy bill in '13 on Secretary Nagel's advice. Brandeis revealed in an address before the New Century Club in Boston the unfairness of the new measure. It penalized people deprived of a rudimentary education in their home countries by oppression or poverty. Its purpose was to restrict immigration from Mediterranean and Southeastern Europe. Literacy was adopted as the yardstick because the protagonists knew that many of those they aimed at would fail.

The movement thus springs from the conception or claim of race superiority. It involves necessarily race discrimination and must lead to race antagonism. How dan-

gerous such a conception of race superiority becomes
the present war bears witness.

Although Congress did not see it in this light, Wilson did.
Brandeis' work in 1915 was not less diversified by reason
of the intensity of his Zionism. The year would have been
crowded without it because earlier projects remained uncompleted and Wilson needed him.

From the civics and economics lesson he gave congressmen at the price-maintenance hearing in January, Brandeis
plunged into the turmoil of the garment trade situation in
New York. On the day after the Board of Arbitration held a
session he testified before the New York State Factory Investigating Committee for a minimum wage law. And the
next day he appeared again before the United States Commission on Industrial Relations, sitting at City Hall.

State Senator Robert F. Wagner, was chairman of the factory investigation committee and Alfred E. Smith the vice-
chairman. The Supreme Court had not yet rendered a decision in the Oregon minimum wage case but— answering
Smith's question— Brandeis had no doubt the legislation was
identical in principle with state laws governing hours, child
labor and factory safety. All were limitations upon liberty
of contract, and such restrictions represented the difference
between liberty and license.

> The liberty of each individual must be limited in such
> a way that it leaves to others the possibility of individual
> liberty. The right to develop must be subject to that lim-
> itation which gives to everybody else that right to de-
> velop. The restriction is merely an adjustment of the re-
> lations of one individual to another.

Manufacturers were objecting because they had not
thought out the proposition. They were deluded by such
phrases as "the law of supply and demand," which was a
half-truth like "liberty of contract." They were mistaken in

assuming that their expenses would be increased. Just as
clients of his own had realized that they did not get their
money's worth from child labor or other cheap labor the ob-
jectors would come to the same conclusion.

> Anything which is of better quality, which costs a
> little more, gives a larger percentage of value than a
> thing that is cheap. It is one of the curses of the poor that
> they have to buy poor things; and it is precisely the same
> in regard to human labor and human service as in regard
> to merchandise. . . . Not only is the employee worth
> more but the employer exerts himself to make the em-
> ployee more efficient. . . . A man is careless and waste-
> ful of a cheap thing. So, too, cheap labor is treated care-
> lessly and wastefully. Nobody would think, for instance,
> of expecting a good performance from a horse unless
> the horse is well-fed.

The federal commission's current phase of inquiry was the
centralization of industrial control and its bearing on the
prevalent labor unrest. Under the questioning of Frank P.
Walsh, Brandeis pictured the modern gigantic corporation as
a bulwark against the growth of unionism, a power divorced
from its thousands of stockholders shirking responsibility,
a danger to society, a state within a state. The chief cause of
unrest was industrial absolutism.

Spurious efforts to democratize ownership resulted in making the workers' condition worse. The small stockholders,
recognizing their lack of influence, left the management to
its own devices, and only a scandal could dislodge it. They
might be innocent in fact but socially they were not and they
must be held responsible for the acts of the corporation.

This brought Brandeis to the bat once more against bigness. The giant units, creatures of finance, were controlled
by men, who, even if they had a social concern, could not
manage properly because of the diversity of their interests
and inability to become intimate with the facts of the busi-

ness. Prevented mainly by human limitations, they tried to cover too much ground.

> I doubt whether anybody who is himself engaged in any important business has time to be a director in more than one large corporation. If he seeks to know about the affairs of that one corporation as much as he should know, not only in the interest of the stockholders, but in the interest of the community, he will have a field for study that will certainly occupy all the time that he has.

Then again, while benevolent despots might introduce certain reforms, improvement merely of the physical and material condition of the workingman could not dispel unrest. Any social or industrial system must be directed toward the development of manhood. It must always be remembered "that the United States is a democracy and that we must have, above all things, men." Profit-sharing was not the way; the workers must participate in the government of the trade, in decisions as to the conduct of the business and their own condition.

Walsh asked: "Past experience indicates that large corporations can be trusted to bring about these reforms by themselves?"

Brandeis answered: "I think all of our human experience shows that no one with absolute power can be trusted to give it up even in part. That has been the experience with political absolutism; it must prove the same with industrial absolutism."

Industrial democracy had to be won, and if a union could not do it that was proof that the corporation was too large to be consistent with the public interest, too powerful in its financial influence to be useful to the state. Hence the government must step in. But legislation could not accomplish much unless it set a limit on the size of corporate units. And no effort of the workers to secure industrial democracy would be effective so long as concentration of power persisted.

One of the commissioners wanted him to clarify the meaning of industrial democracy. Did it mean that the worker would have a voice in the affairs of an industry?

"Yes, sir. And not only a voice but a vote; not merely a right to be heard but a position through which labor may participate in management."

He held up the protocol in the garment trade as an accomplishment to be striven for by others. Under that system both sides conferred to solve the trade's problems. There was general recognition of the fact that conscious wrongdoing on either side was uncommon, and a joint obligation to remedy conditions which had developed into conflicts, not merely to find equity. The essential of direct dealing between employer and employee, as a prelude to understanding each other's contentions, was achieved under the protocol. Though manufacturers and union men differed radically and intensely they sat down together.

> They have the same respect for one another which opposing lawyers have for each other. Their conflict does not create enmity. The men, though contending for exactly the opposite results, become friends.

A common mistake was to deduce a wrong motive from a wrong effect. Often it was not the intent that was wrong but the results sought. "People fail to recognize true values," Brandeis said.

What the employer needed most was to have labor understand the problems of his business and disabuse workers of exaggerated notions of profits; put a competent representative of labor on his board and make him grapple with a specific problem.

> A few years ago, when union leaders were demanding from my client an increase in wages and I asked them:

"How much do you think the employer ought to earn before he increases your wages?" they named a figure which was far above his actual earnings, and I said to them: "Gentlemen, the books are open. If you can find either that there is more being earned, or can show a way in which the employer can earn more than he is earning, the balance shall go to you."

He reverted to his favorite theme of scientific management which, by increase in production, would afford workers the opening to demand a larger share. Labor should therefore insist upon its adoption.

And this was only a step toward the workers' goal, as he conceived it. There must come a time when labor would hire capital instead of capital hiring labor.

The members of the commission, submitting their reports were unable to agree on a program.

The garment industry called him back. Deadlocked on the question of the right of a man to his job, it brought to the Board of Arbitration the case of a manufacturer who had laid off his workers on the pretext of reorganizing his shop and then hired back those of his choosing. The Board heard testimony, talked it over at lunch, listened to additional witnesses, dined and discussed again and delivered a unanimous judgment. Brandeis urged a spirit of fairness and the rule of reason in determining whether or not a regular employee should be discharged. He avoided defining what was fair and reasonable as any such attempt would lead rather to injustice than to justice in the long run. This must be left to the good sense of men familiar with the particular facts because the facts would vary in particular cases. To codify what was reasonable would require taking into consideration such infinite possibilities that the mind of man could not in advance justly determine the rule to be applied. The rules would become so numerous that the mere selection or application of a rule would present a difficulty almost insurmountable.

The condition of the industry was chaotic— barbaric, he called it. Piece-work prices had not been standardized but were being made separately in each shop, so that in a sense there were fifteen hundred competing unions when there should be collective bargaining. Another problem was equal division of work and the regularization of employment. This was wrapped up in the control of labor supply and the admission of apprentices. No solution could be found by shifting the burdens from employers to employees or vice versa. Each side should as far as possible withhold insistence upon rights and consider in the first place its duties.

But this pronouncement did not leave the workers certain as to what they ought to do. The advice to be fair and reasonable could not check unemployment, which was becoming more and more widespread. A crisis confronted the protocol. Two weeks later the discharge of pressers from another shop brought up the question: What constitutes a regular employee? The manufacturers' association called for another session of the Board, but the question was referred back to the contestants.

The paper on which the protocol was written began to crumble. It was less than five years since the signing of the treaty designed for enduring peace. Once more the union appealed to the arbitrators, asking for decisions "in a language so explicit that no party is able to misconstrue or misinterpret the meaning."

But in May, a few days before the Board was to sit again, the association notified the union that in view of illegal stoppages and other acts it considered their mutual relations severed.

A cackle of criticism came from the trade press. The arbitrators were characterized as false prophets. The relationship between employer and employee had been built on sophistry, casuistry and ethereal concepts often communicated over the long-distance telephone. Social uplifters and alleged industrial statesmen had been tolerated to formulate the rules for making cloaks. Manufacturers should extricate themselves from this labyrinth of fine-spun theories and make adjustments themselves by united action.

Brandeis was in Washington. A carbuncle developed on his face and instead of going to New York he proceeded home. With Lincoln Filene, Bloomfield and Moskowitz he held a conclave— a new agreement must be evolved or there would be a strike. Moskowitz advised against calling it a protocol. Like the German word *Kultur* it had been badly advertised, and both sides were tired of it.

The tempest was stilled awhile, the union and the association agreeing to Mayor Mitchel's appointment of a council of conciliation. The council included Felix Adler, Professor Kirchwey, Judge Walter C. Noyes, Charles L. Bernheimer, Henry Bruère, and Brandeis. They concluded that the principles of industrial efficiency and of respect for the human rights of the workers must be applied jointly, priority being assigned to neither. Peace and progress depended upon giving complete loyalty in the effort to reconcile both. Hence the employer must retain the right to hire and fire but the worker must be safeguarded against oppressive exercise of these functions.

The recommendations were accepted and the threatened strike was called off. A collective agreement succeeded the protocol.

The trouble with labor was that it failed to train its energy on the right steps, to work even for the removal of its most dreaded curse, unemployment, which had now settled on the country like a plague. A meeting for the jobless held at Cort Theatre in Boston was symptomatic of the times. Brandeis told the audience that unemployment in 1915 was a tragedy of peace as deep and far-reaching as the tragedy of war; and only an exaggeration of the normal condition. Society had allowed this great cause of misery to remain untouched and labor itself had been remiss. If unions would only add to their demands regularity of employment the best minds of the country would be directed toward the invention of methods to achieve continuity.

> Irregularities may be overcome, some of them entirely eliminated, and where some remain the state may step in and by state insurance and state employment take up the slack and assure for every man a real opportunity, instead of a paper opportunity, in this country.

Brandeis was again needed in Washington. The newly appointed Federal Trade Commission was getting ready to function but disagreed on its policies. The acting chairman, Edward N. Hurley of the Illinois Manufacturers' Association, invited him to address them on the commission's powers; to suggest how to organize, proceed, and maintain contact with the commercial world. One of the members was Brandeis' friend, George Rublee, a recess appointee.

First Brandeis wanted to clear up the belief that business should be able to procure official sanction or advice in advance of entering upon projects likely to come under the prohibition of the Sherman Law. "It sounds very alluring," he said, but it would be a dangerous power for this commission of three businessmen and two lawyers to assume. Such questions were of a legal nature and must ultimately be decided by the Supreme Court. Moreover, no problem could be decided properly unless all the facts were properly set forth; the commissioners were not expected to be prophets and to determine what the facts were going to be or whether the plan would result in a restraint of trade. To get at truth the other side must be fully represented, which was impossible, because the people who eventually would be affected were not available.

Businessmen running round in circles as if they did not know whether what they intended was in restraint of trade could ask their hearts, and not their lawyers; and nineteen times out of twenty they would know. The president of one of the largest trusts had said to him four years ago:

"Now, you have been speaking in favor of this Sherman Law and I have been going around and trying to find out what I can do and I can't get any advice as to what I can do." And he said, in rather a pleasant enough way, but in certain ways rather sneering, "Perhaps *you* can advise me." I said, "I can advise you perfectly, but it is a question what advice I can give you. If you ask me how near you can walk to the edge of a precipice without going over I can't tell you, for you may walk on the edge and all of a sudden you may step on a smooth stone or strike against a bit of a root sticking out and you may go over that precipice. But if you ask me how near you can go to the precipice and still be safe, I can tell you, and I can tell you that whatever mishap comes to you, you will not fall over that precipice."

The same man had taken advice to avoid risks in other business matters. Why should he expect more from the Sherman Law than from any other law? "I think our Supreme Court will hold a good many things to be legal which men, without full investigation, have held bad," Brandeis said.

He told the commission that its greatest work would be to investigate the facts of trade and bring them out before they came to "a really tight situation" and harm was done. The business community could then understand the real situation in regard to their business. If the question of costs were studied, he believed that five-sixths of all the cut-throat competition and the desire for a combination would be eliminated. Proper systems of bookkeeping and accounting should be worked out for each line of business. Proper trade associations could bring out the actual demand, supply, and capacity in any given line. At present there was a lack of comprehensive knowledge and consequent disorganization; men kept secret what would be beneficial for the public to know.

Certain businessmen once came to him for advice on how

to stop price-cutting. He suggested that they pool their data on production, inventory, price, and give the information to a secretary for publication in a monthly report.

> Well, they have done it and for some years it healed the trouble in that particular business, and those people are just as independent as can be. If I manufacture this month I want to know how many tons there were left over at the beginning of last month; what the demand was; where, and in a general way, whether for export or domestic, and I want to know that just as well as I want to know how to spell or how to make my product in a different way.

The commission would do a valuable service by investigating the character of the thousands of trade associations. On the basis of such information the Department of Justice and the courts could act. If the condition was held illegal and the facts showed it ought to be legal, Congress would have the invitation to correct the situation. All investigations should be of the cards-on-the-table variety, none in an invidious sense; not to detect wrongdoing but to get the facts. When one of the commissioners announced that the lumber trade had submitted a statement, Brandeis said it would be perfectly proper to put trained investigators on the job to find out just what the conditions were.

As time went on he shared the general disappointment in the way the Federal Trade Commission was functioning. It was not strong enough. Its effectiveness would depend largely on the selection of permanent counsel. At his suggestion Stevens, who had failed of election to the Senate, had been named special counsel. If Rublee and Stevens could stay, the Federal Trade Commission was bound to prove to be a valuable government instrument. Monopolistic practices would be nipped and the Supreme Court would have the benefit of impartial studies when rendering judgments. Statutory and case law would be brought into harmony with economics.

When Brandeis fell ill in Washington that spring he was performing a service to Wilson. To save the administration from the embarrassment of a scandal in the Treasury Department he had been called into secret conference with McAdoo and Gregory over the Riggs National Bank, the largest and perhaps the oldest bank in the District of Columbia. McAdoo and the Comptroller of Currency found irregularities and illegal practices in the Riggs National, which in turn charged discrimination in being omitted from the customary distribution of District funds. McAdoo wanted Brandeis to act as special counsel and advise on the legal issues as they came up, but Brandeis waited for a sign from Gregory. And Gregory was mighty pleased. About two months later the bank brought suit to enjoin McAdoo and the Comptroller from attempting to wreak personal vengeance and wreck its business.

Amid apparently conflicting statements from the Treasury and the Attorney General's office Brandeis' appointment as adviser to Gregory came out in the open. The hostile press tried to make it seem that the two departments were not in accord. Friendly newspapers pointed to the case as a struggle between the Federal Reserve Bank system and the Morgan-Rockefeller interests behind the National City Bank and its allies, including the Riggs National. There was talk in Washington that the bank could not stand probing; that it lent money freely to congressmen and other government officials.

The case came to trial. Untermyer defended McAdoo and the Comptroller. Brandeis had generous things to say about the other counsel's skillful conduct, and Untermyer was outspoken in admiration for "the big, broad way" in which Brandeis dealt with the situation.

At Mayor Curley's bidding Brandeis delivered the Fourth of July oration in Boston. McAdoo celebrated the day by worrying over the Riggs case and the damage to the Treasury's prestige caused by a campaign of vicious press agentry designed, he felt, to curtail the Comptroller's powers, hamper the national banking system, and injure the administration. He wanted to forestall an investigation by Congress. As long as Riggs had sent copies of its bill of complaint to every member of Congress and every bank, and an enormous amount of prejudice had been aroused against his department, why should he not distribute his affidavit? The Treasury's side of the case had been handled badly by the newspapers. The court might delay too long. It was an uncomfortable summer that McAdoo spent in his camp in Maine. But calm Brandeis counseled patience; it would be wiser to distribute the affidavits after the decision, when they would get more consideration; moreover, the decision might be full enough to make it the best of all documents to circulate.

In the end McAdoo and the Comptroller were vindicated. Brandeis was paid four thousand dollars on account.

Gregory had further use for him after the government's suit against the United Shoe Machinery for dissolution under the Sherman Law was dismissed. A new case was being prepared by Gregory and George W. Anderson under the Clayton Act, and Brandeis was sent galley proofs of a petition for injunction against the company's unlawful practices. He made suggestions and sat back to enjoy the prosecution vicariously.

Brandeis recovered from an illness with the tonic satisfaction of his daughter Susan's graduation from Bryn Mawr College and Elizabeth's completion of her first year at Radcliffe with high marks. He was happy to have his family united again in the companionship of the summer vacation at South Yarmouth, and he liked to go boating with the girls.

Susan planned to spend a year campaigning for woman's suffrage. Her father campaigned for Governor Walsh's reelection. The platform of the state Democratic Party contained a pledge of continued allegiance to the savings bank insurance system, which now permitted policies to be taken out in $1,000 units in each of the issuing banks. Year after year the insurance companies attacked the state appropriation for administration to make policyholders feel that the banks were unsafe, and yet company agents used the appropriation as an alleged argument against the cheapness of bank-issued policies. Walsh had proved himself true to the program of improving the worker's condition and curbing the power of wealth and privilege, Brandeis said. Walsh had strengthened the workmen's compensation law, taken a far-seeing attitude toward public service corporations, and facilitated reorganization of the New Haven and the B. & M. The best evidence of his intelligent appreciation of the community's needs was furnished by his appointment of Joseph B. Eastman to the Public Service Commission.

When Brandeis appeared on platforms with Walsh he reiterated that it was unusual for him to take part in political campaigns. But this year progressive principles were at stake. The defeat of Walsh would pave the way for the restoration of the régime of Cannon, Boies Penrose and "Boss" Barnes. The Republican candidate was Samuel W. McCall, late of the Ballinger committee.

Republican newspapers naturally belittled the value of Brandeis' support. Congressman August P. Gardner, campaigning for McCall, thought it important, however, to pay attention to "the exclusively virtuous Mr. Brandeis" and to revive distorted history with: "The strangest and most miraculous feat on record is the somersault turned by Brandeis, the opulent and occult organizer of the United Shoe Machinery octopus, when he landed before the footlights as Brandeis, the penniless public's proud trust pulveriser." McCall won.

That fall Brandeis spoke also for suffrage at Tremont Temple and Faneuil Hall, telling how his conversion came through the experience of finding the aid of women in his public work effective and often indispensable. "Indeed, they have shown great aptitude specifically in things political. Can anyone find in the political life of this Commonwealth finer work of organization or more public-spirited devotion than that exhibited by the women in the present campaign?" Two powerful arguments sustained the demand for equal suffrage, he said: the right of women to have full share in determining the conditions under which they and their children live, and their duty to bear responsibility for those conditions.

When suffragists sought to commit him to the proposition that votes for women would lessen the frequency of war, reason controlled his enthusiasm. He was not sure there would be any important difference; the causes of war lay far deeper than the absence of the franchise.

He spoke in Philadelphia at a memorial meeting for Frederick Winslow Taylor. It was a large gathering but labor was not represented. Taylor had worked to increase men's productivity and enable them to earn higher wages, enjoy more leisure, postpone the age at which children went to work, but he encountered opposition from those he wished to help. The people who were undertaking to carry the cause forward must adjust Taylor's truths to the workers' requirements and gain the consent of those to whom the truths applied. It would take time to convince labor that greater productivity was desirable; perhaps twenty-five years. Disciples must be patient.

Brandeis used a banquet of the Boston garment unions and employers to admonish the workers to realize that first of all a business had to make a profit. If they cooperated to bring profits they were entitled to a fair share. Fairness in the division meant strong organizations on both sides.

In New York, where the protocol and Board of Arbitration continued in the dress and waist industry, Chairman Brandeis sat for a two-day session, still nursing the protocol as the means to a common understanding. He also had occasion to see how the municipal reforms inaugurated by Mayor Mitchel were operating. Mitchel's achievements would have to be made known to the people if Tammany Hall was to be kept at bay for another term. The task was difficult; it needed writers and talkers. But Brandeis felt that in this great city a thousand people could be found to enlist— men and

women competent to understand, willing to study, able to
express the results of their study. The immediate gain would
be New York's but an inestimable service would be done for
the whole country.

In contrast to this optimism was Brandeis' worry over the
Supreme Court's delay in deciding the Oregon minimum
wage case. Mrs. Evans said to him one day, when they were
out sailing off South Yarmouth, that the most sinister thing
in the United States was the suspicion of the workers that
they were not getting justice from the courts.

"Yes, you are right." He looked straight ahead. "It's the
country's greatest danger."

Incidentally, he strongly believed in an appointed judiciary.
But as long as judges were elected and the state made no
provision for campaign expenses, candidates should not be
beholden to individual contributors. The expenses must be
borne by some part of the community; why not by the
lawyers? They were usually best able to determine fitness
and most disposed to observe the proprieties.

He was scheduled to address the Chicago Bar Association,
convening at Northwestern University in January, 1916. His
topic was "The Living Law." He wished he might be able
to tell the assemblage that the court had sustained minimum
wage legislation. The trouble was, the law was not living.
It had not kept pace with the rapid development in political,
economic and social ideals. Legal justice had failed to con-
form to contemporary conceptions of social justice. Since
the adoption of the Constitution the ownership of the tools
of production had passed from the workman to the employer.
Legal science— the unwritten or judge-made laws— ignored
the new social needs, and courts continued to apply eight-
eenth-century ideas of individual liberty and the sacredness
of private property.

Where statutes giving expression to the new social
spirit were clearly constitutional, judges, imbued with

the relentless spirit of individualism, often construed
them away. Where any doubt as to the constitutionality
of such statutes could find lodgment, courts all too frequently declared the acts void.

He showed in this Chicago talk how the natural vent of
legislation was stopped by the invoking of constitutional limitations. Hundreds of statutes attempting to adjust legal rights
to the demands of social justice had within a few years been
nullified. Hence the clamor for the recall of judges and of
judicial decisions and for constitutional amendments to curb
the power of the Supreme Court. (Senator James A. Reed of
Missouri had offered one providing that no federal law be
declared unconstitutional unless two-thirds of the court so
agreed. Senator Joseph L. Bristow of Kansas sought a popular determination of any law declared unconstitutional by the
Supreme Court, and Theodore Roosevelt supported him.
Congressman Victor L. Berger of Wisconsin proposed that
the House of Representatives have final authority over all
laws.)

But courts were coming to a better appreciation of social
needs and instead of reasoning from abstract conception were
drawing on life. Here Brandeis turned the pages of his own
experience in convincing the Supreme Court of the reasonableness of the earlier Oregon statute and the maximum hour
laws of Illinois, Ohio and California. He referred also to the
New York State reversal on legislation prohibiting night work
for women, the Court of Appeals stating frankly that it had
been presented with facts (in a Brandeis brief) not in evidence
in the original case in 1907, though it might have taken judicial notice of them even then.

But the struggle for the living law must still be waged.
The Supreme Court of the United States showed by its
recent decision in a labor case "the potency of mental pre-
possessions." He cited examples bearing out a popular insistence that the court lacked an understanding of modern

industrial conditions— decisions from which his friend Holmes eloquently dissented.

Specialization in the legal profession in the past fifty years had brought to the bench men unequipped with economic and social knowledge, and their judgment suffered through a similar failing in counsel presenting cases before them. The blind were led by the blind. So it was not surprising that the laws, as administered, fell short of contemporary needs. Judges and lawyers must study economics and sociology and politics.

Holmes in '97 had put it this way— "the man of the future is the man of statistics and the master of economics."

Holmes never bothered to measure up to the prophecy. Brandeis took him seriously.

When the judgeship was offered Holmes the news came, he said, like a stroke of lightning and changed the course of his life. Brandeis, too, did not dream of appointment but his course was already fixed.

Chapter XVI

THE NOMINATION FIGHT (1)

WHEN Supreme Court Justice Joseph R. Lamar died, almost at the moment Brandeis was delivering his speech in Chicago on the living law, friends besought him, in view of his closeness to the administration, to get favorable consideration for someone to whom the constitutionality of minimum wage legislation would not need to be argued. They suggested Julian W. Mack, Learned Hand, Samuel S. Seabury. A Chicago attorney who feared that the governor of Illinois was on the list begged Brandeis to avert a calamity. Brandeis' position was that Attorney General Gregory was a thorough lawyer, careful in his recommendations, and that there was no danger. Intimates of the President understood that Taft was being regarded as desirable, but there were six Republicans on the bench and only two Democrats.

Brandeis happened to be in contact with Gregory that January on a more personal matter— to congratulate him on the outcome of the jury trial of New Haven directors prosecuted under the criminal clause of the Sherman Law. It seemed a great achievement to have obtained a disagreement over five of the directors, although six others were acquitted. He expected to be in Washington on the twenty-eighth for a dinner party at the McAdoos.

At this time Brandeis was much incensed with the suffering of Jews in Europe, and he was especially active in the movement to establish an American Jewish Congress. On the twenty-fourth he was in New York, addressing a mass meet-

ing at Carnegie Hall. That day he received a telephone call
from Boston. George W. Anderson had an important message
from Gregory— where could they meet? Brandeis was headed
for Bridgeport, to another Jewish meeting, and Anderson
could speak to him there.

A momentous series of events had led to the telephone call.
President Wilson had informed Gregory that he wanted
someone from New England for the Supreme Court vacancy.
Gregory replied that Brandeis was the man, not only as an
outstanding lawyer but as a liberal; that there should be a
liberal on the bench to voice the convictions of a large part
of the people; that Holmes was not really a liberal, nor was
he so regarded by the liberals of the country. But there was
"bound to be a fight" over confirmation, Gregory said, and
Wilson knew it. Accustomed to rely on his Boston adjutant
in New England affairs, Gregory summoned Anderson for
a consultation. Of course Anderson admired Brandeis but he
questioned the expediency of the appointment, for Boston
would oppose a Kentucky Jew and there was "bound to
be a fight."

McAdoo also proposed Brandeis and assured Wilson that
though stiff opposition would be put up by the financial interests, because they regarded the President's adviser-in-gen-
eral as a dangerous radical, the Senate would confirm. A good
many others probably mentioned Brandeis' name to Wilson.
But the President had been keeping him in mind for more
than two years, during which time Brandeis had been close
at hand, virtually living at the Hotel Gordon in Washington.
Wilson had a chance to discern his merits and the detachment
of his zeal. "A talk with Brandeis always sweeps the cobwebs
out of one's mind," he said. Wilson was aware the progressives felt he had made a mistake in naming McReynolds who
became, according to their lights, a reactionary. The selection of Brandeis would make amends. Wilson had great faith
in Gregory's judgment, and Brandeis was the only one he
discussed with his Attorney General.

Gregory and Anderson drank a few highballs together
and parted without coming to a decision. Next morning,
when Anderson was walking off the drinks, a clerk rushed
out of the Department of Justice building and said the Attorney General was anxiously trying to reach him. The
President wanted a report sooner than expected. He was preparing to leave for the West. What was Anderson's answer?
Privately Anderson thought Brandeis would be of greater
usefulness if he remained out of the court, but he made the
recommendation. Gregory made it to Wilson, and Wilson
was satisfied.

At once Anderson was dispatched to Brandeis. In Bridgeport the justiceship was tendered. To Anderson's surprise
the assent came quickly. A single word was telegraphed to
Gregory: "Yes."

The news Brandeis took to Otis Place brought a thankful
sigh from his white-haired wife. No one knew better than
she his capacity for work and his unflinching drive to the
limits of that capacity. Nearing sixty, he was tackling the
problems of Zionism with the same energy, persistence and
physical exertion he had concentrated on earlier causes. Nature had already given him warnings in his recent illnesses.
It was inevitable, as he grew older, that he would be obliged
to give up this kind of work.

When friends compared the limitations of the office with
the uncircumscribed scope of a free lance battling for the
right, he smiled. To Edward Filene, who advised him not to
lock himself up in a court, he said, "No one declines an invitation to the Supreme Court." His jocular tone glossed over
the refusal, more than fifty years before, of another Jew,
Judah P. Benjamin, favored by President Franklin Pierce.
He was glad Wilson wanted to make the appointment and
was convinced, all things considered, he had done well to
accept. Yet he was not entirely sure he ought to be congratulated.

On the twenty-eighth his nomination was sent to the Senate, and that evening at the gay dinner of the McAdoos, Wilson, beaming, presented him to Justice Hughes and Justice Mahlon Pitney as their future associate. The guest whose name was flashed in late-edition headlines smiled in the flicker of the social spotlight. The next morning's papers carried stories on the impending fight.

They told of the dismay of Democratic senators, who were expected to support the President's choice of a radical and socialist. There was a rumor that Senator Lodge would lead the Republican opposition; another that Lodge feared to do so lest Brandeis beat him in a senatorial race, and still another that Weeks, the other Republican senator from Massachusetts, would lead it because of his banking connections. The suspicion was voiced that Wilson named Brandeis to pay off a private obligation or else to win the Jewish vote in the 1916 election. The looming objection to the nominee was "a lack of judicial temperament."

Wall Street was stunned, and newspapers accustomed to expressing its point of view lost no time in doing so again. The *New York Press* regarded the appointment as an insult to the members of the court— Brandeis was "a man of furious partisanship, of violent antagonisms, and of irredeemable prejudices" which utterly disqualified him from acting in a judicial capacity, "where nothing but calm, cold reason should dominate the mind." If Wilson did not withdraw the nomination the Senate should throw it out. The *New York Tribune* said: "It would be a misfortune if he carried to the Supreme bench the narrow, mistaken attitude toward the vital industry of transportation which he took when he was serving as adviser to the Interstate Commerce Committee." The *New York Sun* satirically suggested that Wilson was trying to test the vigilance of the Senate; the appointment was utterly unfit. The *Boston Herald* asserted that few of Brandeis' friends would claim him to be judicially minded. "It is as a controversialist rather than as a dispassionate weigher of facts and arguments that he has achieved distinction. This is not the type of mind which has proved most serviceable in the deliberations of the Supreme Court." The *Boston Transcript* regretted that the exigencies of the approaching presidential campaign should have caused Wilson "to attempt to force upon the Supreme Court one whom the Senate is reported to have been unwilling to confirm as a member of the Cabinet." The *Detroit Free Press* called Brandeis least fit for the cold, dispassionate work of the court. It was a political debt to be paid for swinging the progressives in 1912. The Senate should now stand between the country and "this prostitution of patronage to partisanship."

The reactions of the friendly press were just as interesting. The *New York World* recalled that Hughes, in his day as a lawyer, had also been feared by selfish and corrupt interests. It was important that there should be judges whose point of view was not determined by tradition. Brandeis was undeniably a radical— "and it is because he is a radical of unusual ability and character that his elevation to the bench will be regarded by most people with emphatic approval." The *Springfield Republican* observed that a man of his type in the highest court of the land "would tend to make every trade unionist, every Socialist, every Anarchist even more loyal to our Government and to American institutions." The *Indianapolis Star* predicted that with Brandeis on the bench the country might expect "some red-hot dissenting opinions now and then." The *San Diego Sun* lamented: he would be burying himself in a standpat court in the futile rôle of a dissenter.

Protests against confirmation were reported to be pouring into the Capitol. The old charges of 1912 were revived and laid before the Senate Committee on the Judiciary in executive session. Although McAdoo prevailed on him to request open hearings, Brandeis preferred to leave the fight to others. He went to New York to attend to Zionist and Consumers' League matters, stopping at the Goldmark home. A reporter for *The Sun* asked if he had heard of charges. He said: "I have nothing to say about anything, and that goes for all time and to all newspapers, including *The Sun* and the moon."

He did not believe the opposition was based on racial grounds. Nor did it appear to him when representatives of the United Shoe Machinery bobbed up in Washington distributing pamphlets that his old enemies were bent on spite. No, they were afraid of him. To them it was like putting the robes on Eugene Victor Debs.

First to speak out was Louis A. Coolidge, treasurer of the United. "It is customary," he said, "to consign crooks to jail and not to the bench."

Mellen's attitude was different: the appointment was excellent:

> He was always on the opposite side from me, but my personal relations with him have been most cordial, for he has always been courteous and decent. Even if he has been a radical before his appointment he is sure to become a conservative after he is sworn into office. I can see no reason why his appointment should not be confirmed.

Newspaper polls of the Senate showed thirty-six opposed, from nine to fourteen doubtful. Some Democratic senators, notably James A. Reed of Missouri, Hoke Smith of Georgia, and John K. Shields of Tennessee, were known to be hostile. Some doubted that he belonged to their party. Senator Lee S. Overman of North Carolina, acting chairman of the judiciary committee, said a committee vote at that time would surely reject the nomination; but a sub-committee would be named, hearings would be held, and opinions might be changed. The insurgent bloc in the Senate was not united for Brandeis. La Follette and Norris were delighted, but Albert B. Cummins of Iowa held back because of the still rankling feeling of Mid-Western railroad commissioners that Brandeis traduced them in the five percent rate case. William

S. Kenyon, also of Iowa, wavered. William E. Borah of Idaho wired Clifford Thorne, then chairman of the Iowa railroad commission:

> Give me the facts with reference to the conduct of Louis D. Brandeis in the five percent case. I will treat the information as confidential unless you consent otherwise.

Thorne came on to Washington eagerly. Meanwhile the financial clique was devising a form of presentation which would use a front of upstanding Bostonians to screen its enmity and construct a case of unprofessional conduct. Brandeis stayed over in New York long enough to sit as chairman of the dress and waist industry's Board of Arbitration. Then he resigned, cancelled all speaking engagements, and retired from public activities for the duration of the contest. The Senate sub-committee scheduled hearings to begin February ninth. Sidney W. Winslow of the United Shoe Machinery hurried to Washington, burning to be heard.

Brandeis was not eager for the office. He would have preferred to be let alone till he was sixty-five, which meant altogether. But the coming of the battle convinced him of the correctness of his instinct that he could not afford to decline. Refusal would have been tantamount to deserting the progressive forces. With regard to the struggle over confirmation his feeling now was like that of the fabled mountain woman who loved a good fight and, seeing her husband wrestle with a bear, cried out, "Go it husband— go it bear!" Brandeis was inclined to be the interested spectator, with the inside knowledge that the bear in this instance represented the concentrated power of the financial community.

Allegations of unprofessional conduct, which the bear could be heard growling in the clinch, sounded humorous. Brandeis had said of himself that he pursued a new way of practicing law which the grumblers could not understand. He told a friend: "My record will stand on its merits. I have no skeletons in the closet. There is nothing I have done, my family has done, or my wife's family, that won't bear scrutiny— not even anything adverse that a man might not be responsible for." If a habit of studying problems as a whole was not evidence of a detached mind and judicial temperament, so much the worse.

Now the drama opened in the committee room in the Capitol. Senator William E. Chilton, Democrat, of West Virginia, sat as chairman. Thorne was called up first, and led by Senator Cummins he responded to questions with alacrity and bitterness. He charged Brandeis with being "guilty of infidelity, breach of faith and unprofessional conduct in connection with one of the greatest cases of this generation." Without warning to other counsel Brandeis, "who participated in the cross-examination from our side of the table, who was employed by the Interstate Commerce Commission," had declared that the railroads' revenues were smaller than was consistent with their prosperity and the community's welfare. "I considered that concession practically fatal."

Senator Thomas J. Walsh, Montana progressive Democrat, asked whether Brandeis' statement might have implied either that the rates were not high enough or that the management of the roads was inefficient. Thorne admitted that Brandeis did not concede the carriers were entitled to higher rates; adequacy of the revenues was first considered.

Adequacy of net revenues was meant, not gross revenues, Walsh pointed out. He was joined in this effort at clarification by Senator Fletcher, who knew Brandeis from the Ballinger case.

Thorne went on to say that an appraisal of railroads by the I.C.C. was under way and many valuation cases would doubtless come before the Supreme Court. "If you gradually pack that tribunal with men possessing preconceived notions . . . as to extremely high returns . . . it is going to be very costly to the American people." He said Brandeis had com-

THE BLOW THAT ALMOST KILLED FATHER.

A cartoon by Rollin Kirby from the New York World

mitted himself to the proposition that a net return of seven and one-half percent was inadequate— "niggardly" was the word he quoted. Thorne did not like Brandeis' "sarcastic fling."

Walsh brought out that a seven and one-half percent return meant five percent for dividend and two and one-half percent for other purposes; that what Brandeis meant by a niggardly surplus was the amount above dividends.

"I believe that he is committed to this idea that the earnings should be very large and larger than the commission unanimously said was adequate," Thorne continued. "The Supreme Court has, in recent years, taken the position that a merely nominal compensation is not sufficient. It must be substantial."

"Briefly," Walsh summed up for him, "your position is that he would be too favorably inclined toward the contention of the railroads?"

"Unquestionably I think so."

Some of the sting of Thorne's criticism was removed by the next witness, Ex-Lieutenant-Governor John M. Eshleman of California, who had been head of his state's railroad commission during the advance rate case. Eshleman said:

> I have never been able to tell why Mr. Thorne felt just the way he did about the conduct of this case, and I have yet to find a single man connected with railroad regulation, up to this time, who agrees with Mr. Thorne's position.

Eshleman reminded the senators that Brandeis had not recommended the five percent increase, that all rates were still being made in the dark in the absence of valuation and it was impossible to determine where to grant an advance. If Brandeis had taken any other than an impartial attitude between the parties Eshleman would have thought him failing in his duty. He wondered why Thorne attributed unworthy motives to Brandeis.

Cummins saw the difference: Eshleman conceived of Brandeis' function as being judicial, whereas Thorne believed that he and Brandeis were associated in defence of the public.

Frank Lyon, counsel for the I.C.C. in the ten percent case and for a shipper in the five percent case, said Brandeis' function was to ascertain the truth on both sides. The remark about surplus was inconsequential and no one paid much attention to it except Thorne. Brandeis was interested in obtaining sources of revenue to increase the net and found cattle cars being hauled for one or two cents a car-mile between Chicago and New York. At this Walsh brightened up with an observation that Thorne represented cattle-shippers upon whom Brandeis tried to put additional but justifiable loads. Cummins persisted. He said Brandeis had done more than develop the facts on both sides— he expressed conclusions.

Here in the committee room sat the baronial figure of Clarence Barron. Walsh looked at a list of witnesses and remarked that there were some who knew little about the nominee at first hand. "Mr. Barron, I have in mind, was called here because he is the editor of a newspaper which contained an editorial commenting on the propriety of this nomination. I assume that he has little, if any, direct and positive knowledge."

"Excuse me, did I understand you to say 'little'?"

Walsh did not want the committee's time to be taken up with listening to opinions. Cummins said Barron was sent for to give an account of himself for publishing the editorial. Fletcher objected to hearsay evidence.

When Frank Lyon finished, Barron put in: "Mr. Chairman, may I be permitted to tell the little I know?" He had ten galley proofs in his hand.

Someone was ahead of him, a New York lawyer named Thomas C. Spelling, who wanted to read a record of Brandeis' views on constitutional law as expressed before congressional committees. Fletcher told him to hand it in—"We can read, you know." But the witness called attention to Brandeis' opinion that banking may be considered interstate commerce. Did anybody else think so?

Cummins: "Yes, there are people who believe that."

Such a view was absurd, the lawyer said. It evinced a lack of a clear understanding of the Constitution.

Barron pushed forward. He described himself as a farmer, residing in Cohasset and "connected" with the *Boston News Bureau*, the *Philadelphia News Bureau* and the *Wall Street Journal*. He admitted writing an editorial entitled, "An Unfit Appointment," which called the nomination an insult to New England and to the business interests of the country. He had said that one thing to be thankful for was that the nomination would help bury Wilson at the next election. The editorial asserted that Brandeis, as counsel for the Western opposition to the United, threatened government prosecution unless the United gave these manufacturers rebates. Brandeis became a kitchen cabinet to assist Wilson and the Department of Justice in prosecuting and persecuting the United. Brandeis was the leader of all the political and financial forces smashing the credit of the New Haven and B. & M. systems. It was not necessary to uncover the grave of Patrick Lennox or reopen the Warren settlements to demonstrate his moral fibre. It was necessary only to point to the life insurance scandals where Brandeis appeared "first as a public agitator summoning the policyholders and next . . . in defense of the life insurance company with a retainer in his pocket." Any Senator who thought him fit for the bench was invited to visit Boston for a day "and learn how Brandeis has garnered his wealth."

The committee wanted to know what facts he had as the basis for this editorial, and Barron said:

> About ten years ago Mr. Brandeis warned me that I must be particular concerning what I said about him in the financial field and concerning his financial statements— in fact, in general and particular in regard to

his record; and ever since I have endeavored to comply with his request and have been very careful, and therefore I had the court records of Massachusetts examined and have kept on file in my safe memoranda in relation to what was of record as to Mr. Brandeis, so that it might be useful and in order that upon it I might be able to speak when it was required.

Chilton: "Have you and he been enemies?"
Barron: "Not at all. I have not spoken with him for thirty years."

He offered to read a letter he had written concerning his investigation and was willing to say, privately, to whom he wrote it. Chilton refused to take anything privately. Walsh objected to introducing the letter in evidence; names of investigators and the public records were admissible, but not views based on the record. Did Barron have any personal knowledge of the facts he referred to? Fletcher and Chilton tried to pin him down. He had none. But he suggested the names of people to call in.

Barron proceeded to picture how the Brandeis firm fraudulently obtained the signatures of a dying old man, Patrick Lennox; how Brandeis was paid to help the New Haven ruin and capture the New York & New England "and thereby establish a transportation monopoly in New England"— and Mellen should be called to prove this. Mellen telegraphed the committee that he had no authentic information. "I am not at all unfriendly to Brandeis and I know nothing about his career except hearsay." The opposition did not press for Mellen.

The Boston lawyer who Barron said was thoroughly familiar with the Warren affair was Hollis R. Bailey, Harvard Law graduate of the class of '78 and attorney for Ned Warren. He said the plan which Brandeis helped his partner Sam Warren devise resulted in a breach of trust. The beneficiaries suffered a loss of some hundreds of thousands of dollars, while Sam earned $75,000 to $100,000 a year as against the $10,000 income he had from his law business.

Fletcher tried to show that the terms of the lease were favorable and Ned received over a period $50,000 to $200,000 a year. But, Walsh said, as business fell off Ned, originally satisfied with the arrangement, needed more money for buying "things for the art museum."

Senator C. D. Clark, Republican, of Wyoming, who turned a friendly ear to Barron, asked Bailey if he knew the general opinion of the Boston bar. Walsh interrupted; the question should be more specific. Fletcher said they could not accept an opinion of another's opinion. Bailey answered:

> That he is a very able lawyer; that he is a man of keen intellect; that he is an able advocate; that he is not entirely trustworthy. I think that about covers it.

He told how as a student a year behind Brandeis, when the latter's "eyes gave out . . . I acted as his eyes, you know, and in that way acted as tutor for him."

Winslow came on. He read a long prepared statement into the record, reciting a history of Brandeis' participation in his company and giving no hint of Brandeis' real reason for resigning except the imputation of a new retainer. He added:

> Never during his connection with the company did he express disapproval of their acts, methods or policy. On the contrary, the company's method of conducting business met with his full approval.

He said Brandeis acted unprofessionally and dishonorably in using knowledge acquired during his connection with the United to attack the company for his new clients. He quoted liberally from Brandeis' defence of the United before the Massachusetts legislature in 1906 but omitted mention of Brandeis' behind-the-scenes negotiations for Jones and Mc-Elwain.

He denied as absolutely false Brandeis' assertion that the

United acquired Plant's patents through control of the money market.

The footwork on the thick carpets of Wall Street was not heard by the public. Paul D. Cravath, of the law firm which represented Kuhn, Loeb & Company and handled most of the important work in the financial district, was engaged by unknown parties to read through all of Brandeis' writings and pick out the damning spots. The Kuhn-Loebs and the Seligmans would much rather have had Louis Marshall nominated. The Street agreed on Austen G. Fox, another New York lawyer, to take charge at the hearing. Ostensibly he was selected by a Boston group of fifty-four citizens, mostly lawyers, who sent a petition to the Senate via Lodge. There was no one big enough in Boston. Sherman L. Whipple was unavailable.

The Senate sub-committee agreed to let Fox marshal the opposition provided Anderson, having Gregory's confidence, brought out the other side for the committee. Both attorneys were to act without compensation from the government.

Once Anderson made it clear he was not appearing for Brandeis, he pitched into a cross-examination of Winslow and demonstrated that the tying clause long antedated the organization of the United company and "would not have excited the comment of any lawyer as being unusual or probably illegal in 1900, would it?" Anderson repaired some lapses of Winslow's memory, and the witness repeatedly tried to dodge questions, not admitting that he and Brandeis split on a question of policy but acknowledging that Brandeis in criticizing the company later did not need the information obtained as counsel: the leases were practically public documents on file in every shoe manufacturer's office. Winslow denied knowing in 1906 that Brandeis had shoe manufacturer clients, but the company's pamphlet quoted Brandeis as saying at the Massachusetts hearing:

I have an infinitely greater interest in the shoe manufacturing business as counsel for a large number of shoe manufacturers than I have in this company— an infinitely greater interest.

Anderson offered the pamphlet in evidence as part of a publicity campaign against Brandeis' reputation and for its value in showing that its circulation influenced people's opinion of Brandeis. He squelched one lie after another. Winslow admitted the pamphlet was sent to every member of Congress and had been issued because Brandeis fathered anti-trust legislation which ended in the passage of the Clayton Act. This reminded Cummins of the time Brandeis appeared before the Senate interstate commerce committee:

> He gave a great performance when he talked— the most comprehensive review of the subject which I have ever known, in the course of which he illustrated some of his views by reference to the United . . .

While Fox was in New York to obtain for the committee an official list of the persons who employed him, Moorfield Storey (suggested by Barron) told the tale of the Goldsmith suits against the New England Railroad, of a suit brought against the Austin Corbin estate for compensation promised for the use of Goldsmith's name, and a settlement made by the New Haven.

Storey paralleled this hiding behind Goldsmith with the use of Glavis as a shield for the retainer from *Collier's Weekly*. He described Brandeis' reputation at the Boston bar as that of an able and very energetic lawyer "ruthless in the attainments of his objects, not scrupulous in the methods he adopts and not to be trusted." He said there was a long-standing lack of confidence in him among a representative class of men in that part of the country. When Walsh supposed that the New Haven's powerful influence shaped this attitude Storey retorted that the feeling had started earlier than the New Haven fight, had become intensified with time, and was

shared by A. Lawrence Lowell, who signed the petition, and
some of the largest trustees and leading lawyers in Boston.
True, all of the Law School faculty, but one, endorsed Brandeis. Dean Pound had come from the Dakotas only a few
years before and, like Frankfurter, the young man from New
York, was unfamiliar with Brandeis' reputation among practicing lawyers.

> He has always been very courteous to the school. Mr.
> Brandeis is an attractive person and he has been interested
> in this law school and has helped it, and I fancy he en-
> joys the confidence of those professors. Some of them
> have never been in practice with him.

With McClennen, Brandeis' partner, on the ground Anderson was able to elicit significant facts. Had not Storey been
counsel for one of the Warren brothers, Fiske, in the suit
brought by Edward? Fiske and Sam both were lessees of the
paper mill. It was a perfectly fair arrangement of the Warren
property, Storey said. Nothing in the trial reflected on Sam
Warren or Brandeis. There was apparently no reason for
suggesting independent counsel for Edward. The family was
united and harmonious, and the common practice for lawyers having the confidence of all parties to a family settlement was to represent them all. Storey said he would have
done "perhaps very much as Mr. Brandeis did if I had been
in his place."

Whipple testified. He had been counsel with Hollis Bailey
in the same case and disagreed with Bailey that Brandeis
framed the Warren lease to give Sam an advantage over his
brother. The entire transaction was "free from any taint of
dishonest motives or intentional fraud." Whipple had also
served in the Lennox matter, for James Lennox, after the
assignment to creditors. At the time Whipple disagreed with
Brandeis' procedure in putting into bankruptcy a man who
thought Brandeis should be acting for him, but later Whipple
saw that Brandeis had been misunderstood in his desire to be

attorney for the situation and did not really desert a client.

The broad view Brandeis took was not quite the human view, Whipple said. Brandeis' love of looking after everybody concerned was easily misconstrued. His course would not have been judged wrongly "if Mr. Brandeis had been a different sort of man, not so aloof, not so isolated, with more of the comradery of the bar, gave his confidence, said to them, when he was charged with doing anything doubtful, 'Boys, what do you think about it?' and talked it over with them. . . But Mr. Brandeis is aloof; he is intensely centered in carrying out his own ideas and his own ideals . . . and he does not, so far as I know, consult with anybody or take them into his confidence, and he will do things of a startling character."

The Lennox case was the best example, Whipple said. He would never have understood Brandeis' position that a lawyer's duty extends not only to the debtor but to every creditor if he had not gone to Brandeis for an explanation. Brandeis would never vouchsafe one word unless somebody asked him. It was unfortunate that Brandeis "instead of resting in the security of the purity of his own mind . . . has not cultivated association with gentlemen who are equally honest. . . ." It seemed to Whipple that Brandeis wrapped himself in the self-sufficiency of his conscience and after working out a problem gave little thought to the effect on other minds— "and sometimes I have thought he took a delight in smashing a bit the traditions of the bar which most of us revere but many of which I think ought to be smashed."

Through Cummins and Walsh it was shown that Brandeis had let Lennox know he represented some of the creditors; that it was the accepted practice of an attorney at the request of a failing debtor to draw up the assignment and act as attorney for the assignee.

Anderson told the committee that the Brandeis firm was generally regarded as one of the leading law offices in Boston, the spot to which the prize men of Harvard Law School were attracted for the past twenty years. Brandeis could have had one of the largest incomes in New England had he chosen to devote himself entirely to his lucrative law practice. Was not his "reputation" the result of his dealing with "great public evils up there that the rest of us did not have the time, ability, courage or disposition to go after?"

Not entirely, Whipple answered; but Brandeis had antagonized powerful interests whose feeling of bitterness was very unpleasant. The Boston lawyers who signed the remonstrance were sincere, but they misunderstood Brandeis, and many were identified with large proprietary interests. His own opinion was that the nominee was able, learned, conscientious, highminded. The most striking feature of Brandeis' career was unselfish and unswerving devotion to the uplift of the less fortunate. On the bench he would exert a strong influence establishing ideals to which he had devoted his recent years.

Back from New York, Fox announced he was now in a position to give the names of the persons he represented. The list contained Lowell, Charles Francis Adams, Francis Peabody, Roger S. Warner, and others. They were the ones who had circulated the petition. Warner, son of Joseph B. Warner, whom Brandeis had opposed in the New Haven fight, notified Fox of his employment.

The readers of *Harper's Weekly* were getting a lively slant on the proceedings from Hapgood, who wrote that he had gone to the bottom of the same charges several years back. Once understood, these accusations "redounded all the more to the glory of a great lawyer, a noble citizen and one of the bravest and most disinterested of men." The defamers were dress-suit patriots who "preferred mud without courage." Nearly all were trustees for estates with large holdings in the New Haven, its associated banks, or the United. Hapgood said Lowell knew absolutely nothing about the subject but was loyal to his dinner parties and family associations; that Major Higginson was the man at whose bidding gentlemen acted, and "gentlemen will be gentlemen."

The liberals of the country, in the less organized way of liberals, contended for Brandeis by letter, editorial and conversation. Paul U. Kellogg of *The Survey* engaged Frances Perkins, who happened to be out of a job, to gather signatures for a memorial to the Senate. In an incredibly short time this capable woman compiled a roster of social workers, publicists, manufacturers and labor leaders, headed by Newton D. Baker, ex-mayor of Cleveland and president of the National Consumers' League.

This made good publicity but it was a mere murmur beside the detonating statements produced by Fox.

He read off the names of members of the Boston bar handed to him by Lodge.

The tenor of their opinion was: "We do not believe that Mr. Brandeis has the judicial temperament and capacity which should be required in a judge of the Supreme Court." His reputation did not have their confidence, they said. A character witness, Edward W. Hutchins, described them as men of standing. Anderson identified them more sharply as having been connected with United, Old Dominion and Gillette affairs, with the John Hancock Life Insurance Company, and so on. He said the Hutchins law firm, one of the oldest in Boston, represented the vested interests and a large part of the community's wealth; that Brandeis had been the subject of an advertising campaign in the *News Bureau* for ten years, and had engaged in a good many controversies "which have brought him a very large degree of enmity, have they not?"

Hutchins: "I think so. Yes."

And was bad blood engendered in and about Boston in the New Haven fight?

"Yes, a good deal."

The Barron newspaper and advertising agency machinery provided unusual facilities for attacking a man, Anderson went on. A great many people had been led to regard the critics of the New Haven as destroyers of property and values.

Anderson had in his pocket a letter from Arthur D. Hill, former district attorney in Boston, and even if it did not seem wholly fair he thought he would take his chances with it.

According to Hill, Brandeis was universally acknowledged as one of the ablest in legal learning and effectiveness but was not generally popular with the bar. Many considered him unpleasant to deal with in business matters and unscrupulous in professional conduct. Hill was inclined to doubt whether this view had a solid foundation. Many of Brandeis' opponents were Hill's personal friends and he believed them mistaken. The real basis, he said, was that Brandeis was a radical and a Jew. To spend a considerable part of one's career in attacking established institutions would alone account for a very large measure of unpopularity, Hill said. "It would be difficult, if not impossible, for a radical to be generally popular with Boston lawyers or to escape severe adverse criticism of his motives and conduct." Barron's skillful and long-continued press campaign for the New Haven management cumulated hostility by mere repetition. "When you add to this that Mr. Brandeis is an outsider, successful, and a Jew, you have, I think, sufficiently explained most of the feelings against him."

Hill called Brandeis a merciless antagonist, fighting up to the limit and "with great technicality . . . without perhaps always a keen regard for fair play." On the other hand, Brandeis would make a great judge because of his legal acumen, deep sympathetic insight, power of careful analysis, ability to see facts and the law in their larger relations, capacity for taking a broad judicial view of any question to which he applied his mind, and "an unusual grasp of those social and economic conditions which underlie many of the most important questions with which the Supreme Court will have to deal." Hill's final touch was that he differed with Brandeis politically.

Not a breath of radicalism was blown by the opposition. None of its witnesses ventured on the quicksands of economics. From a safe brink they tossed red herrings. To illustrate Brandeis' lack of straightforwardness Hutchins cited his appearance for Glavis instead of for *Collier's*. Mark Sullivan, who had been Hapgood's associate editor, testified that Brandeis' relation to the magazine was fully known in Washington and to the press. No admonition of secrecy was ever made. Anderson brought forth Hapgood, who fully refuted the charge of concealment. Fox declined to cross-examine him.

From first-hand knowledge of that case Fletcher asserted that *Collier's* could not have had any standing before the Ballinger committee as a party to the Glavis complaints. Senator John D. Works, Republican, of California, who was substituting for Senator Clark, disagreed. Then Fox's assistant, Kenneth M. Spence, tried to link Brandeis with the newspaper release which Ballinger's stenographer Kerby had given out. Chilton and Fletcher showed by the record that Brandeis had never given advice on that score, and Chilton wanted Fox to say frankly whether he meant that Brandeis conspired to have Kerby act as a detective in Ballinger's office. The answer was indirect.

The embattled Bostonians went back to the Warren affair. William S. Youngman, another attorney who had served Edward Warren, said that Sam Warren, an honorable man, was deceived by Brandeis. Youngman was unaware, till Anderson told him, that Sam was second in his class at Harvard and a good lawyer. He squirmed when Anderson challenged his assertion that Brandeis chloroformed Sam's conscientious scruples. Youngman had been hired by Barron in 1913 to investigate Brandeis and report on the Glavis, Lennox and insurance matters, but he denied knowing how Barron intended to use the information.

Dignified old General Albert E. Pillsbury testified to Brandeis' reputation for unbounded audacity and duplicity.

Fox: "Of what, sir?"

Pillsbury: "Of duplicity, double dealing. A man who works

under cover so that nobody ever knows where he really is
or what he is really about. I haven't ever heard him accused
of cheating in money transactions."

Pillsbury said he began hearing things about him thirty
years back but did not remember having had professional relations with him. But Anderson reminded him of the Boston
Elevated in 1902, when Pillsbury was its counsel and Brandeis
balked its plan. Pillsbury forgot. Some things left no impression on his mind, he said. Anderson flashed a contemporary
pamphlet issued by the Public Franchise League. Still Pillsbury had no recollection of the controversy. Dim, too, was
his memory of the gas interests, clients of his when Brandeis
fought them over inflated capitalization.

Pillsbury: "Mr. Brandeis, as I have said, has appeared very
often in the character of a friend of the people and has very
often been reputed to be under pay."

Anderson: "Have you any instance of that?"

Pillsbury: "Nothing whatever. I know nothing about the
facts."

He simply founded his opinion on what he had heard;
never tried to run down any of the rumors or the remarks
of his friends. Unwilling to lay his friends open, he was,
however, pressed into mentioning J. H. Benton (former
counsel for the New Haven, Anderson observed).

According to Hutchins the downfall of the New England
Railroad played a major part in the formation of the nominee's reputation. The lawyer who brought Brandeis into the
case, William J. Kelly (since become a judge of the Supreme
Court of New York), told his story to the committee: Brandeis was not employed to wreck the New England— it had
already been badly wrecked by self-benefiting directors, represented by Moorfield Storey.

To prove that Brandeis took two sides on the question of
railroad mergers and covertly worked for Harriman, Fox
subpoenaed Waddill Catchings, who in 1907 went to partner Nutter for help on Illinois Central proxies. But Catch-

ings said, "The hardest interview I had during the whole campaign was with Mr. Brandeis in convincing him of the justness of our cause." The experience lasted two hours. "I had occasion to retain other lawyers and no one ever raised that question."

One of the stockholders whom the proxy-gatherer solicited was a solid Bostonian named Francis Peabody, who said Sam Warren had been a great friend of his from Dedham Polo Club days. Peabody gave his proxy to Fish and did not believe that Brandeis had no connection with Harriman. He testified that he lost faith in Brandeis after the Warren trial, and that Boston's admiration for his brilliant advocacy of Glavis' case cooled off when it was learned that *Collier's* paid him. Peabody said Brandeis "made almost a practice" of concealing his clients' identities, "which struck me as being disingenuous and not entirely honorable."

Answering Fox, Peabody said, "I once sat a long time hearing Mr. Anderson attacking the New Haven road."

Fox: "I thought it might be interesting to note that Mr. Anderson and Mr. Brandeis had been connected with each other in one of the matters here under investigation."

But when Anderson admitted that he foolishly invested in New Haven stock despite Brandeis' disclosures and did not enter the merger fray until late in 1913, Fox realized it was better to hew to the line of unprofessional conduct. (Anderson had two growing boys and the low level of old reliable New Haven stock tempted him.)

The story of the Gillette Safety Razor Company was brought up. The attorney for the director who had been deprived of a promised vice-presidency testified that Brandeis drew up the agreement and later admitted it to be legally non-enforceable. Fletcher showed that the witness did not want to leave an impression of bad faith on Brandeis' part but a belief that Mr. Gillette prevented the fulfilment of the pact.

Then Kenneth M. Spence, somewhat more aggressive than

Fox, used Barron's exhumation of the Equitable Life episode as evidence of double dealing. He resurrected the suit of a policyholder who charged the insurance company with the same abuses which Brandeis had condemned publicly. He matched this with Brandeis' court appearance in behalf of the company. Here was a photostat of a ten-dollar check which another policyholder paid Brandeis after the protective committee was formed— the inference being that pay was accepted for a pretended public service.

McClennen took the floor and recited facts. Slow-spoken, he gave a conviction of thoroughness. Profuse in details, he made an open effort to stick to history and avoid the rôle of defender. A feeling arose in the room that the nominee himself was speaking through his partner.

When McClennen was graduated at Harvard in '95 as first in his class, Professor Thayer told him to see Brandeis, whose office was one of a handful of the most desirable in Boston to enter. In five years McClennen became a member of the firm. In 1901 the firm became correspondent for the Equitable's New York attorneys. The relations still continued. At no time did the company remonstrate over Brandeis' speech against its practices or his work for the protective committee. The activities of that committee were in no wise checked by the policyholder's suit, which at first turned on jurisdiction. Most of Brandeis' recommendations for reform were accepted by the management and many were enacted by the New York legislature. The ten-dollar check had no bearing. It was in payment of advice on whether to take the cash-surrender value of a policy. Fox accepted as true McClennen's statement that Brandeis received no money for the crusade.

McClennen recalled that when he applied for the position one of the things he had heard about was Brandeis' good work on the New York & New England Railroad. Fox objected to his testifying to matters which took place when he was still in law school. McClennen's measured reply was: "I am afraid I will be the first witness who testified who has not told a great many things learned otherwise than by personal observation. I got this fact [that Brandeis' part in the suit ended in June, 1893] from the diary in the office." Judge Kelly did not learn from Corbin about the New Haven's connection until the latter part of that year.

Next McClennen delved into the annals of the United Shoe Machinery and showed that the tying clauses, carried over from one of the constituent companies and dating back to the Civil War, were never questioned until 1906, and that Brandeis was not asked for an opinion on the legality of the United's operations under the Sherman Law until about that time. McClennen picked flaws in Winslow's testimony and with the help of dates in the office diary and memoranda Brandeis had made of telephone talks with Winslow he straightened out the story.

Walsh understood that the opposition was trying to prove Brandeis unfaithful in going over to the shoe manufacturers and that McClennen intended to show that Brandeis had always worked with them. Winslow, Barron, et al. spread the tale that Brandeis deserted the United for a new retainer. And so Anderson, feeling that the committee was entitled to know what steps Brandeis took to be free of motives attributed to him, drew out of McClennen the fact that the Shoe Manufacturers' Alliance paid $2,500 to Brandeis, who then returned the money out of his own funds and credited his partners with their share.

McClennen: "Mr. Brandeis has a definite percentage of the profits, and while we can stand it for him to give his time to public causes, he has thought that perhaps it was a little hard on the rest of us to ask him to give his time to public causes when there was a client ready to pay him for those same services."

There were other stories to reconstruct but McClennen yielded for the present. Stephen S. Gregory, a Chicago lawyer who had taken over the practice of Chief Justice Fuller and was a former president of the American Bar Association, extolled Brandeis' character and good name. But Fox observed that Gregory never practiced in Boston.

However, Melvin O. Adams, a Boston lawyer for thirty-eight years, who had known the nominee all that time, said the Massachusetts bar unanimously considered him very able, of profound learning, and a large portion believed him to be actuated by lofty purposes, honest and trustworthy; but that the group which included Peabody were "in the network of State Street."

Asa P. French, who followed Adams as United States attorney in Boston, testified he had not once heard Brandeis' reputation assailed by an impartial critic, one whose opinions or interests had not been antagonized by Brandeis. "We have what I may call an aristocracy of the Boston bar . . . they cannot, I think, consider with equanimity the selection of anybody for a position on the great court of the country from that community who is not a typical, hereditary Bostonian."

To these testimonials Fox could reply only by asking Adams and French if they had read the documents in the Lennox case. Fox had no questions to ask of Thomas J. Boynton, former attorney general of Massachusetts, who said he had not heard ill of Brandeis until the United circulated its pamphlet.

Newton D. Baker dwelt on Brandeis' standing with social workers— as the greatest lawyer of their group, a detached and highminded man. Baker presented a brief with the signatures Frances Perkins had gathered. There were Walter Lippmann, Reverend Percy Stickney Grant, Reverend John Haynes Holmes, Rabbi Stephen S. Wise, Ernest Poole, Hamilton Holt, Walter Weyl, Lawrence Abbott, Florence Kelley, Belle I. Moskowitz, Lillian D. Wald, Morris Hillquit, Frederic C. Howe, George W. Kirchwey, Owen R. Lovejoy, Henry Bruère, William J. Schieffelin, Professor E. R. N. Seligman, Oscar Straus, Charles R. Crane, Adolph and Sam Lewisohn, among others.

Eye-witness evidence came from Joseph Walker, member
of the Massachusetts legislature from 1904 to 1911 and the
Speaker for two years. He had been in the Brandeis fights—
had written a pamphlet against the gas companies, opposed
the New Haven's trolley acquisitions, campaigned for savings bank insurance— facing with Brandeis the bitterness of
the financial lords. As a legislator he always relied on information brought by the Public Franchise League, another
thorn in State Street's flesh. He had no social or political relations with Brandeis, who "got in wrong" for his work.

> We must realize also, in addition to these leaders of
> finance, 7,000 stockholders of the New Haven in Massa-
> chusetts and their stock was dropping. They were afraid
> of an investigation. They wanted to keep things quiet,
> and they laid a great deal of the blame on Mr. Brandeis
> for originating a situation which was not his fault.

Walker said Brandeis' reputation stood as high as any
man's in the state before these matters came up. More businessmen lost confidence in him after the decision in *Muller
v. Oregon* and his constant activity for social welfare legislation.

Fletcher asked, "There were a great many stockholders of
the New Haven railroad among the lawyers?"

"Yes, sir."

William Whitman, whom President Cleveland appointed
to the Equitable board, came to the hearing to praise Brandeis'
perseverance and faithfulness in working for the protective
committee without pay. It was all for the benefit of the company, in friendly consultation, aiming to rehabilitate it, and
"we did it," he said.

Cummins suspected Brandeis of having appeared before
congressional committees to protect someone's interest. His
connection with the American Fair Trade League, which
backed the Stevens price-maintenance bill at the last session,

came under review. Chilton asked Edmund A. Whittier, an officer of the League, whether Brandeis had been paid by them or any of the members. Whittier answered him with complete assurance, and Anderson showed that no client of Brandeis' was a member. Fox asked about Gillette. Not even Gillette. Subpoenaed by Chilton, William H. Ingersoll gave the senators a glimpse of the economic philosophy which sought to prevent hundreds of thousands of small merchants from being suffocated by the monopoly ambition of big price-cutters.

Ingersoll: "I have had law business in Boston which I have tendered to his office but he has always declined to take it, saying that he did not want to have any possible criticism . . . not wanting to mix the business and the public things in which we are working."

Cummins: "That is to me remarkable."

Ingersoll: "Well, suppose he did take it and then you asked the questions as to whether he was acting down here for anyone who is a client of his?"

Cummins: "It is a remarkable thing that he, in declining to take your business, should put it on the ground that you were interested in a bill that was before Congress."

Ingersoll: "I cannot say that he put it that way; but he declined the business, anyway."

McClennen answered Fox's insinuations on the Lennox case by reading the stenographic notes made at the first meeting of James Lennox and Brandeis in 1907; and the notes of the second meeting, at which Brandeis showed he was interested only in a square deal for all concerned. The records proved that Brandeis was counsel for no one but the assignee. But Fox hinted that the law firm's fees, totaling $43,852.88 in four years, were more than it would have received as Lennox' attorney.

James Lennox testified, giving a story at variance with McClennen's. Lennox had a faulty memory.

Turning to the next matter McClennen said the draft

of the reorganization plan for the Warren paper business was in the handwriting of Sam Warren, who had unusual mental capacity. "Of course, you realize that Mr. Sam Warren was likely just as good a lawyer as Mr. Brandeis at that time." Senator Fletcher repeated Youngman's innuendo that a man of high integrity like Warren would not have entered into the arrangement without being chloroformed by Brandeis; and Fletcher wondered whether such a man was subject to hypnotic influences. Youngman came back, saying there were misleading omissions in McClennen's testimony; that Brandeis failed to give the heirs an inventory of the estate, that at Brandeis' advice the trustees began to charge a selling commission, and that the depreciation of the book value was "one of the devious ways of getting money out of the heirs into the hands of Mr. Brandeis."

On the New Haven question again, Anderson proceeded to show how Brandeis declined compensation from General Lawrence, the B. & M. stockholder who had enlisted him against the merger. From McClennen Anderson attempted to wrest an office secret to offset Peabody's and Pillsbury's talk about sailing under false colors.

Anderson: "I ask you now what he did in his own firm with relation to his having freedom to advocate the public interests as he saw them, with reference to this employment."

McClennen: "It does not seem to me that that matter is of any consequence here."

Senator Works: "Was the firm paid for service to Mr. Lawrence as distinguished from Mr. Brandeis?"

McClennen: "Yes . . . it was simply that Mr. Brandeis paid the firm what he thought would have been an appropriate charge to Mr. Lawrence had he made any."

Anderson: "That is, Lawrence paid nothing and Mr. Brandeis put into the firm treasury how much?"

McClennen: "Is that of any consequence?"

Works: "It is not of any consequence to me."

Anderson: "It is to me."

McClennen: "May I say that it was a substantial amount?"

Works wondered how Brandeis could do this and yet appear for Glavis presumably in the public interest but paid by another.

"On the contrary," Fletcher said, "I think it is fair to state that Mr. Brandeis never at any time gave anybody to understand that he was appearing in that case for the public."

Anderson followed through: "Gentlemen, don't you want to put the amount in there?"

The total was $25,000, paid to the partners in Brandeis' own checks.

A new source of opposition came from the Anti-Saloon League. Reverend James Cannon, Jr., of Blackstone, Virginia, felt duty-bound to the large church and temperance constituency represented by the League to bring to the senators' notice information recently come into his possession. He did not say how it came but he exhibited photostats of dockets showing Brandeis' employment in 1891 by the Massachusetts Protective Liquor Dealers' Association and the New England Brewers' Association; and other photostats taken at the Boston Public Library of arguments Brandeis made that year on the liquor laws.

Cannon admitted that having been an attorney for a liquor association twenty-five years ago was not in itself disreputable, but the fact that Brandeis was a lobbyist for the liquor traffic would not look well in a biography. He was concerned not so much with the particular case of '91 as with the sweeping statements Brandeis then made, such as: "Liquor drinking is not a wrong. . . . Trust your licensing boards. Make your laws reasonable so that men may obey them." Since stating these views on prohibition Brandeis had said nothing to controvert them, Cannon pointed out, and "what we ask is to have judges whose minds are unbiased on this question and will give the subject-matter fair consideration before them."

The question must finally go to the Supreme Court for

settlement, and he doubted whether "we could get a decision from him without prejudice."

Fletcher: "Of course, you can conceive that a judge on the bench might have some views as to what he believed the law ought to be, but still would enforce the law as it is written?"

Cannon: "Yes, I think that is true . . ."

The hearing came to a feeble close in the middle of March. Spence submitted a summary of proof as to Brandeis' connection with the Old Dominion. He quoted Brandeis as saying to William F. Fitzgerald, the broker who opposed consolidation with Phelps-Dodge: "Fitz, you had better come over on the other side. That's where the big money is. I have got on the bandwagon and you had better do the same."

Fitzgerald now testified that Brandeis favored withholding the engineer's report and advised him to take a portion of the $50,000 expense money. "I told him to go straight to hell and I left him." Fitzgerald advised his partner that if they took any of the expense money and concealed the report Brandeis would have a stranglehold on them for life. "I am not persecuting him, although I dislike him very much."

Senator Walsh brought out that the consolidation worked out successfully and the property was one of the great copper-mining enterprises in the world. As for the bandwagon—"Really, then, as I understand you, what was meant by the language used by Mr. Brandeis on that occasion was an expression of opinion that it would be a good business proposition to get the two projects together and you ought to get in and advocate that?"

Fitzgerald: "Possibly."

Walsh: "That you would make some money?"

Fitzgerald: "That he was conserving my interests in giving that advice."

Fox would not let go of the bandwagon but his witness denied he meant to suggest that Brandeis conspired with Phelps-Dodge. McClennen referred to office diaries and gave

the history of the fight against Bigelow and Lewisohn, the
suits brought against them by the new board for recovery of
promotion profits, and the steps taken to finance improvements in the mine.

Cummins: "I hope it is not improper for me to say that
Mr. Fitzgerald's testimony did not make the slightest impression on me. I did not see anything in it so far as the suppression of the report was concerned."

Charles Sumner Smith, president of the Old Dominion,
testified the next day about the engineer's report and its availability to stockholders.

He said Brandeis was not responsible for withholding it
from the newspapers. He himself was.

The last stand was taken by Edward R. Warren (not of
Sam Warren's family), who quit the Public Franchise League
in the dispute with Brandeis over the capitalization of the
consolidated gas companies. He had worked with Brandeis
nights and Sundays "in the most intimate way" when suddenly, near the end of the legislative session, without Warren's divining "the real motive or what actuated Brandeis
to change his opinion at that late hour," Brandeis' personality
carried the League's executive committee on a compromise.
"Mr. Brandeis has a wonderful magnetism when he speaks
and he has a wonderful way of carrying his points, and he
carried those men right off their feet."

The Massachusetts Board of Trade remained opposed to
the concession, Warren said. If the Board and the League
had stood together the capitalization compromise might not
have gone through. Brandeis by his silence led the legislature to think that the Board and the League agreed.

But Walsh showed that Warren had no direct information,
and McClennen produced a letter which Brandeis had written
on the very day of his appearance before the legislators— a
letter summing up his statement that while the Board of
Trade could not favor the compromise bill the League felt it
was better to amend a bad law than run the risk of having

it stand unrepealed. Walsh dismissed the whole affair as inconsequential. Fox nodded.

And so the hearing was declared closed. But not before Fox presented a communication addressed to the Senate judiciary committee:

> The undersigned feel it their painful duty to say to you that in their opinion, taking into view the reputation, character and professional career of Mr. Louis D. Brandeis, he is not a fit person to be a member of the Supreme Court of the United States.

It was signed by William Howard Taft, Simeon E. Baldwin, Francis Rawle, Joseph H. Choate, Elihu Root and Moorfield Storey. Another letter calling Brandeis unfit was signed by Peter W. Meldrum. The august significance of the rebuke could not be missed: the seven had served as presidents of the American Bar Association.

Chapter XVII

THE NOMINATION FIGHT (2)

NO WORD of complaint came from Brandeis during the month and a half in which the grave-diggers made their excavations. Although their fury and intensity sometimes pained him the performance revealed to the country the mercenary forces he had been fighting— and this gave him some comfort. Now and then he talked to his secretary, Miss Malloch, about the testimony and they were amazed at the distortions. Several times McClennen wired him for his recollection of certain incidents. Aside from this he made no attempt to help his cause although he could have explained many matters easily. He would have gone before the sub-committee gladly had he been asked. He reflected that they did not want him.

The only time he expressed scorn was in Lincoln Filene's office, where Bloomfield took him one day for lunch. Filene mentioned Lowell's belief that President Wilson had made the nomination in gratitude for Brandeis' obtaining "some papers" for him. Brandeis remarked, "Lowell is a paper king." And that was all.

Justice Holmes was chagrined at the conduct of the opposition and the defamation of a good man. He could not forebear to show his friends he was upset.

Fox and Spence, working on a brief, thought they had Brandeis beaten. In the course of the hearing someone communicated with them and mysteriously requested a secret meeting. He said he had documents relating to Wilson and a Mrs. Peck which could be used effectively. Fox declined. It might involve the honor of the nation and, moreover, apparently did not bear on Brandeis' professional conduct. At times those who had retained Fox criticized him for not pushing the fight hard enough. He took the attitude that he was not prosecuting anyone, simply laying facts before the committee. It seemed to Spence that Fox could have made out a better case, but was either too dignified or too lazy; that the Lennox case was proof positive of disgraceful conduct and unworthiness.

The brief declared Brandeis guilty of duplicity. Copies were showered on lawyers over the country. It cited violations of the canons of professional ethics. "The nominee has represented interests opposed to the public welfare and has been guilty of sharp practice." As an instance of his sudden shifts in position there was that initial conversation between Ingersoll and Brandeis, and the speech at the advertising club which Brandeis made in favor of price-maintenance to Ingersoll's surprise.

The *Wall Street Journal* deplored Brandeis' lack of delicacy— "the average lawyer would withdraw in order to save the President further embarrassment" but this one was determined to get the job.

It was now April. The sub-committee reported to the full committee, and they were divided: Chilton, Walsh and Fletcher for confirmation, Cummins and Works opposed. No one knew how long it would be before action was taken.

Chilton correlated and organized the 1,316 pages of testimony given by forty-three witnesses. First he disposed of the Warren case, finding no breach of trust, a fair agreement which worked out justly, as Sherman L. Whipple conceded; so did Moorfield Storey. Brandeis exerted no improper influence. Chilton devoted considerable space to the United, particularly Winslow's misstatements and public insinuations as to why Brandeis left the company.

The most significant fact in this case is that Mr. Brandeis voluntarily and with no prospect of profit to himself gave up his connection with a profitable client as soon as he became convinced that the policy it was pursuing, and would not change, was wrong. Four years later, and again without desire for profit to himself, he gave his assistance to the effort to stop what he believed would be the future and increasing effect upon the community of the wrong policy. It may well be asked: How long does an employment mortgage the lawyer's conscience?

The Lennox case was also analyzed at length. Chilton gave a flowing narrative stressing James Lennox' deceptions and obstructions, the hiring of separate counsel by Patrick Lennox on the day the assignment was recorded ("This showed a clear understanding that Mr. Brandeis was not counsel for Patrick Lennox, and there was nothing to distinguish between Patrick and James T., in that respect") and the inevitability of bankruptcy proceedings. Whipple had said Brandeis was upright throughout.

The events in this case were due entirely to the fact that the debtors went back on the plan to which they agreed and under which the matter was taken up, namely, to devote their property fully and without hesitation to the payment of their debts. They were never deserted in any way.

As for concealing *Collier's* payment, Chilton referred to the understanding of the Ballinger committee that Brandeis did not appear gratis for the public; to general knowledge that Glavis was not in a position to pay for five months of continuous work by a man of Brandeis' calibre; to *Collier's* allusion to itself in its columns as the employer, and to Hapgood's quoting Finney of the Interior Department as saying, "Mr. Hapgood, I have no respect for you, I think that you and your newspaper have gone into this merely for sen-

sational purposes, but I want to tell you that you have a
great lawyer." Chilton pointed out that *Collier's* felt it imperative to verify Glavis' charges, having taken the legal and
moral responsibility of presenting them. The Ballinger committee "did not ask Mr. Brandeis who was paying his fee
because then it made no difference."

Chilton made short shrift of the suggestion of impropriety
in receiving information from stenographer Kerby. He
showed how circumspectly Brandeis acted, how faithful
Kerby was to a higher obligation.

> There are no limits to suspicion, but there are rules
> of evidence as well as just ways for determining the
> probatory effect of facts. Shall we ignore the proved
> facts and indulge a suspicion in order to condemn the
> nominee? I cannot. The facts in this matter leave no
> stain upon Mr. Brandeis.

And Brandeis was not employed to wreck the New York
& New England Railroad. The procuring of Illinois Central
proxies bore no relation to the New England railroad situation. The charge of responsibility for the New Haven's
financial collapse had no foundation. The charge that he acted
unprofessionally in the Gillette case was farfetched. In the
Equitable case he consistently acted for the best interests
of the company, and the protective committee was not designed to be antagonistic to it, and Brandeis' work as the
Equitable's attorney in specific cases had nothing to do with
its management.

Chilton held that Thorne's complaint had no merit. The
I.C.C. letter of employment itemized Brandeis' duties to produce facts omitted by the carriers which might help the other
side, to see that all sides and angles were presented, to emphasize any aspect which in his judgment required it. Brandeis
served the commission, not any of the parties. Evidence was
prepared by various counsel separately. Counsel separated
again to prepare briefs and arguments. Thorne grouped all

the carriers and struck an average income which was not available to many roads below the average, whereas Brandeis stated the revenues in detail and classified the carriers by size. Counsel for shippers and their clients recognized the correctness of Brandeis' position. Besides, the increase sought by the roads was denied on the grounds urged by him. "Later, in the light of the new conditions created by the European war, a part of the increase sought was granted, against his opposition." Brandeis had performed his duty fully. The I.C.C. did not complain. If he was culpable so was the commission. If he advised them to do wrong and they did so, the shocking conclusion must be that they endorsed the wrong or were incompetent.

Fitzgerald had wasted his venom. Regarding the Old Dominion, Chilton wrote that the insinuations were so entirely unwarranted that the entire committee thought it unnecessary to hear the facts in reply.

Chilton took notice of a recent editorial in the *Wall Street Journal* comparing the Lennox betrayal with "the present standards of his Teutonic ancestors." The newspaper said Lennox paid Brandeis $10,000. Chilton answered: "Absolutely false." Barron had fostered a systematic advertising campaign and yet the committee, after examining all the available witnesses suggested by him, found "absolutely nothing in the conduct of Mr. Brandeis to warrant Mr. Barron's opinion and absolutely nothing to reflect upon Mr. Brandeis' character as a man or a lawyer. . . . I am not willing to endorse a campaign of slander." The advertising had influenced others to give adverse opinions, and it was natural that bitter antagonisms developed when Sherman Law construction and the duties of the states concerning industrial combinations were burning issues. On the other hand, testimonials were received from members of bench and bar, professors, businessmen, labor leaders, people in all walks of life, from every part of the country.

Finally, the allegation that the nominee lacked judicial

temperament. This, said Chilton, could be determined only by experience.

> No one can tell whether a great lawyer will be a great judge until he has been tried. It seems to me there is more in the life of Mr. Brandeis as shown by this record to incline one to the belief that he has the qualities of a good judge than there is to the contrary. It is remarkable that friend and foe alike speak of his great ability as a lawyer. The late Chief Justice Fuller advised one seeking a lawyer in the East as follows: "Go to Boston and see Mr. Louis Brandeis, as I consider him the ablest man who has ever appeared before the Supreme Court of the United States. He is absolutely fearless in the discharge of his duties."

Fletcher concurred in Chilton's report. Walsh vigorously wrote one of his own.

But Cummins wrote that while Brandeis' "intellectual power and high learning" were admitted by everybody, in the five percent case he was employed "to take the public side of the question, that is to say, he was to present the side opposed to the claims of the railroads" and instead practically decided the suit in favor of the roads. Then again, a due regard for professional propriety would have prevented Brandeis from accepting employment from anyone to attack his former client, the United. The whole Lennox transaction was condemnable, Cummins said. Brandeis failed to recognize his plain obligation to tell the Ballinger committee he was in *Collier's* employ. Brandeis had no corrupt motive in the handling of the Warren estate but he was not at liberty to defend the lessees when Edward Warren made a claim against them. Nothing in the testimony on the Illinois Central proxy business reflected in the slightest degree upon anyone involved, and Cummins was not disposed to hold Brandeis responsible in the New England Railroad case but could not fathom his motive for paying his partners $25,000 for taking up the merger campaign without receiving compensation.

> All I can say of the singular performance is that Mr.
> Brandeis furnished the opportunity for serious criticism
> and at best indicated that his view of duties and respon-
> sibility was somewhat abnormal. It is not strange that
> those who looked at the incident from the outside were
> skeptical and suspicious.

Nothing in the other matters warranted comment, Cummins wrote, although some were "possibly of doubtful propriety." He had the profoundest admiration for Brandeis'
strength of mind, scope of knowledge, and most of his sociological and economic views— and regretted to oppose confirmation. But Brandeis had lost the confidence of so large an
element of his profession and of the country "as to vitally
impair his usefulness as a justice of the Supreme Court."

Works, in his separate report, disagreed with Cummins
over the five percent rate case but shared his view on the
Warren controversy. He believed Peabody's testimony on
the Illinois Central; absolved Brandeis of guilty knowledge in
the conspiracy against the New England Railroad but chided
him for not suspecting. He charged Brandeis with a deliberate
attempt to deceive the Ballinger committee and the nation.
Collier's was kept in the background and Glavis to the fore
"to make it appear to be a 'conservation movement' in the
public interest and not a defence of *Collier's* against a threatened libel suit, which was beyond doubt what *Collier's* were
paying for."

Quite the opposite, Works found, was Brandeis' course
in the merger matter, but equally open to suspicion and criticism. There was concealment in both cases. If the public knew
he paid his partners $25,000 it would have supposed the
money was made up to him in some other way. Refusal of
compensation from the Shoe Manufacturers' Alliance "was
evidence that in his own mind such an employment was
wrong." Nor could Works understand why he paid his firm

—Drawn by Boardman Robinson

THE OLD GANG: "Things have come to a pretty pass."

From "Puck," June 17, 1916

money out of his own pocket in this case, too. Brandeis persistently used his former client, the United, as an example of the evils of trusts and showed a lack of "a due sense of the proprieties so necessary to be observed by members of the profession." There was conclusive evidence, also, that Brandeis had been regularly retained and employed by Lennox. The fees in prospect under an assignment were a strong temptation. "Whether it influenced Mr. Brandeis to advise that course no one can tell."

Works wanted to be fair. Brandeis had made enemies of lawyers and friends among the poor and lowly. The protests of men of high standing must be considered. By intolerant and offensive methods, by concealments and desertion, Brandeis defied the plain ethics of his calling.

> His course may have been the result of a desire to make large fees, but even this is not clear. . . . To place a man on the Supreme Court bench who rests under a cloud would be a grievous mistake. . . . Whether suspicion rests upon him unjustly or not his confirmation would be a mistake. It is agreed against him that he is not possessed of the judicial temperament . . . the temperament that has made him many enemies and brought him under condemnation in the minds of so many people would detract from his usefulness as a judge. He is of the material that makes good advocates, reformers, and crusaders, but not good or safe judges.

In contrast stood a statement by ex-Governor David I. Walsh that before Brandeis engaged in public activities "he had already achieved a position at the Massachusetts bar which would well have warranted his appointment to the Supreme Court at the age of forty. He is a great lawyer and a great citizen. Is not this a combination for a great judge?"

A brilliant lawyer could easily escape calumny by drifting with the tide; the man who never represents the public in a great forensic contest "never has these troubles"— so said

Senator Walsh. Brandeis was a vigorous, aggressive, relentless antagonist— "moreover, he has been successful."

> The real crime of which this man is guilty is that he has exposed the iniquities of men in high places in our financial system.

Senator Walsh's separate report pointed a finger at Bigelow of the Old Dominion, who had to give up $2,000,000 misappropriated from stockholders. It was reasonable to assume that a person of such importance had influence in the financial circles and social set of Boston. And the exposure of the New Haven— "doubtless most of the wealth and culture were arrayed on its side"— but Barron, the paid press agent, was the only witness to question the purity of Brandeis' motives. And there was Winslow of the United, possessed with the idea that Brandeis was bound to him forever. Great industrialists commonly believed they might ensure the support of lawyers on public questions by putting them on the payroll. And Storey— still bearing animosity over Corbin's fight on the New England Railroad directors whom he and Simon E. Baldwin defended.

Strangely, these senatorial proceedings did not venture to produce the name of Morgan.

The judiciary committee recessed after getting the reports. Its long delay of action gave a hint of struggle. The ostensible reason, more time to study the testimony, failed to hide the fact that recalcitrants refused to budge. Wilson was said to be determined to put them in line. Again the committee convened— and adjourned without voting. Senator Henry F. Ashurst, Democrat, of Arizona, denounced the Republicans as filibustering until the party conventions would be over. On the floor he exchanged caustic words with Senator Sutherland. Said Ashurst:

> If the nominee had been a person who all his life had been steering giant corporations around the law there would have been a yell of approval from the Republican

side, but there having been sent in the name of a man
who has consecrated his life to the poor people of this
country, casuistry must be restorted to, and then all the
delay that can be conjured up is resorted to.

It developed that the Democratic members of the committee were the ones who were taking up the time at the
meetings. Cummins said the eight Republicans had offered
again and again to vote.

Only a minority of the ten Democrats was usually present.
Reed of Missouri was ill. Shields of Tennessee was also kept
away by illness. And Hoke Smith of Georgia admitted: "I
say frankly for myself that there has never been a time that
I have been ready to vote for a report favorable to Mr. Brandeis."

It was now evident that the administration did not have
solid party support. Senator Robert L. Owen, Democrat, of
Oklahoma, asserted in the Senate that the committee members of Republican persuasion were approving the corporations' concerted assault— "the most vicious and unjust assault
ever brought against a nominee for a judgeship," against one
who desired justice done the common people by incorporated
wealth. But there was no covering the Democratic defection.
A number of Senators resented Wilson's monotheistic leadership and they were unwilling to do him a service. Others may
have been swayed by the prejudice of their home states.

The nomination had been pending three months. Twice
more the judiciary committee postponed voting. It was likely
that they would report without recommendation. Wilson began to call in senators (Overman and Simmons) to persuade
them in the name of progressivism. Before summoning others
he wrote the warmest tribute he ever tapped out on his type-
writer. Addressed to the chairman, Charles A. Culberson,
Democrat, of Texas, it was meant for all the Senate and all
the nation. It took a wide swing at the character and motives
of the people who brought the charges. Wilson said he had
investigated them in 1913 and they were unfounded:

They proceeded for the most part from those who hated Mr. Brandeis because he had refused to be serviceable to them in the promotion of their own selfish interests and from those whom they had prejudiced and misled.

Wilson said he knew what he was doing when he named Brandeis; and knew by associating with him his extraordinary ability, clear-sighted counsel, grasp of economics, moral stimulation:

> He is a friend of all just men and a lover of the right; and he knows more than how to talk about the right— he knows how to set it forward in the face of its enemies.

Still the Democrats were not ready for action. Sutherland made a motion to reopen the hearing. He had information that Brandeis gave a legal opinion to Louis K. Liggett prior to the merger of the United Drug Company and the Riker & Hegeman chain of drug stores in February of that year. The nomination was now recommitted to the sub-committee, and William E. Borah sat in place of Cummins.

The facts were that Anderson, as United States attorney, looked into the proposed merger during the preceding fall, sensing an anti-trust case, and found an instrument of power, which, if abused, might be a Sherman Law violation. Liggett appeared before the Senators and testified he went to Anderson with his attorney, Frederick E. Snow, to lay his cards on the table. Snow endorsed the legality of the project but suggested that Liggett get an outsider's opinion, Brandeis.' In December, 1915, Liggett received a letter jointly signed by Brandeis and Snow and forwarded to Anderson, deeming the proposed purchase of the chain "lawful beyond any reasonable doubt." The merger was accomplished. In April, Anderson reported to Washington, still sure the company could go into any community and cut prices till its ruined local competition and took possession of the field. Liggett said his stores were doing only five percent of the country's retail drug business. The Brandeis-Snow opinion regarded it lawful for the company to develop a wide demand for its goods by selling them under trademarks and through exclusive agencies.

Answering Borah, Liggett said the engagement of Brandeis made no change in his merger plan. Answering Works, he said he did not know what Brandeis' fee would be. Then Snow was questioned, and he told how he had opposed Brandeis in most of Boston crusades. He submitted the same facts laid before Anderson, and Brandeis saw no violation. Snow said he found Anderson's report lacking in material facts and again called in Brandeis, who advised sending another letter asking Anderson also for the basis of his conclusions. This was sent in March, after the close of the confirmation hearing.

Works smelled a rat. "I suppose the filing of this joint opinion was to modify the views of Mr. Anderson, was it not?"

Snow answered: "Mr. Brandeis thought Mr. Anderson was a very open-minded man but I said at the time I did not think it would have any effect on him."

Borah took up the scent: "But Mr. Brandeis and yourself were not able to satisfy Mr. Anderson that it was not in violation of the Sherman Anti-Trust Law."

Snow: "We certainly were not."

Borah: "Then, in so far as you employed Mr. Brandeis to modify the views of Mr. Anderson you did not succeed?"

Snow: "I did not employ him for that purpose."

Borah: "I thought so."

Snow: "I employed him because I was advising my people to go ahead and complete this merger. . . . I wanted to have my opinion confirmed by someone else."

Anderson stepped up as a witness. He said he had had more differences of opinion and "violent but friendly" controversies with Brandeis than with any other man living, except perhaps with Whipple. "I think I later told him chaffingly that I hoped that when he got on the bench he would not attempt to rule such bad law as he had tried in this case to make me adopt." Anderson added that he had the profoundest respect for his ethical perception, character, analytical power and gift for illumination. "I go to him whenever I am at a loss . . ."

Interstate Commerce Commissioner Harlan was called at Chilton's suggestion. Chilton asked: "Did you employ him— was it your understanding that he was to be employed— to represent any one side or to represent the commission?" Harlan said he did not understand Brandeis was on either side but in the public interest. "It never occurred to me that he represented one side or the other." His services were "eminently satisfactory." Brandeis gave practically a year's time to the exclusion of everything else. "I think we got from him, and the public got from him, the best that was in him."

Works did not let Harlan go so easily, but made several tries at pinning him down to say that the I.C.C. engaged Brandeis to protect the public interest by helping the shippers.

"Well," said Harlan, " 'the public interest' is a little broader than the mere shipping side." And when Works attempted to identify the two, Harlan observed that the shipper usually came with a special interest.

Walsh got the answers he wanted: that the commission did not regard Brandeis as faithless to it or the public; that far from being improper for Brandeis to say that railroad revenues were not on the whole adequate, it was "precisely the sort of view that we looked to counsel to express" and if the net incomes of the carriers were not sufficient that was something the commission ought to know. To Works he explained that the question whether revenues were adequate in the public interest was a very different one than the reasonableness of rates existing or proposed. But Works did not give up. Again with the shippers in mind he asked, "Mr. Brandeis was admitting away that side of the case, in broad terms, was he not?"

On the basis of the day's testimony Chilton, Fletcher and

Walsh sent another favorable report to the full committee; Borah and Works to the contrary. There was nothing out of the ordinary in the Liggett matter, Chilton wrote, and no suggestion of anything improper; and Harlan's evidence made it perfectly clear that Thorne's charge could not be sustained.

Wilson set his jaw. The Republican vote was a foregone conclusion. The divided Democrats were his problem. He sent for more Senators; called in McAdoo and told him to hurry the malingerers. They must stand by the President. He called in Henry Morgenthau, Sr., to get Hoke Smith, who was difficult because of personal differences with Wilson and because of anti-Jewish feeling in Georgia following the murder trial of Leo Frank. McAdoo had recently failed to whip up support for the appointment of George Rublee to the Federal Trade Commission (Rublee's share in the price-maintenance bill killed his chances) and this defeat was ominous.

It was late in May but it was chilly. Brandeis went to Washington, to Hapgood's apartment, where Reed, who had opposed Rublee, arranged to meet him. The night Reed came in his bearing was antagonistic, but as they talked his face changed. He did not seem to be seeking light on any particular subject, the conversation skirting on the general political situation. Then Reed realized he had been keeping his wife waiting in a carriage downstairs for an hour and a half. His goodnight was quite friendly. Reed was a key man, and the switch was important.

Morgenthau believed he succeeded with Smith and understood the senator would try for a recommendation from the ten Democrats on the committee. In fine fettle Morgenthau proceeded to find Brandeis; he had a plan, a political masterstroke. In New London, Connecticut, he met Brandeis and urged that immediately after confirmation he declare himself a candidate for senator from Massachusetts. Lodge was up for re-election. Brandeis could get the labor vote and win public vindication, at the same time taking over a doubtful state which the Democratic Party needed badly. Brandeis asked if the suggestion came from Wilson. He was glad it did not. The only promise he made Morgenthau was "prayerful consideration."

In Boston there was a movement to hold a Jewish mass meeting and invite Dr. Eliot to preside— Eliot the first citizen of the land, next to the President. Anderson was asked to see him. Eliot twiddled his thumbs and observed that the nomination was unwise. But this was not the question now. Quite so; he would give his answer later. He declined. However, he wrote Chilton a letter praising Brandeis' "practical altruism" and saying that rejection, in view of the circumstances, would be "a grave misfortune for the whole legal profession, the court, all American business and the country." Anderson felt that though the letter probably had no effect on the committee it restored Brandeis' cheer.

One Eliot was worth many Lowells and the solitary Harvard Law professor who held back from endorsing Brandeis was no match for the rest of the faculty. Dean Pound wrote a letter deprecating the emphasis friends put on the nominee's social views and stressing his greatness as a lawyer. Brandeis' article in 1890 on the right to privacy had done nothing less than add a chapter to the law. The Oregon brief achieved a revolution in technique. In sheer legal ability Brandeis would rank with the greatest justices of the court. The eminent members of the Boston bar who participated in his continued reappointment to the Law School's visiting committee could not have been ignorant of the charges. Their present objections must be "the unconscious product of fear of his practical views and aversion to his social and public activities." The student body openly protested that President Lowell did not represent campus opinion.

On May twenty-fourth Chilton, having the assurance of Reed, Smith and other doubtfuls, moved in committee for a favorable report to the Senate. Shields came up from Ten-

nessee in time to make a solid Democratic vote of ten yeas.
The Republicans— Borah, Sutherland, Cummins, Works,
Clark, Knute Nelson, William P. Dillingham of Vermont,
and Frank B. Brandegee of Connecticut— all voted nay.
Hardly anyone doubted now that every Democratic senator
would fall in line. This would suffice for confirmation and
the Republicans would therefore consider it bad policy to
put up further obstruction.

At this stage the *New York Times* balked at the imminent
prospect of a judge who held a view of the court's function
differing from its own. The Supreme Court must be a conservative body. To supplant conservatism by radicalism would
be to strip the Constitution of its defences. The *New York
World* retorted by referring to the Dred Scott decision— "the
wholly gratuitous effort of a few conservators of the institution of slavery."

The committee's minority report to the Senate held that
the facts made confirmation impossible; no previous nominee's
honesty and integrity had been so seriously questioned. "It
must be evident to any thinking and unbiased mind that this
appointment has resulted from something other than the qualifications of fitness of the appointee for the office."

Marshall, Story, Taney, Matthews: Chilton recalled that
their nominations were attacked as viciously in their time.
It was easy enough to make charges unless, of course, an
appointee had not the capacity and courage to take part in
the major issues of the past quarter-century. Works had mentioned Brandeis' resting under a cloud. What about Root?
Chilton reminded the Senate that in 1902 Moorfield Storey
joined in conclusions of a damaging character concerning
"Root's Record in Philippine Warfare," yet Root subsequently held high governmental posts, was now president of
the American Bar Association and was probably acceptable
to all who opposed Brandeis.

By unanimous consent agreement in executive session the
Senate met at five o'clock on the afternoon of June first to

vote without debate. In fifteen minutes it was over: 47 yeas,
22 nays. Only one Democrat deserted— Newlands, who rose
to explain that despite his admiration he did not regard Brandeis as a man of judicial temperament. The only Republicans
who voted for him were La Follette, Norris and Poindexter;
the only New Englander, Hollis, Democrat, of New Hampshire. Hollis announced that Clapp would have voted yea if
present. Lodge rose to say Weeks would have voted nay.
Borah, too, was absent, but not Warren G. Harding, Charles
Curtis, nor Albert B. Fall.

Brandeis heard the news from his wife. He had left the
office at four-thirty and taken the train for Dedham. She
received a telephone call from Miss Grady and so, when
he arrived, she properly dropped the salutation "Demby"
and greeted him with a "good evening, Mr. Justice!" The
news shocked neither. Their thoughts were of the new life
they would enter, of giving up Dedham and the house in
Otis Place. And now that the battle was over he wondered
why this and that person had not come out in his support.

Four days later they went to Washington for the ceremony of induction on a Monday noon. First, in the robing
room, Chief Justice White administered the oath of allegiance
to the Constitution in the presence of the associate justices.
Holmes gave him the welcoming smile of a dear friend.
Hughes held out his hand in friendship, too. There was
undoubted civility from the others: McReynolds; Joseph
McKenna, who had been lifted out of California politics by
McKinley; William R. Day, who had come from a judicial
career in Ohio— a Roosevelt appointee; Willis Van Devanter, former Wyoming politician named by Taft, and
Mahlon Pitney, New Jersey judge, the last of the Taft con-
tributions.

At the end of the line, wearing the black silk robe, Brandeis entered the familiar semi-circular courtroom in the Senate wing of the Capitol and passed the marble columns flank-
ing the dais to sit beside the clerk of the court. The room

was crowded to the aisles. Brandeis could see his wife and daughter Elizabeth, his brother Alfred, Pauline Goldmark, Gregory, Anderson, and Newton D. Baker, who was the new Secretary of War. As steps in the ceremony the Chief Justice announced the appointment, the clerk read the commission, and Brandeis took the judicial oath:

> I, Louis D. Brandeis, do solemnly swear that I will administer justice without respect to persons and do equal right to the poor and to the rich; that I will faithfully and impartially discharge and perform all the duties incumbent upon me as associate justice of the Supreme Court of the United States according to the best of my abilities and understanding.

The marshal conducted him behind the justices, all bowing as he went by, to the black-leather, high backed chair at the extreme left of the Chief. He sat down beside Pitney, secure on the bench which had been delaying decision on the Oregon minimum wage law.

Chapter XVIII

FIRST YEARS ON THE BENCH

MRS. BRANDEIS sewed up the old green flannel bag and took it to Washington when they moved. The justice could use it for carrying papers to the Saturday court conferences. They rented an apartment in Stoneleigh Court on Connecticut Avenue. A Negro messenger named Poindexter, left behind by Justice Lamar, was given continued tenure of office. To Felix Frankfurter fell the privilege of selecting a secretary from the Harvard Law School graduating class, and Calvert Magruder was chosen. Miss Malloch in the Boston office was instructed to dispose of the few thousands' worth of stock which Brandeis held, such as American Telephone & Telegraph, and his single share of United Shoe Machinery pfd., and to manage his approximately two-million-dollar investment in municipal, state and federal bonds. He wound up his partnership relations, taking his 30.47 percent share of fees charged up to June first, and collected from Attorney General Gregory the balance due him for services rendered in the Riggs Bank matter. A week after he took his seat the court restored the Oregon case to the docket and adjourned for the term.

He had resigned from Mayor Mitchel's conciliation committee and was succeeded by Judge Mack. He retired as trustee of the Utilities Bureau which Morris Llewellyn Cooke conducted in Philadelphia. He gave up membership in the National Economic League. Ties must be snapped though interest in the world outside the court would never cease. He pledged himself to give several thousand dollars for the work of the Law School. And he accepted the honorary presidency of the American Jewish Congress.

Early in July Brandeis addressed the Zionist convention in Philadelphia where the project of a million-dollar stock corporation to develop the economic possibilities of Palestine was adopted. The British ambassador, Sir Cecil Spring-Rice, had told him that His Majesty's government favored Jewish settlement. Wilson had also given him assurances. Brandeis described the program for the acquisition of land as linking "the teachings of Moses with the philosophy of Single Tax" —the land purchased by the Jewish National Fund would remain in perpetuity as the heritage of the Jewish people, leased for an annual ground rental to be paid to the community and used for community purposes; in case of transfer the occupant would sell only his improvements.

From impassioned public advocacy he suddenly took to silence. In mid-July, after his pleading for Jewish unity and rights at a meeting at Hotel Astor in New York, the dissident voice of Judah L. Magnes called out in the assembly: "There are higher things than the Supreme Court of the United States!" Personal criticism could not sting Brandeis, but he no longer was a private individual; as a justice he must avoid exposure to cheap disparagement. Thereafter his activities and consultations would take place behind his own door. Through de Haas, Rabbi Wise, and Mack he maintained contact.

It was disappointing to see a long strike in the New York garment trade deal a deathblow to the protocol that summer, but a collective agreement healed the breach. It was satisfying to learn that the railroads were practicing scientific management. According to Ivy L. Lee, former assistant to the president of the Pennsylvania system, the carriers' net operating income for the year had increased by $308,000,000, about a million dollars for each business day. "Mr. Brandeis," Lee said, "has been a far better friend to the railroads than either he or they knew."

Brandeis had the confidence of his optimism. The crusades of yesteryear were not to be counted as so many closed books. Aftermaths would come, worth watching. Nor were his wings clipped; for the freedom to agitate for social justice he had gained a share in the power to deliver it. This was something of value despite the fact that the court was being reproached, denounced as a judicial oligarchy, preserver of property rights as against human rights. He was eager to get to work. There was much to be done. And much had to be left behind; the unjust attacks on Wilson during the current presidential campaign made him feel this keenly. But the struggle against his confirmation convinced him that the renunciation was well worth while.

The fact that the justiceship by itself was a big enough task was made clear in August, after General Pershing's punitive expedition into Mexico, when Wilson asked him to serve on a commission to meet the representatives of the Carranza government and settle the border difficulties. He consulted the Chief Justice, then at Lake Placid, who barred the way. Then he went to the White House, and late the same day the President released a letter from Brandeis saying he found the state of the court's business to be such that it was his duty not to undertake this important constructive task. He told his intimates he was very sorry. In Washington the talk was that the Chief did not want any of the court involved in political questions.

Sailing and paddling off South Yarmouth, Brandeis enjoyed the meditative calm of the water. The summer recess did not mean all rest and play, for each justice had stacks of petitions to consider. While war was smashing the structure of European civilization and threatening to strike home, he had nothing to do with the preparedness movement, one way or the other. Pacifism was in his wife's department. She was a charter member of the Massachusetts Women's League for Peace and Freedom. His thought was that the current period of prosperity afforded favorable conditions for systematic experimentation to overcome the greatest cause of waste and suffering in America—irregularity of employment.

October came. Daughter Susan entered the law school of the University of Chicago after her year of suffrage work. Elizabeth went back to Radcliffe. Father and mother were in their modest apartment in Washington which served as both a home and a study. The term began. Brandeis was no longer the newest newcomer; Hughes had resigned to run against Wilson, and John Hessin Clarke (Ohio railroad lawyer and federal judge) was nominated and seated within ten days. Brandeis now sat to the Chief Justice's extreme right.

Holding the scales over a lawsuit differed little from his customary perspective on cases, despite incredulous enemies. They looked for victory. He looked for the common welfare. He had recently restated his formula— that in every controversy nominally between employer and employee "there is a third party, the public," whose interests were paramount; parties of the first and second parts should not be permitted to make settlements injurious to the public, which always had a reserve moral right to be heard and if necessary to interfere. On the bench the justices heard both sides of an issue and listened to the inward voice of the law.

As the nine justices foregathered in the conference room on Saturdays to discuss cases, first the Chief spoke and then his associates in the order of seniority. When the time for voting came the order was reversed. If the Chief stood with a majority he designated the justice who should write the controlling opinion, a composite of their views. The minority made arrangements among themselves. As Holmes once said, a division did not mean that some of the justices "were not doing their sums right, and, if they would take more trouble, agreement inevitably would come." Instead of mathematical certainty in a rarified atmosphere there were nine human beings with nine different minds.

In December the court divided on an order of the Interstate Commerce Commission, five holding for reversal. Holmes wrote the opinion. Brandeis voted with dissenters Pitney, Day and Clarke. On the same Monday he delivered several unanimous opinions. His first sustained the police power of Iowa in forbidding the sale of ice-cream containing less than the prescribed percentage of butterfat. Another upheld the police power of New Jersey in requiring a registration fee of non-resident automobilists using the state's highways. During this term he wrote twenty-one opinions for the full court (except that McReynolds disagreed twice) and joined in seven dissents, mostly with Clarke.

He gave his own first dissenting opinion on May 21, 1917, in a case involving the New York State compensation law. The majority, speaking through Van Devanter, rejected an award of damages to a New York Central Railroad section hand on the ground that the Federal Employers' Liability Act covered the field and granted the right of recovery only if the railroad were at fault. In sum, Congress offered no protection to employees injured without fault on the part of carriers and prohibited the states from affording it. Brandeis reasoned that Congress did not intend by its silence to supersede state provisions. He traced the origin, scope and purpose of the federal law to prove his point. He went behind state compensation laws to show their necessity as demonstrated by the "world's experience." What he wrote was a sociological essay with copious footnotes. Upon the states fell the financial burden of dependence, the heavier burden of demoralization and social unrest, and the duty to avert misery and promote happiness. Moreover he cited cases to indicate that Congress had not pre-empted the whole field. Uniformity was not desirable. The subject of compensation in industry was one peculiarly appropriate for state legislation. Only Clarke concurred.

Brandeis meant for the court to catch up with the break with the past. He inserted a passage on social studies as having "uncovered as fiction many an assumption upon which American judges and lawyers had rested comfortably."

In June, just before the term closed, he wrote another dissenting opinion. McReynolds held that the State of Washington in prohibiting private employment agencies from taking fees from workers deprived the agencies of property in violation of the due process clause of the Fourteenth Amendment. Regulation of the business was proper, McReynolds said, but this was destruction. Of the four dissenters McKenna merely referred to precedents. Brandeis regarded the invalidation of a statute enacted in the exercise of the state's police power as too serious a matter to pass by without extended statement. Was the measure arbitrary? "The judgment should be based upon a consideration of relevant facts, actual or possible— *ex facto jus oritur*. That ancient principle must prevail in order that we may have a system of living law." Documenting his opinion with citations from government bulletins, magazine articles and books, culled by personal research, Brandeis described the evils of the private agency system and the unsatisfactory attempts to regulate it. The problem of the people of Washington was "the chronic problem of unemployment," accentuated in that state "by the lack of staple industries operating continuously throughout the year and by unusual fluctuations in the demand for labor, with consequent reduction of wages and increase of social unrest." The state Supreme Court and the federal District Court had sustained the statute. Weight must be given to this for they must have been familiar with local conditions and needs in establishing the reasonableness of the law. Holmes and Clarke agreed.

In this fashion the quest of social justice which Brandeis had started upon as a lawyer he continued as a judge. The technique, if not the arena, remained the same. Was it futile if he spoke only for a minority? By implication any championship was initially a minority action. Clothed in the prestige of an opinion coming from the highest bench, it could travel far. On such momentum the campaign of education could push its way into the nation's thinking, penetrate the lecture halls of law schools and germinate among future jurists. In the pages of the United States Reports the opinion would stand as a fixed finger pointing to truth, urging a turn-about. Even the Supreme Court was capable of change.

That same spring cases under two Oregon labor statutes were decided. By an equally divided court judgments for the state were affirmed against violators of the minimum wage law. Brandeis, whose place among Oregon's counsel had been taken by Frankfurter, did not share in the consideration and decision because of his prior participation. And when Frankfurter argued for the state's new law setting a ten-hour day for both men and women factory workers, Brandeis again sat back. The issue had no longer come to be looked upon as a contest between capital and labor— so ran the argument— but a concern of the state as an organic whole. The court's attention was invited to the body of experience covered by a 400-page brief. McKenna, Holmes, Day, Pitney and Clarke sustained the law; the Chief Justice, Van Devanter and McReynolds registered dissent. McKenna wrote that the record contained nothing to support the contention that the law was neither necessary nor useful for the preservation of health.

Once more the "Brandeis brief" triumphed. Mrs. Kelley of the National Consumers' League said she would have regarded the decisions that day as miracles "if I did not know, from the inside, the long story of genius, wisdom and hard work beginning nearly ten years ago."

But in the following term Brandeis was impelled to assert the legality of labor's elementary rights. The United Mine Workers of America attempted to win over the workers in West Virginia coal mines running in competition with union mines in neighboring states, but the Hitchman Coal & Coke Company had made non-membership in the union a condition of employment; if a worker joined the union he must leave the employ. This was the popularly designated "yellow dog" contract. The company sought to enjoin the efforts of John Mitchell, president of the union, and other organizers to unionize its mine without its consent. The District Court granting the injunction was reversed by the Circuit Court of Appeals. But the Supreme Court upheld the injunction. Pitney cited decisions, from which Holmes had dissented, which maintained the freedom to make yellow dog contracts as part of the constitutional rights of liberty and property; the union violated these rights of the company in conspiring to subvert the workers' status and cause breaches of contract.

Though the District Court held the union itself illegal under West Virginia law and the Sherman Law, Brandeis disproved both findings. The alleged conspiracy was a lawful purpose to improve the condition of workingmen by strengthening their bargaining power and extending the range of union power. Unionizing a shop meant inducing the employer to enter into a collective agreement with the union; it implied his formal consent. The end was lawful; the strike or equivalent economic pressure was a lawful means. For a union to induce men to join with the intention of ordering a strike unless the employer consented to a closed union shop was not coercion, in a legal sense, any more than was the employer's threat to refuse employment unless an applicant consented to a closed non-union shop. As an employer might withhold from the men an economic need— employment— so the workers might withhold from him an economic need— labor. The company's whole case rested on individual agreements secured under the same pressure of economic necessity which it sought to prevent the union from using.

Pitney recognized that the workers could terminate their contracts at will and also strike but that this did not give a third party the right to organize them and instigate a strike. Brandeis answered: there was no evidence whatever of any attempt to induce them to violate their contracts; until a worker actually joined the union he would not be obliged to leave his job. "There consequently would be no breach until the employee both joined the union and failed to withdraw from plaintiff's employ." The union's plan probably was to secure assurances from individuals that they would join when a large number should have consented to do so and then strike unless plaintiff agreed to a unionized mine. "Such a course would have been clearly permissible under the contract." That it was justifiable "should not, at this day, be doubted." Holmes and Clarke concurred.

There were other first principles which the majority still doubted, and one was the power of Congress to prohibit the interstate shipment of child-made goods. Holmes scoffed at the notion that the child labor law of 1916 was unconstitutional, a meddling with states' internal affairs. As soon as the products crossed state lines they entered the domain of national welfare and encountered the public policy of the United States expressed by Congress. Joining with Holmes were McKenna, Brandeis and Clarke. The dominant voices of the five other justices, in striking down the law, precipitated a crusade for a child labor amendment to the Constitution.

Sometimes Brandeis thought it useless to dissent. The court voided a contract fixing the resale price of patented articles bought by a store from a phonograph company. While Holmes disagreed, as with earlier decisions of a similar nature, Brandeis acknowledged that the precedents settled the law. This was "an economic question," he said. "To decide it wisely it is necessary to consider the relevant facts, industrial and commercial, rather than established principles. On that question I have expressed elsewhere views which differ from those entertained by a majority of my brethren." But he did not inject these views into his opinion, such was his judicial temperament. If the law was believed to be operating harmfully "the remedy may be found, as it has been sought, through application to the Congress, or relief may possibly be given by the Federal Trade Commission, which has been applied to."

His appeal to the "facts peculiar to the business" saved the Chicago Board of Trade from the clutches of the Sherman Law. The Department of Justice contended that the Board's rule fixing the price of grain each day at the closing quotation was an illegal restraint of trade. Every trade regulation imposed a restraint, Brandeis said. The test of legality was whether the restraint destroyed competition or regulated and thereby promoted it. To determine this the court must consider the facts. He analyzed them and found the effect of the rule to be beneficial. The decision was unanimous.

And now came the climax of the fight against the United Shoe Machinery Company. The suit was for dissolution under the Sherman Law—and Brandeis and McReynolds were pressed into impotence by etiquette. The Chief Justice, McKenna, Van Devanter and Holmes found a combination of non-competitive machines, the leases falling within patent rights, and common control not obnoxious to the law. Day, Pitney, and Clarke said the leases ought clearly to be condemned, and Clarke gave the history of the United and its transaction with Plant, the formidable competitor. If Brandeis and McReynolds could have joined the three dissenters the United would have been ordered dissolved. Monopoly stayed perched on its throne of shoe machinery.

Some time later a decree came up for review, enjoining the United from making leases violative of the Clayton Act. Of course, Brandeis could not pass on his own handiwork, but his stepping down did not hinder. The decree was affirmed by a vote of seven to one, McKenna alone holding back.

Out of the war in Europe arose a case of unfair competition which showed, incidentally, the differing thought-processes of Holmes and Brandeis. The court held, where the International News Service copied Associated Press dispatches, that there is a property right in news enduring as long as the news has commercial value. In a separate opinion Holmes, denying that news is property, agreed that a specified number of hours should elapse after original publication unless credit were given to the source. Brandeis fully dissented and stood alone. He delivered a long opinion— that after voluntary communication news was as free as the air to common use; there was no obligation to disclose the source; to create a new rule of law might open the door to greater evils than that of appropriation, such as the curtailment of the free use of knowledge. He brought out a fact which the others chose to ignore: that foreign governments had closed the channel of war news to the International, and the innocent readers of newspapers served by it would have been deprived of information of the greatest importance. The propriety of some remedy appeared to be clear, he said, but courts were ill-equipped to determine the limitations of a property right in news, while a legislature might regard newsgathering as a public utility and impose certain obligations upon an agency like the Associated Press which distributed news only to its restricted membership.

Thus his dissenting opinions came to be distinguished by social concern.

Being a jurist was not enough. A social philosopher was not enough. He was also a statesman without portfolio, as the war years proved. After America's entry in the war he conferred on Palestine's prospects with Arthur Balfour, who arrived with the British mission and who was calling himself a Zionist. Wilson also promised help. Brandeis kept up a running conversation by cable with Chaim Weizmann, British Zionist leader, distinguished chemist and director of the Admiralty laboratories, who had attained definite political influence. Late in 1917 the final draft of the Balfour Declaration, favoring a Jewish national home in Palestine, was cabled from Whitehall to the White House for Wilson's approval. Wilson waited for Brandeis. The Declaration was proclaimed only after revisions by Wise and de Haas had been endorsed by their "silent leader."

As early as October the President designated Brandeis to

compile data with Colonel House for use in determining the basis of eventual peace. In this way not only were plans laid for the restoration of Palestine as a cooperative commonwealth but guaranties for the rights of minorities in other countries were prepared. Officials representing the Polish cause came to him for support of an independent Poland. Spokesmen for Yugoslavic nationalities eagerly presented their claims in his little study. There came Thomas G. Masaryk, the Bohemian leader, whose name had been familiar to Brandeis since '99, when Masaryk, a university professor in Prague, risked his position to defend a Jewish cobbler sentenced for "ritual murder." Masaryk was an old friend of Charles R. Crane and wanted Wilson's help for Czech recognition. From Masaryk and the other visitors Brandeis drew information which prompted the State Department to express sympathy for the oppressed races of Austria-Hungary in their struggle for freedom. He soaked in an immense amount of geographical, ethnical and historical data. He helped Masaryk generously and later had a hand in drawing up Czechoslovakia's declaration of independence. After the Bolshevist coup in Russia it was widely reported that Brandeis would be sent there as minister plenipotentiary to bring Russia back to the Allied side. It was newspaper talk. Crane went.

As a member of the government Brandeis accepted the war. The United States could have stayed out of it, he realized, but he thought it would not be good for us if Germany were not checked. He shared the widely held view that a German victory would set the clock back. Secretary of War Baker gathered a group of younger men about him, including Frankfurter, Walter Lippmann and Stanley King, who would rush to Brandeis for suggestions. This was typical. Brandeis did not proffer advice; others applied to him. His advice extended like many invisible wires into many government bureaus. He conferred a good deal with McAdoo and he convinced Wilson that McAdoo was the man for director-general of the railroads. (His own brother was in the grain administration.)

Brandeis broke his rule in behalf of Herbert Hoover, whom Norman Hapgood had met in London and told to see the justice. Hoover impressed Brandeis as a capable man who had come through an ordeal, who seemed to know more about the European situation than all of his previous visitors. Hoover had no important friends in the administration. The country was then about to enter the war and Hoover was too valuable to lose. Brandeis reached McAdoo, Baker and Gregory and told them to bring Hoover to Wilson's attention. Thus he helped Hoover, appointed food administrator soon after, to climb to political fame.

Brandeis did not wholly approve the government's war policy. He was opposed to the expeditions into Russia and Siberia. Wilson's Fourteen Points were good, the armistice message wrong, the peace treaty bad. Indemnities should not have been imposed; if the United States had not gone into the war there might have resulted a better peace, but with her help the Allies were enabled to dictate an oppressive treaty. The principle of self-determination, meritorious in itself, was applied too hurriedly, erroneously. Instead of separate new nations, federated states could have been established in the nature of *zollvereins*.

While the slaughter of war was still making progress, the collaboration of Colonel House and Brandeis piqued Senator James E. Watson, Republican, of Indiana. Reports of their activity was notice to the country, he said, "that these two men shall sit in the council chamber of the nations when the great peace treaty is settled. A piqued Watson was a caustic Watson. He wanted the truth about the President's purpose because Brandeis, he knew, was an ex-near-Socialist. Immediately after the armistice the newspapers headlined Wilson, Lansing, Root, Brandeis and House as the prospective negotiators. One editorial attacked the President for surrounding himself with Jewish advisers and condemned the choice of

Brandeis as "not acceptable to something like half the American public for the reason that his type of mind is understood to be pacifist and altogether too tolerant of sentimental tenderness toward the down-and-out. This . . . may be sadly out of place in the coming peace council." Brandeis was not sent to Versailles. Wilson told Rabbi Wise, "I need Brandeis everywhere but I must leave him somewhere."

As soon as court closed in June, 1919, the justice sailed for Palestine with de Haas. In London he met Weizmann. In Paris he arrived on the day the Germans were signing the Treaty of Versailles; he called on Wilson, House, Balfour and French and Italian officials. Wise, Frankfurter and other American Zionists had preceded him to Paris to persuade European Zionists to adopt Brandeis' program of social justice as the basis of a mandate for Palestine. The program sought to secure the land, its resources, and the utilities for the whole Jewish people, to guard these against capitalist exploitation, to encourage cooperative enterprises, grant political equality to all inhabitants, afford free immigration, and finally achieve, after a period of transition, a commonwealth. The Zionists could not agree among themselves.

While the question of the mandate hung fire pending a treaty with Turkey, Brandeis resumed his journey. At Alexandria he met Colonel T. E. Lawrence and General Edmund H. H. Allenby. The military machinations of the British disturbed him. Treading the soil of Palestine he was stirred to the heart and he dedicated himself afresh to the dream and task of rebuilding. Practically, he thought of introducing an irrigation system and wiping out malaria. The settlements convinced him that despite the devastations of fifteen hundred years the land could again flow with milk and honey and much besides. Character, developed by centuries of suffering, could supply what Palestine had lost. But the road was economic.

Back in Paris he sought out Balfour to report that the British military authorities were violating the pledge of the

Declaration. Balfour took action. Back in London he clashed with Weizmann on method, objectives and administration. Saddened onlookers saw the passionate Weizmann confronted with the determination of Brandeis, and they worried over the conflict.

Next summer (1920) the World Zionist Conference was held in London and a large American delegation attended. As soon as Brandeis landed Weizmann hastened to confer with him, plead with him to raise money. Money must be found for reconstruction. With Lord Chief Justice Reading, Brandeis evolved a financial and economic plan to give three-year control to a committee of distinguished British Jews, some not previously connected with Zionism. Weizmann kissed his hand and assented.

Brandeis presided at the conference and declared, "We have come to the time when there are no politics that are valuable except the politics of action." He outlined the re-organization plan. That night, while Brandeis was asleep, Weizmann arranged a meeting with some of the principals and presented a substitute scheme. Brandeis felt betrayed. To his associates he said, "Lloyd George might lie, but not to his cabinet."

He returned to the States with the knowledge that the American delegation was split. The hostile element set to work to oust his régime in the Zionist Organization of America; and abetted by Weizmann, who arrived in 1921, they succeeded in the overthrow at the Cleveland convention that year. A vote of confidence in Brandeis was denied, whereupon Mack read Brandeis' resignation as honorary president, submitted his own as president, and called off the names of thirty-seven others who quit the executive committee. "Our place," Brandeis wrote, "will then be as humble soldiers in the ranks where we may hope to hasten by our struggle the coming of the day when the policies in which we believe will be recognized as the only ones through which our great ends may be achieved." But he needed no cue to proceed with comprehensive plans of his own for economic development. This intensive work for Palestine was compressed between court terms.

Out of the war came many cases involving civil liberties, prohibition, taxation, the railroads; and new concerns arising from the economic carnage of the world Armageddon "for democracy." Through it all he never was too busy to keep up daily communication with Miss Grady at the State House in Boston and watch over the affairs of savings bank life insurance.

To Emma Goldman and Alexander Berkman, convicted of violating the conscription law, he granted permission to appeal. But the war power of Congress was paramount, as the Chief Justice stated in a unanimous opinion in the Selective Draft Cases. To Holmes and Brandeis was assigned the writing of opinions sustaining the government in Espionage Act prosecutions, but only when they were convinced of "a clear and present danger" of obstructing the conduct of the war. They parted company with their colleagues over the conviction of perpetrators of a leaflet protesting the use of American soldiers to crush the Russian revolution. The majority upheld sentences to twenty years' imprisonment; the minority of two preferred "free trade in ideas." Again, where the managers of an inconsequential German newspaper in Philadelphia were convicted for publishing false reports to promote the success of the enemy, Brandeis found nothing but feeble changes in copied news items.

> To hold that such publications can be suppressed as false reports, subjects to new perils the constitutional liberty of the press, already seriously curtailed in practice under powers assumed to have been conferred upon the postal authorities. Nor will this grave danger end with the passing of the war . . . an intolerant majority, swayed by passion or by fear, may be prone in the future, as it has often been in the past, to stamp as disloyal opinions with which it differs. Convictions such

as these, besides abridging freedom of speech, threaten freedom of thought and of belief.

Holmes agreed with him; to Clarke it was simply a case of flagrant mistrial in the high tension of "the late deplorable war."

So it was with the distribution of a Socialist Party circular describing the war as "the price we pay" for remaining out of the party. Brandeis discerned peril in permitting juries to make such statements of opinion punishable by declaring them false statements of facts; this "would practically deny members of small political parties freedom of criticism and of discussion in times when feelings run high and the questions involved are deemed fundamental. . . . Mr. Wilson, himself a historian, said before he was President and repeated in *The New Freedom* that: 'The masters of the Government of the United States are the combined capitalists and manufacturers of the United States.'" Holmes joined him there again but let him stand alone in a case where an official of the Nonpartisan League was convicted under a Minnesota statute for making an anti-war speech. The state law which Holmes sustained was to Brandeis a violation of a right guaranteed by the Constitution; it in fact proscribed the teaching of pacifism for all time. The decision was inconsistent coming after the court had held, against the states, that employers were protected in discriminating against unions and businessmen in conducting private employment agencies. "I cannot believe that the liberty guaranteed by the Fourteenth Amendment includes only liberty to acquire and enjoy property," Brandeis wrote.

The revocation of the second-class mail privilege of the *Milwaukee Leader*, a newspaper published by Victor L. Berger, former Socialist congressman, was one of the strokes of post office tyranny which disturbed him. It was another case of "false reports" to obstruct recruiting and aid the enemy. The evidence convinced Clarke and a majority, but Brandeis saw that a decision giving the Postmaster General power to declare a newspaper guilty of violating the Espionage Act would enable him to become "the universal censor of publications." The larger question was "whether in times of peace our press shall be free." If administrative officers might exercise such powers, "in every extension of governmental functions lurks a new danger to civil liberty." Holmes agreed in substance with this view and briefly expressed his own— without footnotes.

Aside from individuals whose conflicts with the legal process became *causes célèbres*, was the nameless herd, suffering in a distraught world of wornout economics and struggling against the high walls of capitalistic domination. When in England Brandeis had noticed a rapid trend toward the recognition of the right to regularity of employment. Birkenhead, the Lord Chancellor— a very conservative gentleman— made a noteworthy admission in this respect. Great Britain was far ahead of the United States in grappling with the grave problems, and Brandeis felt that her solutions would be a great help to this country. In the heydey of prosperity Americans rarely took time to think; in suffering sometimes they did. His idea was to do away with day labor, obliterate the distinction between the salaried man and the wage earner by declaring the right to continuity of employment. Why didn't the employers themselves seize upon it as an anti-Bolshevist measure? The trouble was that the situation called for a different vision than that of stock-ticker patriots.

As concentration of industrial power increased, the restive workman sought justice in trial by combat— the strike— and also achieved some measure of support from legislative bodies. The Clayton Act restricted the use of injunctions in labor disputes, but the court held that this did not permit a union to instigate sympathetic strikes against an employer's customers. "Congress had in mind particular controversies, not a general class war," Pitney said for the majority. And thus a prop intended to equalize before the law the position of workers and employers as industrial combatants was kicked down. Brandeis went into the facts of the industry here involved—newspaper press machinery; there were only four manufacturers in the field in this country, the complainant running an open shop and the three others threatening to break with the union unless union conditions applied to their competitor. Nothing could be plainer than that the employees and the affiliated unions had a common interest and were refusing to work on articles whose production constituted an attack on their standard of living.

When Arizona became a state it adopted a civil code similarly protecting labor against injunctions. The court held the provision unconstitutional as permitting the violation of a property right, in this case by noisy and successful picketing of a restaurant, and depriving the owner of liberty and property. With great pains Brandeis historically traced the development of judicial recognition of labor's rights as the struggle for improvement was balked by injunctions at every stage. The new state of Arizona determined to prevent the injection of judges' economic ideas, translated into law. The state was free to prohibit labor injunctions and remold the rights of property to meet the changing needs of society. So Brandeis thought.

After Wilson's ideals and body were shattered the new era of normalcy marched in. Senator Harding became President, and Brandeis kept his eye on the business news in his morning paper. A brief item exposed the condition of the country to anyone who could read: it told of 2,344,000 motor vehicles having been produced during the first eleven months of 1922. He pointed it out to a friend. Where was the money coming from? We were not earning it as a nation. Brandeis saw that eighty percent of Americans were being exploited for the remaining twenty percent; that the new bonds—national, state, municipal—were simply a mortgage held by the few on the many.

Wilson, shortly before his death, wrote Brandeis an optimistic note:

With the comradeship and assistance of men like yourself (if there are any more) I believe that many good
and great things can be accomplished, and that thought
makes me not a little confident of the future, and I am
grateful for the assurance and guidance of your friendship.

On the other hand, the doleful voice of a liberal newspaper
editor sighed at the fate of Brandeis the judge buried under
reaction. "What a decade for Louis D. Brandeis, citizen!"
The alleged victim did not look at it that way. He was glad
to be where he was. Accepting existing institutions, he believed in seeking betterment within their broad lines rather
than a universal remedy such as state socialism. Remedial institutions were apt to fall under the control of the enemy
and so become instruments of oppression.

But adherents of orderly, peaceful, democratic evolution
became alarmed at the drift of the court with regard to
progressive legislation. Four appointees of Harding ascended
the bench. Taft was named Chief Justice on the death of
White, and he wrote the opinion striking down the Arizona
anti-injunction law. After Clarke resigned to take up work
for the League of Nations, Senator Sutherland was confirmed
on the same day he was nominated. The entrance of his old
opponents did not seem dramatic to Brandeis, though there
was irony in the situation. He had a smile for each of them.
Pierce Butler, formerly a Minnesota railroad lawyer, succeeded Day; Edward Terry Sanford, Tennessee judge, followed Pitney. With this changed personnel a new majority
invalidated an act of Congress authorizing the Minimum
Wage Board of the District of Columbia to prescribe wage
standards as an unconstitutional interference with freedom
of contact. Liberals had been led to believe that the Oregon
cases were vindications of their faith, but now the court
turned back and plucked a precedent which had been thought
forever interred.

Sutherland spoke. He scorned the brief and the mass of

reports in favor of the policy. He said "our own reading has disclosed a large number to the contrary"; the court was concerned with validity, not desirability. Chief Justice Taft, who surprised many by dissenting, declared that the decision on the Oregon maximum hour law was the controlling case, and that it was not the court's function to void congressional acts "simply because they are passed to carry out economic views which the court believes to be unwise or unsound." Holmes had doubts about the social benefits of the District of Columbia statute but deferred to the weight of opinion reasonably held by reasonable men. Brandeis said nothing. His daughter Elizabeth had become secretary of the Minimum Wage Board after graduating from Radcliffe with highest honors, and because of this tinge of personal interest he took no part.

Sutherland was again spokesman for the majority in deciding that a stonecutters' union committed an unlawful restraint of trade by calling a strike against the plaintiff's nonunion products. Brandeis said the law prohibited only unreasonable restraints. "The propriety of the unions' conduct can hardly be doubted by one who believes in the organization of labor." With Holmes concurring in dissent Brandeis pointedly reminded the court it had held that the Sherman Law permitted capitalists to combine fifty percent of the country's steel industry in one corporation and almost the whole shoe machinery industry in another corporation.

> It would, indeed, be strange if Congress had by the same Act willed to deny to members of a small craft of workingmen the right to cooperate in simply refraining from work, when that course was the only means of self-protection against a combination of militant and powerful employers. I cannot believe that Congress did so.

Brandeis had used the United States Steel and the United Shoe Machinery cases as horrible examples on another occasion and in doing so he revealed the chasm between him and

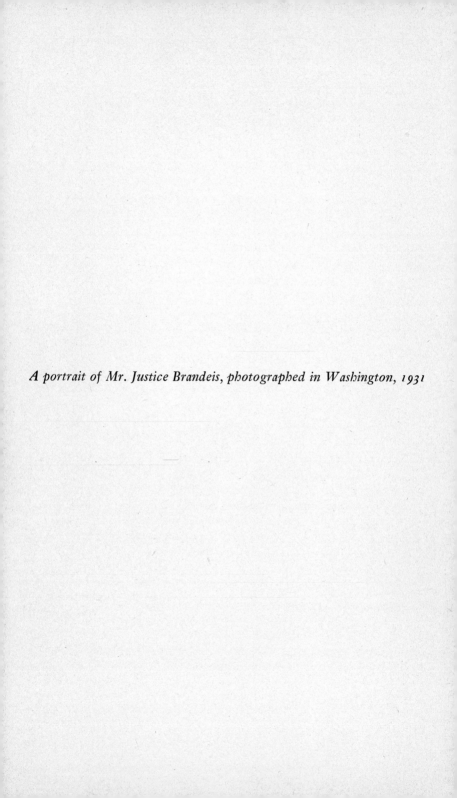

A portrait of Mr. Justice Brandeis, photographed in Washington, 1931

most of his associates in an understanding of economics and industrial life. While they sustained the government's anti-trust suit against an association of hardwood lumber manufacturers as a combination in restraint of trade, Brandeis regarded it as cooperation for rational competition. Joined by Holmes and McKenna, he said the Sherman Law certainly did not command the blind pursuit of competition. The manufacturers' plan for exchange of information on sales, prices, production and supply on hand was akin to the government's own bulletin service on other commodities— it provided the smallest concern with trade facts, it substituted research for gambling, it made possible intelligent conduct under competitive conditions. Refusal to permit cooperation might lead the lumber concerns, frustrated in their efforts to rationalize competition, to enter the inviting field of consolidation. And there would be another huge trust like the court-approved steel and shoe machinery combinations.

The crippling of the Federal Trade Commission in its task of preserving the competitive system was another judicial stroke which he tried vainly to stave off. But as the years brought another change in the court's personnel he won his contention in favor of trade-association cooperation.

The newcomer, given majority opinions to write in validating the plans of cement and maple flooring manufacturers, was Harlan Fiske Stone, former dean of Columbia Law School, who had spent a short time as a member of the law firm of Sullivan & Cromwell before President Calvin Coolidge appointed him Attorney General and later made him a justice. Coming from a firm which had been active in trying to prevent Brandeis' confirmation, Stone formerly shared the belief that he was "a wild man," a propagandist and emotional reformer. On the bench he found Brandeis as dispassionate a lawyer as himself, trying to make the law responsive to the changed social forces and the dominant economic considerations, and he came under Brandeis' influence. Stone rapidly became known as the new liberal on the court. He was confident that in time a majority would follow the road hewn by Holmes and Brandeis. What Holmes knew intuitively Brandeis demonstrated with painstaking, and Stone himself had had the good fortune to be able to study questions while other lawyers, bent on victories for their clients, could not acquire an impartial grasp.

Dissent was not the only avenue to contributions to the growth of the law. There was the daily routine, less sensational but measurable despite its obscurity to laymen. In the sphere of railroad regulation this was notably true, for Brandeis' experience and technical equipment won recognition from his colleagues, and many opinions entrenching the powers of the Interstate Commerce Commission came from his pen.

After the war he favored retention of federal control of the railroads, as of major industries, to prevent the chaos and unemployment of sudden disruption. Wilson sought his advice, but he was chary; the reports of his refusal, however, were exaggerated— Wilson was physically incapacitated from asking too often. But years before, when the President wanted him to suggest a New Englander for a vacancy on the Commission he proposed Joseph B. Eastman. Governor Walsh said Eastman was badly needed at home, and Wilson asked for another choice. It was George W. Anderson. And when Anderson attained a judgeship, which was more to his taste, Wilson asked Brandeis if he could now have Eastman. In 1919 Eastman came to Washington to fill the unexpired term. President Harding had someone groomed for the post, a favorite of Senator Lodge, but James L. Richards of Boston worked to get the entire New England delegation to back Eastman for reappointment for the full seven years. The Hoover administration came in and Republicans put up another fight to oust him. Richards again came to the rescue. Eastman's views were not popular with the administration. He was known as a public ownership man, but his opponents had high regard for his ability and integrity. He disagreed often with his fellow-commissioners and became a writer of dissenting opinions, even as Brandeis.

When Congress returned the roads to their former owners by the Transportation Act of 1920 the commission's functions were enlarged to ensure adequate service. It was authorized to apportion joint rates among the carriers on the basis of individual needs, and it issued an order granting New England roads an increased share of the through rates on freight moving between New England and the rest of the country. An Ohio railroad attacked the constitutionality of this grant of authority— unsuccessfully, for the unanimous court, speaking through Brandeis, held that a road's "just share" must be determined by the commission with an eye to preserving the whole transportation system.

An I.C.C. rule apportioning freight cars equally among bituminous mines in times of car shortage and prohibiting carriers from placing for loading at any mine more than its ratable share, including private cars, was likewise held valid. "The object of the rule," Brandeis said, "was not to equalize fortunes but to prevent an unjust discrimination in the use of transportation facilities and to improve the service." Mc-Reynolds alone thought "it was foolish."

The difficult and controversial business of determining the value of a public utility for rate-making purposes called for analysis and exposition, and even prophesy, from the justice who strove to avert burdens from falling on either investors or consumers. Since 1898 the court had been proceeding under a rule enunciated in *Smyth v. Ames* entitling a utility to a fair return on its value. In 1923 the court decided that the Public Service Commission of Missouri had reduced the rates of a telephone company to a point where they were confiscatory. In providing an inadequate return the commission deprived the company of property in violation of the due process clause of the Fourteenth Amendment. McReynolds, delivering the opinion, said the value of the property at the time of the rate hearing should have been taken as the rate base; the Commission erred in excluding the increase in cost of materials and labor during the war. Brandeis concurred in the result but differed fundamentally on the method for determining whether a prescribed rate was confiscatory.

The rule of *Smyth v. Ames*, he said, was legally and economically unsound. It had failed to protect either capital or the public. It led to the attempt to prove the present value of a utility by estimating the reproduction cost—which involved exercising judgment instead of ascertaining facts. The result was arbitrary.

Originating in the dark days of guesswork, before regulation became scientific, the rule was adopted as a bulwark against inflated claims and swollen prices such as preceded the panic of '93. A long depression followed and the price level slumped. But as it rose again the principle operated in the opposite direction. Commissions began to suspect and reject the delusive calculations of engineers and their predictions, after the war, of a new plateau of prices at various percentages above the 1914 level. The Massachusetts Public Service Commission declared that "capital honestly and prudently invested" must be taken as the controlling factor in fixing the basis for fair rates. To take reproduction cost instead, Brandeis pointed out, might subject investors to heavy losses "when the high war and post-war price levels pass and the price trend is again downward."

This was considered a bold utterance in 1923—annoying to such prosperity mongers as may have noticed it. But the man of statistics was talking. American experience did not justify the prediction of a plateau, he said, and in a footnote:

> The course of prices for the last 112 years indicates, on the contrary, that there may be a practically continuous decline for nearly a generation, that the present price level may fall to that of 1914 within a decade, and that, later, it may fall much lower.

He clarified the legal issue. What the investor devoted

to the public was not specific property but capital embarked in the enterprise. What the Constitution protected was this capital. The rate base should therefore be the amount prudently invested— "prudent" not being used in a critical sense but with a view to excluding dishonest or obviously wasteful expenditures. This would bring stability in place of "the wild uncertainties of the present method" and "the fickle and varying judgments of appraisers, commissions, or courts." Instability was a standing menace of renewed controversy. Moreover, the community could get efficient service only if the managers of the utility were free to devote themselves to the problems of operation and development. Finally, as the measure of a compensatory rate he urged "the annual cost, or charge, of the capital prudently invested." In this long and carefully constructed opinion Holmes concurred.

The difficulty of applying the rule of *Smyth v. Ames* was manifest in the court's effort a year later to relate depreciation charges to present value. Again McReynolds spoke for the majority, and Brandeis and Holmes dissented in favor of a workable rule. Brandeis maintained that legal science could solve the problem of a just depreciation charge for utilities in much the same manner as life insurance companies provided a reserve to meet any margin of error. If the rule of prudent investment were applied and the amount set aside should prove inadequate the utility would be permitted to earn the annual cost of any new capital invested. If the amount should prove excessive the income from the surplus reserve would be credited to reduce the current capital charge, much as a policyholder benefited under mutual insurance. "Thus justice both to the owners of the utility and to the public is assured."

The campaign for the prudent investment theory kept up through the years, and with Stone on the bench Brandeis generally had two supporting voices. The water rates of Indianapolis came up next and the court, clinging to present or reproduction value, held that the value of the company's property "for a reasonable time in the immediate future" must also be taken into account. Brandeis observed that Aladdin's lamp was missing.

Next the court held that rates limiting the returns of the Baltimore street-car system to 6.26 percent on its valuation were inadequate. The state public service commission had based the allowance for annual depreciation on original cost. The court said the plainly right thing to do was to base it on present value. Brandeis delivered a long lecture in accountancy, thoroughly annotated, with footnotes occupying almost as much space. Holmes and Stone concurred in his dissent.

Longest of all was his exhaustive dissenting opinion in the case of the St. Louis & O'Fallon Railway. Under the Transportation Act carriers earning an income exceeding six percent of their valuation were required to pay half of the excess into a fund to be administered by the I.C.C. for the benefit of weaker roads. The O'Fallon denied it had earned an excess and disputed the method of valuation used by the majority of the commission. McReynolds said the commission had failed to discharge its duty in applying the law; it had acted as an arbiter in economics in rejecting current or reproduction costs. But the mandate from Congress which the majority of the court held incumbent upon the I.C.C. was not so simple as McReynolds stated it; nor was it stated accurately. Not only did the O'Fallon itself concede that Congress did not make value measurable by reproduction cost, but Congress clearly intended that the commission weigh the realities of railroading. Brandeis' microscopy isolated ten separate aspects of the problem and to each he devoted thoroughgoing analysis fortified by reference to authorities and ample quotation from railway trade journals. The fine lines of an intricate case were saved from the blur of confused thinking. Distinctions were made patent— between functional depreciation and physical depreciation, between measure of value and evidence of value. His opinion endeavored to do more than express the dissenting side; it aimed to teach and convince. It was a work of intellectual painstaking, of rigorous plodding for lucidity. Only the twenty-seventh draft satisfied him.

He tucked away the other drafts in a little storeroom which once was the kitchenette of a two-room apartment. This place was now his study, on the floor above his living quarters in Florence Court, an apartment house on California Street. Both rooms of the study were small, hemmed in by bookshelves reaching to the ceiling. In one the secretary-for-the-year worked; in the other, the justice. They were like two students in library alcoves. Light came in from a narrow courtyard. Up early, the justice sometimes entered with a magnifying glass in hand, looking for a particular volume of reports. When darkness came he switched on the green desk lamp; the top light was never used and it was in a state of disrepair. Here where the infinite pains of silent labor were applied some former tenant slept. In the kitchenette reposed stacks of manuscript and corrected proofs. The O'Fallon opinion was not a unique product; Brandeis took as much care with less important cases. And he reminded the secretary to check up carefully every allegation of fact and every figure lest the respondents, when they petitioned for a rehearing, point to some *i* not dotted or *t* not crossed.

Chapter XIX

THE STATES, THE NATION, AND DEPRESSION

H OLMES once spoke of "the loneliness of original work"
and "the solitude of thought." Holmes and Brandeis
were not gemini on Washington's zodiac, however much
their names were joined. Both abstained from social functions and the President's receptions. Together they went on
auto rides through Virginia's countryside. The visits of the
Brandeises to the Holmeses in the redbrick house on I Street
were frequent, and a long friendship matured into the
deepest kind of affection. Sometimes when Holmes was blue,
which was unworthy of the cigar-puffing philosopher, Brandeis cheered his spirits by inciting him to turn a neat dissenting opinion. Holmes in his literary library on the second
floor rear sat at a desk in the corner and let the traffic of
contemporary life rumble along.

The trouble with him, Brandeis reflected, was that he
thought *in vacuo,* so one day Brandeis spoke up: "You say
you're always trying to improve your mind and yet you stick
to reading literature. If you want improvement I'll give you
something different to read." The Department of Labor had
just issued a bulletin on the textile industry. Brandeis recommended it to him. "And after you've read it take a trip
through Lowell and Lawrence and see the conditions for
yourself."

Holmes agreed that it probably was not good for him to

be reading the same sort of thing continually, but when the bulletin arrived he looked at it and changed his mind.

Holmes saw little difference between Brandeis and himself. He said he had called attention to the need to cope with economic forces long before Brandeis. After his retirement in his ninety-first year he remarked, without relinquishing the end of a fragrant and well-smoked cigar, "I stated my opinions briefly. I didn't believe in footnotes. But our aims were the same. . . . I still think he's a really good man. We're friends."

Holmes observed the constitutional propriety of letting legislatures make social experiments "in the insulated chambers afforded by the several states" though these efforts might seem futile or their objects noxious to him. If police powers were not stretched too far the Fourteenth Amendment should not be used by judges to blight the community's desires.

So it was on the rock of tolerance that the court often split. But tolerance was not enough. A finding that a law was "not unconstitutional" could hardly suffice for Brandeis. He must establish its validity by probing beyond the record and amassing data independently. The effect of his method was threefold: it helped make the public aware of the long-range implications of the issue, it provided lawyers with a cue for future cases, it gave body to a negative vote and breathed life into it as a cause forever marching on.

On a rare occasion their independent approaches took the two comrades to opposite sides. They disagreed on the Minnesota law proscribing the advocacy of pacifism. They sat in judgment on war-begotten laws of Iowa, Ohio and Nebraska prohibiting grade-school instruction in German, and while Brandeis stood with the majority in refusing to uphold the conviction of guilty teachers, Holmes dissented. Again, when Holmes spoke for the court sustaining a conviction under the federal anti-narcotic law, Brandeis objected that the prosecution must fail because the alleged crime was the fruit of the criminal conspiracy of government agents to induce its commission.

In another case where Holmes wrote the decision Brandeis dissented sharply and alone. The deed to a house in the anthracite region of Pennsylvania reserved the right to remove coal under the premises. The state passed a law forbidding mining within city limits in such a way as to cause the sinking of a dwelling or of immediately adjacent land. Holmes held that since the statute destroyed rights of property and contract it went too far and constituted a taking for which compensation should be made; a strong public desire to improve the public condition did not warrant achieving the desire "by a shorter cut than the constitutional way of paying for the change."

Owen Wister in his life of Theodore Roosevelt snatched at this to prove the existence of a natural gulf between the two justices which sentimental persons failed to recognize. Brandeis, in approving the Bolshevik short cut, revealed his "Oriental mind," Wister said. By the same token the legislature of Pennsylvania which enacted the law and the state's court which upheld it were composed of Oriental minds.

Brandeis' chain of reasoning was this: Coal in place was land; the right of an owner to use his land was not absolute; when the uses, owing to changed conditions, seriously threatened the paramount public welfare the state could prohibit them. The state so doing did not appropriate property, it merely imposed restrictions. With a further change in local or social conditions the restrictions could be removed and the owner would be free to enjoy his property again. "The propriety of deferring a good deal to tribunals on the spot has been repeatedly recognized. . . . Nor can existing contracts between private individuals preclude exercise of the police power." Holmes rested his conclusion on the assumption that the power could not be exercised here unless a reciprocity of advantage obtained between the owner of the restricted property and the rest of the community, and that such reciprocity was absent. Brandeis cited cases where no reciprocal advantage was given to owners of oil tanks, a livery stable, a billiard hall, an oleomargarine factory, a brewery— "unless it be the advantage of living and doing business in a civilized community."

States' rights was not a fetish with either. The Constitution provided a system of federated sovereign states— and it was the Constitution that they were expounding. Even though the oxcart and the horse and buggy had faded in the face of autos and continent-spanning railways, and industry had lost its purely local significance in the acceleration of interstate commerce, the states must be saved from federal encroachment. The historical reason furnished the legal basis. Wisdom dictated the continuance of this demarcation. Brandeis' belief in the small unit extended to government as well; within the compass of the state it was easier to cope with locally varying problems confronting the people. States must be allowed to police their social conditions and use the taxing power to correct economic conditions. In centralization, as in industrial monopoly, lurked the evils of inefficiency and the danger of tyranny.

National prohibition was wrong because it was national. Liquor was a local issue to be solved as the community saw fit. Brandeis' views on how the liquor question should be handled remained as they had been in '91, but many commentators thought that in writing the decisions in leading prohibition cases he departed from liberalism and exhibited a New England strain of austerity. But the Eighteenth Amendment made prohibition the law of the land and these were questions of constitutional law. When repeal came Brandeis was relieved.

And yet the country might have fared better under the amendment and the Volstead Act if Harding had not followed Wilson as President. This was his private opinion, resulting from the ruthlessness of enforcement, the illegal conduct of government officers, and the reaction of the public.

In a memorandum prepared for Wilson he outlined a desirable procedure under the law. Section 2 of the Amendment provided for concurrent power of enforcement by Congress and the states. He wrote, "The intention was that each government should perform that part of the task for which it was peculiarly fitted." The federal government's part was to protect the United States from illegal foreign importations and each state from illegal introduction of liquor from another state; this would require its entire energies. "The protection of the people of a state against the illegal sale within it of liquor illegally manufactured within it is a task for which the state governments are peculiarly fitted; and which they should perform." It involved diversified action and adaptation to the habits and sentiments of the people of each state.

Such were his distinct positions from the standpoint of law and of political science. Bishop Cannon probably would have given a cookie to know his social attitude. Brandeis considered drink (along with unemployment and low wages) one of the three main causes of misery for the workingman. Early in 1920 he suggested that *The Survey* conduct an inquiry into a small city (Grand Rapids was selected) to determine the effects of a year's freedom from these causes and learn what else must be done to make this a livable world. He contributed money for the investigation.

Well pleased with the reports of Winthrop D. Lane and Bruno Lasker, he turned the attention of *Survey* readers to the need for arresting the current tendency towards centralization. He put it this way in a letter:

> The great America for which we long is unattainable unless that individuality of communities becomes far more highly developed and becomes a common American phenomenon. For a century our growth has come through natural expansion and the increase of the functions of the federal government. The growth of the future— at least of the immediate future— must be in

quality and spiritual value. And that can come only through the concentrated, intensified strivings of smaller groups. The field for special effort should now be the state, the city, the village— and each should be led to seek to excel in something peculiar to it. If ideals are developed locally the national ones will come pretty near taking care of themselves.

Brandeis was as scrupulous as any of his associates in resisting the gravitational tug of one's own philosophy. But when the justices passed on the conflicting claims of the federal and state governments the results of nine constitutional tests were not always uniform. Where science did not preempt the field there was room for the personal equation. As for Brandeis, he clung to his conception of the Founding Fathers' intent and substantiated his conclusions with "the logic of realities."

He urged his companions of the conference room to slough off the shackles of precedents which no longer could apply because of new facts arising since the first enunciation of a rule. "Modification implies growth. It is the life of the law." Where the court in adhering to an old rule prevented Congress from permitting state compensation laws to govern maritime accidents of a local nature, he could see no relief "until another amendment of the Constitution shall have been adopted." Where a precedent nipped a Pennsylvania law licensing steamship ticket sellers, construed as a burden on foreign commerce, Brandeis asserted there was no command that "we err again," and he recorded a long list of cases bearing on the commerce clause in which the court "explained away its earlier decisions."

And where a state law standardizing bread sizes was invalidated he urged on his fellows an appreciation of the facts which were essential to the understanding that should precede judging.

Sometimes, if we would guide by the light of reason,

we must let our minds be bold. But, in this case, we have
merely to acquaint ourselves with the art of breadmak-
ing and the usages of the trade. . . . Much evidence referred to by me is not in the record. . . . It is the history of the experience gained under similar legislation.
. . . Of such events in our history, whether occurring
before or after the enactment of the statute or the entry
of the judgment, the court should acquire knowledge
and must, in my opinion, take judicial notice whenever
required to perform the delicate judicial task here involved.

To decide, as the court did, that the law was unnecessary,
burdensome and not calculated to effect its purpose "is, in my
opinion, an exercise of the powers of a super-legislature— not
the performance of the constitutional function of judicial
review."

All within the bounds of courtesy and respect for a colleague's honest but opposite conclusions, disagreement could
be vigorous, fervent, crusading. The spectacle of dispute and
its disquieting effect on the citizen, who was supposed to
look to the highest court for certainty, paled beside allegiance to the Constitution. A five-to-four decision was a confession— that on Olympus sat nine earthly men. But more
important than the shattering of a myth was the compelling
duty to insist that the court honor its functions. "Hitherto
powers conferred upon Congress by the Constitution have
been liberally construed," Brandeis reminded the majority
when they put "an exceedingly narrow construction" on the
authority to tax incomes under the Sixteenth Amendment.
Here was frustration of the popular will indeed. The old in-
come-tax law which Joseph H. Choate had described as a
communist march was later invalidated and the upshot of the
court's action was the adoption of the Amendment, under
which Congress enacted a new law. One provision treated
corporation dividends issued in the form of stock as income
— the court voided it.

Brandeis understood the workings of corporate financial management too well to be misled by the argument of Charles Evans Hughes as counsel and the syllogism of five of his brethren. Stock dividends were income, not capital, and he took time to describe the operations of a company blessed with accumulated profits. If stock dividends were to be exempt "the owners of the most successful businesses in America will, as the facts in this case illustrate, be able to escape taxation on a large part of what is actually their income." The people of the United States did not intend this. And finally, "the high prerogative of declaring an act of Congress invalid should never be exercised except in a clear case."

He was just as severe in objecting to the misuse of executive power, in resenting the President's trespass of the Senate's prerogatives. Wilson had removed a postmaster while the Senate was in session and without its consent, and in so doing stirred the fires of a Vesuvius as old as the Constitution itself— the debate over the power of removal. The cases offered a choice between two policies with long lines of precedents and arguments on both sides, and in addition the issue was confused by something unintelligent Justice Peckham had written.

Chief Justice Taft delved into Clio's records and delivered a long opinion upholding the presidential arm. McReynolds also turned the yellowed pages and wrote a lengthy conclusion to the contrary. Brandeis not only burrowed into the background of American government and stamped his dissent with eighty-seven footnotes but called up the spirit of 1787 in condemning "the arbitrary or capricious exercise" of executive power. Holmes endorsed the findings of the dissenters' exhaustive research. Stone silently sided with Taft and privately felt that the President ought to be able to remove any scud from office, from a Cabinet member down. Stone thought Brandeis would have agreed had he ever been an attorney general.

Brandeis' main thesis was the maintenance of a free government. The purpose of the Constitutional Convention in adopting the doctrine of the separation of powers was not to promote efficiency— "not to avoid friction, but, by means of the inevitable friction incident to the distribution of the governmental powers among three departments, to save the people from autocracy." Distrust of an almighty president was manifest in the conviction then prevailing that "the people must look to representative assemblies for the protection of their liberties."

Political idealism made Brandeis realistic. The people must often look for protection against their representative assemblies. This was poignantly true in times of economic stress when civil liberties were ground between property rights and radical movements advocating political change. The tendency of legislatures in a paroxysm of patriotism to create a pariah class of criminal syndicalists was as wrong as the prejudice of judge, jury and community against defendants in a criminal action who happened to be radicals. Disseminators of unpopular social, economic and political doctrines were as much entitled to their rights as citizens who conformed. And yet the court sustained state laws denying these rights while it repeatedly voided laws inhibiting business. Brandeis had in mind the Nebraska bread case, the Pennsylvania mining case and the Washington employment agency case among others. He believed: "The powers of the courts to strike down an offending law are no less when the interests involved are not property rights but the fundamental personal rights of free speech and assembly."

In a democracy public discussion was a citizen's duty. Brandeis recognized this as a cardinal principle of the American system of government. But without freedom to think, speak and join together discussion would be futile. The conviction of Charles E. Ruthenberg, leader of the Communist Party of America, under a Michigan law, came before the court on a writ of error; Ruthenberg died and the writ was dismissed. Charlotte Anita Whitney, an organizer of the Com-

Mr. Justice Holmes and Mr. Justice Brandeis
One of the last photographs taken of Oliver Wendell Holmes

munist Party of California, was also convicted of criminal
syndicalism and she appealed. At first the justices decided
that they lacked jurisdiction to review the state court's judgment because no federal question appeared. The want was
supplied, and upon a rehearing the California law was found
not to be repugnant to the Fourteenth Amendment. Brandeis
agreed that Miss Whitney's activities were punishable in the
light of the evidence, but he could not subscribe to a sweeping suppression of freedom and a denial of the right to as-
semble with a party advocating the desirability of a prole-
tarian revolution by mass action far in the future. In a separate opinion (Holmes concurring) he said:

> Those who won our independence believed that the
> final end of the state was to make men free to develop
> their faculties, and that in its government the deliberative
> forces should prevail over the arbitrary. They valued
> liberty both as an end and as a means. They believed
> . . . that the greatest menace to freedom is an inert
> people . . . that the path of safety lies in the oppor-
> tunity to discuss freely supposed grievances and pro-
> posed remedies; . . . they eschewed silence coerced
> by law— the argument of force in its worst form. Recog-
> nizing the occasional tyrannies of governing majorities,
> they amended the Constitution so that free speech and
> assembly should be guaranteed.

Fear of serious injury could not alone justify suppression. "Men feared witches and burned women. It is the function of speech to free men from bondage of irrational fears."

> Those who won our independence by revolution were
> not cowards. They did not fear political change. They
> did not exalt order at the cost of liberty. To courageous,
> self-reliant men, with confidence in the power of free
> and fearless reasoning applied through the processes of
> popular government, no danger flowing from speech

can be deemed clear and present unless the incidence of the evil apprehended is so imminent that it may befall before there is opportunity for full discussion. If there be time to expose through discussion the falsehood and fallacies, to avert the evil by the processes of education, the remedy to be applied is more speech, not enforced silence. Only an emergency can justify suppression. Such must be the rule if authority is to be reconciled with freedom. Such, in my opinion, is the command of the Constitution. It is therefore always open to Americans to challenge a law abridging free speech and assembly by showing that there was no emergency justifying it.

Miss Whitney's lawyers might have presented the question whether there actually existed a clear and imminent danger of serious evil as the most important issue and might have required this to be determined by the court or the jury.

Brandeis' new statement of this principle of Americanism, fashioned in literary travail— the phrases whittled and re-arranged for best effect— stirred many thoughtful persons who were troubled lest the repressive tactics of capitalism soon would give the country no choice but between two forms of dictatorship. The democratic process sorely needed reaffirmation. Congratulations came from many quarters. Senator Borah, repenting his sin of 1916, also praised the opinion. Its persuasiveness induced the Governor of California, so the story went, to give Miss Whitney a pardon.

Borah said privately of his *faux pas:* "I have only to say that I was misled by statements and by the appearances which the statements seemed to produce. I think, with a more thorough investigation, I would have arrived at a different conclusion. At any rate, I am free to say, as I have said before, that the vote against Mr. Brandeis is one of the votes which I have cast since I have been here that I have deeply regretted."

However high Brandeis' utterance might rank in the literature of freedom the concept did not make headway in the court, neither in a case involving the pacifist conscience of an applicant for citizenship nor in another concerning the invasion of privacy by a prohibition agent. With Holmes' majestic dissent in the Rosika Schwimmer case he wholly agreed. And when Brandeis protested against wire-tapping, which the majority did not deem a form of "search and seizure" and self-incrimination forbidden by the Fourth and Fifth Amendments, Holmes and Stone supported him. The situation was perfect. He could speak for a living Constitution, its guaranties adaptable to a changing world; he could declare his hatred for espionage. When those amendments were adopted for individual protection against specific abuses, seizure was effected by breaking and entry, and incrimination by torture; but now instruments had been invented more tyrannous than writs of assistance, more subtle than the rack. With scientific progress other vicious forms of invasion might evolve "by which it will be enabled to expose to a jury the most intimate occurrences of the home. Advances in the psychic and related sciences may bring means of exploring unexpressed beliefs, thoughts and emotions."

The makers of our Constitution undertook to secure conditions favorable to the pursuit of happiness. They recognized the significance of man's spiritual nature, of his feelings and of his intellect. They knew that only a part of the pain, pleasure and satisfactions in life are to be found in material things. They sought to protect Americans in their beliefs, their thoughts, their emotions and their sensations. They conferred, as against the government, the right to be let alone— the most comprehensive of rights and the right most valued by civilized men.

The fact that the physical connection with the telephone wires was made outside the petitioner's premises was immaterial; "search and seizure" could not be limited in definition to the confines they had in 1787. It was also immaterial that the intrusion was in aid of law enforcement. "Experience should teach us to be most on our guard to protect liberty when the government's purposes are beneficent." And should the government let its officers break laws and breed contempt for them? To declare that the end justified the means— "to declare that the government may commit crimes in order to secure the conviction of a private criminal— would bring terrible retribution. Against that pernicious doctrine this court should resolutely set its face."

The political philosophy set forth by the Constitution held the allegiance of not only Brandeis the judge, but Brandeis the man. He admired the twenty-five delegates who did the actual work of the Convention, who were familiar with all historic attempts at instituting republican government, who had the ability to express themselves and deliberated without publicity. It was an ideal setting. They wrought a document which this latter-day expounder colloquially described as all right, still all right for present purposes. But it had to be interpreted properly. Even the Fourteenth Amendment was satisfactory if properly construed.

No strain on the imagination was needed to understand why he ignored Bryan's preference for him as a presidential candidate in 1920 and why he passed in silence La Follette's intimated desire to have him for a running mate in the 1924 election. Aside from Fighting Bob's demand for congressional veto power over Supreme Court decisions, and the unattractiveness of the vice-presidency, Brandeis was content to stay where he happened to be; more than content— eager. He had no ambitions. He was happy at his work, mindful of a leverage surpassing political régimes. When newspapers carried a quotation from him endorsing his old friend's record he was vexed. The statement was dug up from the 1912 campaign and, without a datemark, looked like a current political utterance.

The restrictions of judicial office were not irksome. A free man on the bench actually lost little by not being a private citizen and less by not being an elected executive. Some people went to the extreme of thinking of a judge as all-powerful; but freedom to act could never exceed inherent limits. Nor was it hypocritical to hold a private opinion which followed a channel different than that of one's action as a servant of the state.

In 1921 the Brandeises permitted the wife and children of Nicola Sacco to use their Dedham home. Sacco was in the Dedham jail at the time. He and Bartolomeo Vanzetti, both anarchists, had just been convicted of murder, and Mrs. Evans had become deeply interested in them during the trial. What thoughts Brandeis may have harbored on the innocence of the shoeworker, Sacco, and the fishpeddler, Vanzetti, or on the prejudice of the ruling forces in the Commonwealth of Massachusetts, bore no relation to the requirements of the Constitution, the limitations of the Judicial Code, and the due legal processes of the state.

Mrs. Evans discussed the case only once in his presence. Mrs. Brandeis told her later it would be better not to mention it again because it might come before Louis in the court. In 1927 the date was set for electrocution. Arthur D. Hill, counsel for the condemned men, could not obtain a writ of habeas corpus from Judge Anderson, then on the Circuit Court of Appeals. It was summertime; the justices of the Supreme Court were on vacation. Only one signature was needed for a stay until the application for a writ of *certiorari* could be considered by the full court. Holmes was in his boyhood home at Beverly Farms. Two days before the execution date he sat on his porch listening to Hill's story. All the while his heart responded his duty reminded him that as a judge of the United States he had no authority to meddle with a state matter.

He was somewhat offended by letterwriters who "with the confidence that sometimes goes with ignorance of the law" supposed he had "a general discretion to see that justice is done."

The next day Hill hurried to Brandeis, whose summer home for the past few years was at Chatham, on the tip of Cape Cod. Brandeis declined because people close to him were involved but he was convinced also that there was no federal question. Stone, reached on an island off Maine a few hours before the men went to their death, felt so, too. And so did Mrs. Evans.

The roundup of alien radicals begun by Attorney General A. Mitchell Palmer, the Red-baiting pursued by his successor, Harry M. Daugherty, the scandals of the Harding administration, and the inflation of the Coolidge years were reflected glints from the spearheads of triumphant industrialism. America lost her sense of values. Idealism lay in the dust. Money, bigness, integration, dominance, and pleasure became the accepted prizes of life. The building of a wholesome society, swept aside by the war, was an academic memory, a fused picture of ruined columns and uncompleted temple. Here and there men and women held their tenets steadfast, some clinging to the simple morals of Aesop's Fables learned in childhood, others to a philosophy of maturity. Persisting in the pursuit of industrial democracy when the din of prosperity roared through the land, Brandeis put great stock in an awakened moral sense of the social-minded intelligentsia.

That force, combined with an awakened economic sense of organized labor, could break down the stupid belief that business evils, such as espionage, were inevitable ills which a Christian should bear with resignation. In the summer of '24 he saw depression and suffering ahead. The probable thinking period could be used by the free weeklies and dailies to tackle the problem of irregularity while others concentrated on trade cycles. "Steel Output in U. S. Fluctuates Rapidly"— so ran a newspaper headline. Here was the crime of highly organized monopolistic business as expressed in steel production figures. Where were the economic statesmen? The coun-

try was offered only the vision of the Street and the pater-
nosters of princes and politicians. It was necessary to look
among persons with a moral or an economic concern to find
a lever for vanquishing the citadel of prejudice against the
proposed principle. William H. McElwain had recognized
the moral "must" as soon as it was called to his attention and
within five years achieved, through thinking and courage,
complete success in regularizing employment.

Brandeis regarded improvement in workers' conditions not
as a goal but as an incident to the striving. Material welfare
was valuable mainly as a means of increasing opportunities
for development. The clear objective was to make man free
— a self-respecting member of a democracy, and worthy of
respect. "The great developer," he wrote to his friend,
Robert W. Bruère, "is responsibility. Hence, no remedy can
be hopeful which does not devolve upon the workers participation in responsibility for the conduct of business; and
their aim should be the eventual assumption of full responsibility— as in cooperative enterprises. This participation in and
eventual control of industry is likewise an essential for obtaining justice in distributing the fruits of industry."

After the post-war coal and railroad strikes Brandeis had
a plan for preventing the recurrence of similar crises; not
by crippling unions and prohibiting strikes but by industrial
sanitation. Employers should accept trade-unionism formally; cease the use of private detectives and armed guards;
discontinue the resort to injunctions. The withdrawal of
delusive measures of protection, which were discouraging to
constructive thought, would remove irritating causes of discontent and spur employers into resourcefulness. It would
also tend to correct conditions which left the employer and
the community open to the arbitrariness of unions. Another
way to narrow the field of conflict to manageable proportions (and soften the temper of the parties) would be for
society to stop putting its eggs in one basket.

As against the American passion for bigness and integration, safety lay in industrial, financial and territorial decentralization with protective federation. It lay in the maintenance of independent substitutes, in the small unit, in diversification. Society should insure itself against the arbitrariness of coal barons or miners by further development of hydroelectric power and the alternative use of oil; against the arbitrariness of railway executives and workers by further development of water transportation, the automobile, the air service. Where possible, insurance against interruption of supplies should be effected by storing adequate quantities. Brandeis remembered how he protected Rand-Avery from its workers' ultimatum by getting timetables printed in advance of the usual peak season.

In an exceptional case adjustment by negotiation might prove unattainable. What then? Not force, physical or legal, but passive resistance. The sure remedy for the arbitrary demand of an excessive price for an article or service was doing without. Emergencies called for courage and powers of endurance. Brandeis observed that walls, mercenaries and laws had never succeeded in affording for long protection to a fear-ridden, comfort-loving people. Justice and independence — we must love these more than goods or ease.

But by '27 the country had paid for its great material prosperity by falling into a state of comfortable servitude. In the spring of '28 unemployment figures, as he analyzed them, presented a terrible picture. Ex-Governor Walsh, now in the Senate, read excerpts from *Survey Graphic* describing conditions in various parts of the United States. He called for a government building program. With unemployment thus forced upon public attention Brandeis thought that the right to continuous work should be vigorously championed; raised above the right to dividends; given an equality with rent, interest and taxes; asserted as a moral right in a civilized community. It was essential to the emancipation of labor. If the right gained recognition economic and social invention would quickly devise the means of securing its enforcement.

There was danger that Secretary of Labor James J. Davis might misinterpret the unemployment figures. There was danger in listening to soothe-sayers such as Owen D. Young of the General Electric— which was among the worst and least justifiable offenders. President Hoover had also talked— but as a trumpeter for big business; he was really a serious factor in producing the current unemployment and irregularity. In these respects the United States was the most reckless of all countries. Americans had sinned most in worshiping easy money.

In the spring of '29 Brandeis wrote to an old friend that unemployment would be the nation's greatest concern for the next decade. In the fall the stock market crashed. Commodity prices tumbled. It was the due-date of the first instalment of retribution. Economic chaos hushed the bombast of the practical men. Then voices began to find themselves, each to assert the true reason for the depression, and as they spoke more workers were laid off. Unemployment was generally regarded as a consequence of distress. On the contrary, Brandeis maintained that irregularity was its greatest contributing cause.

In those distressful days he saw also the need for stopping the waste of commercial life-insurance companies and its grievous burden on wage-earners. The educational campaign for the savings bank system was still on, was still necessary. As the demand for his book, *Other People's Money*, picked up, he induced Crane to turn back the royalty rights and he donated them to Miss Grady for use by the Massachusetts Savings Bank Insurance League. As the depression continued the old-line companies suffered an enormous percentage of lapses and lost ground to the twenty-one banks which kept up a steady increase in number of policies and amount of insurance in force.

The lines deepened in Brandeis' face, the wrinkles in his forehead became grooves, his hair whitened; but brightness shone through the shadows of the eyes and the voice was not tired. A visitor to his study, dejected by the forlorn world outside, was always treated to optimism. The depression would do some good, Brandeis said; people were already realizing the inadequacy of things material and turning attention to spiritual values. A renewed striving for the good life would bring revaluations and new directions of effort.

Some of the great American idols had begun to be revalued. There was Henry Ford. He succeeded as a businessman but failed in his social obligations— to his employees and to the community; he felt no responsibility toward Detroit, let it default— the only city in the country to do so. But Brandeis never wasted words on anti-social individuals. He preferred to talk of policies, and characteristically saw the sunny side of bad ones— even of Hitlerism. Democracy and the Jews were gaining, the world over, from Nazi performances— a fine exhibit of autocracy.

Zionism had plunged him directly into the workings of government and economic processes. He had more than a finger in the Palestine pie. By '29 half a million dollars of his money had gone into it, and he considered this his best investment. Long parted from the politics of the movement— his group, constituting a minority fraction of the Zionist Organization and merely paying dues on time, devoted themselves to specific undertakings for Palestine's economic development. This was his great adventure in a life which, he said, was now beginning to seem long. In this he found romance: creating opportunities through which a people worthy of the land might build it up. "Some say, 'How can you expect success in so small a country?' To my mind the smallness of the country contributes greatly to the probability of complete success. The problems are all compassable. None is so big in bulk, so complex, that wee man seems inadequate for the task."

With Nathan Straus, Felix Warburg and others he called for capital to be used in definite projects. A wholesale cooperative needed to be formed to bring down the cost of living; he emphasized speed—the money to start it should be collected in thirty days. A medical unit could wipe out malaria—he drew largely on his own funds. There was a plan for the hydroelectric harnessing of River Jordan for power and irrigation. Money was needed also for building and loan associations, for cooperative societies of producers and consumers. He financed a survey of Transjordania with an eye to Palestine's future requirements. In 1930 he gave $15,000 to the Histadruth, a labor federation, to provide Jewish agricultural workers with more employment. He no longer had doubts as to whether supplying the settlers would weaken character and make them dependents instead of self-reliant pioneers. Of course, confidence did not mean certainty. "Empire builders must take risks," he said.

Generous though his companions in the adventure regarded him, he was stern and exacting, intolerant of mistakes. Friends said, "The Old Man is a tyrant," but said it with a nuance of feeling. He maintained his refusal to let the so-called Brandeis-Mack group become entangled with the administration of the Zionist Organization. But when Zionist leaders besought him to make peace—the debt was huge, morale low, membership reduced, Louis Marshall dead, and the British government seemed to be catering to the Arabs—he relented. The Cleveland convention in 1930 marked the revival of the prevailing influence of Judge Mack, Rabbi Wise, Robert Szold and the other adherents. Brandeis took no personal interest. He was absorbed with economics in action, thrilled with Palestine's picture of health in a world of depression.

Contrasted with his direct part in Palestine's internal affairs was his position as a circumscribed spectator of the vast undertaking of reconstruction in America. He could step in only where the Constitution permitted. The monstrous débâcle, the concentration of industrial control, the disparity between productive capacity and consumptive ability bore out his observation, "Man's works have outgrown man."

He kept abreast of economic thinking, often by first-hand contact with the thinkers. Many persons active in public life and scholarly pursuits came to him, in the same open spirit as visitors reaching out for intellectual growth. Under the stimulus of the crisis experimentation took place. Brandeis reflected that it was one of the happy incidents of the federal system that a single courageous state might, if its citizens chose, serve as a laboratory and try novel social and economic experiments without risk to the rest of the country.

Chapter XX

EXPERIMENTS

W ERE the states "still masters of their destiny"? The phrase was Brandeis'. Doubt was raised by the court's disposition of a number of earlier cases. When Oklahoma extended protection to farmers' cooperatives the court took it away. Brandeis deplored the frustration of this effort at economic democracy: cotton growers, excluding capitalist control of their cooperative ginnery, socialized their interests by an equitable assumption of responsibilities and an equitable distribution of benefits. Holmes and Stone joined him in dissent. Pennsylvania's law came next, imposing a gross-receipts tax on corporations operating taxicabs but not on individuals in the same business. Owen J. Roberts was of counsel for the taxi company which challenged the statute, successfully. Once more the three dissenters urged more latitude for the states.

Pennsylvania's fear of corporate power, expressed in laws since 1840, gave Brandeis his text:

> The apprehension is now less common. But there are still intelligent, informed, just-minded and civilized persons who believe that the rapidly growing aggregation of capital through corporations constitutes an insidious menace to the liberty of the citizen; that it tends to increase the subjection of labor to capital; that, because of the guidance and control necessarily exercised by great corporations upon those engaged in business, individual

445

initiative is being impaired and creative power will be
lessened; that the absorption of capital by corporations,
and their perpetual life, may bring evils similar to those
which attended mortmain; that the evils incident to the
accelerating absorption of business by corporations outweigh the benefits thereby secured; and that the process
of absorption should be retarded.

The court might think such views unsound, but its job was
to determine constitutionality. It nullified another state law—
of New Jersey, fixing fees to be charged by employment
agencies; and another— of Minnesota, regulating the price
of milk.

In 1930 there were new changes in personnel, always a
source of speculation. Illness obliged Taft to resign in February, and President Hoover called back Hughes, with criticism from the progressives, to serve as Chief. Sanford died
in March, on the same day as Taft, and to this vacancy
Hoover sought to elevate Judge John J. Parker of the Circuit
Court of Appeals; but labor denounced him as a friend of
yellow-dog contracts and the name was withdrawn in favor
of Roberts, the Pennsylvania lawyer who had made a national reputation in the investigation of the Teapot Dome
oil scandal. During the next term Hughes and Roberts, with
Holmes, Brandeis and Stone, formed a majority nucleus standing together in several liberal decisions, invalidating California's red-flag law and Minnesota's gag law, and sustaining
Indiana s chain-store tax and a New Jersey statute which
restricted insurance agents' commissions. When Brandeis
finished delivering the opinion in the insurance case McReynolds, as spokesman for what appeared to be the new minority, snapped out: "No rational person could uphold such a
law."

The majority view that insurance was affected with a
public interest and states might regulate the rates inspired
hope of a revival of welfare legislation; and hope that other

businesses would be found subject to regulation. More to the point was Brandeis' declaration that the presumption of constitutionality must prevail in the absence of facts persuasive enough for overthrowing the law.

Curiously the cry of crippling the police power came from Butler, Van Devanter, McReynolds and Sutherland when the other justices held constitutional the Minnesota law for the suppression of "a malicious, scandalous and defamatory newspaper." Butler cited the New Jersey case as to the presumption of validity. He said the court was required to assume that conditions in Minneapolis justified discontinuance of *The Saturday Press;* to his opinion he appended its last editorial, which vilified Jewish gangsters and public officials as being in cahoots. The paper had issued only nine numbers in its drive on gambling and racketeering in that city when it was legally declared a nuisance and enjoined from further publication.

As counsel for Minnesota was arguing his case Brandeis asked him how a community could secure protection from a combination of officials and criminals if free discussion were not allowed.

"Of course there was defamation," Brandeis said. "You cannot disclose evil without naming the doers of evil." Here was not a scandal of the kind that appeared too often in the press but a matter of prime interest to every American citizen. "What sort of a matter could be more privileged?"

"Assuming it to be true," counsel put in.

"No," the justice insisted, "a newspaper cannot always wait until it gets the judgment of the court. These men set out on a campaign to rid the city of certain evils."

"So they say."

"Yes, of course, so they say. They went forward with a definite program and certainly they acted with great courage. They invited suit for criminal libel if what they said was not true. Now, if that campaign was not privileged, if that is not one of the things for which the press chiefly exists, then for what does it exist? As for such defamatory matter being issued regularly or customarily, how can such a campaign be conducted except by persistence and continued iteration?" The Chief wrote the controlling opinion, the composite views of himself, Holmes, Brandeis, Stone and Roberts. The pity of it was that one of the editors, Howard A. Guilford, whom an unconstitutional law might not stifle, was later mortally suppressed by a shotgun.

If a liberal bloc existed in the popular mind, a mirage could be dissipated. The accession of Hughes and Roberts, it soon developed, did not herald a new trend. Each justice voted according to his own understanding. The makeup of the majority continued to be as fluid and variable as in the old days.

In 1932 national distress had deepened and responsiveness was expected from the court, but the principle of roughshod individualism, of *laissez-faire* economy, still seemed rooted. Sutherland spoke for a large majority who found that Oklahoma's law requiring a certificate of public convenience and necessity for any new firm manufacturing ice aimed to prevent competition and fostered monopoly as against consumers. Brandeis drew on his knowledge of business; where interest and depreciation charges on plant constituted a large element in cost of production, the financial burdens incident to unnecessary duplication of facilities and the division of possible patronage among competitors brought high unit costs, unreasonable rates and poor service. In his opinion, the requirement of a certificate therefore promoted the public interest. It prevented waste; it averted the crowding of a locality with resultant price-cutting and the destruction of small firms by powerful corporations. Where monopolies obtained, as among other public utilities, they were under the effective control of a commission, which could terminate them.

If the Oklahoma legislature decided that conditions justified the conversion of a private calling into a public one and the

Mr. Justice Brandeis in the study of his summer home at Chatham, Massachusetts, in July 1935

curtailment of the right to enter it when the necessity for another plant did not exist, the usual presumption of validity should apply, Brandeis said. The power "seems indispensable in our ever-changing society." The state could enter the ice business to secure an adequate supply for its inhabitants; it could use the lesser power of preventing individuals from wantonly engaging in the business and making impossible a dependable source; it could exert the taxing power and thereby drive out all individual dealers by the unequal competition and in effect bar private enterprise altogether. The principle to follow was that the state's power extended to every regulation of any business reasonably required and appropriate for the public protection.

The opinion by Sutherland held that the state was not entitled to dispense with "certain essentials of liberty," such as the right to go into a private business like ice manufacturing, "in the interest of experiments." Behind the veil Brandeis saw the justices intruding their differing view of public policy and exercising "not the function of judicial review but the function of a super-legislature." His realistic opinion was heavily annotated with references to studies in refrigeration, trade journals, association reports, economic treatises, and current books and magazine articles.

The *Washington Post* criticized him for supporting with "curious logic" this Oklahoma law which ventured "dangerously near to socialism." He "put his economic theories ahead of the Constitution" and gave "a dissertation on hard times. . . . The justice took occasion to air his personal views on the American economic structure, with only a casual reference to the legal point at issue." What annoyed the *Post* was the eighth section of Brandeis' opinion, starting thus:

The people of the United States are now confronted with an emergency more serious than war. Misery is widespread, in a time, not of scarcity, but of overabundance.

These words were not uttered in a judicial drone. With intense feeling, Brandeis gestured as he spoke. In past economic emergencies, in the era of scarcity, the danger was excessive prices. But the long-continued depression brought "unprecedented unemployment, a catastrophic fall in commodity prices, and a volume of economic losses which threaten our financial institutions."

> Some people believe that the existing conditions threaten even the stability of the capitalistic system. Economists are searching for the causes of this disorder and are re-examining the basis of our industrial structure. Most of them realize that failure to distribute widely the profits of industry has been a prime cause of our present plight. But rightly or wrongly, many persons think that one of the major contributing causes has been unbridled competition.

As the footnotes showed, he was not offering ideas as his own but a selection and synthesis of others' conclusions: the overexpansion of industry without a corresponding increase in the people's consumptive capacity, the impossibility of overcoming irregularity in employment unless production and consumption were more nearly balanced, the insistence that "there must be some form of economic control." And many thoughtful businessmen insisted that all stabilization projects must prove futile unless a check were put on the embarking of new capital in an industry where capacity already exceeded production schedules.

> Whether that view is sound nobody knows. The objections to the proposal are obvious and grave. The remedy might bring evils worse than the present disease. The obstacles to success seem insuperable. The economic and social sciences are largely uncharted seas. We have been none too successful in the modest essays in industrial control already entered upon. The new proposal

involves a vast extension of the area of control. Merely to acquire the knowledge essential as a basis for the exercise of this multitude of judgments would be a formidable task; and each of the thousands of these judgments would call for some measure of prophecy. Even more serious are the obstacles to success inherent in the demands which execution of the project would make upon human intelligence and upon the character of men. Man is weak and his judgment is at best fallible.

But because of experimentation great achievements had been made in the exact sciences— a reminder that "the seemingly impossible sometimes happens." Free and encouraged, these experiments attested the value of the process of trial and error.

Some people assert that our present plight is due, in part, to the limitations set by courts upon experimentation in the fields of social and economic sciences; and to the discouragement to which proposals for betterment there have been subjected otherwise. There must be power in the states and nation to remold, through experimentation, our economic practices and institutions to meet changing social and economic needs. I cannot believe that the framers of the Fourteenth Amendment, or the states which ratified it, intended to deprive us of the power to correct the evils of technological unemployment and excess productive capacity which have attended progress in the useful arts.

Denial of the right to experiment was fraught with serious consequences. The court could exercise this high power but — "we must ever be on our guard, lest we erect our prejudices into legal principles." And Brandeis repeated himself: "If we would guide by the light of reason, we must let our minds be bold."

Only Stone joined with him. Holmes had recently retired

— withdrawing from the world, he said. The traditional conservatives and the doubtful liberals more than sufficed to stay the state's hand.

Benjamin N. Cardozo, chief judge of the Court of Appeals of New York, was selected by Hoover in the difficult duty to find a successor to Holmes. The Senate confirmed him unanimously, without discussion or roll-call. Cardozo regarded Brandeis as standing "with the few great judges of his country and the world," the originator of a method of solving constitutional law problems "which, if followed, would keep the law responsive to changing human needs. In his work on the bench he has shown this method in action." The new associate did not sit on the Oklahoma case, but as the term drew out and another judicial year went past an occasional triumvirate of dissenters was established.

In March, 1933, Franklin D. Roosevelt took over the spoliated stables and locked the doors, declaring a bank holiday. The depression, which the good nature of the American people shied from calling a panic, had become critical. The new President summoned counselors from academic groves and elsewhere to formulate a program. Frankfurter, who had supported him in the election campaign, was said to be an important adviser, and significance was attached to Frankfurter's close relations with Brandeis. Twenty years before, when Wilson arrived to usher in the New Freedom, it was Brandeis who had the President's ear. Time brought new rôles. Freedom still went begging. The justice enjoyed the news that on the day all the banks of the nation were shut the insurance departments of Massachusetts savings banks were able under "the Brandeis law" to make payments— and they did so.

In the period of transition a case involving Florida's new system of graduated taxes on chain stores was decided against the state. Roberts wrote the opinion. There was a minority— of the expected three. But Brandeis spoke only for himself and covered more ground than the legal issues at bar. The majority refused to acknowledge that "the undisclosed pur-

pose" of the statute was to discriminate against large corporate chains. Brandeis emphasized the point that Florida's
chief aim in using the taxing power was not revenue but protection of independent stores from capitalistic corporations
by subjecting the chains to financial handicaps which might
conceivably compel them to withdraw from the state. The
privilege of engaging in intrastate commerce as a corporation
could be granted or withheld by the state as it saw fit; it had
the power to prohibit excessively large chains and could use
the more temperate remedy of taxation to prevent their domination.

The prevalence of the corporation in America has led
men of this generation to act, at times, as if the privilege
of doing business in corporate form were inherent in
the citizen; and has led them to accept the evils attendant upon the free and unrestricted use of the corporate
mechanism as if these evils were the inescapable price
of civilized life, and, hence, to be borne with resignation. Throughout the greater part of our history a different view prevailed.

Brandeis delved into the legislative history of limitations
on corporations and produced an abundance of footnotes to
show how the fears of the people were put into law; and how
finally states trafficking in charters for revenue ("The race
was one not of diligence but of laxity") effected a general
lessening of restrictions. The removal of limits on size and
activities resulted in giant corporations whose size alone gave
them a social significance and in such concentration of economic power that "so-called private corporations are sometimes able to dominate the state." He paid a tribute to A. A.
Berle, Jr., and Gardiner C. Means as able, discerning scholars
who demonstrated this in their recent book, *The Modern
Corporation and Private Property*. He mentioned Thorstein
Veblen and Walther Rathenau as other men of insight and
experience who were alarmed at the growing separation of

ownership (of shares widely dispersed) from control (in the hands of a few) and the approaching rule of the corporate system by a plutocracy. The process of absorption had advanced in the United States so far that two hundred corporations controlled directly about one-fourth of the national wealth, and these in turn were "actually dominated by a few hundred persons— the negation of industrial democracy." Other writers showed the coincidental concentration of individual wealth, and he echoed their belief "that the resulting disparity in incomes is a major cause of the existing depression."

Among these two hundred corporations were five of the plaintiffs in the Florida case: Great Atlantic & Pacific Tea Company, Louis K. Liggett Company, Montgomery Ward & Company, United Cigar Stores Company and F. W. Woolworth Company. "Against these plaintiffs, and other owners of multiple stores, the individual retailers of Florida are engaged in a struggle to preserve their independence— perhaps a struggle for existence." The citizens of the state, in subjecting chains to the handicap of higher license fees, might have done so for the preservation of competition or for a broader purpose.

> They may have believed that the chain store, by furthering the concentration of wealth and of power and by promoting absentee ownership, is thwarting American ideals; that it is making impossible equality of opportunity; that it is converting independent tradesmen into clerks; and that it is sapping the resources, the vigor and the hope of the smaller cities and towns. . . .
>
> The encouragement or discouragement of competition is an end for which the power of taxation may be exerted. And discrimination in the rate of taxation is an effective means to that end.

Decisions by which the court had sustained the states and the federal government in laying taxes to favor certain industries or forms of industry were cited by Brandeis. He said business must yield to the paramount interests of the community in peace as in war. And when a business became harmful by excessive size, as a state might conclude bigness in retail merchandising menaced the public welfare, the state could curb it. The state had the right also to draw the line between capitalistic corporate chains and cooperative chains of individual stores; they were as fundamentally different as economic absolutism and industrial democracy. The way of cooperation "leads directly to the freedom and the equality of opportunity which the Fourteenth Amendment aims to secure. That way is clearly open."

Through his peroration came the beat of deep conviction.

There is a widespread belief that the existing unemployment is the result, in large part, of the gross inequality in the distribution of wealth and income which giant corporations have fostered; that by the control which the few have exerted through giant corporations, individual initiative and effort are being paralyzed, creative power impaired and human happiness lessened; that the true prosperity of our past came not from big business, but through the courage, the energy and the resourcefulness of small men; that only by releasing from corporate control the faculties of the unknown many, only by reopening to them the opportunities for leadership, can confidence in our future be restored and the existing misery overcome; and that only through participation by the many in the responsibilities and determinations of business, can Americans secure the moral and intellectual development which is essential to the maintenance of liberty. If the citizens of Florida share that belief, I know of nothing in the Federal Constitution which precludes the state from endeavoring to give it effect and prevent domination in intrastate commerce by subjecting corporate chains to discriminatory license fees. To that extent, the citizens of each state are still masters of their destiny.

The unpredictable court on the same day it handed down the Florida tax decision reversed a decree against Appalachian Coals, Inc., a selling agency for one hundred and thirty-seven coal producers which had been prosecuted under the Sherman Law. Hughes wrote that this was an honest, cooperative effort to remove injurious practices and make competition fairer in an industry suffering from deplorable conditions. "The intelligent conduct of commerce through the acquisition of full information of all relevant facts may properly be sought by the cooperation of those engaged in the trade." The court thus gave force to a view long before expressed by Brandeis in a dissenting opinion. "The interests of producers and consumers are interlinked; when industry is grievously hurt, when concerns fail, when unemployment mounts and communities dependent upon profitable production are prostrated, the wells of commerce go dry," said Hughes. Only McReynolds was unconvinced.

The planners in Washington hailed the decision as a harbinger of judicial approval. Scarcely two weeks had passed since Roosevelt's inauguration. There was reliance also on an earlier case where the court, in an opinion written by Brandeis, unanimously upheld the power of the Secretary of Agriculture under the Packers and Stockyard Act to prescribe rates to be charged by commission buyers and sellers. Legislative price-fixing was apparently valid. Might not Congress regulate industry and agriculture where the states were impotent or hamstrung?

As the states adopted measures to cope with their local dilemmas the march of adjudication began. The first emergency law coming up for review was a Minnesota statute establishing a two-year moratorium on mortgages and challenged as a violation of Article I, Section 10, of the Constitution, which forbade states to pass laws "impairing the obligation of contracts." Hughes said the contract clause must be construed in the light of the relation of the emergency to the constitutional power. "Emergency does not create power. Emergency does not increase granted power or remove or diminish the restrictions imposed upon power granted or reserved." The constitutional question was whether the power possessed by the state embraced this particular exercise of it in response to particular conditions. He reasoned that if a state could give temporary relief from enforcement of contracts in the presence of disasters due to physical causes (fire, flood, earthquake) "that power cannot be said to be nonexistent when the urgent public need demanding such relief is produced by other and economic causes." The situation in Minnesota furnished a proper occasion; the legislation was temporary in operation and limited to the emergency which called it forth. Brandeis, Stone, Roberts and Cardozo supported him.

The conservative dissenters were horrified. Congress had already abrogated the gold clause in all obligations. They feared the implication of the moratorium decision and "the potentiality of future gradual but ever-advancing encroachments upon the sanctity of private and public contracts." They said they would be neglectful of their duty if they failed to spread upon the permanent records of the court the reasons which moved them to disagree. In a long opinion Sutherland declared, "A provision of the Constitution does not admit of two distinctly opposite interpretations"— one thing at one time, an entirely different thing at another; it must be taken as it was meant when framed and adopted; periods of depression had always alternated with years of plenty. "If the provisions of the Constitution be not upheld when they pinch as well as when they comfort, they may as well be abandoned."

Hughes retorted by quoting Marshall:

We must never forget that it is *a constitution* we are expounding . . . a constitution intended to endure for ages to come, and consequently to be adapted to the various *crises* of human affairs.

Two months later the court split again— the same five justices forming the majority— over the New York Milk Control Law, under which a board set a minimum price of nine cents a quart to consumers. Other states had adopted similar statutes, and additional importance attached to the case by virtue of the bearing it might have on the Agricultural Adjustment Act, authorizing the Secretary of Agriculture to fix the selling price of milk in various milk sheds. The New York law sought, as a part of its plan to remedy evils in the industry, to prevent destructive price-cutting by the stores. A grocer was convicted and fined for selling two quarts and a loaf of bread for eighteen cents and he appealed on the ground that the law conflicted with the due process clause as an unwarranted interference with his liberty. The court held, in an opinion by Roberts, that the milk industry was subject to control for the public good; the power of the state to regulate business in the public interest extended to the control of price, where price regulation was a reasonable means. Roberts said "a state is free to adopt whatever economic policy may reasonably be deemed to promote public welfare, and to enforce that policy by legislation adapted to its purpose. The courts are without authority either to declare such policy or, when it is declared by the legislature, to override it." They were, in fact, incompetent to deal with its wisdom. "The Constitution does not secure to anyone liberty to conduct his business in such fashion as to inflict injury upon the public. . . ." McReynolds led his confrères in dissent.

Supporters of Roosevelt's New Deal legislation, watching the court for auguries, joyously received these successful tests of depression laws. But hope was based on despair, not on ability to practice the jurist's art of distinguishing cases. We were a public of groping citizens, not of constitutional lawyers. The progressive forces identified their aims with the liberalism of several of the justices and were certain the others would not dare block national recovery. Brandeis' record on unionism, wage and hour standards, social insurance, regulation of competition and other *desiderata*, and the presence of about half of his former secretaries in administration councils— these were considered substantial reeds. Stone and Cardozo were also trusted. Hughes had taken on the mantle of Marshall in a crucial period in American life. Doubts about Roberts were allayed by the milk decision. As for the four economic standpatters— they were no more likely to "follow the election returns" than their colleagues— but if they attempted obstruction and mustered only four votes the New Dealers would be safe. And yet safety seemed to lie in avoidance of the court.

Washington correspondents put Brandeis' name on the wires with misleading frequency. His influence on the fashioning of the New Deal and the share of his disciples in its direction were overstated. From the beginning he regarded the program— apart from the question of constitutionality-- as having been drawn up too hastily. The desperate condition of the country when Congress sat in extraordinary session to pass the President's bills did not excuse headlong drafting nor condone poor results. Many hands put their contributions in, but not enough minds came together; there should have been more mature deliberation. To credit Brandeis with the spiritual paternity of, for example, the National Industrial Recovery Act was to ignore the United States Chamber of Commerce and the familiar aspiration of big business to govern industry autonomously under suspension of the antitrust laws. To take for granted his assent to this and to the vast undertaking of the Agricultural Adjustment Administration was to forget his strictures against bigness, the danger of placing too much power in the hands of one man. The danger was not alone of tyranny but of inefficiency; with too much to be done and too little time for it, arbitrary rules had to take the place of thinking. Planning could not encompass every contingency. It apparently failed to foresee in cotton-crop reduction, for instance, the lessening of the amount the ginneries and the railroads carried, and worse—the creation of a large body of dependents. Legal validity was something else.

Wisdom lay in method. The end must rectify the means. If Brandeis were in the field as in 1912 he might have contrived a sharply differentiating policy, such as regulated competition vs. regulated monopoly, which chagrined Teddy Roosevelt. Of course, Brandeis would have needed a Wilsonian welcome.

As a judge he could still put his private views into private circulation. Many callers in these days were public officials. What happened to ideas picked up at Mrs. Brandeis' Sunday teas was a matter of individual taste and of competition with the other ideas that flowed to the eager, receptive man in the White House. It would hardly surprise Brandeis, after sitting down in a corner with a man anxious for light, to see by the papers that the advice was wasted.

As a judge he applied legal principles to legal cases. The first controversy to reach the court under the National Industrial Recovery Act involved the delegation by Congress to the President of power over interstate commerce. Was the delegation unwarranted? Article I of the Constitution vested legislative powers in Congress. Section 9C of the N.I.R.A., regulating the petroleum industry, authorized the President to prohibit the interstate shipment of oil produced in excess of quotas set by the states. Thousands of executive and administrative orders had been issued by New Deal agencies and there was doubt as to the firmness of their footing.

Questioning government counsel in the Texas "hot oil" cases Brandeis wanted to know what criterion was to guide the President, what findings had been made to warrant his orders, whether any official publication contained orders and codes. "Is there no place where you can get them or find out what the regulations are? . . . Well, is there any way by which one can find out what is in these executive orders when they are issued?" He examined a copy of the petroleum code. There was nothing in it to show the grounds on which the President acted in approving it. The court should have all the facts and not a mere conclusion of the administration.

Early in January, 1935, the New Deal received its first blow. Hughes delivered an hour-long opinion nullifying Section 9C. Congress had set up no standard for the President's action; it did not require any finding by him as a condition of his action. Instead of declaring a policy, Congress gave him unlimited authority to determine the policy and lay down the prohibition, or not, as he might see fit— "and disobedience to his order is made a crime punishable by fine and imprisonment." Regardless of the assumption that the President would act for the public good, the best of motives was not a substitute for constitutional authority. If Congress could grant the power of Section 9C nothing could stop it from selecting as grantee some officer other than the President and someone whose power need not be restricted to the transportation of oil but other commodities as well, and not merely transportation but other subjects of legislation.

While Congress was able to leave to selected instrumentalities the making of subordinate rules within prescribed limits and in accordance with an established policy, the decision held that the essential legislative functions were something "Congress manifestly is not permitted to abdicate." But even if the N.I.R.A. gave the President a star by which to govern his course, circumstances under which he could proceed, he must still make findings of fact to show that his orders complied with those conditions. Cardozo dissented: a standard was not lacking, and the President was not required to state his reasons for exercising the granted power. The eight other justices held that the President as a delegate of Congress "necessarily acts under the constitutional restriction applicable to such delegation."

Having exposed the weakness of the Recovery Act and incidentally shown how it could be revised, the court proceeded the next day to hear arguments on the constitutionality of the keystone of the New Deal monetary policy— a law abrogating the gold clause in public and private contracts. Holders of railroad, industrial and government bonds and of gold Treasury certificates which were surrendered under protest demanded payments in gold or the equivalent in terms of the present currency, which had been devaluated by the Gold Reserve Act. One hundred billion dollars pledged in gold— if the law suspending gold payments was void, the obligations would now total $169,000,000,000 in currency. For three days in a crowded courtroom tense with the awareness of a great occasion lawyers solemnly invoked the principles of the Constitution. As against the impairment of contracts and the taking of property stood the sovereign power to coin money and regulate the value thereof. Attorney General Homer S. Cummings pleaded with the court to avert catastrophe and "stop the terrible consequence of deflation."

Newspaper emphasis raised readers' interest to the height of the question's importance. The public discovered the position of the Supreme Court in American life, and in the life of the Roosevelt administration. The nervous suspense as Mondays passed without decision gave dramatic color to the nine guardians of the American system of government.

Four justices had shown in the moratorium case a preview of their attitude. But no one expected McReynolds to lose his temper and declaim, "The Constitution as we have known it is gone!" The outburst came when Hughes finished rendering the majority opinion upholding the power of Congress to invalidate provisions of contracts interfering with the exercise of its authority to establish a monetary system.— "Contracts may create rights of property," Hughes said, "but when contracts deal with a subject-matter which lies within the control of the Congress, they have a congenital infirmity." Did the gold clauses constitute an interference? This was the paramount question. The answer depended on an appraisement of economic conditions and on determination of facts. And here the judgment of Congress bore a reasonable relation to a legitimate end.

The government's own contracts— such as the Fourth Liberty Loan bond on which a plaintiff sued for gold payment— were considered separately. Here the government altered its own pledge and in this respect the law was invalid; but the claimant had not shown actual damages.

Stone once remarked that the justices did not make their intellectual differences personal differences. Brandeis regarded the court as a harmonious one, despite disagreement sometimes expressed with strong feeling. To the public it was obvious that McReynolds was inclined to be irritable at times. But a friendly spirit pervaded the conferences, thanks to the tact of the Chief. Brandeis thought Hughes the best Chief Justice he had ever known.

To the world outside, confronted with economic insecurity, intellectual differences mattered little. It wanted bread. For the security of a million railway workers Congress used its power over interstate commerce to pass the Railroad Pension Act. Roosevelt said it was drawn crudely and he signed it with reluctance. The Supreme Court of the District of Columbia ruled that the law exceeded the authority of Congress by applying to workers in both interstate and intrastate commerce. On appeal the government lost again. Roberts left the camp of Hughes, Brandeis, Stone and Cardozo and in the company of the four conservatives decided that the act imposed an arbitrary burden on the carriers for social ends; the pension system was not a regulation of transportation— it stretched the commerce clause of the Constitution beyond common sense.

Hughes bespoke the minority view that the gravest aspect of the decision was that it did not merely condemn the defective features of this law but denied to Congress the power to pass any compulsory pension act for railroad workers; the majority raised "a barrier against all legislative action of this nature" by placing "an unwarranted limitation on the commerce clause."

Supporters of the pending social security bill were not altogether panicky. Their measure rested on the taxing power. But the majority had ominously branded the "failure to distinguish constitutional power from social desirability" and flatly said that matters of social welfare lay outside the orbit. The fundamental consideration assumed by the dissenters— "that industry should take care of its human wastage"— was dismissed. Roberts was pivotal. How would he vote the next time? Was it in his hands to make or break the New Deal?

Much was taken for granted in these speculations. And while the enormity of a single judge's influence rekindled the periodic resentment against the court's veto power and suggested the requirement of a greater majority, six or seven votes for invalidation would increase the difficulty of blocking dangerous laws should that necessity befall. Every crisis revived the same prescription, and there was talk again of enlarging the court by the addition of "dependable liberals." People forgot how Holmes disappointed the first Roosevelt in the Northern Securities case. The talk went for naught.

Long before an N.R.A. case was presented, and without reference to the validity of codes that were being established by industries, Brandeis naturally was glad to know what his old friends in the cloak trade were doing. The principle of voluntary cooperation within industry had been imbedded in the protocol, and now the cloak code recognized labor's welfare as essential to rehabilitation. An excellent provision to safeguard hour and wage standards called for a guarantee of rates by wholesalers to contractors who maintained the scale. There was a plan to bring retailers into the program by requiring them to retain N.R.A. labels in the garments. (The idea of white sanitary labels originated in the protocol era.)

The main purpose of industry was to extend employment and make it secure, lessen seasonal recessions, and provide for workers' earnings at reasonable weekly amounts sufficient for fifty-two weeks' living. Retailers should be induced to prolong the seasons and change such fictitious lines of demarcation as Easter and Thanksgiving, after which production at legitimate prices usually ceased. Without a provision for unemployment reserves stabilization could never take place; it was a normal adjunct to the extension of employment and the security of a living to the workers. And as this was a function of management, contributions to the reserve should be made by employers only and assumed in their prices. Very much as management set up reserves for the depreciation of machinery and for interest on capital invested, the human element must likewise be provided for through a continuous allowance, while working, for periods of idleness.

Still, the constitutional question remained to be answered — when a specific case should arise. The N.R.A. had been popularly described as the effect of a long line of dissents by Holmes and Brandeis. That the court would throw it out in these times was "unthinkable . . . suicidal." But the government was chary of putting its luck in the crucible.

Holmes in his withdrawal from the world and immersion in murder mysteries occasionally asked callers, "What is this N.R.A. I hear about?" McReynolds, talking to reporters, said the mystery of the New Deal reminded him of the student who told his professor he once knew what causes the aurora borealis, but forgot.

Meanwhile the administration's record of performance failed to square with its intentions, notoriously in regard to collective bargaining. Frank P. Walsh criticized the steel code as a means of welding the monopolistic and anti-union program of the United States Steel Corporation. Borah attacked the whole enterprise as a handicap to the little man and the consumer and a boon to big business. During the period of the N.R.A. profits rose faster than payrolls and concentration of industry gained pace. Industrialists boasted that no federal law had ever been able to regulate production, but their wail against the powers vested in the President was falsetto. The call for decentralization would have been more consistent coming from Brandeis.

Near the end of the two-year span of the Recovery Act the government found the temerity to follow a lumber-code case up to the Supreme Court, then abruptly changed its mind and decided to run the gauntlet with chicken dealers convicted of violating the live-poultry code.

On a memorable day in May three unanimous decisions were handed down. Roosevelt's purpose in packing the Federal Trade Commission with friendly members was cramped when the court, speaking through Sutherland, ruled against his arbitrary removal of a Republican. The Frazier-Lemke Act, not a New Deal measure, providing for a five-year stay on farm mortgage foreclosure proceedings, was held void as applied; despite the argument that widespread foreclosure would cause farms to fall into the hands of corporations and reduce independent farmers to a peasant class, Brandeis reasoned that the property and the debt were both taken from the creditor. He said, "The Fifth Amendment commands that, however great the nation's need, private property cannot be thus taken even for a wholly public use without just compensation"— resort must be had to proceedings by eminent domain; the burden of relief afforded in the public interest might be borne by the public through taxation. In the third decision, the chicken case, the court pierced the heart of the N.R.A.

Hughes chose to ring the knell. He told why the section authorizing the President to approve "codes of fair competition" was unconstitutional regardless of the grave national crisis which confronted Congress.

"Extraordinary conditions may call for extraordinary remedies" but "do not create or enlarge constitutional power," the Chief Justice said. The codes were not simply a plan for voluntary effort within trades but for "the coercive exercise of the law-making power." The codes had standing as penal statutes.

It was clear why the eight justices who had nullified unwarranted delegation of power in the Texas "hot oil" case could not let Congress give the President "an unfettered discretion to make whatever laws he thinks may be needed or advisable for the rehabilitation and expansion of trade or industry." Cardozo joined them now because here was "delegation running riot."

Hughes pointed out that the Recovery Act did not define fair competition. It dispensed with such procedure as the Federal Trade Commission must follow in determining unfair methods of competition and such standards as the Interstate Commerce Commission must observe in issuing orders supported by findings of fact. The matter was left to trade groups, with authority to enact the laws they themselves deemed wise. Proponents of a code might roam at will, the President approving or disapproving as he chose.

Penalties were confined to code violations in transactions affecting interstate or foreign commerce, but in this case the butchering and the local sale of chickens, both taking place in the State of New York, were held to be transactions not directly affecting interstate commerce and therefore remaining in the domain of state power. If the commerce clause were not so construed "the federal authority would embrace practically all the activities of the people and the authority of the state over its domestic concerns would exist only by sufferance of the federal government." Thus, with virtually no limit, "for all practical purposes we should have a completely centralized government."

By this reasoning the hours and wage provisions of the live poultry code, as they applied to persons not employed in interstate commerce and not in direct relation to it, must fall. If the cost of doing intrastate business were subject to federal control all the processes of production and distribution entering into cost could likewise be controlled. Answering the contention that federal legislation on wages and hours was necessary because of the diversity of state standards, Hughes said—

> It is not the province of the Court to consider the economic advantages or disadvantages of such a centralized system. It is sufficient to say that the Federal Constitution does not provide for it . . . the recuperative efforts of the federal government must be made in a manner consistent with the authority granted by the Constitution.

The decisiveness of the decision not only chopped the head off the N.R.A., it shook the ground under the New Deal. Roosevelt caustically told his press conference that the court had thrust the country back into the horse-and-buggy stage where ninety percent of trade was intrastate and no social questions were presented on a national basis. It rested with the country, he said, to decide whether this government should have the powers that were vested with every other national government in the world. He did not openly advocate a constitutional amendment. While others did, many were reminded of the fate of those powerful national governments— dictatorship— and were thankful that the nine justices, though they differed in economics, stood in an unwavering line behind the political form of this nation.

A week after the decision the court term closed. And life went on.

Brandeis could no longer visit Holmes and find him philosophically waiting for his sunset. It was night.

Chapter XXI

TOWARD THE FUTURE

B RANDEIS went back to Chatham and to his old sweater
and knickers. A stroll across the dunes and a deep breath
of vitalizing salt air renewed contact with nature and gave a
pleasurable sense of wellbeing in his seventy-ninth year. In
the wooden dwelling which was their real home he and his
wife had the company of their daughter Elizabeth and her
family. In a house nearby were Susan and her husband and
children. Family life, which he had always cherished, in Boston as in Louisville, was thus integrated for the summer.

A woolly, white-haired justice playing with his grandchildren might be a subject for a Joshua Reynolds, but no artist
had persuaded him to pose in all the years of his fame.

Susan was married to Jacob H. Gilbert, a New York attorney, and both were practicing law in that city. When Susan
argued before the court in 1925 her father remained in the
robing room. Elizabeth met Paul A. Raushenbush as fellow-
students in economics at the University of Wisconsin. They
married and obtained appointments to the faculty, and in that
progressive environment furthered the principle of unemployment reserves.

The reunion was never complete without Mrs. Evans, the
dearest friend of the Brandeises. Talk ranged wide, but no
fresh topic was started at dinner lest the justice pass his usual
bedtime.

His prompt departure for the open spaces of his fifteen
acres at Chatham was not an escape from Washington, except

in a physical sense; nor did a man of mature philosophy need geographic perspective. While the administration wrestled with the colossus of the general welfare he kept thinking of the menace of a centralized government and the handicap of America's size. He talked of Denmark, Palestine, insurance, and the small unit. The country should go back to the concept of federation, letting each state reach for self-development and evolve its own sound policy. There were enough good men in Alabama, for example, to make Alabama a good state. But the tendency was to put responsibility on the federal government.

Visitors went away with sharp impressions. He was dead against the American idea of concentration and specialization in one area with resultant wastelands. Each community should try to become a microcosm— where there was wheat there ought to be a mill. He was dead against chain stores and other methods of robbing a town of a well-rounded life. If the withering hand of outside control were withdrawn the people would have sufficient opportunities for growth. Always he reverted to this point. Always his first thought was of man.

Through the maze of New Deal experimentation some of his concepts managed to forge ahead. His old friend Senator Fletcher, at the head of a committee investigating the stock market, drew an argument from *Other People's Money* for federal regulation of securities and exchanges on the basis of congressional power over the mails. (A fifteen-cent edition of Brandeis' book became a best-seller in Washington, spreading his ideas to one hundred thousand new readers.) The banking act of 1933 separated deposit banking from investment banking. The securities act of the same year— written by three protégés of Frankfurter: James M. Landis, a former Brandeis secretary; Thomas G. Corcoran, a former Holmes secretary, and Benjamin V. Cohen— regulated the issuance of securities and required the filing of data for the protection of investors. In 1934 Representative Sam D. Rayburn's stock exchange bill became law. Early in 1935 another old friend, Senator Burton K. Wheeler, chairman of the interstate commerce committee, introduced a bill to tax bigness.

Wheeler proposed a graduated excise tax on the net capital return of corporations on the ground that concentration of corporate resources was "the very negation of democracy" and social and economic evils were "inherent in size itself." He offered his bill primarily to provoke discussion and lead to an experiment in decentralization.

Meanwhile the House committee was busy with a measure — again drafted by Landis, Cohen and Corcoran, and sponsored by Rayburn— to eliminate holding companies from the public utility field. President Roosevelt echoed Brandeis' thought: regulation of these private empires was impossible; they must be dealt a death sentence. The President stigmatized holding companies as a device "which can give a few corporate insiders unwarranted and intolerable powers over other people's money." They substituted absentee ownership for local surveillance. This system of private socialism must be destroyed in order to avoid government socialism. The utility bill would reverse the process of centralization and restore independent enterprises.

But the question of taxing bigness lay neglected by the administration until, suddenly in June, 1935, Roosevelt announced a program, somewhat confused by the description "wealth sharing," which otherwise bore an unmistakable Brandeis imprint. The President declared in a message to Congress that "size begets monopoly." Small businesses must not be stamped out or the competitive economic society would cease. Existing revenue laws had done little to prevent the unjust concentration of wealth or to break up the power of "relatively few individuals over the employment and welfare of many, many others." In addition to gift and inheritance taxes and intercorporate dividend taxes, he urged a graduated tax on corporations and eventual elimination of all unnecessary holding companies. Men close to the White House believed that Roosevelt had become definitely converted and was now committed against the evil of bigness.

Whatever Congress did with the program, at least the issue had been publicized and recognized. It looked like a good beginning. Senator Borah created some fog by talk of monopoly when the evil was bigness, and others harangued for redistribution of wealth. What was concentration of wealth compared with concentration of control? The fight must be for redistribution of economic control. And the ground was broken.

Both the tax and the utility laws passed with modifications. Brandeis strongly believed in compromise. But his conception of compromise was to go along with the other man only if they were both going in his own direction. In the struggle over the securities bill Landis stuck to a pet provision for a ten-year liability period during which investors could collect damages. After considerable harassing by Wall Street he relented, with a show of reluctance, and cut it down to two years— but succeeded in diverting the enemy's fire from other drastic provisions. Such Machiavellian deftness was worthy of an apt pupil of a skillful master.

Landis also had the quality of thoroughness. When he was secretary to the justice he was not content with the hearsay legend that Brandeis started work at five o'clock in the morning. He resolved to test it, and after staying up late at a New Year's Eve celebration he returned to the office. Waiting in his incongruous evening clothes he eventually heard a key in the lock. The justice let himself in, nodded to Landis in the customary way, and sat down to his papers. Landis looked at the time: the legend was correct.

The contagion of Brandeis' thinking caught Senator Robert F. Wagner on unemployment insurance, although there had been no direct contact between them since 1915. This social reform was not to be a federal undertaking, both for constitutional and for practical reasons. In its original form in 1934 the Wagner-Lewis bill laid a five percent tax on payrolls as an incentive to the adoption of state laws conforming to specified standards. The purpose was not primarily to ensure unemployment payments but to induce employers to regularize employment. In Wisconsin Paul Raushenbush and Elizabeth had worked out a plan whereby each employer built up his own reserves and paid benefits only to his own workers, the rate of his contributions to the fund diminishing as his account with the state increased. Thus the steadier the employment, the lower the tax. Brandeis' early plan was inducement by agreement; the new one was inducement by taxation. The bill was intended to effect the creation of such reserve funds and it allowed employers to credit against the tax their contributions under state laws.

But there were two schools of thought on insurance, the other stemming from European laws and described by Elizabeth Brandeis as being based on the assumption that unemployment was an "incurable malady for which legislation can provide only a palliative." The opponents of reserves asserted that the mission of insurance was not to attempt the impossible feat of abolishing unemployment; many advocated the pooling of premiums paid by employer and employee alike into state-wide funds out of which compensation would be made to the jobless. Social workers did not seem to have the idea clear; they had always been slow to grasp regularity. They gave Roosevelt a wrong steer and he, after approving the bill initially, let it die in committee. However, Wagner had been able to give currency to the Brandeis tenet that a provision against unemployment should be considered as a charge on industry.

The Brandeis theory was that business enterprises needed incentives to efficiency instead of opportunities to shift their burdens; the weakness of insurance was the danger of lapsing into bad ways because of a feeling of safety and ease. Wagner's new bill finally passed as the Social Security Act of 1935. By holding the door open to pooled insurance it permitted employers to put their responsibilities upon the pool—in other words, upon the consumer. Only a three percent (maximum) payroll tax was imposed. The states were given latitude in setting up their systems. Employers were allowed a ninety percent credit as an offset to their state contributions. A federal subsidy was to be allocated among the states as grants-in-aid of administration. The state funds were to be deposited with the United States Treasury.

A similar technique was adopted in the Guffey Coal Act to stabilize bituminous coal mining. This law taxed mine operators' sales and allowed a ninety percent drawback where operators maintained the wage and hour provisions of the industry's former N.R.A. code. Here was reliance on the taxing power to restore a portion of the Recovery Act; an attempt to work within constitutional limits so far as known. To escape Supreme Court condemnation Congress revamped other legislation— restricted the A.A.A. to interstate commerce and avoided delegation of power, extended the N.R.A. to facilitate voluntary codes, passed new railway-pension, farm-moratorium and hot-oil laws washed clean of obviously unconstitutional spots.

Rugged individualists watched in ambush for the appearance of social measures and, when they saw red, whooped with a cry of communism and flung their legal tomahawks. Interested parties were entitled, surely, to challenge a law. And no constitutional issue could be decided without a case in point. As the bitterness of conflict spread, opposing industrial and political forces made the court their battleground, almost their storm-center, on the eve of a presidential election. At this juncture the floodlights on the Capitol were rivalled by the blazing whiteness of the eleven-million-dollar marble Parthenon which the public treasury had newly lavished on the judicial process. There across the park stood the American oracle, gifted to direct the drama of the nation's destiny.

Despite his private view of the unwisdom of the A.A.A., Brandeis opposed its invalidation. Whereas the court in 1936 held unconstitutional the use of the federal taxing and spend-

ing power directly to regulate and control agricultural production as an invasion of states' rights, Stone regarded the decision, written by Roberts, as "a tortured construction of the
Constitution" and a usurpation of legislative functions. Brandeis and Cardozo stood by him in dissent.

The next New Deal case to be decided involved the Tennessee Valley Authority, sued by a group of preferred stockholders of an Alabama electric power company. These stockholders challenged the legality of a contract which their
company had made with T.V.A. Chief Justice Hughes wrote
the opinion upholding the government's authority to build
Wilson Dam at Muscle Shoals and dispose of electric energy
generated there without invading the reserve rights of the
states. Brandeis concurred in the conclusion, but he was convinced that the stockholders had no right to attack the government through a suit against their company. Stone, Cardozo, and Roberts agreed with him that the court's jurisdiction did not extend to such a case. He urged that "we re-
frain from passing upon the constitutionality of an act of
Congress unless obliged to do so in the proper performance of
our judicial function, when the question is raised by a party
whose interests entitle him to raise it." McReynolds was the
lone dissenter. He said the grounds for jurisdiction were clear
and the contract was invalid.

Brandeis devoted a large part of his opinion to specifying
the rules under which the court had avoided constitutional
questions pressed upon it. These were salutary rules. One
branch of the government could not encroach on the domain
of another without danger.

When the Bituminous Coal Conservation Act, the so-called
Guffey act, came up six justices, led by Sutherland, declared
that the tax it levied on coal sales was in effect a penalty for
non-compliance with the wage and hour standards which
were to be established. These provisions would regulate not
interstate commerce but intrastate industry. Of the majority,
the Chief Justice said that interstate price-fixing of coal, which

was linked with the labor regulations, was within the power of Congress and could stand alone. On the last point Cardozo, Brandeis and Stone agreed with Hughes, but on every other question presented in this case their opinion was that the suits were brought prematurely. Cardozo wrote that the court's opinion "begins at the wrong end . . . the complainants have been crying before they are really hurt." He quoted Brandeis' dictum in the T.V.A. case.

Another New Deal law, the Municipal Bankruptcy Act, was voided in a five-to-four decision. McReynolds held for the majority that the law, permitting sub-divisions of states to readjust their debts, usurped the states' sovereignty. Cardozo, joined by Brandeis and Stone, pointed out that the law provided for the consent of the states.

On the last day of the court term the New York State minimum wage law for women was decided. In view of the court's pronouncement in the Guffey case that industry was the special province of the states hopes had been running high. Dean Acheson, a former secretary of Justice Brandeis, argued for several other states which had similar laws. Brandeis listened to opposing counsel dispute whether the New York statute differed from the District of Columbia law which had been voided in 1923. He did not agree with Butler, who spoke for a majority of five, that the old case controlled the new; that freedom of contract was impaired. Brandeis, Stone and Cardozo joined with the Chief in holding that there was a difference.

But Stone asserted with Brandeis' and Cardozo's concurrence that the years which intervened since the 1923 decision afforded opportunity to learn the effect of insufficient wages on the entire economic structure of society. Stone cited instances where the court had upheld limitations put on freedom of contract in the public interest, notably price regulation in the New York milk industry. Regardless of the merits of the minimum wage statute as a remedy, Stone said the legislature "must be free to choose." Many legislative bodies had found wage regulation an appropriate corrective for serious social and economic maladjustments growing out of inequality of buying power, and this fact "precludes, for me, any assumption that it is a remedy beyond the bounds of reason." He could not imagine "any grounds other than our own personal economic predilections" for saying that contracts of employment were not a proper subject of legislation.

Thus ended a term in which the three steadfast dissenters sought to impress on their colleagues that the court was over-reaching itself.

As the justices departed for their summer haunts the court was once more pitched into public controversy. The unpopularity of the last decision was manifested widely, and people generally recognized the impasse created by the court. Was a constitutional amendment the only relief? The leaders of the major political parties in the ensuing presidential campaign ventured to approach the issue cautiously. Hughes had said in his separate Guffey opinion that if the people desired to give Congress powers to regulate intrastate industries and labor relations "they are at liberty to declare their will in the appropriate manner, but it is not for the Court to amend the Constitution by judicial decision." He made clear, however, that for Congress to control state activities which affected interstate commerce only indirectly would be to subvert the fundamental principle of the Constitution.

Brandeis recalled in 1932 that "in only two instances— the Eleventh and the Sixteenth Amendments— has the process of constitutional amendment been successfully resorted to, to nullify decisions of this Court. . . . It required eighteen years of agitation after the decision in the Pollock case to secure the Sixteenth Amendment."

The present great controversy could not be defined accurately as the New Deal vs. the Constitution. If the New Deal should fall by running athwart the federal system and attempting recovery by arrogating national sovereignty, the evils of the economic structure would abide despite invalidation. On the other hand, many who crowded round the Constitution in a patriotic surge plainly wanted an interpretation to preserve their vested privileges. In the ample scope available properly drafted laws might be properly construed. The issue, then, was the Constitution vs. the Constitution. If the conflicts of the country were turning all eyes on the Supreme Court, this was the point on which to focus.

But here was a justice who felt that the people should not look to the law and the courts for the real solution of their problems but rely on themselves. Their greatest handicap, Brandeis believed, was low moral standards, especially the plane of business morality; the dominance of materialism; the relaxation of religious control where this was the only check. Industrialism had brought about an increase in the fiduciary relation; positions of trust were betrayed. A decline in the state of civil liberties accompanied this. The Supreme Court could curb excesses but neither the court nor the enlargement of the government's powers could create a free people. Instead of amending the Constitution, Brandeis would amend men's social and economic ideals.

Instead of worshipping at the eleven-million-dollar temple the people would do better by attending to the Delphic oracle. On the slopes of Parnassus stood two pillars, one bearing the inscription, "Know thyself"; the other, "Nothing too much." Americans had ignored both admonitions.

Brandeis was willing to be called a Jeffersonian. Albert Jay Nock's biography expressed what he felt about "the first civilized American"— a man whose concept of government he admired; whose mind was far-reaching and even foresaw the conservation problem which would come up after the disappearance of free land. Lincoln had great qualities of heart but was comparatively an ignorant man, an unlearned man. Brandeis looked to the time when citizens would have as little need of government as possible, the government restricted within certain limits, helpful but not all-powerful.

He liked to think of the Scandinavian countries, where the socialist governments were not socialist in action— they did not have to be; independent groups worked out the answers. Cooperatives (about which Brandeis had first learned from Beatrice Potter Webb's study, "The Cooperative Movement in Great Britain") possessed the virtues of self-reliance, social good, and avoidance of authoritarian oppressiveness. The tendency was much in the direction of Kropotkin's scheme of mutual aid. With cooperatives flourishing by the side of an economic system of competition, the answer to the currently advertised panaceas could be found. When people were good enough to become good socialists they would not need socialism. Brandeis' political and economic vision was closer to anarchism. It was practical democracy.

"Success in any democratic undertaking must proceed from the individual," he wrote. "It is possible only where the process of perfecting the individual is pursued. His development is attained mainly in the process of common living." Democracy substituted self-restraint for external restraint. It demanded "more exigent obedience to the moral law than any other form of government."

The New Deal, like the Old, sometimes flirted with antisocial bigness and the idea of pressure from the top, depending upon whose counsel happened to be followed. Power over the community crushed individual liberty. Man was the loser whether paternalism was governmental or corporate. Even where a large unit (attained usually by force) managed to be efficient it was unwholesome; generally it was inefficient. And the United States was least suited to planning— huge and disorganized. We had never settled down.

The ability of big men was overrated. Officials were put into jobs too big for them. True, we must have individuals as leaders— leadership by consent, and the consent must be actual. Here again Brandeis centered on the development of the mass of men. He had a firm conviction of their educability; the less important the man, the more educable; such

a person lacked the arrogance of the mighty and his curiosity
was not blunted. Education was not especially difficult. "You
can make things clear to others when they are clear to you,"
Brandeis told a visitor. He spoke as one who all his mature
life had been a teacher.

In the field of law he believed that the best opportunities
for the next twenty years lay in teaching; six of his ex-secre-
taries were on law school faculties. He remembered his own
"first public works" in legal education and the widened horizon he grasped by hearing Emerson, in quavering voice, read
a lecture. In all fields the expansion of education and democracy was coextensive. Jefferson in the retirement of his old
age lay the foundations of the University of Virginia; by
coincidence Brandeis undertook to further the growth of the
University of Louisville.

In 1925 he and his brother started on a task befitting the
Adolf Brandeis family since for nearly three-quarters of a
century it had stood in Louisville for culture and, at least
in Uncle Lewis, for learning. With this underlying sentiment
he believed that if they might have ten years to work in,
the preliminaries could be accomplished— and the rest left
to Alfred's descendants and the centuries.

Money alone could not build a worthy university; too
much or too quick money might mar one, particularly "foreign money." Growth could not be imposed. It must proceed
mainly from within. Broaching the project to his brother
he wrote:

> To become great, a University must express the
> people whom it serves, and must express the people and
> the community at their best. . . . The desire for worthy
> growth must be deeply felt by the executive officers and
> members of the faculty. It must be they who raise the
> University standards and extend its influence. But the
> desire may be stimulated by suggestion; and achievement
> may be furthered by friendly aid. Thus, there is a large
> field for the efforts of those outside the University whose

capacity, experience and position give them a wider
view and bolder vision; whose positions enable them to
secure for the University's projects the approval and
support of the community; and whose means enable
them to furnish financial aid. From them may come also
the encouragement without which few achieve and that
informed, friendly supervision without which few per-
severe in the most painstaking labors.

The family service he and Alice had in mind was "to take
the part of the ever-helpful, sympathetic friend who, with
thought, tact and patience, will awaken aspiration and encourage effort." They would be glad to give "such part of
our surplus income as may be wisely applied in the undertaking."

The money required will doubtless increase with the
expanding functions and character of the work. But in
this connection the service of money will resemble that
of water in agriculture— always indispensable, always
beneficent to the point where it becomes excessive, but
of little avail unless there be an appropriate cultivation,
and unless the operations be conducted with good judgment.

"The aim must be high and the vision broad," he said.
Through the department of sociology the university could
purpose to influence the life of Kentucky socially and economically; through the department of fine arts and music,
to promote "that development which is compounded in the
term Culture;" through a library of World War history, to
influence the political life of the state and nation "by a deep
and far-reaching study of history, and inquiry into the Causes
and Consequences of present ills, and a consideration of the
proper aspirations of the United States and of the functions
of the State;" through the department of English, to increase
in the community a general appreciation of good books and

of mental and spiritual enrichment. Brandeis conceived of the local university as the most hopeful instrument for any attempt to break up the tendency toward centralization and substitute "intense development of life through activities in the several States and localities."

The University of Louisville could serve this end if it were essentially Kentuckian.

> For this reason everything in the life of the State is worthy of special enquiry. Every noble memory must be cherished; thus the details of Kentucky history, political, economic and social, become factors of ultimate importance. The biographies of its distinguished sons and daughters, including as such those who have lived and achieved elsewhere, are matters of significance. The University Library should grow rich in Kentuckiana. It should become a depository of unpublished manuscripts and like possessions associated with the life of the State and the achievements of Kentuckians.

Therefore Brandeis gave liberally not only for books but for binding, shelving and cataloguing. The library loomed in his mind as the means of raising the institution's standards. On the library he concentrated. He adopted the procedure of sending checks for deposit in a special account to be drawn on by his brother as needed, considering this a wiser course than sending the money direct to the university. While the younger Louisville Brandeises and Dembitzes were to take on the responsibility of publications in other departments, he looked to Alfred for personal gathering of Kentuckiana. He wanted him to make as a special concern the raw materials of books— reports by state, county and municipal bureaus, annual reports of public service corporations, banks and private businesses— publications largely uncopyrighted and usually treated as of ephemeral (if any) value; in these sources the real history of the community was recorded, and by their close and continuous study the important political, economic and social facts would evolve, and thus "the experience which is to become our teacher is to be gained."

> There has been in America in general a failure to recognize the value of such material— or, at all events, a failure to make a systematic collection of it. . . . The reason is that the collection of the uncopyrighted involves far more knowledge, imagination and effort . . . requires the kind of knowledge which you have, the thought which you will give— and the eternal watchful interest without which a really valuable collection cannot be built up. It must be the work of an individual who really cares. . . .
>
> To attain it will not be possible in the relatively few years which you and I are likely to live. But what we are to think of is the library as it will be twenty-five or a hundred years hence. . . .

He took care of the law school library himself and provided bound volumes of transcripts of records and copies of briefs filed with the Supreme Court. With his remarkably large accumulation of war documents, pamphlets and books he established the Alfred Brandeis World War Library. A separate library of government documents which he had wisely saved through the years was donated as another memorial to his brother. He gave also rare original documents on international relations and material on the liberation of nationalities in the war. Memorials were set up by him in honor also of men who had influenced his early life: William N. Hailman, his principal in the old German American Academy (library of German literature); Albert R. Cooper, his early mentor in English literature; Louis H. Hast, who cultivated in Louisville an appreciation of great chamber and orchestral music; and his uncle Lewis (library of Palestine— Judaica, stressing the rebirth of Palestine, now "a laboratory of the social problems that have harassed the world").

Spanning music, literature and the fine arts— Brandeis

started the fine arts library with another fund and presented many books on the arts of antiquity— he established also a railroad library as a tribute to pioneers of the Louisville & Nashville, which made the city's name a household word "and gained for it honorable mention throughout the financial world." In 1935, ten years after the laying of the figurative cornerstone, the libraries of Louisville were proclaimed by the university. Brandeis' wide range evidenced itself: from the classics to a collection on organized labor covering 700 volumes and 1,000 pamphlets. For he meant to make the university a seat "not only of learning but of adventure in all fields of intellectual and spiritual endeavor."

Back in Washington, for his own light reading he dispatched his secretary to the Library of Congress for some book on the Greek tyrants, including legends. Mrs. Brandeis often read to him for an hour a day. They came upon the story of Periander, king of Corinth, who put his royal foot down on excessiveness and never let his governors go beyond certain safe bounds in ruling conquered lands. Brandeis called for an economic survey of ancient Rome and for a study of the communes of Lombardy. Still the student of history, he drew many inferences for the present. Attica, Rhodes, Egypt — his talk flowed with place-names of olden times and a broad knowledge of their problems. He understood why Periander forbade people from the country to flock to the city; how Greece grew in greatness through men who stayed at home. Once he said, "I've just finished the best book I've read in twenty years." It was Zimmern's "The Greek Commonwealth."

But books were rarely stepping-stones to philosophy. Life came first, sometimes propelling him into an intuitive leap, and then he turned to books for further information. Ancient history corroborated experience. It was insurance companies, not the cities of Greece, that taught him the value of the small unit. It was the New Haven railroad— which in 1935 had to file a petition under the bankruptcy law because its resources were still being drained by non-railroad properties and because, instead of meeting competition by using its mind it throttled competition. (Like an ancient curse: the twin evils of bigness and banker-management). It was savings bank insurance which reenforced his thesis. The system was flourishing at the end of March, 1936, with $116,241,378 insurance in force, representing 129,956 policies issued by twenty-three banks, with agencies in eighty-four other savings banks and eighteen trust companies and national banks. The capital assets were diffused, instead of concentrated, with a resulting closer supervision of investments and a relatively higher net return than that of the commercial companies. During the first quarter of 1936 the system wrote over thirty percent more insurance than in the first quarter of 1935, while the companies wrote in Massachusetts thirteen percent less.

Brandeis remembered that many years ago, driving through the state with his father, sister and a nephew to the town of Peru, the highest point in Massachusetts, he met a man who had gone to Boston to make his mark but returned to his own community and prospered. Brandeis could think of many Americans who reached success without straying. One might name William Allen White as an example of a man who stuck to his little Emporia, Kansas, and became a national influence. Perhaps the brightest men stayed at home. As for himself, he was sure he would have done well had he remained in Louisville.

There was no dodging the fact that he chose Boston because Boston had cultural impressiveness. But the arid stretches between the oases in America could very well be fertilized by decentralization, local development, industrial democracy, and the prime consideration of man. In the matter of vocational training he would remark, for example, that it was not enough to enable a peasant to become an agriculturalist; he must be given an opportunity to become a cultured person.

A secretary, reading over the printed proof of an opinion the justice was preparing, pointed out a split infinitive, saying he had no objection himself. Brandeis let it stand. Culture

did not call for the stuffed shirt of dignity. In the late morning after a short walk with Mrs. Brandeis on his way to court
he would hop into a hired automobile (not a corporation taxi)
and wave goodby to her through the back window. He took
along sandwiches of her making. In the conference room he
often slipped off his coat before buckling down to work. In
the courtroom, while an associate justice might be droning
out a decision, he pored over books and kept the page-boy
scurrying for more. He brought over his old gooseneck desk
lamp from the old court, regardless of the new surrounding
splendor.

In his letter-writing his informality, and frugality, were
evidenced by the use sometimes of half of the folded sheet
of court stationery. He disdained unnecessary telegrams. The
letters which his colored messenger took to the postoffice
daily stacked high. As a correspondent he was punctual.
His simplicity and directness made one ashamed not to avoid
superfluity and ostentation.

His mind gravitated toward the hard core of fact. It was
so in his estimates of men. He might call one charming or
entertaining but if the man was working toward a wrong
end the adjective served to dispose of the subject. Another
might have a bevy of admirers generally agreeing that their
man was well-liked in Washington; to Brandeis it was much
more important that he possessed ability, knowledge and
courage. In any appeal to Brandeis' judgment oratory lacked
force; he shut out eloquence— his conclusions were based on
matters brought to his attention.

"A statute valid as to one set of facts may be invalid as to
another," he said in an opinion deciding a Tennessee railroad case. The road was bound by state law to pay half
the cost of constructing underpasses on the theory that it
benefited by improvements in the community. "A statute
valid when enacted may become invalid by change in the
conditions to which it applied." Here the elimination of
grade-crossings was for the advantage of federal-aid high-

ways and motor-vehicle competition; traffic and revenue depleted, the railroad now required protection. Here was the realistic approach, an arterial principle reaching beyond grade-crossings— one which might well travel the course of the law and free living Americans from dead premises.

The Chief saw that "the facts of life assume a greater importance than formulas" with Brandeis, and "throughout his career he has exhibited a prodigious and uninterrupted activity. . . . He seeks to make his account of his researches a guide to every traveler over the same road." With serene confidence Brandeis kept at his work, conscious of clarifying the roadmap for future generations and convinced that the idea of bigness was at last losing hold, the illusion of grandeur fading.

His warmest advice to any young couple was that they should settle in a small town. The Roman notion of a little summer villa of one hundred and twenty rooms was out of date, he said.

After eighty years of living Brandeis lost none of his optimism or faith in the resourcefulness of men and women to attain the American ideal.

BIBLIOGRAPHY

Books, Articles and Statements by Brandeis

OTHER PEOPLE'S MONEY AND HOW THE BANKERS USE IT. Frederick A. Stokes & Co., New York, 1914. A collection of articles published in *Harper's Weekly* between Nov. 22, 1913, and Jan. 17, 1914.

BUSINESS—A PROFESSION. Small, Maynard & Co., Boston, 1914, 1925; Hale, Cushman & Flint, Boston, 1933. Addresses and articles, 1902-1916.

THE SOCIAL AND ECONOMIC VIEWS OF MR. JUSTICE BRANDEIS, edited by Alfred Lief. Vanguard Press, New York, 1930. Judicial opinions, etc.

THE CURSE OF BIGNESS: MISCELLANEOUS PAPERS OF JUSTICE BRANDEIS, edited by Osmond K. Fraenkel. Viking Press, New York, 1934. Including an almost complete bibliography.

———

LIABILITY OF TRUST-ESTATES ON CONTRACTS MADE FOR THEIR BENEFIT, written with Samuel D. Warren. *American Law Review*, July, 1881.

THE WATUPPA POND CASES, written with Warren. *Harvard Law Review*, December, 1888.

THE HARVARD LAW SCHOOL. *Green Bag*, January, 1889.

THE LAW OF PONDS, written with Warren. *Harvard Law Review*, April, 1889.

THE RIGHT TO PRIVACY, written with Warren. *Harvard Law Review*, December, 1890.

THE ANTI-BAR LAW. Argument before Joint Committee on Liquor Law, Massachusetts Legislature. Privately printed, Boston, 1891.

HEARINGS on the Care and Management of Public Institutions of the City of Boston before Committee of the Board of Aldermen. City Document, 1894. Argument, vol. 3, pp. 3625-3649.

NOTES ON BUSINESS LAW. Massachusetts Institute of Technology, Boston, 1894-6.

TARIFF LEGISLATION NOT NEEDED. Statement before House Committee on Ways and Means, Jan. 11, 1897. Tariff hearings, 54th Cong., 2d Sess., pp. 2081-4.

SUBWAY CONTROVERSY: Shall the Boston Elevated Railway Company be the Servant or the Master of the People? Associated Board of Trade and Public Franchise League, Boston, 1902.

THE EXPERIENCE OF MASSACHUSETTS IN STREET RAILWAYS. *Municipal Affairs*, winter issue, 1902.

THE MASSACHUSETTS SYSTEM OF DEALING WITH PUBLIC FRANCHISES. Address at Cooper Union, New York, Feb. 24, 1905. (Typewritten copy.)

CONSOLIDATION OF GAS COMPANIES AND OF ELECTRIC LIGHT COMPANIES. George H. Ellis Co., Boston, 1905.

LIFE INSURANCE: THE ABUSES AND THE REMEDIES. Policy-Holders Protective Committee, Boston, 1905.

INDUSTRIAL COOPERATION. *The Echo*, Filene Cooperative Association, Boston, May 1905.

LETTER to *The Nation*, New York, May 1, 1905.

THE GREATEST LIFE INSURANCE WRONG. *The Independent*, Dec. 20, 1906.

SAVINGS INSURANCE BANKS FOR WORKINGMEN. *Charities and The Commons*, Feb. 16, 1907.

FINANCIAL CONDITION OF THE NEW YORK, NEW HAVEN & HARTFORD RAILROAD COMPANY, AND OF THE BOSTON & MAINE RAILROAD. Privately printed, Boston, 1907.

STATEMENTS on the New England transportation monopoly before committees of the Massachusetts Legislature (1907-09) and the Massachusetts Commission on Commerce & Industry (*Boston Journal*, Dec. 13, 1912).

THE PROPOSED RAILROAD MERGER: WE NEED MORE MINDS, NOT FEWER. *New England Magazine*, May, 1908.

MASSACHUSETTS' SUBSTITUTE FOR OLD AGE PENSIONS. *The Independent*, July 16, 1908.

BOSTON & MAINE PENSIONS. *The Survey*, June 19, 1909.

INVESTIGATION of the Department of Interior and of the Bureau of Forestry. 61st Cong. 3d Sess. (1910), Senate Doc. 719, Serial vol. 5892-5900. Arguments, pp. 4903-23, pp. 5005-21; brief, pp. 5041-182.

HEARINGS before Interstate Commerce Commission: Proposed Advances in Freight Rates by Carriers, 61st Cong., 3d Sess. (1910), Senate Doc. 725, Serial vol. 5905-12. Brief, pp. 4753-845; argument, pp. 5251-278.

SCIENTIFIC MANAGEMENT AND THE RAILROADS. The Engineering Magazine, New York, 1911.

USING OTHER PEOPLE'S MONEY. *New York American*, Nov. 28, 1911.

MEMORANDUM ON REGULARIZATION OF EMPLOYMENT, 1911. (Typewritten copy.)

THE NEW CONCEPTION OF INDUSTRIAL EFFICIENCY. *Journal of Accountancy*, May, 1911.

FIRST ANNUAL REPORT, Joint Board of Sanitary Control, New York, 1911. Foreword by Brandeis.

THE SPIRIT OF GET-TOGETHER. *American Cloak and Suit Review*, Sept. 1911.

LETTERS to *The Survey*, March 15, 1909; April 29, 1911; March 12, 1912; Nov. 13, 1920.

HEARINGS before Senate Committee on Interstate Commerce: Laws Regulating Corporations, Persons, and Firms Engaged in Interstate Commerce. 62d Cong., 2d Sess. Statement, Dec. 14-16, 1911, pp. 1146-291.

AN ILLEGAL TRUST LEGALIZED. *The World Today*, December, 1911.

SHALL WE ABANDON THE POLICY OF COMPETITION? *Case and Comment*, Feb. 1912.

HEARINGS before House Committee on Investigation of the United States Steel Corporation, 62d Cong., 3d Sess., Report 1137. Statement, Jan. 29-30, 1912, pp. 2835-72.

TRADE UNIONISM'S NEXT STEP. *The Boston Common*, March 2, 1912.

HEARINGS before House Committee on Patents: Oldfield Revision and Codification of the Patent Statutes, 62d Cong., 2d Sess. Statement, May 15, 1912, pp. 1-25.

PRIMER OF SCIENTIFIC MANAGEMENT, by Frank B. Gilbreth. Constable & Co., London, 1912. Foreword by Brandeis.

LABOR AND THE NEW PARTY TRUST PROGRAM. *La Follette's Weekly Magazine*, Oct. 12, 1912.

EFFICIENCY IN YOUR HOME AND IN YOUR BUSINESS. *New York American*, Dec. 10, 1912.

COMPETITION. *American Legal News*, Jan. 1913.

THE SOLUTION OF THE TRUST PROBLEM: A PROGRAM. *Harper's Weekly*, Nov. 8, 1913.

HEARINGS before Interstate Commerce Commission: 5% Rate Case. 63d Cong., 2d Sess. (1913-14), Sen. Doc. 466, Serial vol. 6581; arguments, pp. 5233-66; pp. 6328-35. Revenues of Rail Carriers in Official Classification Territory, I.C.C. Docket 5860.

LETTER to *New York Times Annalist*, Jan. 26, 1914.

HEARINGS before House Committee on Interstate and Foreign Commerce: Interstate Trade Commission. 63d Cong., 2d Sess. Statements, Jan. 30, 1914, pp. 1-21; Feb. 4, 1914, pp. 89-109.

HEARINGS before House Committee on Judiciary: Trust Legislation. 63d Cong., 2d Sess., Serial 7. Statement, Feb. 16, 1914, pp. 637-95; Feb. 25, 1914, pp. 921-52.

LA FOLLETTE'S WINNING OF WISCONSIN, by Albert O. Barton, Madison, 1922. Foreword by Brandeis, 1914.

PRELIMINARY REPORT ON EFFICIENCY IN THE ADMINISTRA-
TION OF JUSTICE, by Charles W. Eliot, Moorfield Storey,
Louis D. Brandeis, Adolph J. Rodenbeck and Roscoe
Pound. National Economic League, Boston [circa 1914].

HEARINGS before New York State Factory Investigating Commission. Statement, Jan. 22, 1915, Fourth Report, vol. 5,
pp. 2877-900.

THE CONSTITUTION AND THE MINIMUM WAGE. *The Survey*,
Feb. 6, 1915.

STATEMENT before Federal Trade Commission on work to be
undertaken by it. April 30, 1915. (Typewritten copy.)

STATEMENTS before United States Commission on Industrial
Relations. Senate Doc. 415, 64th Cong., 1st Sess., Serial
vol. 6929, 6936. Statements, April 16, 1914, pp. 991-
1011; Jan. 23, 1915, pp. 7657-81.

THE JEWISH PROBLEM AND HOW TO SOLVE IT. Jewish Congress Organization Committee, New York, 1915.

AS ESSENTIAL OF LASTING PEACE. *Harper's Weekly*, March
13, 1915.

PALESTINE AND THE JEWISH DEMOCRACY. *The Outlook*, Jan.
5, 1916.

CENTRAL POWER STATION RATES. *The Utilities Magazine*,
Philadelphia, 1916.

LETTER to Robert W. Bruère, Feb. 25, 1922. In *Columbia
Law Review*, vol. 31, p. 1098.

THE RIGHT TO WORK. *Survey Graphic*, April 1, 1929.

Additional References

BIOGRAPHICAL: Boyhood of Brandeis, An Early View of
the Man (interview with Alice H. Grady by Bert Fort),
Boston American, June 4, 1916; The Centennial History of
the Harvard Law School (1817-1917), Harvard Law School
Ass'n, Boston, 1918; Brandeis: A Remarkable Record of
Unselfish Work Done in the Public Interest, by Ernest
Poole, *American Magazine*, Feb. 1911; Louis D. Brandeis Pays

Partners for His Service to People, by Philip J. Halvosa, *Boston American*, Sept. 29, 1912; Just the Man for Judge, by Hamilton Holt, *The Independent*, Feb. 7, 1916; Brandeis, by William Hard, *The Outlook*, May 31, 1916; Brandeis, the Man and Zionist Leader, by Edward A. Filene, *Boston Sunday Post*, July 4, 1915; Louis D. Brandeis: Volunteer Attorney General for the Public Interest, *Hampton's Magazine*, June, 1910; Who Is This Man Brandeis? by Frederick W. Coburn, *Human Life*, Feb. 1911; Louis D. Brandeis, Trouble-Maker, by Judson C. Welliver, *The World Today*, Jan. 1912; Up from Aristocracy, by Livy S. Richard, *The Independent*, July 27, 1914; Mr. Justice Brandeis, The People's Tribune, by Elizabeth Glendower Evans, *The Survey*, Nov. 1, 1931; Pilgrims of '48, by Josephine Goldmark, Yale University Press, New Haven, 1930.

LABOR: Fatigue and Efficiency, A Study in Industry, by Josephine Goldmark, Russell Sage Foundation, 1912, containing the "Oregon Brief"; Meetings of the Board of Arbitration, Cloak and Suit Industry, New York (mimeographed record); Interview by Treadwell Cleveland, *La Follette's Weekly Magazine*, May 24, 1913; The Women's Garment Workers: A History of the International Ladies' Garment Workers' Union, by Lewis Lorwin, B. W. Huebsch, New York, 1924; Settlement of the Cloakmakers' Strike, by Mary Brown Sumner, *The Survey*, Sept. 17, 1910; The Cloakmakers' Strike, by John Bruce McPherson, *Journal of Political Economy*, March, 1911; The New York Cloakmakers' Strike, by Edith Wyatt, *McClure's Magazine*, April, 1911; *The Echo*, Filene Cooperative Ass'n, Boston, March 19, 1913; Law and Order in Industry, by Julius Henry Cohen, Macmillan Co., New York, 1916; Conciliation, Arbitration and Sanitation in the Cloak, Suit and Skirt Industry in New York City, Bulletin 8, U. S. Bureau of Labor Statistics, 1912; Industrial Court of Cloak, Suit and Skirt Industry of New York City, Bulletin 144, U. S. Bureau of Labor Statistics; Letter to *The Survey* from Florence Kelley, May 13, 1916; National Consumers' League Report, Feb. 1917.

INSURANCE: Massachusetts Savings Bank Insurance and Pension System, Massachusetts Savings Bank Insurance League pamphlet, Boston, 1910; Report of Superintendent of Insurance of the District of Columbia, House Doc. 559, 59th Cong., 2d Sess., 1907; The Massachusetts System of Savings-Bank Life Insurance, by Edward Berman, Bulletin 615, U. S. Bureau of Labor Statistics, 1935; Life Insurance for Workers, by Buel W. Patch, Editorial Research Reports, Vol. II, 1935, No. 16, Washington.

ZIONISM: Louis D. Brandeis: A Biographical Sketch, by Jacob de Haas, Bloch Publishing Co., New York, 1929 (contains Zionist addresses by Brandeis); Brandeis in Zionism, by Jacob de Haas, *Menorah Journal*, Feb. 1928.

BALLINGER CASE: The Whitewashing of Ballinger, by Louis R. Glavis, *Collier's Weekly*, Nov. 13, 1909; Achilles and His Rage, by Louis R. Glavis, *Collier's Weekly*, Dec. 4, 1909; The Changing Years: Reminiscences of Norman Hapgood, Farrar & Rinehart, New York, 1930.

BUSINESS REFORM: The Original Plan and Early History of the Federal Trade Commission, by George Rublee, *Proceedings*, Academy of Political Science, Jan. 1926; The Federal Trade Commission: A Study in Administrative Law and Procedure, by Gerard C. Henderson, Yale University Press, New Haven, 1924; The Control of Resale Prices, by Roy W. Johnson, William H. Ingersoll and Gilbert H. Montague, Dartnell Corp., Chicago, 1936.

WOODROW WILSON: The Political Education of Woodrow Wilson, by James Kearney, Century Co., 1926; Woodrow Wilson: Life and Letters, by Ray Stannard Baker, Vol. IV, Doubleday, Doran & Co., Garden City; The Philosophy of Justice Brandeis, by Charles G. Ross, *St. Louis Post-Dispatch*, June 19, 1927; Crowded Years: The Reminiscences of William G. McAdoo, Houghton, Mifflin Co., Boston, 1931; All in a Life-Time, by Henry Morgenthau, *World's Work*, Dec. 1921; The Intimate Papers of Colonel House, Houghton, Mifflin Co., Boston, 1926.

UNEMPLOYMENT RESERVES: Wisconsin Tackles Job Security, by Elizabeth Brandeis, *The Survey*, Dec. 15, 1931; Employment Reserves as Insurance, by Elizabeth Brandeis, *The New Republic*, Sept. 27, 1933; The Wisconsin Idea: Unemployment Insurance Reserves, *The Annals*, American Academy of Political and Social Science, Nov. 1933; Economic Bases of the Wisconsin Unemployment Reserves Act, by Harold M. Groves and Elizabeth Brandeis, *American Economic Review*, March 1934.

MISCELLANEOUS: Report of the Committee of the Whole Board of Aldermen on the Care and Management of Public Institutions, Boston, 1894; The Boston Franchise Contest, by Robert A. Woods and Joseph B. Eastman, *The Outlook*, April 14, 1906; Bulletin No. 4, Civic Federation of New England, Boston, 1906 (on sliding-scale gas rates); The Battles of Labor, by Carroll D. Wright, George W. Jacobs & Co., Philadelphia, 1906; Henry Demarest Lloyd, by Caro Lloyd, Putnam's, New York, 1912; La Follette's Autobiography, Robert M. La Follette Co., Madison, 1913; *New York Times Annalist*, Jan. 27, Dec. 15, 1913; *Strauss Magazine Theatre Program*, March 31, 1913; Report of Investigation of the Financial Transactions of the New York, New Haven & Hartford Railroad Co., Interstate Commerce Commission, No. 6569, 1914; *Jewish Tribune*, Nov. 12, 1926 (Brandeis' 70th birthday number); Massachusetts Courts, Vol. 5, 1927 (Sacco-Vanzetti case); The Filene Store: A Study of Employes' Relation to Management in a Retail Store, by Mary La Dame, Russell Sage Foundation, New York, 1930; The Libraries of the University of Louisville, compiled by Anna Blanche McGill, University of Louisville, 1934; Brandeis and ʻsıǝpuɐɹ The Reversible Mind of Louis D. Brandeis, "The

People's Lawyer," as it stands revealed in His Public Utterances, Briefs and Correspondence, United Shoe Machinery Co., Boston, 1912, 1914; The Documents in the Case, Being Testimony of Public Men in Favor of the United Shoe Machinery Co. (issued by the company), 1915.

NOMINATION: Brief on Behalf of Opposition to Confirmation, by Austin G. Fox and Kenneth M. Spence of New York, 1916; Hearings before Subcommittee of the Committee on the Judiciary of the U. S. Senate on the Nomination of Louis D. Brandeis to be an Associate Justice of the Supreme Court of the United States; Sen. Doc. 409, 64th Cong., 1st Sess., Serial vol. 6926-7 (1916); *Congressional Record*, April 28, 1916.

SUPREME COURT: United States Reports, Government Printing Office, Washington; Mr. Justice Brandeis, essays by Chief Justice Hughes and others, edited by Felix Frankfurter, Yale University Press, New Haven, 1932; Brandeis: Lawyer and Judge in the Modern State, by Alpheus Thomas Mason, Princeton University Press, Princeton, 1933; Brandeis Defends Newspaper Crusading as Minnesota "Gag" Law is Argued, by George H. Manning, *Editor and Publisher*, Feb. 7, 1931; The Business of the Supreme Court, by Felix Frankfurter and James M. Landis, Macmillan Co., New York, 1927.

INDEX